BURIAL RE
of the
EASTERN CEMETERY
PORTLAND, MAINE

Compiled By

William B. Jordan, Jr.

HERITAGE BOOKS, INC.

Other Titles By The Author

Burial Records 1811–1980 of the Western Cemetery, Portland, Maine
History of Cape Elizabeth, Maine

Published 1987 By

HERITAGE BOOKS, INC.
3602 Maureen Lane, Bowie, Maryland 20715
301–464–1159

ISBN 1–55613–067–8

A Catalog Listing Hundreds Of Titles On
Genealogy, History, and Americana
Available Free Upon Request

Show me the manner in which a nation cares for its dead, and I will measure with mathematical exactness the tender mercies of its people, their respect for the laws of the land and their loyalty to high ideals.

Wm. E. Gladstone.

National Register of Historic Places in the State of Maine

This is to Certify that the

Eastern Cemetery

has been reviewed by the Maine Historic Preservation Commission and by the National Park Service in Washington, D.C. and under the provisions of the National Historic Preservation Act of 1966 has been entered upon the National Register of Historic Places on _December 12_ 19 73.

Be it further certified that by inclusion in the National Register the above named is recognized as a part of the Historical and Cultural Heritage of our nation and should be preserved as a living part of our community life and development in order to give a sense of orientation to the American people.

Earle S. Shettleworth, Jr.
State Liaison Officer

TABLE OF CONTENTS

INTRODUCTION

The origins of the Eastern Cemetery, Portland's oldest burial ground, are now unknown. It is evident that the first use of the area for that purpose occured during the seventeenth century prior to the Indian Wars. According to the local historian John T. Hull the burial ground abutted the northern edge of George Cleeve's house lot.

The general poverty of the seventeenth century settlers apparently prevented the use of inscribed grave stones in most instances. At the present time there are no known seventeenth century graves in the Eastern Cemetery. The oldest grave stone now surviving is that of Mary Green who died 23 May 1717. From its design it is apparent that the stone was placed upon the grave many years later. When City Engineer William A. Goodwin conducted his survey of the Eastern Cemetery in 1890 no grave stone existed that pre-dated it.

Local historians, however, have always insisted that the south-west corner bordering Federal Street is the oldest section. There is common agreement that in all likelihood George Cleeve and other early settlers were buried there. In his generally reliable *History Of Portland*, William Willis in 1866 states: "Here the rude forefathers of the hamlet sleep. Here repose the remains of the eminent men and women who have adorned our town during two centuries, ...the humble villager, the noble company of Christian men and women who having passed through the vicissitudes of our many sided life, rest in peace within the bosom of the silent grave."

Burial throughout most of the eighteenth century was very casual indeed. Apparently, no attempt was made to record location of interment until 1772 when the First Parish paid Joseph Noyes two shillings to prepare a plan of known burials. Unfortunately no copy of the plan has survived. Occasionally, scraps of information surface as to burial activities. For example in May 1737, according to William Goold, forty diptheria victims were buried therein. Like so many other eithteenth century interments the location of the graves has been lost.

As to ownership it is recorded that the Rev. Thomas Smith acquired from the George Munjoy heirs most of what is now Munjoy Hill including land south of Congress Street and east of India Street. This of course includes the old burial ground. Despite repeated requests from the selectmen to sell it to the town he refused to do so. The town did however establish a right-of-way from Congress Street to Mountfort Street and named it Funeral Lane. Finally, 6 May 1795, nineteen days before he died, the Rev. Smith deeded the old burial ground, plus the lot bounded by Funeral Lane, Congress Street, and Mountfort Street, to the town for the sum of £17-5-0. The additional tract served as a public common before being absorbed by the cemetery in 1821. On the northeast corner of the common was a town pound and near the center a small building used by the Portland Artillery. On the southwest side was a town school.

Also in 1795 the town authorized the selectmen "to lay out the... Burying Ground into regular plats and divisions, and that the Sextons of the several Parishes be strictly enjoined to conform in digging the graves for any persons to such divisions that some degree of regularity and order may be introduced among the mansions of the dead, and not be scattered over the ground in so confused and irregular a manner as has heretofore been the case." In addition six narrow lanes were laid out running southerly from Funeral Lane to what is now Federal Street. Lastly, that same year, it was established "that hence forward no part of said Burying Yard shall be reserved for particular families, but that the bodies of persons as they die be interred, without distinction as to place, in a regular manner, contiguous to each other, that the ground may include the greatest number of graves possible and be sufficient for many years to come. Provided that notwithstanding that this regulation shall not be confused to restrain any person who may incline so to do, from building Tombs under the direction of the Selectmen." In 1798 when the Town By-Laws were drawn up the method and time of burial, and by whom, as well as the removal of bodies was clearly outlined.

In this period the construction of underground tombs was initiated and would continue periodically over the next thirty-five years. Eventually a total of ninety-five were built with all but ten located in four rows along the northern edge of Funeral Lane.

On occasion sections of the cemetery were set aside for special purposes. At the terminus of Funeral Lane on Mountfort Street twenty-five square rods was set aside in 1795 as the Friends' Ground to accommodate the Quakers. Just exactly how many were buried there is impossible to determine. To this day, as was their custom, the graves are largely unmarked.

Early in the nineteenth century two sections, each known as the Colored Ground, were set aside for the burial of Portland's Blacks. One section is located at the corner of Federal and Mountfort Streets, while the other is at the Corner of Congress and Mountfort Streets. Unfortunately very few of the graves are marked by a stone. Were it not for the burial records their names would be largely unknown. For the most part their grave sites are now lost. Interestingly, some bear old Portland names and were it not for the fact that they are identified as to race in the burial records genealogical problems might arise. One fascinating inscription from a stone destroyed long ago survives as follows: "Elizabeth Freeman, known by the name of Mumblet, died 28 December 1829. Her supposed age was 85 years. She was born a slave, and remained a slave for nearly thirty years. She could neither read nor write, yet in her own sphere she had no superior nor equal, she neither wasted time nor property, she never violated a truth, nor failed to perform a duty. In every situation of domestic trial she was the most efficient helper and the tenderest friend. Good mother, farewell."

In addition the town set aside certain areas known as the Strangers' Ground. More than one such section was apparently so designated. Here were buried the friendless and the poor. Unfortunately the location of these sections is now unknown.

Vandalism is by no means a recent problem in the Eastern Cemetery. The incident rate as well as the magnitude of destruction has of course been greater in this century. On 29 May 1816 the Selectmen published a warning of punishment in the *Eastern Argus* in the wake of a particularly damaging foray by "... some evil minded person or persons...." Portland's "genius loci" of the nineteenth century, John Neal wrote on 28 May 1828 in his newspaper *The Yankee*, an outraged editorial condemning the vandalism of that era. He admonished his fellow townsmen to visit the Eastern Cemetery: "Look about you... and there you may see the very grave stones broken down for sport, and shattered to pieces in play, by mere children, and before the very faces of twelve thousand living people, who are related, every one of them, to those who sleep there, and to whom the outrage is offered.

Just think what might be made of the burial-ground at the top of the hill, if proper and speedy measures were taken. ... Yet, if you were to wander the world over in search of a spot worthy of being set apart for the burial place of a large town, you could not find one more beautiful than this to which I allude....

But enough, they who have any sort of feeling... must be ready to cry out with shame and horror at the coarse and brutal outrage that is offered every day of the week, and every hour of the day, to the tomb-stones and grave-stones there....

If a reward be not offered for the discovery of these wretches, the people of this town deserve to see their wives and little ones dug up and scattered to the four winds of heaven, or launched upon the waters of Casco Bay." Although Neal wrote the editorial more than 150 years ago conditions have not improved.

The cemetery was enlarged for the last time in 1821. Over the next twenty-five years other significant changes were forthcoming. In 1838 the city permitted the opening of a lane for foot traffic from Funeral Lane to Federal Street. That same year it was also decided that in burying so called "strangers" that they be interred two to a grave, one above the other. In 1841 trees were planted for the first time. Despite the fact that more were subsequently set out over the years none survive to the present day. As the area became increasingly urbanized it was necessary to bring forward various physical changes. A granite retaining wall was constructed along Mountfort Street in 1847 and two years later the city's first receiving tomb was built adjacent to the Congress Street entrance.

This so called "City Tomb" is built of field stone and brick with a paved floor. It measures twenty-one feet in depth, eleven feet in width, seven feet in heighth, and is entirely beneath the surface of the ground. An examination of the burial records documents its constant and frequent use. Unfortunately many who were temporarily interred therein have no subsequently recorded resting place. In 1868 the Superintendent of Burials stated in his annual report that the City Tomb contained the remains of 111 individuals. How they were all accommodated strains the imagination.

Entrance to the City Tomb is gained through a small single story Gothic revival board and batten building. Currently it is, like the cemetery itself, in a wretched state of repair. Apparently this receiving tomb was in constant use until the end of the century. Its use is documented as late as 1889.

With the Western Cemetery established in 1829, followed by Evergreen Cemetery in 1852, and Forest City Cemetery in 1858, use of the Eastern Cemetery gradually declined. In 1851 the city halted further burials in the oldest section except under unusual circumstances. According to the Superintendent of

Burials it was impossible to dig a grave anywhere in that area without disturbing an earlier interment. Seven years later the city suspended all burials except in cases of close family ties where it was obvious that space was available. Even this arrangement did not eliminate the problem of resurection coinciding with interment. Naturally, no prohibition existed as to continued use of the tombs. Even here capacity has been strained in a number of cases.

In the rebuilding that followed the great fire of 1866 Federal Street was extended to Mountfort Street. During construction it was necessary to erect a massive retaining wall along the back of the cemetery in 1868. About twelve feet of surface was cut away. Bones and stones were simply carted away with the rubble. Althouth it is obvious that a number of graves were obliterated no record is known to have survived.

Over the years the cemetery has been fenced in various ways but never to prevent casual access. Across the Congress Street side there now exists the battered remains of a cast iron fence that once separated Portland High School from Cumberland Avenue. When the present high school building was constructed in 1918 the fence was salvaged and reerected at the cemetery thanks to the generosity of a public spirited citizen.

Although it is unrecorded when construction took place it is nevertheless evident that a hearse house stood opposite the little Gothic building on Funeral Lane. The earliest mention of a municipal hearse is 1805 when the town authorized the purchase thereof. When this public service was discontinued it is impossible to say but apparently it lingered on until late in the century.

In the latter part of the nineteenth century various individuals took it upon themselves to compile lists of Eastern Cemetery burials and inscriptions. Two of these collections survive in the library of the Maine Historical Society.

Of considerable interest is a manuscript volume compiled by William F. Hoadley about 1903. Although he is responsible for a wealth of errors Hoadley copied many inscriptions and epitaphs from stones that have since vanished. A self-appointed sexton he took a proprietary interest in the preservation of the cemetery. For many years he spent his summers conducting tours for the occasional visitor. When a tomb was opened to receive a new occupant Hoadley had the presence of mind to record the names that appeared on the coffin plates. He died at the age of fifty-two in 1912.

Another selective tabulation of significance was carried out by Stephen Marion Watson late in the nineteenth century.

Originally published in a local newspaper under the heading *Tomb Stone Inscriptions In The Eastern Cemetery, Portland, ME*, it is now preserved in *Portland Scrapbook* II:6-11 at the Maine Historical Society. It lists 274 items with some attempt to preserve the original style. Unfortunately there are a number of errors. As with Hoadley, the Watson list contains inscriptions from stones lost before later tabulations were carried out.

Watson, an antiquarian of some note, published the *Maine Historical And Genealogical Recorder* and was a founder of the original Maine Genealogical Society. He was, for twenty years, librarian of the Portland Public Library. Death overtook him in Chicago 7 June 1920 at the age of 85.

It was not however until the arrival on the scene of William Augustus Goodwin that a thorough and systematic survey was initiated. A native of Athens, Maine, Goodwin graduated from Bowdoin College in 1843 and received his A.M. three years later. Trained as a civil engineer, he was employed in route surveys for the Atlantic and St. Lawrence, York and Cumberland, as well as the European and North American Railway. After serving for several years as a Superintendent of Construction for the U.S. Light House Service he became Portland's City Engineer in 1871. In 1890 Goodwin carried out a monumental survey of the Eastern Cemetery assisted by William S. Edwards.

The Goodwin survey produced not only a listing of 4,136 grave stones, monuments, tombs, and grave sites, but an accurate map of the burial ground with each carefully located thereon.   Dividing the cemetery into twelve sections, A through L, every known grave and tomb was numbered. As a companion to the map a double index was prepared, one alphabetical by name, the other numerical by site. Each listing included all the pertinent information found on the stone. If the grave stone was missinq it was so recorded in the numerical listing. The accuracy of this survey is excellant. The original map, on linen, is in the files of the Portland Park Department.

In producing this revised list I visited and checked each grave on Goodwin's map, making corrections and/or additions where necessary, as well as noteing the stones that have been destroyed or broken since 1890.   The underground tombs presented a special problem. These substantial vaults are in some cases closely packed. The coffins were simply piled one atop another. The Tukesbury tomb, A Tomb 69, contains twenty-eight identifiable coffins. Unfortunately quite a number of the tombs lack monuments listing the people therein. Over the years as repairs have been made to the wooden planks that cover the buried entry ways occasional listings have been made from the coffin plates. Also incorporated in the tabulations are those individuals found in the burial records who have no stone.

Turning now to the matter of burial records one's initial reaction can best be described as annoyance. During Portland's era as a town neither death nor burial records were maintained with any degree of regularity. This improved somewhat in 1832 when the city was incorporated and a Superintendent of Burials appointed for the first time. An examination of the records reveals that improvement was gradual to say the least. The degree of literacy exhibited by some of these functionaries was frequently marginal. Some were extremely original in the spelling of names. Fortunately, in 1890 their record keeping duties were assumed by the city clerk's office.

Prior to incorporation burials were carried out by the various parish or church sextons. In 1824 they were given the additional title of Funeral Porters. However, it wasn't until 1847 that undertakers were included in the city directory. Even then they were grouped under the heading of "City Officers." When checked under their individual names it is immediately evident that their activities as undertakers was strictly part time. Althouth most were sextons, among the others we find a stone mason, a clothier, a cordwainer, and a laborer. The Black community had its own undertaker, Abraham Niles, who later perished on his way to the California gold fields. In 1858 James S. Gould was appointed City Coroner as well as Superintendent of Burials, a post he held until his death in 1892.

One most annoying problem that occasionally appears in utilizing the cemetery and burial records under discussion involves the removal of bodies from one cemetery to another. In 1858 the city offered lots in Evergreen Cemetery in exchange for lots in the Eastern and Western Cemeteries. A number of people availed themselves of the opportunity and moved family members to Evergreen. In the case of John Mussey he built a new tomb in Evergreen Cemetery and proceeded to move family members from their tomb in the Eastern Cemetery along with a massive monument. Not content with a more fashionable sepulcher for his family he tried to ornament their final resting place with honored neighbors. That same year, 1873, he petitioned the City Council to be permitted to move Burroughs and Blyth, the two naval captains who fell in battle in 1813, to Evergreen. Fortunately 185 public spirited citizens presented a petition of protest prompting a negative response to Mussey's extraordinary request.

When transfers did occur a notation to that effect was seldom entered in the burial records. In a number of cases the bodies of small children were simply abandoned. Occasionally family members were left in the Eastern or Western but a monument bears their name in Evergreen.

Unfortunately Mussey was not alone in his removals. Socially prominent and wealthy Henry Deering also transferred selected ancestors from an Eastern Cemetery tomb to a more "appropriate" resting place at Evergreen. Not to be outdone, Adm. George Henry Preble, of Civil War fame, emptied the Preble tomb of everyone but the Commodore, his wife, and the unretrievable dust of an infant child, for burial at Evergreen. He also exhumed Gen. Jedediah Preble, and the general's two wives, moving them with their monuments to Evergreen.

Other individuals, with similar motives, peopled new family cemetery lots with "honored" ancestors. In 1877 the local historian William Goold on the occasion of Adm. James Allen's burial in the Eastern Cemetery commented "I never enter that hallowed enclosure but I feel an impulse to remove my hat, recollecting the declaration of the voice from the burning bush to the youthful Moses, "the place on which thou standest is holy ground." Here not only repose the rude fathers of the hamlet but also the eminent men who, for two centuries, have adorned the town. It was the only place of burial belonging to the town until 1829, when it was estimated that the dead here interred outnumbered the living within the corporate limits.

And here I want to say a word against the removal of the dust of its tenants. This was the chosen spot for their burial. It is marred in places by partially filled graves where relatives have dug (often in vain) for the bones of ancestors, and are forced to be content with the removal of the head-stones. In many instances these stones are lost or are placed in more socially prominent cemeteries, testimonials to a lack of consideration and the epitome of bad taste. Such removals only encourage the thoughtless to commit acts of vandalism."

One removal led to a rather unusual discovery. In the fall of 1900 William H. Hoadley assisted in the exhumation of Capt. William W. Chamberlain for transferal to Evergreen. The captain had been killed aboard his ship by a falling spar on a voyage from Hong Kong to San Francisco. He died 21 August 1856 at the age of forty-one. The ship was off the Hawaiian islands when the fatal accident occurred. The captain's body was placed in a coffin made of southern pine three inches thick and heavily lined with tared canvas. The corpse was encased in five layers of canvas. The tightly wrapped body was then placed in the coffin and packed about with oakum. Five months later the captain's remains were buried in the Eastern Cemetery.

When Hoadley opened the coffin and removed some of the wrappings the corpse was found to be in a perfect state of preservation. The features, except for a blueish tint, were exceedingly lifelike. However, upon closer examination the body was found to be as hard as stone. Two physicians who were in attendance stated that this was the first such case of petrification they had ever seen. Without further disturbing Capt. Chamberlain he was reburied at Evergreen Cemetery.

At this point it is pertinent to comment upon the material included as an appendix. In each case the data has been extracted from the burial records. In 1804 an Alms House – Town Farm was built on what is now Park Avenue near the present Institute for the Blind. A burial ground was established in 1858 called the Alms House Yard. Burials continued to be made until 1874. Throughout the same period some indigent individuals and "strangers" were as usual fitted into the Eastern and Western Cemeteries as well as Forest City. Finally in 1887 the bodies in the Alms House Yard were removed to the Alms House lots in Forest City Cemetery. None of the bodies were identified, no monuments were ever erected, no record exists at Forest City. The only listing is that extracted from the burial records.

Yet another interesting listing extracted from the burial records are the individuals who came to rest at the Maine Medical School at Brunswick and at the Portland Medical School.

In 1881 a state law was enacted requiring Maine municipalities to surrender unclaimed bodies for anatomical purposes. A notice was circulated by the Maine Medical School. Despite the fact that Portland's City Council tried hard to prevent delivery a large number of individuals were surrended until the need ceased in 1921. Once again the only listing is that extracted from the burial records.

Finally, it is disheartening in the extreme to note that preservation-protection of the Eastern Cemetery is a matter seldom if ever addressed by the city government. Spectacular acts of wanton destruction are currently commonplace. Not only are stones and monuments battered into fragments but tombs are opened, coffins demolished, and bones scattered far and wide. Some of the eighteenth century stones have recently been mutilated by "folk art" collectors. Unless the city government, and such local organizations as Greater Portland Landmarks, move immediately nothing will survive this century except the largest monuments.

William B. Jordan, Jr.
11 May 1987

**FRIENDS OF
THE EASTERN CEMETERY**

ABBREVIATIONS

ae – age
b – born
Capt. – Captain
Co – Company
Col. – Colonel
Cpl. – Corporal
d – died/day(s)
d/o – daughter of
gr – grand
GSL – Grave Site Lost
h/o – husband of
Inf – Infantry/infant
KIA – Killed In Action
LME – Ledger Monument
 Eroded
m – month(s)
Maj. – Major
MB – Monument Broken
MBE – Monument Badly
 Eroded
MD – Monument Destroyed
ME – Monument Eroded
MEB – Monument Eroded &
 Broken

Mnt – Monument
nd – no date(s)
NM – No Monument
NS – No Stone
s/o – son of
SB – Stone Broken
SBE – Stone Badly Eroded
SD – Stone Destroyed
sis/o – sister of
TM – Two Monuments
USA – United States Army
USN – United States Navy
w – week(s)
w/o – wife of
wid/o – widow of
y – year(s)

CEMETERY INSCRIPTIONS

A man found drowned. Buried 29 May 1848 ae: c45y. "Buried near the gate." "Strangers' Ground." GSL

Murdered man, name unknown buried 17 June 1849 ae: c35y. Catholic. GSL

Seaman from Bark *ST.JAGO* d 9 Oct 1856 ae: 23yrs. "Casualty by a fall." GSL

An illegitimate female child d 4 Dec 1844 ae: 4m. GSL

Child found back of Munjoy Hill d 24 Sept 1855 ae: c7w. GSL

Infant child d 14 Jan 1858 ae: 2d. "Died in the English steamer." GSL

Remains of man found by excavations at Fish Point. Buried 18 Apr 1854. GSL

Remains of a man, name unknown, who arrived in Portland on board steamer *Governor* from St. Johns, ticketed to Nashua, New Hampshire, buried 11 Aug 1854. GSL

Stranger, name unknown buried 10 Jul 1842. "Drowned." GSL

ABBOTT, Charles d 20 Jan 1861 ae: 55y 10m. GSL

Frederick A. d 25 May 1846 ae: 2y 1m. "Buried in Capt. O. Harwood's enclosure." GSL

Jeremiah S. d 29 Mar 1835 ae: 62y. SBE G:63

Sarah M. w/o Walter d 12 Dec 1840 ae: 30y. SD A-24-13

Susannah wid/o Jeremiah S. d 22 Feb 1844 ae: 74y. SBE G:63

ABRAMS, Ralph d 14 Feb 1866 ae: 93y. GSL

ACORN, Philip s/o Jacob d 26 Sept 1797 ae: 27y. Black. SD L:22

ADAMS, Adeline d/o Moses & Nancy d 10 June 1840 ae: 34y. ME G:38

Ann d/o Charles d 31 Dec 1855 ae: 1y 18d. Black. GSL

Ann D. d/o Rev. Solomon d 12 Oct 1850 ae: 12y. "Died in Boston." ME A Tomb 74

Bartlett s/o Bartlett & Charlotte b 5 July 1806 d 30 Dec 1806 I:201

Bartlett d 27 Jan 1828 ae: 51y. ME A Tomb 46

Benjamin d June 1805 ae: 60y. I:105

Caleb nd "Caleb Adams – 1850" on granite post. F:93 Tomb

Charles H. d 1 Mar 1870 ae: 10y 7m. GSL

Charles P. s/o Moses & Nancy d 11 Sept 1827 ae: 19y. ME G:38

Charles R. N. d 2 Nov 1851 ae: 26y. GSL

Charlotte wid/o Bartlett d 15 Feb 1837 ae: 58y. A Tomb 46

Charlotte W. b 16 Aug 1807 d 10 June 1824 ME A Tomb 46

Cordelia w/o Elijah d 19 Jul 1853 ae: 35y. GSL

Elijah s/o Moses & Nancy d 21 Aug 1813 ae: 10m. ME G:38

Elijah d 13 Dec 1881 ae: 77y. ME G:38

Eliza d/o Bartlett & Charlotte b&d 23 Aug 1812 I:203

1

ADAMS (continued)

Eliza d 17 Apr 1841 ae: 42y. SD A-7-3

Mrs. Elizabeth d/o Timothy Bryant d 17 July 1860 ae: 25y 10m. GSL

F. Crawford Cook s/o Elijah & Louisa d 1 Mar 1832 ae: 16y. ME G:38

George s/o Bartlett & Charlotte b&d 27 Feb 1809 I:202

Harriet McMannus d 7 Mar 1849 ae: 4d. GSL

Harrison d 2 Jan 1849 ae: 39y. Black. GSL

Isaac d 5 July 1834 ae: 61y. TM A Tomb 72

Isabella d/o Robert & Mary E. d 12 Nov 1852 ae: 8m. GSL

Jacob d 5 Mar 1734 ae: 33y. D:18

Capt. Jacob d 12 July 1807 ae: 35y. "Wrecked at Richmond's Island." Unusual stone. K:70

John d 1 Aug 1749 ae: 20y. SBE D:97

John Crawford s/o Elijah d 4 Mar 1852 ae: 15y 7m. GSL

Louisa w/o Elijah d 9 Apr 1840 ae: 34y. ME G:38

Maria G. d/o Moses & Nancy d 14 Nov 1840 ae: 30y. ME G:38

Martha W. wid/o Caleb d 17 Jan 1894 ae: 90y. F:93 Tomb

Mary d 23 Dec 1877 ae: 76y. A-7-5

Mary Arnold w/o Elijah d 11 Oct 1878 ae: 78y. ME G:38

Mary Eustis d/o Rev. Solomon d 28 Aug 1853 ae: 6y. "Buried David Dana tomb." A Tomb 74

Moses d 7 Mar 1820 ae: 53y. ME G:38

Nancy wid/o Moses d 30 Oct 1838 ae: 64y. ME G:38

Nancy d 24 Aug 1847 ae: 83y. Widow. GSL

Paulina w/o Capt. Caleb d 23 Mar 1852 ae: 64y. "Died in Brunswick." F:93 Tomb

Phebe C. d 14 Nov 1848 ae: 30y.

ADAMS (continued)

Black. GSL

Sarah d 1 Jan 1844 ae: 64y. Widow. SBE A-7-4

Sophia d/o Moses & Nancy d 20 Apr 1845 ae: 45y. ME G:38

Susan E. adopted d/o Silas M. d 20 Jul 1849 ae: 6y. GSL

Sarah W. b 10 Dec 1810 d 30 Jul 1815 A Tomb 46

William s/o Moses & Nancy d 30 Aug 1820 ae: 16y. ME G:38

ADIE, Mary A. wid/o Capt. William d 19 June 1861 ae: 54y. A Tomb 6

Capt. William d 2 Feb 1855 ae: 53y. A Tomb 6

AIKEN, Elizabeth S. d/o Robert & Martha d 15 Sep 1833 ae: 1y. SD F:20

AITCHISON, Helen L. d/o William & H. M. d 15 Dec 1841 ae: 4y 3m. ME A Tomb 73

ALAMBY, Mary R. d/o George T. & Martha M. d 21 Oct 1853 ae: 4m 5d. SD H:149

ALDEN, Benjamin s/o Capt. James & Elizabeth d 12 Feb 1822 ae: 16m. SD B-6-5

Charlotte Q. d/o Capt. C. & Nancy d 31 Oct 1821 ae: 2y 5m. SD C:3

Elizabeth wid/o Capt. David d Oct 1804 ae: 68y. SBE B-6-2

Elizabeth Tate w/o Capt. James d 8 Aug 1824 ae: 44y. SBE B-6-2

Franklin d 11 Jan 1820 ae: 17y. "Lost at sea." SBE A-3-18

Rear Adm. James s/o James & Elizabeth Tate b 31 Mar 1810 d 6 Feb 1877, San Francisco, California, USN, Mexican War, Civil War Mmt B-6-4

Capt. James d 27 June 1853 ae: 78y. SBE B-6-1

Capt. John d 19 Oct 1833 ae: 62y. SBE A-3-18

John R. s/o Capt. C. & Nancy d 6 Feb 1825 ae: 2y 5m. C:4

Joshua nd "Lost at sea." SBE

ALDEN (continued)
A-13-18
Sarah Ann wid/o Rear Adm. James d 10 Jan 1889 ae: 73y 11m 30d. Died Somerville, Massachusetts. NS B-6-4

ALEXANDER, Arabella Waterman d/o John & Mary Jane d 13 Aug 1843 ae: 2y 7m. I:196

Arabella W. d/o John d 19 Feb 1851 ae: 5y. GSL

Ellen S. d 21 Mar 1847 ae: 10y. Black. GSL

Emons Brown s/o John & Mary Jane d 5 Mar 1839 ae: 3y. I:195

Henrietta J. d/o Mary d 26 Sep 1852 ae: 17y. Black. GSL

John H. s/o John & Mary Jane d 25 Nov 1832 ae: 13m. I:194

Lizzie d/o William d 12 June 1869 ae: 14y. GSL

Mary d/o widow d 25 Sep 1842 ae: 13m. GSL

Mary d/o wid Mary d 3 Sep 1842 ae: 3y. Black. GSL

Mary Jane w/o John d 29 Oct 1858 ae: 51y. GSL

Simeon d 23 Nov 1845 ae: 36y. "Buried by side Emma Motley's stone." NS H:168

Viola G. d 21 Feb 1851 ae: 8y. GSL

ALLEN, Abigail G. d/o William d 10 July 1863 ae: 5y. GSL

Betsy w/o William d 20 Feb 1848 ae: 56y. "Buried head of Lydia Austin's grave." GSL

Charles H. s/o John & Carol d 13 June 1934 ae: 62y 19d. GSL

Herbert E. s/o Roswell M. d 18 Apr 1864 ae: 3m. GSL

Joshua s/o Capt. Moses & Sarah d 20 May 1805 ae: 21y. "Late of Sandwich, Cape Cod." L:25

Mary A. d/o Samuel & Mary d 10 Nov 1827 ae: 10m. SBE B-10-20

Mary Ann w/o Charles d 10 Feb 1855 ae: 35y. GSL

Sarah d/o John d 17 Nov 1843 ae: 3y. "Buried at head of

ALLEN (continued)
Sarah Codman's grave." NS F:135

William d 24 Aug 1861 ae: 76y. GSL

AMEDEE, Alexander nd, ae: 17y. SBE B-3-11

AMES, Aphia w/o John d 17 Feb 1847 ae: 66y. GSL

Jane d 29 Oct 1843 ae: 33y. "Buried by side of her father." GSL

ANDERSON, Ellen Monroe d/o William d 28 Apr 1859 ae: 2y 5m. Black. GSL

Elsey d 5 Dec 1845 ae: 80y. Black. GSL

Harriet G. d 22 Aug 1853 ae: 42y. Black. SB A-10-28

Isa J. d/o William d 30 Dec 1857 ae: 11m. Black. GSL

John d 21 Aug 1853 ae: 61y. "Buried Anderson tomb." A Tomb 68

John d 22 Oct 1854 ae: 25y. "Buried 4' east of Mother Finney's stone." NS Black. B-10-1

Jonas d 20 May 1853 ae: 36y. "Native of Stockholm - drowned." GSL

Leonard s/o William d 3 June 1860 ae: 11m. GSL

Lewis N. s/o Andrew B. d 9 Feb 1893 ae: 8m 10d. GSL

William J. d 2 Oct 1860 ae: 41y. Black. GSL

ANDRES, Anthoyer J. d/o Peter & Sarah d 6 Oct 1849 ae: 14m. SBE I:69

Augustus E. s/o Peter & Sarah d 4 Oct 1850 ae: 13m 21d. SD I:68

Emma J. d 6 May 1855 ae: 14y 17d. SD I:67

ANDREW, Charles F. d 24 Sept 1863 ae: 16m. GSL

ANDREWS, Augustus E. s/o Peter d 4 Oct 1850 ae: 1y. "Buried near the Friends' Ground." GSL

Charity d 19 June 1862 ae: 84y.

ANDREWS (continued)
GSL

Charlotte d 14 Jan 1859 ae: 84y. NM A Tomb 77

Henry K. d 26 Aug 1849 ae: 42y. GSL

Jane S. d 1 Oct 1852 ae: 18y 8m. GSL

Jonathan d 19 Apr 1820 ae: 50y. C:214

Mary T. wid/o Stephen d 2 June 1845 ae: 42y. GSL

ANDROS, Emma J. d/o Peter d 5 May 1865 ae: 14y. GSL

ANGIER, Ezekiel s/o Oakes d 8 Aug 1843 ae: 3w. ME A Tomb 79

ANGUS, George s/o Dennis H. & Ann d 6 Oct 1834 ae: 6y. SD F:181

Sophia A. d/o Dennis H. & Ann d 25 Nov 1835 ae: 19m. SD F:182

ANLRY, Joseph d 17 Nov 1847 ae: 20y. "Buried Strangers' Ground." GSL

ANNEAR, Lavina E. d 13 Oct 1856 ae: 17y. "Native of Pr. Edward's Island." "Buried at head of Rebecca Mitchell's grave." NS C:79

ANSON, Mary w/o William d 10 July 1837 ae: 37y. "Native of Bedlington, County Durham, England." A-4-5

Mary d/o William d 21 Feb 1844 ae: 20y. "Buried by his stone." NS A-4-6

William d 2 June 1859 ae: 70y. SD A-4-6

APPLETON, David s/o John W. d 5 June 1845 ae: 8m. "Buried Strangers' Ground." GSL

ARMSTRONG, Elizabeth d/o Richard d 13 Mar 1864 ae: 7m. GSL

Frederick D. s/o Frederick d 28 June 1846 ae: 13m. GSL

Jacob L. d 27 Jan 1873 ae: 29y. Civil War: 17th Reg. Maine Inf., Co. A NS C:89

ARNOLD, Mary Hobson d/o Capt. Thomas & Mary M. b 17 June 1798 d 11 Mar 1800 SB L:28

Mary Maria w/o Thomas d 18 June 1798 ae: 22y. SB L:28

ASH, Mary w/o Samuel H. d 22 Dec 1817 ae: 54y. L:43

Samuel H. d 30 July 1822 ae: 46y. L:68

ATKINS, David A. s/o Joshua F. d 15 Aug 1845 ae: 9m. "Buried at head of John Cammett's grave." NS B-12-5

Grace H. w/o Isaiah d 31 Aug 1876 ae: 91y 3m. A-12-4

Isaiah d 7 Jan 1840 ae: 53y. A-12-3

Capt. Isaiah H. d 5 Jan 1851 ae: 36y. SBE A-12-5

Nabby d 7 Sep 1861 ae: 82y. GSL

Nathaniel d 14 Jan 1802 ae: 59y. C:83

Polly d/o late Nathaniel d 24 Apr 1851 ae: 73y. GSL

Smith S. d 15 May 1884 ae: 71y. GSL

ATTWOOD, Mary w/o Bradbury C. d 2 June 1818 ae: 25y. SBE I:211

AULTS, Almira Scott d/o John d 1 Feb 1870 ae: 4m. GSL

AUSTIN, Horace d 12 Oct 1815 ae: 18y. J:45

John d 18 May 1802 ae: 31y. J:44

Lydia d 9 Dec 1834. GSL

AYER, Alice d 7 June 1864 ae: 2m. GSL

George C. s/o Samuel & Sarah J. d 21 May 1815 ae: 6m. SBE K:3

AYERS, Joseph d 31 July 1830 ae: 49y. K:40

BABB, William Henry d 2 Dec 1847 ae: 28y. Mmt A Tomb 57

BABCOCK, Abigail N. Gay d/o Nathan & Abigail S. b 20 July 1807 d 12 Nov 1814 MB A Tomb 21

Abigail S. wid/o Nathan d 5

BABCOCK (continued)
   Feb 1851 ae: 64y. MB A
   Tomb 21
Nathan d 28 Mar 1846 ae: 62y.
   MB A Tomb 21
BACHELDER, Ephraim d 15 July
   1824 ae: 31y. SB B-15-13
Samuel Merritt s/o Capt. Levi
   L. & N. C. d 17 Nov 1856 ae:
   14m. SBE B-8-27
BAGLEY, Abner s/o Abner d 10
   Sep 1843 ae: 1y. "Buried by
   side of Green's stone." GSL
David Brown s/o John B. d 6 Mar
   1846 ae: 4y. GSL
Enoch C. s/o John B. d 8 Nov
   1849 ae: 2y. GSL
John, Jr. d 24 July 1798 ae: 24y.
   GSL
Leah H. d/o John B. & Mary A. d
   1 Sep 1830 ae: 7m. A-6-13
Lewis D. s/o John d 7 Aug 1844
   ae: 3m. "Buried in Family
   Range." GSL
Maria G. d/o John B. d 29 Oct
   1849 ae: 4y. GSL
Mary w/o John d Apr 1804 ae:
   66y. GSL
Mary d/o John B. & Mary A. d 11
   Sep 1837 ae: 1y. A-6-13
BAILEY, Alice Ilsley d/o James
   d 25 Aug 1858 ae: 6m. GSL
Ann T. wid/o Edwin d 18 Oct
   1866 ae: 64y. LME E:6 Tomb
Anna H. w/o Daniel d 7 Sep
   1853 ae: 22y. SD B-14-13
Daniel d 31 Aug 1853 ae: 35y.
   SD B-14-13
Edward s/o Benjamin & Jane d
   3 Nov 1818 ae: 2y. SD K:26
Eliza w/o Hiram d 20 Sep 1824
   ae: 19y. Name misspelled
   Bagley on stone. B-10-14
Eliza A. d/o Benjamin & Jane d
   26 Mar 1819 ae: 9y. SD K:26
Eliza A. d/o Benjamin & Jane d
   17 Sep 1821 ae: 2m. SD K:26
Elizabeth w/o William d 17
   July 1848 ae: 57y. SD C:228
Frank s/o Thomas d 17 May
   1867 ae: 5y 6m. GSL
Henry s/o Benjamin & Jane d 26

BAILEY (continued)
   Mar 1819 ae: 7y. SD K:26
Henry s/o George H. d 29 Dec
   1861 ae: 13m. A Tomb 47
Hollis s/o George d 6 Aug 1850
   ae: 1y. GSL
Hudson d 19 Aug 1798 ae: 48y.
   "Drowned at sea". Revolu-
   tionary War: Continental
   Army; Lt. 11th Reg. Mas-
   sachusetts Continental Line.
   Massachusetts Society of the
   Cincinnati. Name spelled
   Bayley on stone. B-10-13
Irene w/o George H., d/o
   Tristram G. Prince d 7 Dec
   1854 ae: 28y. A Tomb 47
James d 6 Sept 1851 ae: 67y.
   GSL
John Jr. d 3 Nov 1815 ae: 38y.
   SD K:25
Joseph H. s/o James d 2 Nov
   1847 ae: 11y. GSL
Joseph H. s/o Joseph L. d 24
   Sept 1863 ae: 22y. NM A
   Tomb 49
Judith M. C. d/o G. S. & J. S. d
   13 June 1852 ae: 5y. SBE A-
   23-6
Louisa D. d/o George H. d 2 Aug
   1863 ae: 10w. A Tomb 47
Sarah wid/o Hudson d 17 Nov
   1838 ae: 87y. Name
   misspelled on stone. B-10-13
Sarah s/o James d 20 Nov 1848
   ae: 57y. ME A Tomb 10
Thomas d 9 Aug 1813 ae: 26y.
   SD K:27
William s/o Benjamin & Jane d
   26 Mar 1819 ae: 11y. SD K:26
William d 19 Nov 1855 ae: 55y.
   GSL
William H. nd Civil War: 4th
   Reg. Maine Inf., Co. G NS
   K:26
BAKER, Abel d 24 Aug 1812 ae:
   42y. J:70
Abigail 2nd w/o John d 19 May
   1811 ae: 69y. C:48
Abigail d 26 Jan 1838 ae: 80y.
   SD H:16
Abigail wid/o Capt. William d

BAKER (continued)

13 Dec 1871 ae: 92y 5m. SBE A-3-22

Abigail S. d 27 Oct 1869 ae: 88y. GSL

Albert s/o Albert d 28 May 1849 ae: 12y. "Died in Boston." "Buried near Friends' Ground." GSL

Ann Christina d/o Asa & Pamela d 8 Nov 1818 ae: 30y. D:109

Asa d 1 Aug 1826 ae: 46y. D:111

Charles d 10 June 1802 ae: 20y. J:99

Charles H. s/o Charles H. d 14 Mar 1857 ae: 2y 7m. "Buried Joshua Weeks' tomb." A Tomb 79

Cornelia d/o William & Nabby d 28 July 1834 ae: 32y. SBE A-3-21

Dorcas wid/o Josiah d 23 Aug 1830 ae: 58y. SBE J:66

Elizabeth w/o Samuel d 19 Aug 1808 ae: 27y. J:68

Elizabeth wid/o John d 8 July 1815 ae: 63y. F:46

Elizabeth w/o Joseph d 11 Apr 1819 ae: 32y. SBE G:118

Elizabeth H. w/o Josiah d 31 Dec 1850 ae: 43y. A-24-14

Fanny d 4 Dec 1859 ae: 67y. A Tomb 12

Fannie E. B. w/o Joseph E. d 21 Nov 1865 ae: 22y. ME A Tomb 69

Frank E. d 14 July 1882 ae: 23y. GSL

Georgia M. w/o Joseph E. d 11 May 1905 ae: 60y 7m 12d. GSL

Hannah 2nd w/o Samuel d 1 June 1817 ae: 32y. C:45

Harriet C. d/o Thomas & Mary d 21 Feb 1815 ae: 10m. SD J:100

Harriet C. d/o Thomas & Mary d 7 July 1816 ae: 4m. J:101

Henry s/o Josiah & Lydia d 12 Jan 1814 ae: 24y. J:71

Ida Tess d 22 Dec 1869 ae: 4y. GSL

BAKER (continued)

Isabella d/o Timothy & Mahala d 14 Sep 1847 ae: 26m. SBE C:230

John d 22 Oct 1797 ae: 82y. SB C:49

John d 8 Mar 1823 ae: 44y. J:51

John E. s/o Albert d 4 Dec 1841 ae: 3y. GSL

John Kelsoll s/o A. J. K. & Eliza S. b 16 Feb 1829 d 28 June 1831 B-5-30

Joseph d 20 July 1817 ae: 38y. SBE G:119

Joseph D. s/o Joseph & Elizabeth d 22 July 1823 ae: 15y. SBE G:120

Joseph Edwin d 26 Oct 1885 ae: 49y 8m. A Tomb 69

Joseph H. d 23 Feb 1829 ae: 23y. J:49

Joseph S. d 18 Aug 1839 ae: 28y. A Tomb 69

Josiah d 8 June 1824 ae: 83y. Revolutionary War G:47

Josiah d 24 Mar 1842 ae: 30y. A-17-15

Julia R. d/o Albert d 21 Nov 1841 ae: 9m. GSL

Laura E. d/o Alexander B. d 13 Apr 1853 ae: 9m. GSL

Lydia wid/o Josiah d 23 Oct 1827 ae: 78y. C:46

Mary w/o Thomas d 18 June 1818 ae: 36y. J:102

Mary d/o Thomas d 12 Feb 1843 ae: 16m. GSL

Mary C. d/o William P. I. & Ellen C. d 21 Aug 1848 ae: 22m. SBE A-3-23

Mina E. d/o J. E. & Georgia M. d 16 Oct 1887 ae: 19y 10m. C:129

Nabby wid/o Abel d 24 Oct 1845 ae: 75y. J:72

Nancy w/o Col. Thomas d 30 June 1837 ae: 47y. A-8-13

Sally w/o Capt. Thomas E. d 17 Nov 1807 ae: 24y. SBE D:135

Samuel d 12 June 1821 ae: 47y. SB J:50

Susan wid/o Josiah d 31 July

BAKER (continued)
1825 ae: 55y. B-5-20

Susannah w/o John d 15 Mar 1772 ae: 51y. SB C:50

Col. Thomas d 5 Sep 1838 ae: 57y. War of 1812. A-8-14

William s/o Samuel & Betsy d 20 Dec 1801 ae: 15m. SD C:52

Capt. William d Dec 1811. "Lost at sea." SD A-3-22

BALDWIN, Eliza d 18 May 1849 ae: 71y. GSL

Hannah d 30 Dec 1881 ae: 78y. A Tomb 41

BALIN, Joseph M. s/o John d 3 July 1863 ae: 11m. GSL

BALL, Asenath d/o James d 7 Sep 1854 ae: 1y. Black. GSL

Eunice w/o James d 6 Jan 1859 ae: 76y. GSL

BALLARD, Benjamin s/o Benjamin B. d 23 Aug 1851 ae: 5m. GSL

Elizabeth d 22 Apr 1851 ae: 33y. GSL

BANCROFT, Harriet E. d 30 June 1863 ae: 17y. SBE A-3-37

BANGS, Joshua d 6 July 1755 ae: 32y 3m. G:145

Joshua d 29 May 1762 ae: 77y. SD H:128

Mehitable w/o Joshua d 5 Apr 1761 ae: 65y. H:127

Nathan d 6 Mar 1728 ae: 34y. SD H:126

Sophia d 4 Oct 1823 ae: 24y. SBE B-3-12

Tabitha d/o Joshua & Sarah d 15 Oct 1750 ae: 1y 9m. G:143

Tabitha d/o Joshua & Sarah d 5 Jan 1752 ae: 7m. G:141

BANKS, Charles E. s/o John H. d 15 Feb 1858 ae: 16m. A Tomb 6

Mary d 7 Nov 1851 ae: 4y 4m. A Tomb 6

BANNATYNE, James d 29 Oct 1842 ae: 34y. Unusual stone. SB A-7-1

BANNER, Adaline M. d/o James d 14 Mar 1846 ae: 6m. ME A Tomb 25

BARBOUR, Caroline d/o Joseph & Lucy d 6 Sep 1832 ae: 24y. SBE D:50

Caroline w/o Alexander d 17 Nov 1865 ae: 52y. GSL

Charles d 30 Sep 1822 ae: 24y. SBE B-3-1

Elizabeth wid/o Joseph Bean d 6 Mar 1826 ae: 82y. D:88

Francis d 1 Mar 1839 ae: 28y. SD D:51

Joseph d 30 May 1854 ae: 78y. SD D:53

Joseph Bean d 5 Sep 1795 ae: 58y. "Killed in fall from building." Revolutionary War. D:89

Judith w/o Joseph d 18 Apr 1842 ae: 62y. SBE D:52

Lucy w/o Joseph d 4 Oct 1818 ae: 44y. SBE D:49

Lucy E. d/o Joseph & Lucy d 14 Dec 1880 ae: 57y. SBE D:48

Martha w/o Samuel d 23 Jan 1862 ae: 55y. GSL

Mary w/o Alexander d 25 Aug 1826. GSL

Mary wid/o William d 23 Feb 1847 ae: 79y. GSL

Samuel A. d 27 Nov 1856 ae: 30y. GSL

William d 26 Oct 1854 ae: 58y. GSL

BARKER, Mrs. Catherine d 29 Mar 1853 ae: 84y. GSL

Elizabeth A. w/o J. C. d/o Stilman Thorpe d 19 May 1856 ae: 22y 1m 18d. A Tomb 16

John s/o John & Sally d 23 Aug 1804 ae: 5d. SD J:17

Lizzie E. d/o Jacob C. d 31 Dec 1856 ae: 5y 3m 19d. A Tomb 16

Miriam B G. w/o James L. d 6 Aug 1851 ae: 27y. GSL

Sarah wid/o Thomas d 27 Jan 1825 ae: 56y. "Native of Standish." F:133

Sarah d/o Elijah d 18 June 1847 ae: 2y. GSL

Thomas d 25 July 1819 ae: 53y. "Born Stratham, New Hamp-

BARKER (continued)

shire." "Left wife and 12 children." F:132

BARNECILLE, Lucy w/o Edward d 11 Dec 1815 ae: 29y. SBE I:122

BARNES, Cornelius s/o Cornelius & Lydia d 10 July 1820 ae: 15y 11m. I:213

Capt. Cornelius d 2 Dec 1822 ae: 42y. I:212

Ebenezer S. s/o Nathan d 29 Mar 1847 ae: 47y. GSL

James s/o James d 18 June 1847 ae: 7y. MB A Tomb 23

Mary w/o James d 2 Oct 1825 ae: 43y. SBE D:1

Sarah wid/o Capt. Seth d 6 Mar 1836 ae: 65y. H:97

Capt. Seth d 18 Nov 1832 ae: 65y. H:96

Zereda w/o Harris C. d 21 June 1884 ae: 71y. A Tomb 69

BARNETT, Charles d 20 Dec 1854 ae: 32y. Black. GSL

Charles s/o late Charles d 17 Feb 1855 ae: 1y. Black. GSL

BARR, James W. d 2 May 1839 ae: 23y. A-10-20

BARRETT, Abigail d/o James & Anna d 24 June 1810 ae: 15y. D:134

Ann wid/o James d 17 Sep 1822 ae: 55y. D:130

Eliza d/o James & Anna d 13 Sep 1812 ae: 23y. D:133

George W. d 3 Dec 1818 ae: 17y. D:132

James d 30 June 1819 ae: 55y. D:131

Dr. John d 18 Apr 1842 ae: 40y. A Tomb 61

John Henry s/o Charles E. & Elizabeth M. b 29 Dec 1831 d 2 Oct 1852. F:2

Joseph Baker s/o Charles E. & Elizabeth M. d 11 Sep 1840 ae: 5m. F:5

Martha wid/o John d 20 May 1827 ae: 65y. SBE F:6

Mary d/o Edward d 25 June 1851 ae: 17d. GSL

BARSTOW, Charles s/o James d 22 Sep 1842 ae: 5w. GSL

Joshua s/o Timothy & Susannah d 27 July 1810 ae: 10y. J:190

Susan wid/o Timothy d 5 Mar 1848 ae: 80y. SB J:192

Timothy d 9 Aug 1837 ae: 75y. SB J:192

BARTELS, Elizabeth w/o John d 21 Dec 1808 ae: 23y. C:85

John d 8 Jan 1860 ae: 86y. NM A Tomb 54

Nathaniel d 20 Nov 1862 ae: 43y. A Tomb 54

Nathaniel D. d 20 Nov 1862 ae: 43y. A Tomb 54

Sarah H. wid/o John d 31 May 1864 ae: 78y. A Tomb 54

BARTLETT, Alexander P. d 13 Mar 1860 ae: 49y. GSL

Benjamin C. d 16 Feb 1845 ae: 37y. "Buried near Joseph Thaxter's stone." NS B-7-31

Caleb d 14 Aug 1824 ae: 22y. SB B-15-14

Clara E. d/o Alexander P. d 19 Aug 1859 ae: 2y 8m. GSL

Capt. Daniel d 22 May 1809 ae: 28y. SD K:147

George s/o Alexander d 9 Mar 1846 ae: 18m. GSL

George F. s/o Alexander P. d 5 July 1846 ae: 4w. "Buried near the hearse house." GSL

Luther s/o John H. d 17 June 1835 ae: 30y. A-2-27

Oliver s/o Oliver & Mary d 13 June 1829 ae: 7m. SD F:19

Susan d 13 May 1841 ae: 18y 6m. GSL

Thomas s/o Thomas d 29 Aug 1852 ae: 10m. GSL

BARTOL, Ella J. d/o David d 14 Apr 1849 ae: 10m. "Buried by side of Jennet Warren's grave." NS G:28

Jane Soule d/o B. & Rebecca d 27 Apr 1827 ae: 18y. SBE B-3-39

Joseph Gerrish s/o William & Frances A. E. d 19 Feb 1838 ae: 4y. A Tomb 57

BARTOL (continued)

Rhoda T. d 19 July 1847 ae: 9m. GSL

BARTON, Mary d 19 Oct 1833 ae: 69y. SBE A-2-19

BASSETT, Harrison C. s/o Thomas d 27 Jan 1848 ae: 18m. Black. GSL

BASTEEN, Elizabeth d 22 Dec 1861 ae: 82y. K:95

BATCHELDER, Clarence E. s/o George O. d 28 Nov 1860 ae: 8y 10m. GSL

Harry S. d 30 July 1862 ae: 1y. GSL

Mary E. w/o John M. d 17 May 1840 ae: 20y. MD A Tomb 19

Lorna s/o Joseph d 14 Dec 1843 ae: 4y 8m. GSL

BAXTER, Elihu, M.D. d 24 Jan 1863 ae: 81y 9m. Moved Evergreen Cemetery? A Tomb 4

Florence L. d/o J. P. d 12 Sep 1857 ae: 2y 2m. Moved Evergreen Cemetery? A Tomb 4

Jane May d/o Fred E. d 11 May 1868 ae: 2m 22d. GSL

BEACON, Rhoenath w/o Nathaniel d 17 Feb 1847 ae: 59y. A Tomb 9

BEAL, Jane H. d/o Rufus & Jane H. d 9 Mar 1842 ae: 12y 8m. A-17-8

Jane H. d 30 Nov 1888 ae: 96y. A-17-10

Rufus d 13 Dec 1869 ae: 71y. A-17-9

BEAN, Charles s/o John & Jane d 24 Nov 1824 ae: 2y. H:101

Charles S. s/o John F. d 20 Sep 1856 ae: 18m. GSL

Ellen d/o Levi d 11 May 1853 ae: 6y. GSL

Jane wid/o John d 4 Nov 1835 ae: 45y. SB H:102

Jane T. d/o John & Jane d 18 Nov 1825 ae: 12y. H:101

John d 18 Dec 1822 ae: 40y. SB H:100

BEATY, John d 30 July 1825 ae: 4y 6m. SD B-14-23

BECK, Betsy w/o Thomas d 22

BECK (continued)

June 1825 ae: 59y. MEB A Tomb 81

Eleanor #2 w/o Thomas d 3 May 1846 ae: 68y. A Tomb 81

Samuel d 25 Feb 1825 ae: 21y. A Tomb 81

Thomas d 18 Aug 1818 ae: 31y. A Tomb 81

Deacon Thomas d 9 Mar 1830 ae: 70y. A Tomb 81

BECKETT, Edward s/o Charles d 10 Sep 1842 ae: 10m. GSL

Grace, widow b 17 June 1774 d 9 Jan 1849 SBE A-22-1

George W. s/o Sylvester B. d 5 Dec 1849 ae: 4y. GSL

Jane d/o William C. d 3 Sep 1843 ae: 7m. GSL

Martha E. d/o William C. d 25 Aug 1849 ae: 3m. GSL

Samuel S. d 1 June 1848 ae: 40y. "Buried by side of Mary A. Stevens – 1802." NS J:38

Susan S. wid/o Samuel S. d 5 Sep 1854 ae: 47y. "Buried beside husband." NS J:38

William d 13 July 1814 ae: 39y. GSL

BEEMAN, Dorcas w/o Abraham d 19 Apr 1812 ae: 42y. I:55

BEHRENS, Herman F. s/o Frederick & Julia b 14 July 1862 d 4 Sep 1863. SBE J:154

BELFORD, Annie D. d/o Davis & Judith d 25 Apr 1834 ae: 22y. ME A Tomb 23

Charles E. s/o Davis & Judith d 21 June 1819 ae: 18m. ME A Tomb 23

Davis d 26 Mar 1841 ae: 59y. ME A Tomb 23

Francis P. d 30 Nov 1892 ae: 77y. "Died San Jose, California." ME A Tomb 23

Judith T. d 26 May 1882 ae: 97y. "Died Santa Clara, California." ME A Tomb 23

Louisa D. d 24 Dec 1844 ae: 29y. ME A Tomb 23

Marie T. d 14 May 1873 ae: 53y. "Died San Jose, California."

BELFORD (continued)
ME A Tomb 23

BELL, Benjamin d 10 Feb 1873 ae: 72y. GSL

Hannah w/o Jacob d 28 Aug 1824 ae: 56y. B-12-7

Henry d 7 Dec 1854 ae: 52y. A Tomb 6

Sarah W. w/o Benjamin d 8 June 1872 ae: 68y 8m. SB B-13-8

BELMORE, inf d/o John & Lucy d 1 Mar 1837 ae: 14d. SD B-3-42

John s/o John & Lucy d 29 Dec 1835 ae: 7m. SD B-3-42

Margaret d/o John & Lucy d 6 July 1836 ae: 3y. SD B-3-42

BENJAMIN, John d 9 Apr 1853 ae: 58y. GSL

BENMORE, Ann d 27 Oct 1853 ae: 17y. Black. GSL

BENNETT, Andrew d 27 Oct 1851 ae: 37yrs. GSL

Kesia d 8 Apr 1847 ae: 82yrs. GSL

Mary C. d/o Edward H. d 4 Mar 1850 ae: 5m. GSL

BENNISON, George s/o Robert d 23 Jan 1849 ae: 3yrs. A Tomb 7

BERRY, Amos Strout s/o Josiah & Eunice d 12 Aug 1828 ae: 11m. C:16

Dorcas d/o Burdick & Sally d 20 Aug 1804 ae: 19m. SD D:40

Eliza w/o William B. d 25 June 1834 ae: 38y. A-24-4

Eliza S. d 29 Nov 1877 ae: 80y. A-24-2

Elizabeth d 9 Aug 1831 ae: 89y. MD A Tomb 18

Ellen L. d/o Joseph & Nancy d 30 Apr 1838 ae: 1y 10m. SD D:9

Huldah J. d/o Josiah & Eunice d 19 Nov 1831 ae: 3y. C:17

Jeremiah b 16 Nov 1742 d 23 Dec 1816. D:43

Joanna b 12 Aug 1738 d 10 Oct 1818. D:43

Joseph d 27 Mar 1871 ae: 79y. SD D:12

BERRY (continued)
Joshua d 14 Feb 1740 ae: 30y. GSL

Maleon B. s/o William B. & Eliza d 9 Aug 1831 ae: 11m. A-24-4

Mary d 9 Dec 1850 ae: 69y. GSL

Mary L. d/o Joseph & Nancy d 31 Aug 1840 ae: 5m. SD D:8

Nancy w/o Joseph d 2 July 1852 ae: 58y. SD D:11

Nancy C. wid/o Edward d 29 Feb 1868 ae: 73y. NM F:96 Tomb

Rebecca d/o Jeremiah d 7 Dec 1803 ae: 33y. GSL

Sally, widow d 29 June 1843 ae: 68y. GSL

William B. d 28 May 1863 ae: 73y. War of 1812. A-24-3

BERRYMAN, John d 9 June 1856 ae: 50y. "Native of St. Johns, New Brunswick." "Buried at head of E. Clarke's grave." GSL

BIBBER, Hannah B. w/o Joel C. b 1797 d 1872. A-20-6

Joel C. b 1796 d 1840. A-20-5

Joel C. s/o Thomas M. d 1 Feb 1869 ae: 7w. GSL

Joseph H. s/o William d 27 Oct 1852 ae: 1y 8m. GSL

Lucy Ann d/o William A. d 18 Sep 1854 ae: 15m. "Buried at head of Job Randall." NS A-11-15

Wellha J. w/o Joel d 16 Sep 1860 ae: 51y. GSL

BICKENTON, Circia D. w/o Thomas, d/o Oliver Clapp d 28 Sep 1853 ae: 24y. GSL

BICKFORD, Betsy w/o Joseph d 10 Apr 1830 ae: 27y. F:3

Mary w/o Aaron d 30 Dec 1752 ae: 26y. D:100

Rebecca w/o Job d 29 Oct 1817 ae: 79y. SD G:116

BIGELOW, Lucy E. d/o Samuel & Sally nd. SD H:25

BIRD, Pamelia w/o William d 20 Aug 1839. A-6-15

Thomas d 25 June 1790. Hanged for murder. GSL

BIRD (continued)

William d 27 Dec 1848 ae: 53y. "Died in Saco." "Buried by side of wife." NS A-6-15

BISHE, Charlotte R. d/o John & Mercy d 29 Nov 1832 ae: 4y 6m. SBE B-4-18

BISBE, Rev. John d 8 Mar 1829 ae: 36y. First Universalist Church. SBE B-4-19

BLAKE, Caroline E. d/o John & Lydia d 4 Sep 1833 ae: 17m. J:81

Charles B. s/o Francis & Lavina d 2 Oct 1842 ae: 5y 3m 6d. SD B-3-18

Eliza w/o Thomas d 31 Aug 1821 ae: 31y. G:114

Eliza B. S. w/o Capt. Nathaniel d 14 Oct 1888 ae: 80y 11m. A Tomb 26

Ethel Elizabeth d 18 Apr 1903 ae: 9y 8m 21d. A Tomb 26

Francis d 28 Apr 1857 ae: 60y. B-3-22

Frederick B. s/o Nathaniel & Eliza d 1 Jan 1869 ae: 30y. A Tomb 26

Frederick W. d 2 Feb 1864 ae: 38y. Civil War: 16th Reg, Maine Inf., Co. F. B-3-16

George H. s/o Nathaniel d 1 Jan 1909 ae: 73y 2m. Civil War: 7th Battalion Maine Lt. Artillery A Tomb 26

Georgianna d/o Nathaniel d 13 June 1881 ae: 34y. A Tomb 26

Harriet Lavina wid/o Herbert, d/o Gardner & Hannah Floyd d 19 Jan 1949 ae: 86y 1m 26d. A Tomb 26

Harry N. s/o Herbert & Harriet d 3 Jan 1962 ae: 78y 12d. A Tomb 26

Herbert Clinton s/o Joseph H. d 29 May 1912 ae: 26y 6m 9d. A Tomb 26

Joseph H. s/o Nathaniel & Eliza d 20 Sep 1922 ae: 72y 10m 22d. Civil War: 1st Reg. Maine Vet Vol. Inf., Co. A. A Tomb 26

BLAKE (continued)

Joseph R. s/o Samuel d 31 Jan 1847 ae: 1y. GSL

Lucy E. w/o Rolin d/o late Oliver Blake d 3 Feb 1852 ae: 24y. GSL

Mary d 3 Nov 1853. GSL

Mary w/o Nathaniel d 12 July 1843 ae: 59y. A Tomb 26

Mary L. b 1818 d 16 Mar 1882. A Tomb 26

Nathaniel d 19 Mar 1845 ae: 65y. A Tomb 26

Capt. Nathaniel d 27 Aug 1887 ae: 76y 2m. Civil War: 9th Reg. Maine Inf., Co. I. A Tomb 26

Oliver d 17 June 1848 ae: 58y. "Fell dead in the street." SBE D:23

Samuel s/o S. A. d 6 Dec 1854 ae: 9y. GSL

Samuel s/o Samuel d 15 Sep 1842 ae: 3m. A Tomb 26

Samuel R. d 5 Aug 1868 ae: 37y 9m 22d. Civil War: 19th Reg. Maine Inf., Co. F. B-3-23

Sarah C. d/o Francis & Lavina d 17 May 1853 ae: 31y. B-3-21

BLANCHARD, Mary w/o Moses d 4 Jan 1756 ae: 19y 6m. G:47

Mary E. d/o Joseph B. d 7 July 1855 ae: 1y 4m 13d. GSL

BLASDELL, Susannah wid/o Nicholas d 17 Aug 1822 ae: 83y. J:74

BLOOD, Elder Caleb d 6 Mar 1814 ae: 59y. SBE J:48

Eleanor d/o Rev. Caleb & Sarah d 29 Apr 1813 ae: 29y. SBE J:47

BLUEFIELD, Charles H. s/o Simeon & Susan d 14 Aug 1853 ae: 5m. GSL

Mary d/o Simeon & Susan d 1 Sep 1860 ae: 1y 2m. GSL

Mary E. d/o Simon & Susan d 14 Sep 1858 ae: 4w. GSL

BLYTH, Capt. Samuel, RN killed in action on 5 Sep 1813 ae: 29y. War of 1812: *H. M. S. Boxer.* LM H:7

11

BODGE, Almarin s/o Albert d 27 Feb 1845 ae: 9m. A Tomb 69

BOLAN, inf ch/o John d 22 Oct 1855. GSL

inf ch/o John d 25 June 1860 ae: 5dys. GSL

Bridget w/o John d 1O Sep 1862 ae: 34y. GSL

John s/o John d 1 July 1859 ae: 9m. GSL

John s/o John d 3 Feb 1855 ae: 3y 5m. GSL

Charles E. s/o John d 29 June 1858 ae: 1y 4m. GSL

BOLTON, Eliza A. d/o Thomas & Martha d 11 Aug 1824 ae: 18m. H:122

John N. s/o late Thomas d 17 Dec 1861 ae: 25y. GSL

Martha w/o Thomas d 22 Feb 1848 ae: 53y. SBE H:123

Thomas s/o Thomas & Martha d 3 June 1829 ae: 12y. H:121

Thomas d 13 June 1859 ae: 66y. SB H:124

BOND, E. F. d Aug 1821 ae: 16m. B-4-17

Eliza d 30 June 1807 ae: 33y. LME F:105 Tomb

Estha wid/o John d 25 Jan 1825 ae: 78y. B-4-16

Mary Jane d/o John & Mary A. d 2 June 1814 ae: 23m. B-4-17

BONNEY, Betsy B. b 18 Feb 1809 d 18 Jan 1887. SBE B-7-26

Henrietta d/o Marshall d 30 Mar 1846 ae: 2y. GSL

Joel d 9 Apr 1824 ae: 83y. B-6-10

Mary Ann d/o Marshall d 20 Aug 1845 ae: 19y. GSL

BOOBIER, Thomas d 29 July 1835 ae: 36y. A-3-26

BOODY, Henry H. d 12 Jan 1853 ae: 64y 4m. GSL

BOOTHBAY, Georgianna K. d/o Horatio d 23 Mar 1861 ae: 15m 17d. Mmt A Tomb 66

BOOTMAN, Thankful d 21 Aug 1834 ae: 83y. C:246

BOSTON, Henry W. d 30 Apr 1864 ae: 50y. MmtD A Tomb 86

BOSTON (continued)

Sarah w/o Timothy d 14 June 1816 ae: 29y. K:14

Timothy d 7 June 1826 ae: 40y. K:12

BOSWORTH, Almira d/o Joseph & Deborah d 23 Oct 1806 ae: 15y. SD K:32

BOTH, Antoinette J. d/o A. C. d 1 Mar 1886 ae: 32y 5m. GSL

BOWE, William s/o James d 5 May 1841 ae: 2y 3m. GSL

BOWERS, Catherine d 1 Mar 1843 ae: 76y. GSL

Nicholas s/o Nicholas d 24 Feb 1838 ae: 2m. Catholic. C:115

BOWES, James d 1800. Revolutionary War. Black. GSL

BOWLES, Stephen B. s/o Thomas S. & Abiah E. d 19 Sep 1827 ae: 9m. SB E:65

BOYD, Almira d/o Joseph C. & Isabella S. b 8 Aug 1817 d 6 Apr 1826. NM A Tomb 61

Ann Jane d/o James d 17 Feb 1860 ae: 7y 9m. GSL

David s/o James d 22 July 1844 ae: 2y. A Tomb 17

Frances Greenleaf d/o Joseph C. & Isabella S. b 25 Nov 1808 d 11 Dec 1824. NM A Tomb 61

Horatio Erald s/o Joseph & Isabella S. b 17 Apr 1810 d 11 Mar 1833. NM A Tomb 61

Isabella Southgate w/o Joseph Coffin, d/o Dr. Robert & Mary King Southgate b 29 Mar 1779 d 28 Jan 1821. NM A Tomb 61

James Joseph s/o Joseph C. & Isabella S. b 25 July 1798 d 30 Apr 1829. NM A Tomb 61

Jane w/o James d 20 June 1858 ae: 30y. A Tomb 17

Joseph Coffin d 12 May 1823 ae: 63y. NM A Tomb 61

Miranda Elizabeth d/o Joseph C. & Isabella S. b 24 Dec 1812 d 31 May 1830. NM A Tomb 61

Octavia Caroline d/o Joseph C. & Isabella S. b 15 Mar 1815 d 6 Apr 1826. NM A Tomb 61

Robert d 17 Jan 1827 ae: 68y.

12

BOYD (continued)

NM A Tomb 61

Ruth w/o Robert d 10 Aug 1805 ae: 36y. F:105 Tomb

Sarah C. d/o James d 18 June 1866 ae: 3m. GSL

Sarah M. d/o James d 8 Oct 1854 ae: 8m. GSL

William Edward s/o Robert Southgate d 31 May 1845 ae: 1y. NM A Tomb 61

BOYINTON, Nathaniel G. d 28 July 1838 ae: 32y. A-9-19

Lydia d 3 Feb 1830 ae: 3m. A-11-16 1/2

William s/o Nathaniel & M. G. d 11 June 1830 ae: 9m. A-9-19

BOYLES, Yunel d 22 July 1869 ae: 52y. Mmt A Tomb 38

BOYNTON, Hannah w/o Theophilus d June 1794 ae: 27y. SBE C:63

Theophilus s/o Joshua & Rachel d Nov 1797 ae: 33y. SBE C:63

BRACKETT, Abigail wid/o Anthony d 1 Feb 1805 ae: 77y. I:192

Sarah Jane d/o Jeremiah & Sarah d 11 Nov 1829 ae: 11m. G:104

BRACKLEY, Phebe d 12 May 1862 ae: 79y. GSL

BRADBURY, Alden d 30 Dec 1875 ae: 70y. SBE A-15-4

Andrew d 16 Aug 1852 ae: 72y. GSL

Andrew b 1846 d ---- Civil War: 20th Reg. Maine Inf. Co. A. A-7-13

Caroline d/o Alden & Caroline G. d 17 Oct 1837 ae: 21m. SBE A-15-4

Caroline G. w/o Alden d 30 Jan 1841 ae: 35y. SBE A-15-4

Capt. Charles d 10 Sep 1842 ae: 65y. GSL

Charles H. d 9 Oct 1856 ae: 37y. A-7-13

Daniel d 9 July 1845 ae: 74y. SBE F:39

Deborah w/o Andrew d 28 Jan

BRADBURY (continued)

1837 ae: 50y. SBE A-7-12

Dorcas wid/o Thomas d 23 May 1867 ae: 87y. SBE B-2-26

Eliza Ann d/o Thomas & Dorcas d 12 Sep 1828 ae: 19y. B-2-25

Elizabeth wid/o Rowland d 6 Mar 1798 ae: 87y. GSL

Ellen M. d/o Alden & Caroline G. d 16 Sep 1833 ae: 17m. SBE A-15-4

Frances d/o Theophilus & Sarah d 20 Sep 1769 ae: 1y 8d. C:197

Frances d/o George & Mary J. d 23 Sep 1804 ae: 10m. SBE C:19

Francis s/o Daniel & Rhoda d 10 Nov 1846 ae: 36y. F:42

Francis s/o Alden & Caroline G. d 16 May 1851 ae: 21y. SBE A-15-4

Francis H. s/o George L. & Elizabeth d 28 Aug 1842 ae: 2y. SD G:153

George d 17 Nov 1823 ae: 53y. SBE C:24

George A. s/o George L. & Elizabeth d 8 Sep 1841 ae: 2y. SD G:153

George H. s/o George L. & Elizabeth d 14 May 1838 ae: 1yr. SD G:153

George L. d 21 Sep 1850 ae: 48y. SD G:153

George W. s/o George L. & Elizabeth d 21 Apr 1835 ae: 3y. SD G:153

Hannah wid/o Thomas d 15 Sep 1829 ae: 83y. F:43

Harriet d/o Daniel & Rhoda d 11 July 1832 ae: 27y. F:41

Jacob d 30 Aug 1816 ae: 80y. SD G:151

Jane w/o William d 13 May 1839 ae: 21y. A-9-2

John d 14 Mar 1823 ae: 47y. SB G:152

John A. s/o George L. & Elizabeth d 15 Apr 1831 ae: 18m. SD G:153

Lydia w/o Jacob d 11 Jan 1811

BRADBURY (continued)
ae: 61y. SD G:150

Mary w/o George d 28 Dec 1819 ae: 46y. SBE C:23

Mary Kent d/o George & Mary J. d 23 June 1805 ae: 4y. SBE C:18

Rhoda w/o Daniel d 13 Nov 1844 ae: 70y. SBE F:40

Sarah wid/o Theophilus d 22 May 1824 ae: 84y. SB C:27

Thomas d 24 Sep 1812 ae: 76y. F:44

Thomas d 21 May 1852 ae: 77y. GSL

William d 24 Apr 1854 ae: 43y. SB A-9-3

Wyman s/o Reuben & Eunice b 24 Apr 1810 d 4 July 1811 G:149

BRADFORD, Alexander s/o Alexander d 5 Sep 1826 ae: 18y. B-2-1

Almira wid/o Andrew d 12 June 1835 ae: 38y. SD B-2-3

Andrew d 26 Nov 1827 ae: 34y. SBE B-2-2

Benjamin b 1747 d 1820 Revolutionary War. GSL

Charles s/o Andrew & Almira d 4 Aug 1826 ae: 14m. SD B-2-4

Cynthia d/o Ira & Hannah d 22 June 1826 ae: 22y. B-9-34

Elizabeth wid/o N. d 12 Nov 1857 ae: 72y. GSL

Francis s/o George d 28 Aug 1843 ae: 2y. GSL

Capt. George d 4 Aug 1849 ae: 67y. "Died in Bangor." SBE A-8-19

Gilman Rawson s/o Charles d 28 Nov 1845 ae: 3y 9m. GSL

Hannah w/o Ira d 29 Aug 1872 ae: 87y. SD B-9-36

Harriet w/o George d 21 May 1820 ae: 34y. SBE A-8-17

Harriet d/o George & Harriet d 24 Apr 1847 ae: 27y. SBE A-8-18

Henry C. d 13 Jan 1840 ae: 23y. "Lost in the steamer *Lexington*." SBE A-8-18

BRADFORD (continued)
Capt. Ira d 19 Jan 1866 ae: 83y. SD B-9-35

Joan d 26 Apr 1828 ae: 56y. I:136

Joseph d 6 Sep 1847 ae: 22y. "Native of Calais." "Died at the Hospital." GSL

Malvina W. d/o Joseph d 24 Feb 1848 ae: 12y. GSL

Mary H. w/o Richmond d 29 June 1865 ae: 47y. NM A Tomb 53

Mary T. w/o George d 7 Oct 1838 ae: 59y. SBE A-8-17

Nathaniel s/o Nathaniel d May 1825 ae: 21y. B-2-1

Nathaniel d 29 May 1827 ae: 47y. B-2-1

Sarah Jane d/o Joseph d 14 Apr 1850 ae: 12y 8m. GSL

William C. s/o Nathaniel d 1804 ae: 27m. B-2-1

BRADISH, Abiah w/o Maj. David d 27 May 1813 ae: 66y. C:33

Maj. David d 18 June 1818 ae: 73y. Revolutionary War. C:32

Emma S. d/o Levi d 18 Mar 1856 ae: 45y. ME A Tomb 60

Levi d 12 Dec 1851 ae: 77y. SBE C:28

Susannah d 3 Sep 1799 ae: 21y. C:38

BRADLEY, Ezra S. d 16 May 1896 ae: 73y. "Died San Jose, California." MB A Tomb 23

Fanny S. d/o Charles d 9 June 1868 ae: 33y. A Tomb 72

Herbert F. s/o Charles L. d 8 May 1869 ae: 7m. GSL

BRAGDON, Capt. Daniel d 16 Apr 1819 ae: 57y. Unusual stone. K:168.

Mary w/o Robert d 26 Nov 1815 ae: 28y. SBE I:13

Royal L. s/o John G. d 19 Sep 1845 ae: 1y 1m 13d. GSL

BRADSTREET, Nathan D. d 19 Nov 1826 ae: 24y. D:71

BRAGG, Alden S. s/o late George d 28 Mar 1846 ae: 4y. GSL

BRAMHALL, Cornelius d 28 Mar 1761 ae: 53y. I:24

14

BRAY, Oliver b 2 Apr 1776 d 26 Dec 1823. GSL

Sarah R. d 5 Sep 1833 ae: 49y. SBE B-4-12

Theophilus P. s/o Isaac A. d 2 June 1850 ae: 10y. A Tomb 44

BRAZIER, Abigail w/o Harrison d 7 Apr 1823 ae: 46y. H:40

Abigail C. d/o Harrison & Abigail d 6 Aug 1818 ae: 14y. H:105

Ann L. wid/o Harrison d 15 June 1859 ae: 77y. H:42

Enoch d Mar 1804 ae: 43y. GSL

Enoch s/o Joseph d 10 Nov 1843 ae: 22m. GSL

Eunice O. d/o Harrison & Abigail d 28 June 1818 ae: 4y. H:105

Harrison d 8 Nov 1855 ae: 78y. H:41

John H. d 19 Feb 1850 ae: 47y. "Buried in Harrison Brazier's lot." NS H:41

Joseph B. b 1820 d 1897. A-22-5

Joseph R. d 28 Aug 1878 ae: 70y. GSL

Mary L. w/o Joseph B. b 1824 d 1900. A-22-4

Mary L. d/o Joseph B. & Mary L. Ramsey b 1846 d 1911. A-22-3

BRESLIN, Thomas d 14 Nov 1831 ae: 34y. B-7-1

BREWER, David d 9 Nov 1830 ae: 43y. GSL

John s/o John d 26 Aug 1854 ae: 7w. GSL

BRIDGES, Mary M. w/o Wilson d 5 Apr 1862 ae: 30y. A Tomb 63

BRIDLEY, Mary w/o William C. d 1 Sep 1827 ae: 20y. SB B-6-3

BRIGGS, Abner s/o William nd ae: 17y. "Killed on board barque *Nautilus*, from Charleston to LeHavre, by falling from fore yard-arm to deck." GSL

Abner s/o Abner & Sarah d 1 July 1805 ae: 1m. G:100

Catherine S. wid/o John L. d 30 Jan 1849 ae: 52y. GSL

BRIGGS (continued)

Deborah w/o Nathaniel d 11 Feb 1844 ae: 43y. GSL

Henry H. s/o John P. & Dora F. d 16 May 1838 ae: 20m. SBE G:147

Huldah d/o Abner & Sarah d 3 Jan 1821 ae: 13y. G:100

Dr. John P. d 26 July 1838 ae: 46y. G:147

William P. s/o John P. & Dora F. d 19 Nov 1833 ae: 5y. SD G:148

BRITTON, Cynthia E. Pennell d 19 Apr 1899 ae: 33y. SD A-8-15

BROOKS, Alice M. d/o George W. H. d 5 Nov 1863 ae: 23y 7m. A Tomb 30

Ann d 5 Oct 1869 ae: 94y. ME A Tomb 75

Charles Martin s/o Paschal & Clarissa d 19 Feb 1834. SBE B-5-10

Clarissa P. d/o Paschal & Clarissa d 15 July 1832 ae: 13m. ME A Tomb 45

Cotton B. d 12 May 1834 ae: 69y. A Tomb 75

Eliza d/o John d 23 Feb 1844 ae: 10m. A Tomb 75

Elizabeth d/o George d 14 Jan 1843 ae: 6y. A Tomb 75

George d 8 Aug 1837 ae: 40y. A Tomb 75

Harriet d/o William & C. b 3 Feb 1825 d 25 Sep 1826. SD B-9-38

James s/o John d 17 Oct 1842 ae: 14m. A Tomb 75

Jane Williams w/o Cotton B. d 23 Jan 1828 ae: 60y. A Tomb 75

Margaret d/o William d 10 Sep 1842 ae: 5m. GSL

Martha d H. w/o John C. d 16 Sep 1840 ae: 30y. A Tomb 75

Martha Swift #2 w/o John C. d 10 Jan 1845 ae: 31y. A Tomb 75

Paschal d 14 June 1833 ae: 30y. SBE B-5-9

Sarah w/o Stephen P. d 27 Aug

BROOKS (continued)
1849 ae: 40y. A Tomb 30

Stephen P. d 28 Jan 1859 ae: 53y. 10m. A Tomb 30

Stephen S. s/o Stephen P. d 4 Aug 1844 ae: 9y. "Buried J. Ham tomb." A Tomb 30

BROWN, Abbie Rollins w/o John A. Jr., d/o Hiram & Mary A. Reed b 7 Dec 1841 d 25 Jan 1929. A-7-18

Angeline d 1 Feb 1848 ae: 27y. GSL

Ann wid/o Thomas d 29 June 1859 ae: 78y 8m. A Tomb 49

Ann w/o Nelson d 21 July 1866 ae: 56y. F:76

Ann D. w/o Richard D. d 23 Sep 1864 ae: 51y. GSL

Anna Isabella d 4 Feb 1863 ae: 3m 25d. Black. GSL

Asa d 6 Aug 1849 ae: 21y. "Buried near the gate." GSL

Daniel Henry d 15 Dec 1858 ae: 13y 5m. GSL

Eliza d 15 Sep 1842 ae: 40y. Black. GSL

Elizabeth wid/o Andrew d 22 Dec 1854 ae: 86y. GSL

Elizabeth I. w/o Asa d 17 Jan 1826 ae: 24y. SD B-8-6

Frances d 16 June 1845 ae: 29y. Black. GSL

Frances d 14 Mar 1858 ae: 75y. GSL

George E. d 10 Feb 1858 ae: 25y. GSL

Georgianna H. d/o Nelson & Ann d 8 Apr 1851 ae: 5y 7m. SD F:77

Harriet E. w/o William B. d 24 May 1845 ae: 36y. Black. GSL

Helen L. d/o Daniel d 20 May 1852 ae: 3y 6m. GSL

James H. d 24 Nov 1884 ae: 74y. GSL

Jane d/o John d 18 June 1856 ae: 19y 3m. "Native Windsor, Nova Scotia." GSL

Jesse d 11 June 1842 ae: 21y. GSL

BROWN (continued)
John b 15 May 1817 d 28 Nov 1838. Catholic. A-5-25

John s/o John d 25 Oct 1853 ae: 7d. GSL

John A. d 12 Dec 1843 ae: 35y. SBE A-7-19

John A., Jr. b 1840 d 19 July 1880. Civil War: 5th Battalion Maine Light Artillery, 8th Reg. Maine Inf., Co. B. A-7-18

John H. d 9 Feb 1846 ae: 33y. GSL

John J. d 5 May 1864 ae: 19y. Civil War: 29th Reg. Maine Inf., Co. C. SD A-5-25

Joseph s/o L. d 16 Sep 1842 ae: 14m. Black. GSL

Leda R. d/o James d 29 Mar 1856 ae: 21m. GSL

Levi d 10 Sep 1861 ae: 19y. GSL

Mary Ann d 23 July 1860 ae: 53y 4m. Black. GSL

Pamelia A. d/o George d 30 Sep 1854 ae: 2y. "Buried at head of Thaxter's grave." NS B-7-31

Patrick d 10 June 1800 ae: 41y. SB L:24

Peter d 12 May 1846 ae: 60y. Black. GSL

Phebe Alice d/o William F. d 1 Nov 1853 ae: 8m. GSL

Robert A. s/o James d 30 Sep 1863 ae: 3y 8m 23d. GSL

Ruth C. wid/o John A. d 6 Aug 1892 ae: 74y. A-7-19

Sarah B. d/o Jonathan d 3 Nov 1850 ae: 2m. GSL

Sarah E. w/o William d 4 Apr 1848 ae: 22y 8m. Black. GSL

Sarah J. d/o Benjamin d 11 Sep 1846 ae: 15y. GSL

Sarah P. d/o William & Sarah d 7 May 1858 ae: 15y 8m. B-14-29

Susan C. w/o John B. d 14 May 1864 ae: 42y. GSL

Thankful d 14 June 1843 ae: 63y. Widow. A Tomb 31

William d 18 May 1854 ae: 82y.

BROWN (continued)
Black. GSL
William E. s/o Richard & Ann d
2 Feb 1838. F:1
BROWNE, Abba T. d/o George
W. d 5 June 1849 ae: 6y. GSL
Abigail d/o Thomas & Ann d 1
May 1810 ae: 48y. SD F:168
Harriet C. d/o William d 10
June 1845 ae: 35y. "Died in
Philadelphia." "Buried by
side of David Smith's tomb."
F:105
Lydia wid/o Rev. Thomas d 13
Oct 1805. GSL
Octavia w/o William d 9 Jan
1813 ae: 28y. SBE F:169
Octavia S. d/o William & Oc-
tavia d 27 Apr 1829 ae: 16y
9m. SBE F:170
Capt. Thomas d 3 Mar 1849 ae:
79y. "Buried in his tomb."
GSL
Rev. Thomas d 18 Oct 1797 ae:
64y. GSL
Thomas s/o Rev. Thomas d 1
Mar 1849 ae: 81y. GSL
William s/o Rev. Thomas d 14
Nov 1861 ae: 83y. GSL
BRUNELL, Mrs Agnes d 12 Feb
1848 ae: 31y. GSL
BYRAM, Lucretia R. w/o Henry
O. d 8 May 1837 ae: 24y. SD
A-8-5
BRYANT, Caroline Tucker d/o
Timothy d 27 May 1860 ae:
16y. GSL
Edward s/o Jonathan & M. d 6
Sep 1901 ae: 16m. NS D:145
Elizabeth wid/o Jonathan d 10
July 1829 ae: 74y. SD D:140
Freeman d 13 Nov 1825 ae: 23y.
B-8-8
Georgianna A. d/o Joseph d 13
Aug 1850 ae: 2y. GSL
Henry s/o Jonathan & Elizabeth
d 20 Sep 1797 ae: 4y. SB
D:149
James s/o Jonathan & Elizabeth
d 20 June 1798 ae: 18y. D:148
James d 6 Sep 1859 ae: 59y. SD
D:142

BRYANT (continued)
Jonathan d 18 Nov 1825 ae: 84y.
SD D:140
Joseph d 15 Nov 1805 ae: 22y.
D:143
Lemuel d 22 Jan 1805 ae: 29y.
D:144
Mary N. d/o Daniel d 18 Dec
1872 ae: 83y. "Buried John
Dennison lot." A-18-12
Phebe w/o Caleb d 13 Aug 1829
ae: 34y. B-4-21
Rebecca w/o Spencer b 1770 d
26 Oct 1863. SBE A-10-17
Spencer d 22 Mar 1839 ae: 67y.
A-10-16
Susan R. d/o Timothy d 4 May
1858 ae: 20y 11m. GSL
BUCK, Mary w/o Henry d 17 Sep
1822 ae: 48y. B-9-2
BUCKNAM, Julia d 14 Sep 1857
ae: 3y. GSL
BUDDEN, Rachael F. w/o Jabez
d 13 Apr 1856 ae: 26y 11m.
GSL
BUGBEE, Edward s/o Ira D. &
Eliza A. C. d 4 May 1832 ae:
1y. SD C:41
John B. s/o Ira D. & Eliza A. C.
d 10 Feb 1833 ae: 6y. SD
C:40
BUNCH, Ellen F. d/o Charles W.
d 9 Oct 1868 ae: 11d. GSL
BUNKER, David d 29 Dec 1844
ae: 72y. GSL
BUNNELS, Jane d/o Thomas d 21
Mar 1849 ae: 29y. GSL
BUNTEN, Elizabeth wid/o James
M. d 28 Sep 1857 ae: 79y. SD
E:35
BURBANK, Ann d 8 May 1862 ae:
50y. GSL
Caroline Sophia d/o David &
Sophia d 26 Dec 1830 ae: 2y.
SD H:19
John H. s/o Ann d 24 Oct 1860
ae: 16y. "His arm was in-
terred in June." "Buried at foot
of Thomas Bolton's grave."
NS H:124
Lucy A. w/o Rev. John F. d 11
May 1847 ae: 28y. GSL

17

BURDICK, Levi s/o Austin d 1 May 1859 ae: 23y. GSL

BURGESS, inf s/o John d 23 Apr 1857. GSL

Catherine M. d/o Henry S. d 20 Feb 1878 ae: 23y. GSL

Hattie A. d/o Henry S. d 29 Aug 1882 ae: 26y. GSL

Sarah E. d/o Henry S. d 13 Sep 1841 ae: 8m. GSL

BURKE, inf d 23 June 1857 ae: 6w. "Died on board the British steamer." GSL

Elizabeth A. d/o Enoch A. & Elmira d 11 Nov 1849 ae: 2y. Black. GSL

Joseph H. s/o Enoch A. & Elmira d 19 Apr 1852 ae: 3y 3m. Black. GSL

Enoch d 27 Oct 1854 ae: 27y. "Native of Philadelphia." GSL

BURNES, Ada E. d/o William H. & Laura A. d 8 Feb 1854 ae: 15m. SBE F:64

Bennie s/o William H. & Laura A. d 27 Mar 1865. F:65

Gertie V. S. d/o William H. & Laura A. d 20 Feb 1882 ae: 18y 5m. F:65

BURNHAM, Abigail wid/o John d 28 Aug 1798 ae: 53y. J:90

Edward d 22 July 1852 ae: 49y. A Tomb 45

James d 3 Feb 1862 ae: 71y. GSL

Jane w/o William W. d 1 Mar 1828 ae: 25y. B-11-27

John d 29 July 1798 ae: 60y. Revolutionary War. J:91

Mariner d 7 Dec 1859 ae: 29y. GSL

BURNS, Benjamin d 5 June 1830 ae: 50y 5m. SB D:74

Charles Henry s/o James & Eunice d 5 July 1836 ae: 10m. D:13

Edwin d 17 Sep 1906 ae: 71y. GSL

Elizabeth wid/o Benjamin d 31 Jan 1841 ae: 61y 6m. SB D:75

George d 23 Jan 1839 ae: 82y. D:14

BURNS (continued)
George W. d 27 Jan 1871 ae: 77y. GSL

Laura A. s/o William H. d 29 Sep 1907 ae: 73y 8m. GSL

Lucy wid/o George d 1 Dec 1847 ae: 89y. GSL

Martha W. d/o George d 25 Jan 1850 ae: 7y. GSL

Sarah w/o Samuel W. d 8 Nov 1849 ae: 38y. GSL

William H. s/o Henry & Catherine d 7 July 1898 ae: 74y 8m. GSL

BURRELL, Annie E. F. d/o George S. d 21 Feb 1864 ae: 3m. GSL

Elizabeth S. w/o William d 30 May 1848 ae: 29y. A Tomb 69

BURROWS, Capt. William KIA 5 Sep 1813 ae: 28y. War of 1812: *USS Enterprise*. LM H:8

BUSH, Eliza d 26 Nov 1872 ae: 62y. "Buried Tarr lot." GSL

Hannah d 23 May 1858 ae: 32y. GSL

James s/o George d 30 Apr 1847 ae: 3d. GSL

George s/o George d 17 Apr 1850 ae: 3y 3m. Black. GSL

BUSKIRK, Levi s/o John d 8 Aug 1843 ae: 3m. GSL

BUTLER, Abby E. d/o Samuel d 19 Oct 1855 ae: 24y. GSL

Anne d/o John & Ann d 18 Jan 1769 ae: 5y 1m. SD C:217

George d 24 Dec 1842 ae: 35y. GSL

Mary d/o John & Ann b 4 Sep 1765 d 3 July 1767. SD C:216

Rutilless s/o John d 4 Aug 1848 ae: 3m. "Buried near N. Cobb's grave." NS G:133

BUTTRICK, Abba A. w/o John B. d 9 Apr 1858 ae: 31y. GSL

William s/o John B. d 3 Jan 1855 ae: 9d. GSL

BUTTS, Samuel nd. F:93 Tomb

BUZZELL, Charles H. s/o George d 17 Mar 1855 ae: 8w. GSL

William s/o John W. d 22 Aug

BUZZELL (continued)
1855 ae: 4w. GSL
CADY, Julia d/o John d 30 Sep
1854 ae: 4y. "Buried near E.
Greely's stone." GSL
CAHOON, Charles W. d 25 Apr
1877 ae: 53y. F:105 Tomb
Edwin d 29 July 1842 ae: 17y.
"Stranger." GSL
Ellen w/o James d 5 May 1846
ae: 31y. "Buried at head of
Daniel S. Moody's grave." NS
G:10
James d 23 Mar 1847 ae: 32y.
"Buried at head of Daniel S.
Moody's grave." NS G:10
James B. d 28 Jan 1867 ae: 66y.
Mayor - Portland. F:105 Tomb
John s/o James & Ellen d 4 Apr
1846 ae: 8m. "Buried at head
of Daniel S. Moody's grave."
NS G:10
John d 30 Apr 1865 ae: 64y. GSL
Martha wid/o James B. d 26 Nov
1875 ae: 74y. F:105 Tomb
CALDWELL, Abigail w/o Capt.
William d 26 May 1806 ae:
29y. J:87
Charles s/o William & Abigail d
13 Nov 1804 ae: 3m. SD J:86
CALEB, Antonio s/o Antonio d 5
May 1847 ae: 6m. "Buried at
foot of John Russwurm's
grave." NS I:193
Eliza d/o Antonio d 13 Apr 1846
ae: 1y 9m. "Buried at foot of
John Russwurm's grave." NS
I:193
CALEF, Capt. John d 20 May
1865 ae: 89y. SB A-23-4
Mary d 24 Jan 1844 ae: 71y. SB
A-23-5
CALHOUN, William d 29 May
1848 ae: 30y. A Tomb 30
CAMMETT, Betsy w/o Dudley d
22 Nov 1859 ae: 66y. A Tomb
10
Caroline J. d/o Dudley & Betsy d
10 Aug 1876 ae: 40y. A Tomb
10
Charles d 10 Oct 1821 ae: 2y. A
Tomb 10

CAMMETT (continued)
Dudley d 21 June 1819 ae: 70y.
Revolutionary War. I:78
Capt. Dudley d 14 June 1863 ae:
74y. War of 1812. A Tomb 10
Elizabeth w/o Dudley d 30 Mar
1774 ae: 23y. G:46
Elizabeth D. d/o William d 3
June 1849 ae: 12y. A Tomb 10
Elizabeth W. d 21 Feb 1847 ae:
31y. A Tomb 10
Francis d 1845 ae: 26y. "1st Of-
ficer, ship *Saxony*." A Tomb
10
George H. s/o William d 25 May
1873 ae: 43y. A Tomb 10
John d 3 Sep 1831 ae: 38y. SBE
B-12-5
John Thomas s/o John & H. d 27
Dec 1835 ae: 5y. SBE B-12-4
Margaret d 10 June 1843 ae: 25y.
A Tomb 10
Martha H. d 1852 ae: 17y. A
Tomb 10
Mary #2 w/o Dudley d 26 Apr
1824 ae: 83y. I:77
Mary Louisa d/o Capt. William
d 19 Sep 1851 ae: 23y. A
Tomb 10
Mary T. w/o William d 24 Mar
1862 ae: 66y. A Tomb 10
Sarah d/o Dudley & Mary d 25
Mar 1814 ae: 34y. I:83
Capt. William d 6 Apr 1880 ae:
94y 7m. War of 1812. A
Tomb 10
William A. d 6 June 1847 ae:
21y. A Tomb 10
CAMPBELL, Alettea d/o Capt.
William & Elizabeth d 5 Feb
1773 ae: 2y 6m. C:135
Ebenezer s/o William & Jane d
9 June 1800 ae: 15m. H:107
Elizabeth wid/o Capt. William d
3 Apr 1795 ae: 45y. C:136
Elizabeth d 8 Mar 1868 ae: 72y
6m. A Tomb 42
James d 22 Sep 1856 ae: 25y.
"Native Londonderry, Nova
Scotia." "Buried at side of E.
G. Wentworth's grave stone."
GSL

CANE, Joseph d 18 Sep 1849. Black. GSL

CAPEN, Edward d 30 Aug 1823 ae: 46y. H:92

Frances wid/o William b 11 July 1782 d 26 Nov 1839. SD H:156

George d 4 Sep 1842 ae: 2y. GSL

Harriet N. d/o William d 25 Aug 1847 ae: 2y. GSL

Susan B. d/o Edward G. & Elizabeth d 21 May 1853 ae: 45y. SB H:88

Susannah wid/o Deacon William d 7 Oct 1821 ae: 66y. H:90

Deacon William d 1O Mar 1818 ae: 73y. SBE H:91

William d 5 Oct 1828 ae: 54y. SD H:156

CARD, Abbie W. d/o Jacob A. & Harriet K. d 7 Dec 1861 ae: 23y. SD A-15-6

Addie M. d/o Jacob A. & Harriet K. d 15 July 1860 ae: 13y 4m. SD A-15-8

Charles d 7 Feb 1827 ae: 22y. SBE B-1-36

Edward Kent s/o Jacob A. & H. K. d 3 Oct 1848 ae: 7y. B-1-38

Harriet K. wid/o Jacob A. d 10 Nov 1863 ae: 65y. SD A-15-5

Henrietta L. d/o Jacob A. & H.K. d 1 May 1854 ae: 26y. SD B-1-40

Lucy H. d/o Jacob A. & Harriet K. d 22 July 1857 ae: 25y. SD A-15-7

Martha A. w/o Elisha A. d 3 June 1862 ae: 22y. GSL

Sarah wid/o Capt. William d 8 Jan 1847 ae: 84y. SBE B-1-37

Sarah E. d/o Jacob A. & Harriet K. d 24 Dec 1854 ae: 25y. SB B-1-39

Silas L. d 14 Nov 1856 ae: 33y 6m. SBE B-2-30

Thomas S. d 13 Nov 1832. SB B-2-31

Capt. William d 28 May 1816 ae: 56y. SB H:29

William H. d 10 Apr 1828 ae: 2y

CARD (continued) 4m. SB B-2-31

CAREY, Statira G. w/o Joshua E. d 27 Apr 1862 ae: 31y. SD I:66

CARL, Ella F. d/o Charles, Jr. d 26 Aug 1854 ae: 1y. GSL

CARLE, Ada E. d/o James d 9 Aug 1853 ae: 8m. GSL

Charles H. d 23 Dec 1871 ae: 82y 1m. GSL

CARLETON, Caroline E. w/o Samuel L. d/o Estwick & Sally Evans d 13 Sep 1922 ae: 96y. A Tomb 63

Hattie Bell d/o Samuel L. d 21 Sep 1867 ae: 1y 2m. A Tomb 63

Herbert L. s/o Samuel L. d 7 Sep 1865 ae: 6m. A Tomb 63

Kittie O. L. d/o Samuel L. d 2 Aug 1862 ae: 15m 23d. A Tomb 63

Samuel L. s/o Samuel L. d 11 Apr 1908 ae: 85y 6m. A Tomb 63

CARLISLE, Abigail w/o George d 23 Jan 1802 ae: 34y. SD I:36

Lucy wid/o George d 2 Feb 1814 ae: 34y. SBE J:132

CARLOW, John d 4 June 1847 ae: 66y. GSL

CARNIGHAN, Betsy d 21 Oct 1820 ae: 50y. J:45

CARR, Avis B. wid/o John d 22 Mar 1845 ae: 73y. "Buried at side of her husband." NS A-9-21

Daniel d 1 Feb 1849 ae: 74y. "Buried at foot of Z. Marston's grave stone." NS H:32

Francis I. s/o John & Almira nd ae: 3y 6m. B-2-27

John d 19 Jan 1845 ae: 76y. "Buried at side of Aaron Norton's wife." NS A-9-21

Leander C. s/o Daniel d 13 July 1846 ae: 11mos. GSL

Louisa B. w/o Daniel d 11 Mar 1848 ae: 41y. GSL

Moses N. d 2 May 1839 ae: 33yrs. D:136

CARRUTHERS, Ellen d 23 Oct 1842 ae: 24yrs. GSL

Helen R. L. d/o Rev. James & Robina J. d 24 Oct 1842 ae: 24y. A-10-6

Rev. James b 21 Nov 1772 d 29 Nov 1857. A-10-7

Jane d/o Rev. James & Robina J. d 1 Dec 1838 ae: 29y. SBE A-10-4

Robina J. w/o Rev. James d 12 July 1834 ae: 59y. SBE A-10-5

CARTER, Artemus d 18 Mar 1855 ae: 72y. A Tomb 11

Augustus Sumner s/o Artemus & Harriet b 7 July 1812 d 26 Feb 1813. SB K:134

Caleb S. s/o Caleb S. d 1 Jan 1847 ae: 3y. GSL

Charlotte d/o Artemus, Jr. d 23 Aug 1849 ae: 1y. A Tomb 11

David Stoddart s/o Theophilus d 17 June 1814 ae: 7y. J:138

Edward G. s/o Josiah & Jane d 20 Sep 1822 ae: 13m. SB K:137

Edwin d 3 Oct 1835 ae: 31y. SD J:143

George Edward s/o Josiah & Mary M. d 30 Oct 1827 ae: 4y. K:133

George Henry s/o Josiah & Lydia d 20 Sep 1823 ae: 18y. K:133

Georgianna d/o Charles d 16 Aug 1846 ae: 6y. Black. GSL

Jane w/o Josiah d 10 May 1822 ae: 41y. K:135

Josiah d 5 Apr 1863 ae: 90y 2m. SBE K:138

Lydia w/o Josiah d 5 Aug 1808 ae: 31y. SB K:136

Lydia D. d/o Josiah & Jane d 31 Jan 1816 ae: 5w. SB K:137

Mary w/o John d 25 Jan 1850 ae: 42y. "Died North Yarmouth." Black. GSL

Mary M. w/o Josiah d 10 Jan 1828 ae: 38y. K:140

Peter d 2 May 1839 ae: 57y. K:132

Theophilus d 24 Apr 1821 ae: 43y. SBE J:142

CARTER (continued)

William D. s/o Josiah & Lydia d 3 Nov 1818 ae: 15y. SD K:139

CARY, Anna w/o Benjamin d 4 Oct 1803 ae: 28y. GSL

Harriet A. d 18 Dec 1898 ae: 73y 7m 26d. NM A Tomb 43

CHADBOURN, Adela d 17 July 1851 ae: 35y. "Buried with 8m old child." GSL

James d 1 Jan 1835 ae: 53y. A Tomb 81

James K. s/o Timothy & Lucinda b 5 May 1818 d 28 Oct 1819. H:176

Lucinda P. d 24 Mar 1862 ae: 67y. A Tomb 81

CHADWELL, Dorcas wid/o George d 26 Aug 1841 ae: 37y. GSL

Emily w/o Joseph T. d 15 Jan 1857 ae: 28y. A Tomb 69

Frederick A. d 6 Dec 1854 ae: 22y. A Tomb 69

Joseph T. d 15 Mar 1868 ae: 38y. A Tomb 69

William d 10 Dec 1843 ae: 85y. "Buried at head of Charles Chase's stone." NS H:22

CHADWICK, Ann d 29 Jan 1815 ae: 15y. SBE H:151

Elias s/o Samuel d 8 May 1843 ae: 3y 4m. GSL

Elizabeth M. d 26 Jan 1823 ae: 21y. H:153

George d 29 Nov 1853 ae: 59y. "Buried in Chadwick tomb." GSL

James d Nov 1808 ae: 49y. H:153

James Jr. d Mar 1802 ae: 15y. H:153

Joshua W. d 19 Apr 1829 ae: 31y. H:153

Pamelia wid/o William d 12 Feb 1842 ae: 77y. GSL

Samuel d 8 Jan 1860 ae: 62y. "Buried in his tomb." GSL

William Jr. d 26 Feb 1829 ae: 37y. H:153

CHALK, Mary Ann d/o late Windsor Lord d 29 July 1858

CHALK (continued)
ae: 39y 1m. "Died Newton-
ville, Massachusetts." GSL
CHAMBERLAIN, Aaron d 11 Sep
1831 ae: 79y 6m. Revolution-
ary War. SB B-6-17
Anna w/o James d 3 Oct 1804
ae: 36y. GSL
Bethiah d 25 June 1837 ae: 81y.
SB B-6-16
Charles W. s/o Joshua & Hannah
d 9 Oct 1805. SD K:93
Edward s/o Joshua & Hannah d. 4
Apr 1807 ae: 15m. SD K:92
Elizabeth d 11 Sep 1878 ae: 74y.
SD B-7-24
Gilbert d 16 Dec 1849 ae: 9y.
"Buried in Abraham Niles' lot,
north side, north corner."
Black. GSL
Hannah w/o Joshua d 12 Apr
1807 ae: 27y. SD K:91
Capt. John d 14 Sep 1842 ae:
47y. SD B-7-21
John W. s/o Capt. John & Lucy
M. d 6 Oct 1840 ae: 10m. SD
B-7-21
Lavinia w/o Capt. John d 5 Mar
1834 ae: 28y. B-7-19
Lucy M. w/o Capt. John d 26 Jan
1840 ae: 32y. B-7-20
Mary wid/o Capt. E. d 30 Apr
1852 ae: 80y. B-7-22
William M. d 21 Aug 1856 ae:
41y. SD K:128
CHANDLER, -- w/o Capt. Judah
d 30 Jan 1853 ae: 32y. A
Tomb 16
Caleb d 15 Jan 1855 ae: 84y.
"Buried in Timothy Soule's
lot." GSL
Charles s/o Daniel H. d 28 Dec
1843 ae: 10m. "Buried at head
of Bickford's stone." GSL
Charles s/o Joel d 28 Nov 1843
ae: 24y. "Buried by Miss
Cushing's stone." GSL
Charles H. s/o Joseph H. d 29
June 1856 ae: 5y 7m. A Tomb
16
Elden H. d 5 July 1861 ae: 27y.
A Tomb 16

CHANDLER (continued)
Elizabeth d/o David d 16 July
1847 ae: 24y. "Buried at head
of Mary Freeman's grave."
GSL
Ellen A. d/o John d 19 Nov 1847
ae: 3w. GSL
Isabella R. d/o David d 12 Jan
1851 ae: 21y. GSL
Mrs Jane d 15 Oct 1824 ae: 58y.
G:6
Judah nd. A Tomb 16
Pamelia L. w/o Joel d 3 Apr
1849 ae: 72y. GSL
Rebecca wid/o David d 5 July
1863 ae: 96y 9m. A Tomb 16
CHAPIN, Edward P. s/o Henry
M. & M. K. d 7 Aug 1851 ae:
2m. SD K:37
CHAPMAN, Nathan d 25 Jan
1853 ae: 50y. A Tomb 69
CHASE, Abel s/o E. & B. d 9
Dec 1837 ae: 10m. B-14-17
Abel d 2 Apr 1853 ae: 76y. GSL
Abigail C. d/o E. & B. d 23 Nov
1837 ae: 6y. SD B-14-19
Ada E. d/o William W. d 20 Nov
1849 ae: 5y. GSL
Capt. Amos T. d 26 Mar 1840 ae:
29y. SD H:20
Deacon Asa d 18 Oct 1842 ae:
77y. A-19-8
Augustus s/o Salmon & Mary b
23 Aug 1799 d 11 Sep 1799.
J:212
Barrett P. d 31 Aug 1810 ae: 4y.
SBE A-19-7
Capt. Benjamin Tappan d 3 Apr
1821 ae: 35y. "Died of
yellow-fever on voyage from
Cuba." SB H:17
Benjamin Tappan s/o Benjamin
T. & Hannah b 30 Aug 1821
d 21 July 1826. SBE H:18
Benjamin T. s/o John W. &
Sarah I. d 9 Sep 1847 ae: 3m.
SD K:35
Benjamin T. s/o John W. &
Nancy d 4 Sep 1849 ae: 34y.
SD H:21
Betsy d/o Oliver & Betsy d 3
Dec 1818 ae: 23y. SBE K:64

CHASE (continued)

Catherine d/o Abel d 8 Aug 1849 ae: 8y. GSL

Clarissa wid/o Joshua d 28 Nov 1845 ae: 45y. GSL

Cynthia w/o Capt. Amos T. d 20 Oct 1837 ae: 27y. SD H:20

Ellen d/o Charles & Nancy d 26 Sep 1820 ae: 2m. SD H:22

Ellen L. d/o George d 23 Apr 1849 ae: 4y. GSL

Capt. Daniel d 26 June 1845 ae: 37y. GSL

Daniel s/o David d 22 Aug 1841 ae: 2y 6m. GSL

George s/o Salmon & Mary b 29 Sep 1800 d 11 Nov 1819. SBE J:215

George W. s/o George W. d 10 June 1850 ae: 4m. GSL

Hannah M. d 14 Dec 1818 ae: 50y. SBE A-19-7

Hannah M. d 17 May 1847 ae: 25y. A-19-10

James F. d 20 Mar 1847 ae: 6m. GSL

John W. d 7 May 1819 ae: 29y. SD H:21

Capt. John W. d 9 Oct 1881 ae: 72y. Civil War: 13th Reg. Maine Inf., Co. B. K:36B

Joseph A. s/o E. & B. d 1 Dec 1837 ae: 3y. SD B-14-18

Joseph A. s/o Edward d 16 May 1861 ae: 21y. GSL

Joseph M. s/o John W. & Sarah I. d 18 June 1845 ae: 6y 4m. SD K:35

Julia d/o Salmon & Mary b 8 July 1798 d 20 July 1798. J:212

Ludney d/o Abel Jr. d 10 Aug 1847 ae: 2y. GSL

Mary w/o Salmon d 21 Aug 1801 ae: 31y. J:213

Mary Ann d/o Benjamin G. d 13 Feb 1848 ae: 1y. GSL

Mary B. wid/o Samuel Y. d 3 Mar 1865 ae: 65y. F:157

Mary L. d 5 May 1893 ae: 80y. ME A Tomb 78

Nancy wid/o John W. d 1 Nov

CHASE (continued)

1856 ae: 64y 9m. SD H:21

Polly d 10 Nov 1813 ae: 18y. SBE A-19-7

Rufus A. d 1 Apr 1829 ae: 26y. A-19-7

Ruth H. w/o Caleb S. d 30 Oct 1862 ae: 71y. F:105 Tomb

Salmon d 10 Aug 1806 ae: 45y. J:214

Salmon s/o Oliver & Betsy b 25 June 1800 d 25 June 1808. SBE K:64

Samuel Y. s/o Thomas & Susan d 8 Oct 1820 ae: 21y 6m. F:158

Sarah wid/o Deacon Asa d 30 Aug 1860 ae: 77y. A-19-9

Sarah I. d 17 Feb 1893 ae: 83y. K:36A

Sarah M. d 17 Feb 1893 ae: 82y 9m 24d. GSL

Sarah O. d/o Charles & Nancy d 25 June 1838 ae: 13m. SD H:22

Susannah w/o Thomas d 27 Nov 1816 ae: 39y. J:126

William d 22 May 1832 ae: 34y. SBE A-19-7

CHASON, ---- s/o Lewis d 12 Nov 1854 ae: 1y. "Buried at foot of Eliza Stevens' grave." GSL

inf ch/o Lewis d 23 Nov 1854. GSL

CHENEY, George s/o George H. & Sarah D. b 18 Dec 1836 d 9 July 1837. SD A-1-30

Marion Prentiss d/o George H. & Sarah D. b 7 July 1834 d 2 Sep 1835. SD A-1-29

CHICKERING, Alonzo d 14 Aug 1846 ae: 25y. "Buried at side of fence near corner of the ladder house." GSL

Benjamin F. s/o Dana d 6 Sep 1847 ae: 17y. GSL

Benjamin F. s/o late James M. d 10 Dec 1845 ae: 6y. GSL

Dana d 10 Nov 1850 ae: 66y. GSL

James s/o Dana d 7 Oct 1842 ae: 29y. GSL

CHICKERING (continued)
Sarah M. d/o Dana d 30 Nov 1846 ae: 21y. GSL
CHILD, Charles F. s/o Charles W. d 30 Dec 1871 ae: 39y. NM A Tomb 13
Charles W. d 8 Oct 1862 ae: 52y. A Tomb 13
Harriett w/o Charles W. d 28 Dec 1884 ae: 74y. A Tomb 13
Thomas d 25 Dec 1787 ae: 57y. Royal Customs Inspector Postmaster Stone now at G:47. G:78
CHILDS, Rebecca d 5 Sep 1796. L:87
Rebecca wid/o Benjamin d 30 May 1809 ae: 77y. L:86
CHIPMAN, John b 23 Oct 1722 d 1 July 1768. MD D:106
CHISHOLM, Alexander T. s/o Alexander F. & Jane L. nd. J:145
Allan F. s/o Alexander F. & Jane L. d 3 Aug 1853 ae: 5m. J:147
J. F. w/o Daniel buried 5 May 1854. "Died Sacremento, California." GSL
Jane w/o Alexander F. d 4 Sep 1853 ae: 35y. SB J:146
CHITMAN, inf ch/o William d 6 Dec 1854 ae: 3d. GSL
CHOATE, George A. s/o Daniel L. d 29 Jan 1850 ae: 8y. NM A Tomb 52
CHRIST, John d 27 Dec 1848 ae: 40y. GSL
CHRISTIANSEN, Hilma Marie C. d/o Peter d 25 Feb 1891 ae: 2y 2m. GSL
CHRISTIE, George d 15 Mar 1846 ae: 30y. "Death by intemperance." "Native Cape Ann, Massachusetts." GSL
CHURCHILL, Abigail wid/o Capt. Joseph d 6 Aug 1846 ae: 38y. GSL
Helen d/o widow Abba d 31 Aug 1842 ae: 14m. GSL
Henry s/o George A. d 14 July 1862 ae: 15m. MB A Tomb 44

CHURCHILL (continued)
James Edwin s/o Capt. Edward d 4 Aug 1844 ae: 2y 10m. "Buried near the Friends' Ground." GSL
Mary d/o Edward d 4 June 1842 ae: 3y. "Buried by side of Carter's stone." GSL
Mary I. w/o Hollis K. d 21 Nov 1827 ae: 22y. F:74
CHUTE, Frances Ellen d/o Margaret d 6 Apr 1849 ae: 7y. "Buried at head of M. Oxnard's grave stone." NS H:129
CLAHERTY, James s/o late James d 17 Mar 1857 ae: 4y 6m. GSL
CLAPP, Abigail wid/o Elkanah of Mansfield, Massachusetts d 9 Jan 1828 ae: 83y. B-1-11
Albert Smith s/o Oliver & Cynthia d 1 Apr 1835 ae: 3dys. J:196
Andrew L. Emerson b 8 July 1826 d 10 Dec 1893. Mmt A Tomb 83
Asa b 15 Mar 1762 d 17 Apr 1848. Revolutionary War. A Tomb 83
Charles d 20 July 1796 ae: 5y. A Tomb 83
Charles Quincy b 26 May 1799 d 1 Mar 1868. A Tomb 83
Cynthia w/o Oliver d 15 S 1857 ae: 57y. "Buried on the low flat ground." GSL
Elizabeth Burns d/o Oliver & Cynthia d 16 Apr 1835 ae: 19d. J:196
Elizabeth w/o Elkanah d 20 Sep 1810 ae: 38y. A Tomb 83
Elizabeth Wingate Quincy wid/o Asa b 10 June 1764 d 21 Nov 1853. A Tomb 83
Elkanah d 5 Oct 1810 ae: 44y. A Tomb 83
Laura C. d/o Oliver d 3 Sep 1854 ae: 15y 6m. GSL
Oliver Jr. s/o Oliver & Cynthia d 2 July 1847 ae: 22y. J:195
Tamson d 19 Oct 1848 ae: 76y. Widow. GSL

CLARK, Ann d 4 Apr 1843 ae: 54y. Widow. GSL

Archilbald J. s/o John W. & Susan d 1 June 1859 ae: 37y. SB B-9-32

Edward s/o George & Betsy d 27 Sep 1822 ae: 2y. G:97

Elizabeth d/o George & Betsy d 14 June 1820 ae: 2y 4m. G:98

Emeline d/o Thomas d 18 Dec 1843 ae: 12y. Black. GSL

Francis T. s/o Seth & Nabby d 16 Dec 1813 ae: 2y 7m. SD G:93

Frank Maynard s/o Daniel d 28 Feb 1858 ae: 1y 10m. "Buried Samuel Anderson tomb." GSL

George d 20 Oct 1841 ae: 44y. "Killed by fall from mast head." GSL

George d 3 June 1851 ae: 63y. SBE A-15-17

George Albert s/o George & Betsy d 29 Dec 1825 ae: 9y. G:96

Grace G. d/o Charles S. d 1 Sep 1849 ae: 8m. A Tomb 11

Homer J. s/o Dr. Daniel & L. d 12 Aug 1822 ae: 18y 6m. SD B-5-8

Isaac F. d 31 Aug 1841 ae: 27y. G:95

John s/o Robert d 6 Aug 1854 ae: 9m. GSL

Jonas d 24 Aug 1824 ae: 30y. G:99

Louisa A. w/o Isaac F. d 26 Mar 1841 ae: 26y. SBE G:95

Lucy A. d/o James d 16 Aug 1862 ae: 33y. GSL

Margaret W. d/o John W. & Susan d 30 Mar 1850 ae: 24y. SB B-9-31

Mary d/o James & Lucy Simonton d 9 Dec 1896 ae: 75y. A Tomb 5

Nabby d 7 Dec 1816 ae: 28y. SD G:94

Rebecca w/o William d 17 Oct 1817 ae: 31y. I:41

Rebecca B. d/o Samuel & Mary B. d 6 Sep 1806. L:78

CLARK (continued)

Susan P. w/o John W. d 12 Sep 1886 ae: 87y. SB B-9-33

Thomas s/o Thomas & Nancy d 26 Sep 1804 ae: 7m. SD K:145

William d Feb 1840 ae: 21y. B-9-43

CLARKE, Alexander s/o Dennis d 3 Aug 1853 ae: 5m. A Tomb 44

Charles d 27 June 1846 ae: 26y. SD C:154

Elizabeth wid/o Capt. Jacob d 27 Oct 1834 ae: 27y. SBE E:14

Elizabeth d/o Jacob & Elizabeth d 30 Apr 1841 ae: 57y. SB E:16

Mary Ann w/o Robert d 13 Jan 1861 ae: 33y. GSL

Mary G. d 9 Oct 1834. SB E:15

Mary M. w/o Thomas d 4 Sep 1866 ae: 65y. GSL

Patience Chamberlain w/o Capt. Samuel d 5 Sep 1845 ae: 53y. A Tomb 66

Capt. Samuel d 21 Mar 1851 ae: 62y. War of 1812. A Tomb 66

Susan w/o Samuel d 25 May 1815 ae: 24y. C:155

CLARY, Dolly w/o Samuel d 28 Aug 1850 ae: 68y. SD G:91

Samuel d 1 June 1829 ae: 45y. G:92

CLEMENT, Joanna d 19 Jan 1818 ae: 62y. I:14

Capt. Joseph d 27 Apr 1816 ae: 60y. I:14

Marion w/o Samuel d 10 Apr 1862 ae: 41y. GSL

Barbara d/o Samuel d 16 May 1846 ae: 19m. GSL

CLEVELAND, Mary Helen d/o Elias & Emma d 12 Aug 1855 ae: 2m. E:1

CLINTON, Ann w/o John d 17 Aug 1802 ae: 44y. G:49

Lucy d 1 May 1851 ae: 59y. GSL

CLOUDMAN, Mary d/o John d 16 Aug 1856 ae: 1y 9m. GSL

CLOUGH, Elner w/o John d 22 Nov 1827 ae: 64y. SD B-14-10

John d 2 July 1798 ae: 40y. Revolutionary War SD B-14-10

CLOUGH (continued)

Capt. John d 12 Mar 1853 ae: 48y. SBE A-10-27

Josiah R. d 27 June 1858 ae: 66y. SD B-14-12

Polly wid/o Benjamin d 8 Feb 1850 ae: 80y. GSL

Polly A. w/o Josiah R. d 8 Nov 1831 ae: 40y. SD B-14-12

Mrs Rebecca d 8 June 1805 ae: 87y. GSL

COBB, Abigail w/o Samuel d 3 Sep 1766 ae: 80y 5m. Interesting stone. G:105

Abigail w/o Chipman d 12 Jan 1852 ae: 71y. GSL

Daniel s/o Daniel & Nabby d 28 Nov 1810 ae: 21y. "Died at St. Bartholomews." D:129

Daniel d 15 May 1841 ae: 80y. GSL

Ebenezer d 9 Aug 1721 ae: 33y. B-2-9

Edward H. d 18 Jan 1818 ae: 26y. A Tomb 78

Elizabeth w/o Richard d 13 Jan 1850 ae: 54y. A Tomb 78

Ethan A. G. s/o Nathan & O. d 26 Mar 1826 ae: 8m. B-2-17

Eunice w/o William d 22 Jan 1796 ae: 44y. G:135

Frederick s/o Matthew d 21 Sep 1795 ae: 1y. A Tomb 78

Frederick A. d 2 Aug 1848 ae: 47y 5d. A Tomb 78

George d 2 Mar 1843 ae: 25y. GSL

Harriet wid/o William d 1 Aug 1864 ae: 68y. GSL

Harriet W. d/o Edward H. d 4 Jan 1818 ae: 8m. A Tomb 78

Helen A. wid/o Frederick A. d 19 June 1858 ae: 49y. A Tomb 78

Ira C. s/o Benjamin d 5 Jan 1861 ae: 3y 1m 13d. GSL

Isaac B d 30 Aug 1801 ae: 12y. A Tomb 78

Joshua d 19 Aug 1796 ae: 19y. G:134

Louisa w/o Merritt d 20 May 1853 ae: 24y. A Tomb 25

Martha w/o Edward Jr. d 28 Dec

COBB (continued)

1831 ae: 32y. SB A-4-11

Mary E. d/o Lemuel d 9 Mar 1843 ae: 18m. SBE A-3-27

Matthew d 24 Mar 1824 ae: 67y. A Tomb 78

Mehitable wid/o Matthew d 19 Jan 1835 ae: 72y. A Tomb 78

Nathaniel d 16 Dec 1800 ae: 22y. G:133

Richard d 16 July 1837 ae: 48y. A Tomb 78

Ruth I. C. d/o Albert M. & Lizzie S. d 6 Jan 1899 ae: 1y 2m 26d. GSL

Samuel s/o Samuel & Thankful d 5 Mar 1747 ae: 3y. SBE G:140

Samuel b 23 Feb 1683 d Oct 1767. GSL

Samuel d 15 Aug 1889 ae: 88y. "Died Alms House." GSL

Sarah M. w/o Samuel d 9 Mar 1882 ae: 70y. GSL

Smith d 29 June 1846 ae: 76y. GSL

Smith Woodward s/o Daniel & Nabby d Jan 1815 ae: 22y. "Lost at sea." D:129

Smith Woodward d 29 Dec 1819 ae: 82y. Revolutionary War. D:128

Thankful d/o Samuel & Thankful d Oct 1747 ae: 6m. G:142

Thankful w/o Samuel d 13 Feb 1749 ae: 30y. G:139

Thankful d/o Samuel & Thankful d 8 June 1755 ae: 6m. G:144

William d 7 Nov 1802 ae: 51y. Revolutionary War. SD G:129

William s/o Daniel & Nabby d Jan 1805 ae: 21y. "Died at sea." D:129

William s/o Lemuel d 7 Nov 1844 ae: 9w. GSL

William R. d 6 May 1852 ae: 50y. GSL

COBURN, Nathan d 6 June 1827 ae: 28y. H:174

COCHRAN, Ruth w/o John E. d 4 Aug 1857 ae: 39y. GSL

James d 29 Mar 1833 ae: 26y. H:136

COCHRAN (continued)
James s/o James & Harriet d 30 May 1833 ae: 7m. H:136
CODMAN, Anne w/o Richard d 31 Mar 1761 ae: 19y. SBE F:137
Charles d 11 Sep 1842 ae: 41y. SB D:72
Richard d 12 Sep 1793 ae: 63y. SBE F:136
Richard d 9 Sep 1833 ae: 75y. GSL
Sarah Smith wid/o Richard d 10 Sep 1827 ae: 87y. "Youngest d/o Rev. Thomas Smith." SBE F:135
Statira Preble w/o Richard d 15 Aug 1796 ae: 29y. F:142
Susan, widow d 23 Sep 1842 ae: 62y. GSL
William d 12 Nov 1828 ae: 57y. A Tomb 45
COE, Cornelius Barnes s/o George d 16 Aug 1846 ae: 18m. A Tomb 54
Edward R. s/o George & Lydia d 2 July 1852 ae: 12y. A Tomb 54
Eleanor w/o John d 3 Jan 1882 ae: 78y. A Tomb 54
Eleanor A. d/o Kohn d 17 May 1877 ae: 52y. A Tomb 54
George F. M. d 24 May 1869 ae: 40y. Civil War: 25 Reg. Maine Inf., Co. B. MD A Tomb 68
Hattie L. d/o George d 23 July 1875 ae: 19y. A Tomb 54
John d 20 Aug 1847 ae: 67y. A Tomb 54
Mary E. d/o George d 2 May 1852 ae: 23y. A Tomb 54
COFFIN, Florence M. d/o Ivory H. d 10 Sep 1858 ae: 2y. GSL
John s/o Henry d 25 May 1842 ae: 7w. GSL
John H. C. s/o Nathaniel & Mary b 17 July 1812 d 18 Aug 1813 SD G:83
Eleanor Foster wid/o Dr. Nathaniel, Jr. d 1832 H:71 Tomb
Francis s/o Dr. Nathaniel Jr. & Eleanor F. d 1842 ae: 62y.

COFFIN (continued)
H:71 Tomb
Dr. Nathaniel d 11 Jan 1766 ae: 50y. MD H:71 Tomb
Dr. Nathaniel Jr. d 21 Oct 1826 ae: 84y. H:71 Tomb
Patience H. wid/o Dr. Nathaniel d 31 Jan 1772 ae: 57y. H:71 Tomb
William s/o William d 16 Aug 1846 ae: 6m. "Buried Strangers' Ground." GSL
COHLER, Sarah w/o Charles d 22 Jan 1859 ae: 35y. GSL
COLBY, Elizabeth D. d 5 Sep 1888 ae: 81y 7m. A-11-2
Frances C. Drinkwater w/o John C. b 1807 d 1832. Mmt G:4
Harriet d/o Joseph d 31 Sep 1844 ae: 9m. "Buried Family Range." GSL
John C. b 1798 d 1834. Mmt G:4
Jonathan Morss s/o Samuel & Sally nd. A-11-1
Capt. Samuel d 12 Aug 1845 ae: 84y. A-11-5
Sarah M. wid/o Capt. Samuel d 31 Jan 1853 ae: 85y. SB A-11-4
COLCORD, Edward s/o Josiah & Mary d 14 Sep 1804 ae: 11w. SD J:112
George W. s/o John W. d 1 Aug 1872 ae: 16y. ME A Tomb 29
Hannah F. d/o Josiah d 9 Sep 1864 ae: 52y. A Tomb 11
Martha O. w/o John W. d 22 Aug 1847 ae: 32y. ME A Tomb 29
Mary d 2 Mar 1860 ae: 83y. A Tomb 11
Nancy d/o Josiah & Mary d 12 July 1833 ae: 24y. A-24-8
COLE, David H. b 7 Aug 1789 d 9 Jan 1841. A-13-20
Edward F. d 13 Apr 1863 ae: 2y 8m. "Buried Friends' Ground." GSL
Edward P. s/o William W. d 11 Oct 1844 ae: 4m. GSL
Frederick s/o H. G. d 22 Oct 1848 ae: 4y. A Tomb 9
Hannah wid/o Josiah d 17 Mar

COLE (continued)
1865 ae: 84y. GSL
Joanna d 26 June 1843 ae: 89y. GSL
Louisa J. d 11 Dec 1852 ae: 23y. Black. GSL
COLESWORTHY, Anna d 26 Mar 1851 ae: 76y. GSL
Maria A. d/o Samuel H. d 12 Jan 1842 ae: 4y. GSL
COLLAGAN, William H. s/o Capt. William d 14 Sep 1852 ae: 24y. GSL
COLLAR, Capt. Richard d 19 Jan 1730 ae: 55y 26d. F:48
COLLEY, David K. s/o David d 28 Sep 1866 ae: 10m. GSL
Elizabeth A. dau/o Albert A. d 5 Dec 1849 ae: 13m. GSL
Henry Cross s/o Francis & Mary b 23 Dec 1815 d 22 Oct 1816 F:28
Jacob Sanborn s/o Francis & Mary b 29 July 1817 d 19 Apr 1818. F:29
Mary L. d 12 Jan 1835 ae: 29y. F:30
William E. s/o Albert A. d 21 Oct 1847 ae: 1y. A Tomb 35
COLLIER, Richard d 17 Jan 1732 ae: 55y. GSL
Susan Alice d/o Allen d 3 Oct 1858 ae: 15m. A Tomb 53
COLLINS, Arthur d 10 Sep 1843 ae: 28y. "Buried by side of Dearborn's stone." GSL
Barrett C. C. s/o Daniel D. d 29 Dec 1835 ae: 19y. SBE A-3-24
Daniel D. d 18 Sep 1835 ae: 69y. SD A-3-25
Edward s/o John B. d 19 Mar 1842 ae: 2y 8m. "Buried Merritt tomb." GSL
Edith d 21 Jan 1863 ae: 71y. "Died Boston, Massachusetts." GSL
Elizabeth wid/o John d 24 Jan 1859 ae: 80y. GSL
Frances B. w/o Charles C. b 10 Nov 1807 d 4 May 1828. Mmt A Tomb 12
Hannah wid/o Clement d 29 Dec

COLLINS (continued)
1815 ae: 85y. "Formerly of Boston." H:150
Hannah E. d/o Joseph W. d 9 Feb 1845 ae: 17y. "Buried Isaac Sturdivant tomb." GSL
John d 6 Dec 1848 ae: 77y. GSL
John A. s/o John d 15 Dec 1871 ae: 1y 15d. GSL
Lemuel A. d 9 Sep 1843 ae: 28y. SD A-23-7
William s/o John d 9 Feb 1855 ae: 3m. GSL
Susan d/o Allen d 16 Aug 1853 ae: 5d. A Tomb 53
CONANT, Eliza A. w/o George b 1812 d 18 Jan 1852. Mmt A-17-6
George d 14 July 1895 ae: 90y 7m. "Died Freeport, Maine." Mmt A-17-6
Sarah W. d 23 Nov 1897 ae: 67y. "Died Freeport, Maine." GSL
CONE, John G. d 10 Apr 1852 ae: 73y. Black. GSL
CONNETT, Grace M. d/o Rev. George W. d 16 Dec 1877 ae: 8y. A Tomb 53
Louisa H. w/o Rev. George W. d 23 Dec 1895 ae: 66y 6m 13d. "Died New York City." A Tomb 53
CONNOR, Charles F. s/o John d 3 Oct 1855 ae: 24y. GSL
Charles S. W. s/o W. P. & N. F. d 8 Feb 1850 ae: 1m 8d. SD I:204
John s/o John d 1 Mar 1843 ae: 16y. GSL
Richard s/o John d 30 Sep 1855 ae: 22y. GSL
COOK, Antonio d 3 Sep 1847 ae: 68y. Catholic. GSL
Capt. David b 12 Mar 1751 d 27 Oct 1823. Revolutionary War: Con Artillery Massachusetts Society of Cincinnati. Unusual inscription. B-11-10
Dorothea w/o Horatio Gates b 30 Dec 1783 d 13 Aug 1864. B-11-13
Ellen d/o Mary d 7 Nov 1856 ae:

COOK (continued)
5m. GSL

Frank H. s/o Lewis d 6 Aug 1866 ae: 10m. GSL

George H. s/o George H. d 11 Sep 1850 ae: 12y. Mmt A Tomb 71

Herbert s/o Hiram T. d 17 Apr 1869 ae: 7m. GSL

Horatio Gates s/o Capt. David b 12 Feb 1785 d 20 Jan 1863. B-11-12

Lillia d/o Antonio d 30 Jan 1858 ae: 68d. Catholic. "Buried at side of grandmother." K:11

Mary J. wid/o Antonio d 13 Apr 1851 ae: 72y. Catholic. SB K:11

Olive w/o Thomas B. d 10 Mar 1848 ae: 39y. MB A Tomb 23

Salina A. w/o George H. d 27 Aug 1850 ae: 39y. A Tomb 71

Thomas s/o John d 16 July 1849 ae: 23y. GSL

COOLIDGE, Caroline W. d/o William d 30 Sep 1850 ae: 20y. GSL

Jonas s/o Henry & Mary d 28 June 1820 ae: 21y. SD H:53

Priscilla T. wid/o William d 7 May 1875 ae: 80y. H:51B

W. H. d 28 Jan 1861 ae: 43y. GSL

William d 28 Mar 1856 ae: 63y. H:51A

William S. s/o William & Priscilla d 14 Sep 1806 ae: 7m 14d. SD H:54

COOMBS, Hannah w/o James d 23 Dec 1861 ae: 84y. SBE K:131

COOPER, Betsy w/o Capt. Simon d 29 July 1768 ae: 20y. G:146

Sarah J. d/o John S. d 22 Sep 1864 ae: 2y 4m. GSL

CORNISH, Arthur d 23 Aug 1857 ae: 50y. "Died at the Marine Hospital." GSL

CORRY, Abigail w/o Ebenezer M. d 11 Nov 1839 ae: 39y. SBE C:92

Charles F. s/o Ebenezer M. &

CORRY (continued)
Abigail d 10 Oct 1820 ae: 16m. SBE C:92

Ebenezer M. b 7 May 1793 d 12 Jan 1881. SBE C:91

Edward s/o Ebenezer M. & Abigail d 3 Dec 1828 ae: 18m. SBE C:92

Eliza B. d/o Ebenezer M. & Abigail d 16 Sep 1854 ae: 26y. SD C:93

Elizabeth d/o Ebenezer M. & Abigail d 15 Oct 1825 ae: 21m. SBE C:92

Elizabeth T. d/o Ebenezer M. & Abigail d 11 Oct 1821 ae: 13m. SBE C:92

Esther wid/o James d Apr 1809 ae: 43y. C:108

Francis s/o James & Esther d 6 July 1820 ae: 21y. SB C:110

James s/o James & Esther d 25 Sep 1794 ae: 5y. C:109

James s/o James & Esther d Oct 1808 ae: 12y. SB C:110

James d Oct 1808 ae: 52y. SB C:110

James s/o Ebenezer M. & Abigail d 11 Aug 1826 ae: 6m. SB C:92

Josiah s/o James & Esther d 28 Sep 1820 ae: 19y. "Died at Norfolk, Virginia." C:108

Sarah S. d 24 Jan 1857 ae: 66y. GSL

COTA, Fanny W. w/o Daniel d 7 Apr 1847 ae: 31y. SB A-16-9

COTTON, Martha Hudson wid/o Deacon William d 10 Dec 1784 ae: 65y. Name also on monument H:55. H:50

Sarah w/o Deacon William d 3 May 1753 ae: 47y. Name also on monument H:55. SBE H:48

Deacon William d 8 Dec 1768 ae: 58y. Name also on monument H:55. H:49

COULLARD, Olive S. w/o Elijah d 8 May 1859 ae: 25y. GSL

COUSINS, Charles A. s/o Ivory L. & Nancy E. d 31 Aug 1839 ae: 18m. SD B-11-26

COUSINS (continued)

Edward R. d 6 July 1849 ae: 16y. SD B-11-26

George H. s/o Ivory L. & Nancy E. d 19 Oct 1837 ae: 11m. B-11-26

Nancy d 22 Oct 1881 ae: 81y. GSL

COVAL, Micah d 17 June 1847 ae: 65y. A Tomb 2

COX, Abraham d 27 Aug 1858 ae: 68y. "Executed at Auburn, Maine, for murder upon the high seas." GSL

Arthur d 14 Aug 1876 ae: 18y. NM A Tomb 55

Charles F. s/o Josephius d 19 Sep 1863 ae: 10w. A Tomb 55

Elizabeth H. d/o John d 28 Apr 1844 ae: 10m. A Tomb 55

John s/o Josiah & Sarah d 25 Oct 1785 ae: 20y. SD E:60

Josiah s/o John d 20 July 1829 ae: 73y. A Tomb 55

Josiah d 11 Apr 1874 ae: 45y. A Tomb 55

Melville B. s/o Rev. Gershom F. d 16 Dec 1837 ae: 4y. A-6-14

Merritt s/o Rev. Gershom F. d 31 May 1842 ae: 3m. GSL

Nancy d/o Josiah & Sarah d 1 Oct 1775 ae: 18m. SD E:64

Sarah w/o Capt. John d 25 Oct 1763 ae: 40y. Spelled "Cocks" on stone. E:61

Sarah Greenleaf wid/o Josiah d 21 July 1822 ae: 77y. E:63

Sarah T. d/o Dr. Solomon Allen d 4 Apr 1871 ae: 38y. A Tomb 55

Susan d 17 Dec 1850 ae: 82y. A Tomb 55

William s/o Josiah & Sarah b 15 Mar 1770 d 2 Apr 1784. E:64

William L. s/o Josiah d 23 Apr 1864 ae: 3y 6m. A Tomb 55

CRABBE, Jennie O. d 17 June 1858 ae: 19y. GSL

CRABTREE, Lucy w/o Capt. Eleazer b 3 June 1757 d 6 June 1802. SD I:168

CRAIGE, Edmund s/o Robert d 2 Nov 1848. "Died Gorham."

CRAIGE (continued)

Black. GSL

Robert d 24 Nov 1849 ae: 80y. Black. GSL

Mary d 11 Sep 1844 ae: 15m. "Buried at foot of J. Preble's monument." GSL

CRAM, Henry K. s/o Nathaniel O. d 22 Apr 1854 ae: 1y 6m. A Tomb 70

Latimus Morse d 8 Apr 1842 ae: 32y. A Tomb 70

Mary A. d 17 Oct 1811 ae: 3y. A Tomb 70

Mary A. d 30 July 1815 ae: 9m. A Tomb 70

Mary B. K. w/o Nathaniel O. d 13 May 1861 ae: 45y. A Tomb 70

Mary C. d 7 Oct 1827 ae: 17y. A Tomb 70

Mary J. w/o Nehemiah d 1 Mar 1847 ae: 87y. A Tomb 70

Nehemiah d 15 Mar 1848 ae: 86y. A Tomb 70

Nehemiah d 18 May 1863 ae: 80y. A Tomb 70

Octavia K. d/o Nathaniel O. & Mary K. d 7 Aug 1852 ae: 1y. A Tomb 70

Sarah Martin d 16 Dec 1871 ae: 78y. GSL

Susan M. d 21 Dec 1845 ae: 58y. A Tomb 70

CRANDALL, Martha wid/o Capt. Philip d 24 May 1832 ae: 65y. E:59

Capt. Philip d 17 May 1832 ae: 72y. E:58

CRAWFORD, James d 10 Mar 1859. GSL

William d 7 Dec 1865 ae: 58y. MBE A Tomb 42

CRAY, George B. s/o Ira & Betsy d 22 Sep 1820 ae: 3y 8m. Black. SD L:23

CRANEY, Lewis A. d 20 May 1836. GSL

CRESEY, Charles s/o Daniel & Eliza d 24 Mar 1807 ae: 6m. SB I:106

Daniel, Jr. s/o Daniel & Eliza d

CRESEY (continued)

26 Aug 1832 ae: 28y. I:108

Eliza w/o Daniel d 1 May 1829 ae: 49y. I:107

CRIE, Margaret w/o William d 25 June 1822 ae: 54y. I:103

William d 11 Mar 1831 ae: 66y. I:104

CRIPEN, Charles d 11 Aug 1851 ae: 51y. Black. L:17

CROCKER, Enoch d 10 Aug 1853 ae: 61y. A Tomb 26

Leonice w/o William d 14 Nov 1779 ae: 23y. F:166

CROCKETT, Albert d 16 Oct 1838 ae: 26y. B-1-10

Benjamin d 9 Aug 1850 ae: 39y. GSL

Frances H. d/o Benjamin d 6 Mar 1845 ae: 2y 3m. "Buried at head of Henry F. Dupree's stone." NS K:7

Georgianna d/o Benjamin d 3 Oct 1846 ae: 2y 6m. "Buried at head of John Dupree's grave." NS K:9

Henrietta d/o Benjamin d 11 Aug 1848 ae: 2y. "Buried at head of J. S. Dupree's grave." NS K:9

James d 20 Mar 1825 ae: 39y. B-1-15

John d 2 Sep 1830 ae: 41y. B-1-9

Joshua d 30 Mar 1854 ae: 39y. GSL

Loisa w/o Capt. Richard d 3 Nov 1821 ae: 25y. J:191

Martha A. d 17 Nov 1856 ae: 32y 5m. GSL

Mary Jane w/o Caleb d 21 Aug 1842 ae: 20y. A-18-11

Nancy w/o Nathaniel d 4 Jan 1849 ae: 61y. GSL

Sarah wid/o James d 18 Nov 1829 ae: 39y. B-1-16

Sarah wid/o John d 4 Oct 1865 ae: 77y. B-1-8

Sarah Jane d/o Capt. Richard & Loisa d 26 Apr 1822 ae: 1y. J:191

CROSBY, Abigail Bradbury d 8 Nov 1810 ae: 73y. "Relict of

CROSBY (continued)

Capt. Watson Crosby who was lost at sea in the Autumn of 1775." F:45

Mary d/o Daniel d 11 Dec 1805 ae: 31y. SD K:77

CROSS, Abigail wid/o Eben d 24 Dec 1862 ae: 94y 4m. GSL

Amos H. d 27 Sep 1842 ae: 54y. A Tomb 73

Betsy wid/o Joseph d 24 Oct 1828 ae: 58y. A Tomb 73

Caroline M. d/o Robert & Caroline b 5 Aug ---- d 30 Dec 1808. SBE C:177

Cornelia R. w/o Francis H. d 15 Oct 1897 ae: 75y 6m. A Tomb 73

Ebenezer d 9 Jan 1852 ae: 88y. GSL

Francis H. s/o Thomas & Lana d 13 Aug 1889 ae: 74y. A Tomb 73

Frank K. d 26 Nov 1864 ae: 17y. Civil War: "Died in Rebel prison." A Tomb 73

Harnet J. d/o Joseph & Betsy d 3 Oct 1801 ae: 18m. A Tomb 73

Helen L. d/o John B. & H. M. b.25 Oct ---- d 11 Nov 1825 SBE B-5-4

Helen M. d/o Francis H. & Cornelia b 1 June 1845 d 23 June 1855. A Tomb 73

Henry s/o Joseph & Betsy d 3 Apr 1821 ae: 24y. A Tomb 73

Jane wid/o Ralph d 27 Apr 1826 ae: 58y. ME H:159

Jane G. d 4 Dec 1890 ae: 84y 11m. NS H:158

Joseph b 26 Apr 1753 d 3 May 1822. Revolutionary War: Fifer - Con Army. C:87

Joseph d 29 Oct 1819 ae: 51y. A Tomb 73

Joseph H. s/o Joseph & Betsy d 21 Oct 1805 ae: 18m. A Tomb 73

Lelia F. d/o Francis H. & Cornelia R. b 10 Sep 1852 d 6 Aug 1853. A Tomb 73

Leonard d 21 Mar 1867 ae: 80y

CROSS (continued)
10m. A Tomb 73

Lilla H. d/o Francis H. d 6 Aug 1853 ae: 11m. A Tomb 73

Mary K. d/o Francis H. d 19 Nov 1864 ae: 1y 10m. A Tomb 73

Nathaniel d 12 Dec 1841 ae: 76y. A-11-9

Ralph nd. NS H:157

Ralph d 25 Oct 1815 ae: 54y. MD H:159

Rebecca w/o Nathaniel d 4 Oct 1839 ae: 72y. SB A-11-8

Thomas d 6 Apr 1833 ae: 63y. A Tomb 73

CROSSMAN, Angelia d/o Benjamin & Caroline d 11 Sep 1838 ae: 2y 8m. SBE F:61

Elizabeth w/o Joseph A. d 11 June 1854 ae: 78y. SB B-13-4

Joseph A. d 18 July 1831 ae: 85y. Revolutionary War: Con Navy, frigate *Deane*. SB B-13-3

Sarah E. d/o James H. d 10 Oct 1850 ae: 1y. GSL

Theodore s/o James d 1 Apr 1846 ae: 3y 3m. "Buried head of Mr. Thaxter's grave." NS B-7-31

Thomas B. s/o James d 10 July 1852 ae: 5y. GSL

CROSWELL, Joseph d 8 Jan 1815 ae: 73y. I:40

Mary W. d 4 Mar 1824 ae: 33y. I:39

CROWE, Susan W. d/o Richard R. d 6 Dec 1844 ae: 3y 5m. "Buried Smith's tomb." GSL

CROWTHER, Eunice Jane d/o John d 19 May 1841. GSL

CUMMINGS, Alice Ilsley w/o Dr. Ralph W. d/o late Israel Waterhouse d 5 Dec 1857 ae: 31y. "Buried Waterhouse tomb." GSL

Eleanor w/o Dr. Stephen d 31 May 1824 ae: 48y. SBE B-1-1

Eleanor d/o Nathan & Eleanor d 27 July 1830 ae: 2y 3m. A Tomb 77

Eleonora wid/o Thomas d 3 May

CUMMINGS (continued)
1809 ae: 69y. SB F:160

Fitz H. s/o Dr. Stephen d 26 July 1837 ae: 21y. SBE B-1-2

George s/o Thomas d 4 Aug 1843 ae: 6w. A Tomb 47

John M., M.D. b 31 Mar 1812 d 28 Mar 1878. Mmt A-13-1

Margaret d/o Thomas & Eleonora nd. SB F:160

Mary E. d 7 Jan 1868 ae: 48y 5m. GSL

Nancy d/o Thomas & Eleonora nd SB F:160

Stephen, M.D. d 2 Mar 1854 ae: 81y. Mmt A-13-1

Sumner, M.D. b 24 Apr 1800 d 24 Nov 1848. Mmt A-13-1

Thomas d 19 Feb 1798 ae: 64y. "Born Scotland." SB F:160

CUMSTON, Henrietta d/o Henry d 16 Apr 1852 ae: 12y. GSL

Lydia d 12 May 1850 ae: 66y. Widow. GSL

Lydia Maria d/o late Henry d 9 Feb 1842 ae: 6y. GSL

CURRIER, Daniel W. s/o Royal d 19 Nov 1857 ae: 5y 9m. GSL

George W. s/o Royal d 25 Oct 1856 ae: 2y 9m. GSL

John W. s/o James d 18 Oct 1862 ae: 3w. GSL

CURTIS, Ansel H. s/o Ansel H. d 29 July 1850 ae: 2y. GSL

Julianna d/o Rev. Thomas d 15 July 1836 ae: 23y. SD E:3

Rev. Reuben b 1788 d 1835. A-1-3

William C. s/o James d 1 Sep 1867 ae: 10m. GSL

CURWIN, Nicholas d 19 Oct 1704. GSL

CUSHING, Capt. Abner d 16 Sep 1824 ae: 36y. SD A-16-5

Abner Jr. d Oct 1841 ae: 16y. SD A-16-5

Charlotte C. d/o Capt. Abner & Mary B. d 7 Apr 1845 ae: 20y. SD A-16-4

Jacob d -- Feb 1816. SBE I:15

Loring d 7 Apr 1820 ae: 67y. Revolutionary War. SBE I:15

CUSHING (continued)

Lydia wid/o Loring d 1 Dec 1833 ae: 75y. SBE I:15

Mary B. w/o Capt. Abner d 13 Oct 1847 ae: 51y. SD A-16-5

Mary H. d 5 Feb 1857 ae: 66y. SBE I:15

Mary Louisa d/o Capt. Abner & Mary B. d 5 Aug 1841 ae: 20y. A-16-3

Pollis d 9 July 1843 ae: 79y. GSL

Sarah T. d 30 Jan 1874 ae: 83y. SD I:16

William H. d 23 July 1873 ae: 50y. A Tomb 14

CUSHMAN, Charlemagne d 22 May 1845 ae: 68y. MD A Tomb 39

Charles A. s/o Erasmus d 15 Dec 1850 ae: 9y. GSL

Helen d/o Edward T. d 14 Sep 1841 ae: 3y. GSL

Henrietta Augusta d/o Henry d 2 Jan 1849 ae: 8y. GSL

Imogene M. d/o Edward P. & M. B. d 8 Dec 1852 ae: 8m. GSL

James A. s/o Edward T. d 3 June 1850 ae: 10m. "Buried near the gate." GSL

John H. d 12 Dec 1866 ae: 58y. GSL

Levi d 31 July 1843 ae: 19y. ME A Tomb 82

Mary Lewis d/o Henry d 31 Dec 1848 ae: 3y. GSL

Sarah w/o Charlemagne d 19 Sep 1844 ae: 68y. A Tomb 39

CUTLER, Albert M. d 14 Sep 1866 ae: 33y. A Tomb 32

Julia Ann w/o Rev. Samuel d 28 Dec 1830 ae: 24y. Mmt A Tomb 48

CUTTER, Charles L. s/o Levi d 15 July 1850 ae: 6m. A Tomb 48

David Mitchell d 16 Dec 1831 ae: 33y. A Tomb 48

Elizabeth Jane d 8 Sep 1806 ae: 22m. A Tomb 48

Levi d 2 Mar 1856 ae: 82y. Mayor - Portland. A Tomb 48

CUTTER (continued)

Lucretia Mitchell w/o Levi d 13 Apr 1827 ae: 57y. A Tomb 48

CUTTING, Annie E. d/o Frederick B. d 16 July 1867 ae: 8m. A Tomb 7

Laura B. d/o Osborne W. T. d 7 May 1872 ae: 25y. NM F:95 Tomb

DALEY, Bridget d/o Bernard d 28 Jan 1855 ae: 5m. GSL

Emor d 19 Aug 1805 ae: 44y. SB I:22

Mary wid/o Emor d 12 Oct 1828 ae: 66y. SB I:23

Mrs. Olive d 8 May 1839 ae: 62y. SB A-7-10

Thomas S. d 6 Apr 1877 ae: 27y. GSL

DALY, Royal A. s/o William d 27 Feb 1886 ae: 1y 3m. GSL

DAM, Abby A. d/o George W. d 16 Dec 1849 ae: 6y. A Tomb 81

Stephen F. s/o George W. d 21 Nov 1846 ae: 5y. A Tomb 81

Willie s/o George & Fannie d 21 Aug 1862 ae: 6w. J:183A

DAMRELL, Benjamin B. d 11 June 1855 ae: 16y. GSL

Daniel A. s/o John E. & Lydia A. d 15 Jan 1854 ae: 8m. SB B-11-3

Capt. Edward H. d 4 Feb 1825 ae: 66y. SB B-11-5

Elbridge S. s/o John d 10 Feb 1862 ae: 4y. GSL

Frederick M. s/o John E. & Lydia E. d 24 Jan 1856 ae: 1y. SB B-11-3

George H. s/o Daniel d 13 Aug 1848 ae: 1y. "Buried at head of Shea Child's grave." NS B-10-4

Hannah M. w/o Capt. Edward H. d 24 Nov 1863 ae: 79y 4m. SB B-11-5

DANA, Betsy wid/o David d 28 Feb 1862 ae: 84y. A Tomb 74

David d 27 May 1842 ae: 66y. A Tomb 74

David Jr. d 25 Feb 1837 ae: 35y.

DANA (continued)
A Tomb 74

Dexter d 30 Oct 1822 ae: 49y. A
Tomb 74

Elizabeth d 25 Apr 1820 ae: 4y.
A Tomb 74

Elizabeth Ann d/o Thomas
McLellan d 4 Sep 1873 ae:
67y. F:96 Tomb

Ferdinand d 20 June 1855 ae:
33y. A Tomb 74

Mary O. d 6 Sep 1858 ae: 54y. A
Tomb 74

DANFORTH, John M. d 16 May
1860 ae: 34y. "Died Raymond,
Maine." GSL

Walter d 4 Aug 1848 ae: 45y.
"Died at Elm House, a stran-
ger." "Buried at grave side of
Mrs. Stacy - 1842." NS A-6-16

DANIELS, ---- s/o Charles R. d
31 May 1846 ae: 16m. "Buried
near Friends' Ground." GSL

Charles P. d 8 July 1858 ae: 5m.
Black. GSL

Henry d 5 Dec 1880 ae: 72y.
Black. GSL

Henry A. W. s/o Henry d 2 July
1860 ae: 17y. "Died at Reform
School." GSL

James Curtis adopted d/o George
G. d 26 Aug 1847 ae: 4m. GSL

John W. s/o Charles d 18 Sep
1848 ae: 8m. "Buried near the
Friends' Ground." GSL

Sarah w/o Charles R. d 9 Sep
1849 ae: 42y. SD L:62

Sarah d 13 Feb 1893 ae: 82y
10m. GSL

Sarah d/o Charles d 30 May 1842
ae: 2y. GSL

DARLING, Sylvia d 6 Apr 1870
ae: 87y 1m. SBE A-13-24

DAVENPORT, Frederick D. s/o
Edwin d 4 Aug 1848 ae: 1y.
"Native of Cincinnati, Ohio."
A Tomb 17

Edwin s/o Edwin d 26 June 1844
ae: 6m. A Tomb 17

Margaret D. w/o Edwin d 10 June
1844 ae: 24y. A Tomb 17

Mary A. d 10 Dec 1849 ae: 27y.

DAVENPORT (continued)
"Native of Cincinnati, Ohio."
A Tomb 17

DAVEY, Peter d 9 Jan 1863 ae:
46y. GSL

DAVIDSON, Charles d 8 Jan 1859
ae: 53y. A Tomb 17

Martha wid/o William d 7 June
1864 ae: 80y. A Tomb 17

Phebe N. wid/o Charles d 10
May 1881 ae: 75y. A Tomb 17

DAVEIS, Charles G. d 26 Dec
1857 ae: 44y. "Buried side
Samuel Lord's grave." NS J:39

DAVIS, Ann d/o Daniel & Lois b
17 Aug 1793 d 17 Jan 1796
J:200

Annie d 9 Dec 1869. GSL

Augusta H. d/o late John T. d 29
Sep 1847 ae: 18y. NM A
Tomb 47

Benjamin s/o Ezra d 19 Apr 1849
ae: 1y. A Tomb 30

Carrie M. d/o Mahlon d 12 Sep
1865 ae: 11m. GSL

Mrs. Catherine d 11 Aug 1846 ae:
66y. GSL

Charles s/o Solomon & Mary d 4
Apr 1833 ae: 9d. SD L:50

Charles E. s/o late Charles d 4
May 1860 ae: 7y 6m. GSL

David s/o William & Sophia d 29
Oct 1817 ae: 11m. SD G:41

Ebenezer d 14 Nov 1799 ae: 46y.
Revolutionary War: Ensign,
8th Reg. Massachuisetts Con
Line, Massachusetts Society
of the Cincinnati. GSL

Edward #2 s/o Daniel & Lois b
29 Dec 1796 d 13 Sep 1798
J:201

Edward s/o Daniel & Lois d 22
July 1791 ae: 9m 12d. J:202

Edward G. s/o Joseph d 30 Jan
1857 ae: 2y 11m. "Buried east
side Samuel Beckett's grave."
GSL

Elisha T. s/o Barzillai & Phebe
d 22 May 1827 ae: 9m. B-9-30

Eliza E. d/o Solomon & Mary d
15 June 1835 ae: 14m. SD L:50

Elizabeth wid/o James d 26 Sep

DAVIS (continued)

1854 ae: 61y. Black. SD A-15-21

Elizabeth F. d/o Barzillai & Phebe d 27 Aug 1825 ae: 3y. B-9-29

Ellen d/o Keene W. & Eliza d 20 Sep 1835 ae: 2y 9m. F:18

Elmer A. s/o George H. d 7 June 1890 ae: 28y. "Died Boston, Massachusetts." GSL

Elmira V. d 19 Aug 1858 ae: 28y. Black. GSL

Eugene F. d 4 Aug 1871 ae: 7m. GSL

Eunice w/o Nathan d 18 Sep 1805 ae: 21y. SB J:84

Frances E. d/o Rowland E. & Judith I. d 14 Jan 1848 ae: 2y 8m. SB L:61A

George Ripley s/o Capt. Rowland d 2 Oct 1853 ae: 11m. GSL

Hall Augustus s/o George R. d 20 Aug 1853 ae: 3m. A Tomb 59

Hannah, widow d 19 Aug 1844 ae: 99y. A-13-10

Henry s/o George H. d 29 Nov 1853 ae: 12d. GSL

Herbert W. d 11 Feb 1909 ae: 42y. "Died Winthrop, Massachusetts." MD A Tomb 33

James d 1 Apr 1810 ae: 46y. Catholic. GSL

James d 13 Sep 1846 ae: 64y. Black. SD A-15-21

James E. d 12 Aug 1853 ae: 31y 10m. B-9-9

James W. d 21 Feb 1823 ae: 34y. B-9-8

John s/o Thomas d 12 Sep 1841 ae: 10m. GSL

John R. d 16 Dec 1858 ae: 25y. "Buried J. B. Coyle lot." GSL

John W. s/o James W. d 5 Nov 1858 ae: 15m. Black. GSL

Judith I. Murch w/o Rowland b 1822 d 1883. L:61B

L. P. s/o George H. d 1 Sep 1860 ae: 3m. GSL

Lilla S. d/o George H. d 23 Sep 1857 ae: 15m. GSL

DAVIS (continued)

Mary wid/o Capt. Moses d 17 Apr 1885 ae: 82y. "Former w/o John Starbird." A-23-2

Mary wid/o Solomon b 18 Aug 1811 d 5 Jan 1892. L:50A

Mary S. w/o George H. d 24 Apr 1875 ae: 42y. L:67

Sarah Jane d 3 May 1853 ae: 20y. GSL

Solomon b 13 Aug 1805 d 15 Nov 1883. L:50A

Stephen A. s/o Nathan & Eunice b 2 Aug 1804 d 1 Aug 1805. SD J:85

Teazan s/o Thomas d 4 Jan 1849 ae: 2m. "Buried in William Harding's grave." GSL

Walter Ethan s/o William G. d 10 Dec 1854 ae: 2y. GSL

Wendall N. s/o N. J. d 30 Mar 1846 ae: 5m. A Tomb 82

William d 27 Aug 1807 ae: 29y. I:170

William L. s/o Isaac & Mary P. d 23 Aug 1839 ae: 16y 4m. SD A-13-11

William W. d 26 May 1846 ae: 37y. SBE E:11

DAY, Edith R. s/o Henry E. d 12 May 1869 ae: 15y. F:96 Tomb

Elizabeth d 9 Aug 1802 ae: 1y 7m 9d. SD L:30

Elizabeth d 20 Aug 1867 ae: 99y 9m. SB L:32

Ellen L. s/o John d 25 Nov 1847 ae: 6m. F:96 Tomb

Eunice Quinby wid/o Ezekiel b 16 Mar 1783 d 9 Mar 1862. A Tomb 26

Ezekiel d 22 Mar 1842 ae: 70y. A Tomb 26

Hannah w/o Ezekiel d 15 Oct 1806 ae: 30y. F:105 Tomb

Joseph d 28 July 1851 ae: 40y. "Died at sea." A Tomb 26

Lucretia d 22 Jan 1800 ae: 17d. F:105 Tomb

DEAKE, Mary d 19 May 1809. J:219

DEAN, Charles d 1 Jan 1829 ae: 49y. B-9-21

DEAN (continued)

Esther d 31 Dec 1886 ae: 63y. J:207

Fannie w/o George d 29 Dec 1893 ae: 54y. J:206

George d 12 Jan 1890 ae: 58y. Civil War: 15th Reg. Maine Inf., Co. E. J:206

William J. s/o George d 27 July 1867 ae: 6w. J:205

DEANE, ---- d/o Barzillai d 7 Jan 1855 ae: 11m. GSL

Elizabeth w/o Jonathan d 4 Sep 1811 ae: 50y. I:117

Elizabeth d/o Samuel d 24 Aug 1844. "Buried at foot of Samuel Bates' tomb." GSL

Eunice Pearson w/o Rev. Samuel d 14 Oct 1812 ae: 85y. GSL

Jonathan d 2 Aug 1822 ae: 70y. Revolutionary War. I:116

Mary d 29 Dec 1805 ae: 21y. D:141

Mary A. d/o David d 7 Dec 1861 ae: 7w. GSL

Rev. Samuel b 10 July 1733 d 12 Nov 1814. Ledger A Tomb 84

DEARBORN, Henrietta d/o Bradbury d 13 July 1848 ae: 14y. MB A Tomb 23

Sarah N. sis/o Bradbury d 10 May 1850 ae: 55y. MB A Tomb 23

DEARTH, Benjamin s/o Joseph d 30 Mar 1845 ae: 13m. GSL

DEBREMAN, Clara A. w/o Francis A. d 30 Nov 1853 ae: 24y. GSL

DECRENCY, Julius F. s/o Louis S. d 14 Oct 1850 ae: 6y. GSL

DEERING, James J. s/o Noah d 26 Nov 1841 ae: 5y. GSL

John b 13 Nov 1740 d 4 Nov 1784. SBE E:45

Joseph d 6 Dec 1779 ae: 22y. Revolutionary War. SB E:44

Joseph d 17 Mar 1838. War of 1812: Fifer. GSL

DEES, John nd. SD J:194

DELA, Clara d/o Lewis d 8 Oct 1847 ae: 15m. GSL

DELA (continued)

Clara d 11 Nov 1849 ae: 1y. GSL

Clarissa R. d 7 Sep 1837 ae: 44y. SBE E:49

Francis C. w/o Lewis, Jr. d 31 Dec 1849 ae: 21y. GSL

John d 25 Feb 1842 ae: 10y. A Tomb 79

John d 20 Feb 1846 ae: 49y. SD E:52

Sarah H. d/o Lewis d 7 Oct 1855 ae: 4m. "Buried in her mother's grave." GSL

William N. s/o Lewis d 25 Aug 1854 ae: 4m. GSL

DELANO, Barzillai d 24 Mar 1805 ae: 31y. GSL

Barzillai d 1 Oct 1863 ae: 59y 6m. L:77

Frank E. d 22 Feb 1850 ae: 20m. L:77

Frederick s/o Barzillai & Hannah b 23 Mar 1798 d 11 Oct 1802. SB L:72

Hannah wid/o Barzillai d 22 Oct 1831 ae: 86y. L:71

Joanna wid/o Joseph d 21 Mar 1845 ae: 73y. L:75

Joseph d 31 Aug 1831 ae: 58y. L:74

Mary d/o Barzillai & Hannah b 25 Feb 1805 d 14 Feb 1806. SB L:72

Mary E. d/o Barzillai d 14 July 1841 ae: 18m. GSL

Mary E. d/o Barzillai d 12 Dec 1854 ae: 2y 6m. L:77

Moses s/o Barzillai & Hannah b 7 Nov 1795 d 15 June 1800. SB L:72

Moses #2 s/o Barzillai & Hannah b 8 Feb 1803 d 22 Feb 1803. SB L:72

Russell S. d 7 Jan 1855 ae: 11m. L:77

Sally d/o Barzillai & Hannah b 12 Sep 1801 d 7 Oct 1802. SB L:72

Sophronia w/o Barzillai d 26 May 1886 ae: 75y. L:76

Thomas d 23 Mar 1811 ae: 15y. L:73

DELANO (continued)
William Pearson s/o Joshua & Maria d 5 Feb 1823 ae: 24y 4m 6d. B-8-14

DELESNEIR, Bartlett R. d 9 Sep 1841 ae: 2y. GSL

DEMPSTER, James d 24 June 1846 ae: 40y. "Seaman - buried near Hearse House." GSL

DENNACK, Amelia Alice d/o William P. d 10 Sep 1862 ae: 10m. GSL

DENNINGS, Cummings F. d 12 July 1847 ae: 37y. GSL

Harriet L. d/o Cummings F. d 31 July 1846 ae: 22m. GSL

DENNIS, James d 4 Oct 1844 ae: 65y. GSL

DENNISON, Abner L. s/o John & Lillias d 27 Aug 1842 ae: 21y. SBE A-18-12

Albert B. s/o Albert B. d 7 Apr 1857 ae: 1y. GSL

Alfred Lockhart s/o John H. d 27 Mar 1863 ae: 4y 9m. GSL

George F. L. s/o John H. d 28 Aug 1851 ae: 8m. GSL

George T. s/o John & Lillias d 2 Dec 1844 ae: 18y. A-18-13

H. William d 25 Jan 1853 ae: 6y. "Died in New York." GSL

Howard C. d 6 July 1922 ae: 81y. Civil War: Maine Coast Guards, Co. B, Ft. Scammel. GSL

John d 8 June 1882 ae: 91y. War of 1812, Sgt., Brewer's Massachusetts Militia. A-18-13

John F. s/o John H. d 24 Aug 1854 ae: 14m. GSL

Lillias w/o John d 20 Dec 1872 ae: 81y. "Buried John Dennison lot." NS A-18-13

Mehitable d/o John & Lillias d 11 Aug 1896 ae: 78y 10m. "Died Greely Hospital." NS A-18-13

Nancy M. d/o James & Sarah d 14 Sep 1820 ae: 12y. K:112

Virginia d/o Charles W. d 13 May 1842 ae: 4y. ME A Tomb 35

DEEPLE, Charles d 1 July 1871 ae: 39y. GSL

DESANCHEZ, Cosmo d 9 Dec 1848 ae: 24y. Native "of Huamantla, Puebla, Mexico." B-12-1

DEVINE, Charles E. s/o Edward d 18 May 1855 ae: 1y. GSL

Ellen d/o John & Mary d 1 Dec 1835 ae: 2y 7m. Catholic. B-14-1

DICKEY, Horace D. s/o Horace W. & Sarah A. b 31 Mar 1831 d 3 Apr 1832. G:112

DICKS, Joseph Henry s/o Capt. John W. d 4 Apr 1849 ae: 2y. A Tomb 49

Mariah M. d/o Capt. John W. d 8 Sep 1853 ae: 13m. A Tomb 49

DICKSON, Adelaide E. d/o Jacob & E. d 6 July 1854 ae: 17y. Black. SD A-14-18

Louisa d/o Richard & Eliza V. d 9 July 1841 ae: 10y 3m. Black. A-10-32

Samuel W. s/o Richard d 21 Aug 1841 ae: 7m. Black. GSL

Sarah J. d/o Richard & Eliza V. d 25 May 1830 ae: 1m. Black. A-10-32

DIMOCK, William P. d 17 Jan 1859 ae: 1y 2m. GSL

DIMOND, Henry L. d 16 Mar 1832 ae: 23y. SB E:56

DINSMORE, Mary d 11 Jan 1844 ae: 78y. "Buried J. F. Weeks tomb." GSL

Phebe d 11 Sep 1854 ae: 20y. GSL

Sarah A. d 16 Dec 1857 ae: 17y. "Buried at side of Mountfort St." GSL

DIX, Rhoda d 27 Mar 1805 ae: 19y. GSL

DOCKERY, Mary Ann S. w/o James R. d/o Moses & Abigail Plummer b 21 Dec 1799 d 15 Mar 1854. C:61

DODGE, Abigail w/o Benjamin d 20 Jan 1807 ae: 34y. J:121

Benjamin b 1 May 1774 d 1 June 1838. "Born in Exeter, New

DODGE (continued)
Hampshire." J:122

Benjamin s/o Benjamin & Abigail nd. J:120

Betsy w/o Thomas b 1792 d 20 Jan 1872. I:129

Elizabeth J. d/o Thomas & Lydia d 5 Oct 1813 ae: 2y. I:133

Frances E. d/o Thomas & Lydia d 5 July 1829 ae: 1y 9m. I:134

George E. s/o William S. d 19 Aug 1848 ae: 4m. GSL

Harriet d/o Benjamin & Sarah d 17 Oct 1845 ae: 27y. J:113

Helen Maria d/o William S. d 21 Apr 1849 ae: 3y. GSL

Israel s/o Pickering & Sally nd ae: 18y. SB J:46

Jane C. d/o James M. d 24 June 1841 ae: 1y 5m. GSL

Joseph s/o Benjamin & Sally b 9 May 1814 d 28 July 1815 J:115

Lydia d/o Benjamin & Sally b 2 Sep 1812 d 30 Aug 1813. J:116

Lydia w/o Thomas. I:131

Mary d/o Thomas & Lydia d 29 Aug 1818 ae: 10y. I:132

Mary d/o Benjamin & Mary d 11 Dec 1823 ae: 14y. SB B-15-12

Nancy d/o Benjamin & Abigail d 28 Aug 1833 ae: 35y. J:114

Sally d/o Benjamin & Sally d 13 Feb 1810 ae: 1y 6m. J:117

Sally wid/o Pickering d 5 Jan 1843 ae: 75y. SB J:46

Sarah d/o James M. d 21 June 1841 ae: 17m. GSL

Sarah w/o Benjamin d 19 Aug 1846 ae: 67y. J:124 b. 1779

Thomas d 20 Jan 1831 ae: 47y. I:130 b. 1784

DOLE, Andrew T. d 6 Aug 1866 ae: 57y. A Tomb 48

Sophia A. Fosdick wid/o Andrew T. b 27 Nov 1816 d 1 June 1888. A Tomb 48

DORRANCE, Jane Maria w/o Oliver B. d 19 Sep 1848 ae: 40y. A Tomb 48

DOUGHERTY, David E. d 7 Dec 1869 ae: 4y 8m. GSL

DOUGHTY, David J. s/o Thomas & Sarah d 18 Sep 1857. SBE G:121

Mary A. d/o John & Ellen d 12 Sep 1836 ae: 18y. SD G:122

Sarah d/o John & Ellen d 10 Oct 1845 ae: 13y. SD G:122

DOUGLAS, Ellen M. w/o William G. d 22 Feb 1892 ae: 67y. GSL

DOUGLASS, Francis d 2 Sep 1820 ae: 37y. "Accidentially shot, Casco Bay." SBE H:94

Harriet d/o William & Abigail d 12 July 1818 ae: 22y. SBE C:209

John F. d 19 Aug 1854 ae: 18y. GSL

Robert B. s/o John d 22 Dec 1857 ae: 5y 8m. GSL

William W. s/o John & Frances A. d 2 Apr 1836 ae: 7m. Black. A-10-35

DOW, Jedediah d 29 Dec 1842 ae: 66y. GSL

Jonathan s/o Jabez & Dorothy d 24 Dec 1793 ae: 11y 1m. C:144

Jonathan d 10 Feb 1835 ae: 52y. Mayor - Portland. J:36

Letitia d/o Moses G. d 31 Dec 1854 ae: 16y. GSL

Mercy d/o Jabez & Dorothy d 19 Nov 1773 ae: 2y 9m. C:45

Phebe G. w/o Capt. Jonathan d 16 June 1818 ae: 36y 7m 23d. SBE J:35

DOWEL, Robert d 20 Nov 1846 ae: 21y. "Buried near Hearse House door." GSL

DOWNER, Jeremiah d 17 Apr 1837 ae: 23y. B-4-1

DOWNING, William d 9 Jan 1885 ae: 75y. A Tomb 1

DOYLE, Charlotte C. d/o Capt. David d 28 Aug 1855 ae: 7y. GSL

DRAKE, Abba w/o Benjamin d 29 Aug 1843 ae: 59y. "Buried in J. Sturdivant tomb." GSL

Benjamin d 7 Aug 1854 ae: 75y. "Buried Sturdevant - Drake tomb." GSL

DRESSER, Alfred s/o A. M. d 17 Mar 1843 ae: 2y 10m. GSL

Frederick D. s/o Alfred M. d 18 Mar 1847 ae: 20m. A Tomb 47

James d 28 July 1852 ae: 55y. GSL

Jane P. w/o James d 31 Mar 1834 ae: 32y. SB A-2-8

Marcia E. d/o Asa d 21 Feb 1849 ae: 23m. A Tomb 47

Mary T. d 20 Feb 1863 ae: 32y. F:95 Tomb

Seward M. s/o Daniel d 13 Aug 1855 ae: 10d. F:95 Tomb

Susan Jane d/o James & Jane P. d 29 July 1826 ae: 16m. SB A-2-8

DREW, Charles d 9 Jan 1846 ae: 26y. GSL

Elizabeth w/o Daniel d 19 July 1810 ae: 22y. E:27

Harriet Hall d 15 July 1901 ae: 82y 11m 5d. "Died Brunswick, Maine." GSL

Joanna d/o Andrew & Lydia d 11 Sep 1810 ae: 3y. SB E:28

DRINKWATER, Abbie d 11 June 1898 ae: 67y. SBE D:26

Addie H. d/o William W. d 17 Oct 1882 ae: 1y. GSL

Addie L. d/o William W. d 18 Apr 1880 ae: 7y. GSL

Addison b 1812 d 1813. Mmt G:4

Ann Maria w/o William, d/o John & Hannah White d 15 Feb 1845 ae: 37y. J:216

Arhoda w/o Samuel d 3 Feb 1829 ae: 76y. SB C:143

David d 3 Apr 1862 ae: 77y 8m. A Tomb 8

Dorcas w/o Capt. Rotheus d 31 Mar 1823 ae: 24y. "Also their inf child, aged 3 months." B-8-5

Fred A. s/o David d 18 Apr 1895 ae: 77y 9m. A Tomb 8

Hannah w/o Capt. Sewell d 4 Nov 1862 ae: 70y. SB I:72

Jane B. d 31 Aug 1877. A Tomb 8

Julia E. d/o William W. d 18 Mar 1864 ae: 7m. GSL

DRINKWATER (continued)

Juliett d/o William d 3 Mar 1851 ae: 11m. GSL

Lenora d/o William W. d 30 Oct 1882 ae: 15y. GSL

Margaret W. w/o Phineas b 1783 d 1868. Mmt G:4

Margaret W. d/o Phineas & Margaret W. d 22 Dec 1911 ae: 92y 11m 15d. Mmt G:4

Mary wid/o William C. d 4 Feb 1894 ae: 90y 7m. H:39A

Mary T. d/o Levi & Mary d 12 July 1841 ae: 21m. SBE F:183

Mary Webb w/o William C. d 4 Feb 1894 ae: 90y 6m. G:79A

Olive Mitchell wid/o David d 26 Jan 1873 ae: 89y 10m. A Tomb 8

Phineas b 1777 d 28 Nov 1850 Mmt G:4

Capt. Samuel d -- July 1834 ae: 91y. "Pilot on the *U. S. S. Enterprise*." GSL

Sarah w/o Joseph d 10 Nov 1838 ae: 64y. SBE H:38

Capt. Sewall d 7 Aug 1878 ae: 82y. War of 1812. SD D:26

William C. d 27 Aug 1871 ae: 74y 9m. H:39

William W. s/o Sewall & Hannah d 30 July 1902 ae: 79y 11m 11d. NS D:26

Willie F. s/o William d 11 Aug 1853 ae: 6m. SD D:26

DRIVER, Margaret P. w/o Blaxton d 19 Apr 1853 ae: 72y. Black. SD A-13-25

Margaret Parrs adopted d/o Blaxton & Margaret d 23 Jan 1850 ae: 16y. Black. SD A-13-27

DROWNE, Adeline d/o James d 4 Aug 1846 ae: 5m. "Buried Strangers' Ground." GSL

DRUMMOND, William H. s/o Thomas d 5 Aug 1857 ae: 1y 11d. GSL

DUBOIS, Charles W. s/o Edward H. & Charlotte A. b 1860 d 1893. Mmt A Tomb 62

Charlotte A. w/o Edward H. d 28 Dec 1861 ae: 33y. Mmt A

DUBOIS (continued)
Tomb 62
Edward H. s/o Edward H. & Charlotte A. b 28 Oct 1855 d 4 May 1859. Mmt A Tomb 62
DUDLEY, Joseph d 29 Nov 1821 ae: 57y. C:88
DUFFIE, Michael d 5 Oct 1854 ae: 45y. GSL
DUFFY, John d 4 Jan 1838 ae: 65y. SD C:114
Margaret d/o Mary d 12 Jan 1861 ae: 2y. GSL
DUIN, Hannah F. d/o Daniel d 17 Sep 1847 ae: 34m. GSL
DUKE, A. Louise d/o John D. d 23 Oct 1879 ae: 1y. GSL
DUMMER, Mary Caroline C. w/o Charles d 2 Aug 1823 ae: 26y. A Tomb 78
DUNCAN, Elizabeth C. d/o William d 6 Oct 1857 ae: 6m 15d. GSL
George W. d 9 Mar 1807 ae: 29y. D:157
George W. s/o George W. & Peggy b 4 July 1806 d -- July 1807. D:158
DUNCIER, Susan w/o Henry d 12 Nov 1859 ae: 45y. GSL
DUNHAM, Georgianna E. d 12 June 1881 ae: 34y. A Tomb 26
Mary A. S. d 22 Nov 1878 ae: 43y. A Tomb 26
DUNLAP, Charles d 22 Sep 1844 ae: 35y. SBE A-3-20
Charles d 22 Sep 1844 ae: 35y. "Buried in front of J. Martin's yard." NS A-4-9
DUNN, Ellen M. w/o Charles d 11 July 1859 ae: 25y. GSL
George W. d 22 Mar 1848 ae: 1y. A Tomb 81
Joshua d 20 Aug 1880 ae: 87y. GSL
Lydia H. d 5 Nov 1860 ae: 58y. "Buried Friends' Ground." SBE K:181
DUPEE, Abigail wid/o Dr. Henry F. d 15 Feb 1813 ae: 49y. K:8
Dr. Henry F. b 27 Aug 1762 d 24 Mar 1811. "Born in Boston."

DUPEE (continued)
K:7
John S. d 8 June 1821 ae: 36y. "Died at Gorham." K:9
DURAN, Amelia J. d/o William & Francis d 29 Aug 1859 ae: 17y. MD A Tomb 40
Charles F. s/o William & Frances d 17 Aug 1874 ae: 29y 7m. A Tomb 40
Ellen M. w/o William A. d 31 Mar 1862 ae: 25y 3m. A Tomb 40
Frances wid/o William d 10 Sep 1885 ae: 72y 11m. A Tomb 40
Frank A. s/o William A. & Ellen M. d 28 Aug 1859 ae: 5m. A Tomb 40
George E.H. s/o William & Frances d 25 Mar 1865 ae: 24y 5m. "Killed in action - Petersburg, Virginia." Civil War: 17th Reg. Maine Inf., Co. B. A Tomb 40
Mary A. d/o William & Frances d 13 Nov 1838 ae: 9m. A Tomb 40
William d 5 Aug 1882 ae: 80y. A Tomb 40
DURGIN, Hannah w/o John B. d 1 Mar 1858 ae: 25y. GSL
DUROY, Frances A. d/o Marshall M. d 2 Dec 1845 ae: 3y 5m. GSL
DWIGHT, William T. s/o Rev. William T. d 12 Nov 1848 ae: 4y. A Tomb 74
DWINAL, Abigail w/o James d 3 Apr 1849 ae: 66y. SB B-7-12
James d 21 Apr 1849 ae: 69y. SB B-7-13
Margaret P. d/o James & Abigail d 6 Feb 1824 ae: 10y 10m. B-7-10
Russell S. s/o James & Abigail d 22 Apr 1824 ae: 19m. SD B-7-11
William H. d 10 June 1864 ae: 49y. GSL
DYER, inf s/o Samuel d 25 Sep 1859 ae: 7w. GSL
Arthur C. s/o Ezekiel d 11 Apr

DYER (continued)

1860 ae: 28y. "Died Boston, Massachusetts." A Tomb 3

Augustus H. s/o Augustus H. d 29 Oct 1846 ae: 1m. A Tomb 3

Betsy wid/o Ezekiel d 29 Nov 1858 ae: 92y. A Tomb 3

Cordelia d/o Ezekiel & Mary d 20 Jan 1833 ae: 19y. SD B-5-2

Emma Ford d/o Lemuel & Nabby b 1819 d 21 Oct 1877. MB A Tomb 22

Ezekiel d 23 June 1849 ae: 86y. A Tomb 3

Frederick s/o Joseph H. d 28 Aug 1858 ae: 4m. "Buried side of Mr. Foster's grave." NS C:9

Frederick W.H. d 22 Apr 1859 ae: 24y 1m 8d. SBE F:102

Capt. Henry d 21 Jan 1832 ae: 42y. SBE F:104

Jabez s/o Nathan & Eunice d 25 Aug 1811 ae: 16m. SBE B-11-8

James W. d 8 Oct 1838 ae: 2y. SD C:244

John M. s/o Nathan & Eunice d 19 Nov 1828 ae: 12y. SBE B-11-8

Lemuel d 22 Jan 1847 ae: 61y. "Died from a cut in the ankle, while cutting timber in Hiram." A Tomb 22

Lucy d/o Paul & Sarah d 5 Mar 1825 ae: 25y. B-11-20

Margaret d/o David d 22 May 1842 ae: 2y. "Buried by side of N.Boynton's stone." NS A-9-19

Mary #2 w/o Joshua d 26 Oct 1806 ae: 23y. K:84

Nabby Ford w/o Lemuel b 1789 d 1828. MB A Tomb 22

Nathaniel s/o Christopher & Lydia d 3 Apr 1826 ae: 12y. B-3-30

Capt. Nathaniel d 22 Mar 1823 ae: 73y. B-11-7

Olive N. d 9 Oct 1864 ae: 50y 8m. F:99

Rebecca w/o George d 29 Aug

DYER (continued)

1849 ae: 33y. A Tomb 69

Robert Ford s/o Lemuel & Nabby b 1816 d 1820. MB A Tomb 22

Sally w/o Joshua d 14 Oct 1804 ae: 27y. K:85A

Samuel T. d 15 May 1864 ae: 27y. Civil War: 1st Reg. Maine Inf., Co. B. SBE F:101

Samuel W. s/o Samuel T. d 12 June 1864 ae: 10. GSL

Sarah w/o Capt. Henry d 24 Dec 1831 ae: 43y. SBE F:103

Sarah w/o Alvin d 28 June 1842 ae: 25y. A Tomb 79

Sarah d/o Alvin d 10 Aug 1842 ae: 2m. GSL

Sarah, widow d 7 Nov 1843 ae: 48y. "Buried at head of William Thomas' stone." GSL

Seth d 14 Oct 1844 ae: 44y. A Tomb 3

Susan C. w/o Robert F. d 20 Aug 1847 ae: 23y. MB A Tomb 22

William H. d 24 Apr 1859 ae: 24y. GSL

William H. d 28 Nov 1862 ae: 50y 9d. SBE F:100

Willie Wallace s/o Lemuel d 7 Apr 1857 ae: 1y 6m. A Tomb 6

DYSON, Merti s/o George d 9 Aug 1883 ae: 2m. A Tomb 1

EARLY, Jane w/o Cornelius d 13 Feb 1860 ae: 35y. "Buried McDowall's lot." NS B-13-5

William M. d 16 Nov 1894 ae: 53y. NS F:38

EASON, William Prime s/o Charles F. d 13 Apr 1854 ae: 3y 9m. Black. GSL

EASTERBROOK, Thomas d 24 Nov 1853 ae: 21y. "Died Marine Hospital." GSL

EASTMAN, Jane L. d/o Charles F. & Harriet E. d 16 Mar 1844 ae: 7m. Black. SD A-14-19

Susan wid/o Ralph d 5 Sep 1847 ae: 55y. SD K:173

William P. s/o Charles F. & Harriet E. d 13 Apr 1853 ae: 3y 8m. Black. SD A-14-19

41

EATON, Asa d 22 July 1822 ae: 23y. D:68

James D. d 30 Nov 1851 ae: 29y. SD C:238

EDGAR, Nancy, widow d 10 Dec 1843 ae: 69y. GSL

EDGECOMB, Betsy M. w/o Noah d 17 June 1870 ae: 70y. A-24-17

George R. s/o Noah & Betsy M. d 2 Nov 1841 ae: 21y. SBE A-24-18

Hannah Stone d/o Noah & Betsy M. d 12 Dec 1833 ae: 7y. A-24-17

Noah d 15 Jan 1873 ae: 75y. A-24-16

Samuel s/o Noah & Eleanor b 30 July 1800 d 1 Dec 1804. C:42

EDMOND, Laura B. d/o John & Sarah A. d 19 June 1852 ae: 10y. A Tomb 2

EDWARDS, Caroline M. w/o John T. d 30 Mar 1839. ae: 25y. A-4-2

Catherine wid/o William d 15 Aug 1854. GSL

Elizabeth G. wid/o Capt. William d 29 Sep 1860 ae: 50y 9m. "Died Boston, Massachusetts." Black. SD L:12

Ellen C. d/o John T. & Caroline M. d 11 Apr 1839 ae: 1m. A-4-2

Ellen d/o William d 22 May 1842 ae: 9m. GSL

Eustis s/o William E. & Adeline d 9 Aug 1847 ae: 2y 3m. A Tomb 57

Jane w/o William d 1 Aug 1842 ae: 24y. GSL

Joseph s/o William E. & Adeline d 12 Jan 1837 ae: 2y 3m. A Tomb 57

Martha d 11 Jan 1879 ae: 94y. GSL

Mary wid/o Thomas d 13 May 1855 ae: 86y. "...of Boston, Massachusetts." A Tomb 57

Mary J. w/o William d 1 Aug 1812 ae: 24y. SB B-15-17

William d 6 Aug 1848 ae: 66y.

EDWARDS (continued)
Black. GSL

Capt. William d 1 Jan 1853 ae: 38y 4m. Black. SD L:13

ELDER, Alphanetta d/o Erastus W. C. d 15 Oct 1853 ae: (3?)m 5d. GSL

Eleanor wid/o Elijah d 12 May 1859 ae: 86y 5m. MBE G:113 Tomb

Capt. Elijah d 10 May 1812 ae: 40y. MBE G:113 Tomb

Isaac d 3 Oct 1845 ae: 42y. MBE G:113 Tomb

John d 12 July 1852 ae: 52y. A Tomb 39

Mary O. w/o John d 30 Apr 1838 ae: 35y. A Tomb 39

Peter d 12 May 1881 ae: 68y. GSL

Simon M. d 5 Feb 1893 ae: 68y. GSL

Susan M. wid/o John d 12 Jan 1866 ae: 52y. A Tomb 39

William s/o Elijah & Eleanor d 23 Nov 1830 ae: 20y. MBE G:113 Tomb

ELERSON, John d 27 Sep 1841 ae: 45y. GSL

ELLIOT, Charles s/o Zedediah d 26 Mar 1846 ae: 2y. "Buried at head of Elliot Libby's grave." H:144

James s/o Jesse B. d 23 May 1846 ae: 3m. GSL

John s/o Jesse B. d 15 May 1846 ae: 4y. "Buried at foot of Snell Wingate's grave." NS G:23

Mary Ann d/o Jesse B. d 1 July 1846 ae: 2y 4m. GSL

Ralph Alvin s/o Ralph H. & Ruth E. d 26 June 1923 ae: 1y 8m 5d. GSL

ELWELL, Charles d 20 June 1842 ae: 40y. GSL

Hannah w/o Capt. Henry B. d 22 Nov 1780 ae: 32y. SB C:201

EMERSON, Andrew L. d 23 Mar 1835 ae: 33y. #1 Mayor - Portland. A Tomb 83

Edwin s/o Stephen d 17 May

EMERSON (continued)
1848 ae: 17y. GSL
James H. s/o Stephen d 4 June
1841 ae: 7y 2m. GSL
Joseph E. s/o Capt. Joseph &
Rebecca d 2 Aug 1849 ae: 17y
3m. SB A-1-35
Martha w/o F. d 31 Jan 1844 ae:
32y. "Buried by Patterson
stone." NS B-12-12
Mary J. G. Clapp w/o Andrew L.
d 19 Oct 1831 ae: 29y. A
Tomb 83
Rufus d 12 Apr 1859 ae: 79y.
"Buried John Anderson tomb."
A Tomb 68
William L. s/o Andrew L. &
Mary J. G. C. d 22 Apr 1831
ae: 6m. A Tomb 83
EMERY, Ellen w/o William d 11
Dec 1869 ae: 82y. GSL
Harriet C.R. w/o William d 31
Oct 1904 ae: 86y 7m. "Died
Gray, Maine." GSL
Hester A. d/o Joshua d 2 Mar
1846 ae: 35y. "Buried by side
of Rev. Nathan Webster." GSL
James N. s/o Samuel d 25 Feb
1846 ae: 21y. GSL
Joshua d 25 Dec 1858 ae: 84y.
GSL
Sabine d 24 Mar 1868 ae: 34y. A
Tomb 2
Samuel d 15 Jan 1862 ae: 81y.
GSL
EMMONS, Sarah T. w/o Stephen
b 17 Feb 1806 d 5 Oct 1885.
A Tomb 46
ENNIS, Jane d/o J. d 17 Mar 1844
ae: 7m. Black. GSL
ENOS, Emily T. d/o Manuel &
Lucy T. d 11 Sep 1857 ae:
13m. Black. SBE J:220
Lucy T. w/o Manuel d 16 Sep
1857 ae: 26y. Black. SBE
J:220
Vincent J. s/o Manuel & Lucy T.
d 30 Apr 1853 ae: 11m. Black.
SD J:222
EPES, Daniel d 3 May 1799 ae:
59y. GSL
ERSKINE, George d 13 Mar 1819

ERSKINE (continued)
ae: 23y. SB E:7
George s/o Asa & Almira d 27
Jan 1830 ae: 11m 17d. SBE
Huldah wid/o George d 9 June
1837 ae: 75y. SBE E:9
Mary w/o Asa d 10 Jan 1824 ae:
25y. B-3-13
ESDELL, William d 7 July 1863
ae: 87y. GSL
EUSTIS, Frances w/o William d
31 Dec 1835 ae: 31y. SBE G:40
EVANS, Barbara w/o Estwick d
18 Oct 1810 ae: 38y. J:136
Eliza d 28 Aug 1824 ae: 16y.
SBE B-9-6
Eliza wid/o Estwick d 4 June
1842 ae: 44y. A-10-9
James P. d 19 Feb 1852 ae: 71y.
GSL
John d 28 Dec 1824 ae: 40y.
SBE B-9-6
Maria M. d/o Estwick & Sarah d
8 May 1851 ae: 36y. SBE A-
5-15
Thomas M. s/o William & Ju-
dith d 4 May 1820 ae: 5m. SD
C:104
EVERETT, Hannah w/o Oliver d
23 Mar 1806 ae: 35y. SBE E:40
Joseph s/o Oliver & Mary d 31
Aug 1821 ae: 3m. SD E:36
Nicholas d 15 Jan 1860 ae: 49y
4m. "Casualty on the Rail
Road." A-21-9
Oliver s/o Oliver & Hannah b 3
Sep 1804 d 28 Aug 1805. SBE
E:39
Theophilus s/o Oliver & Hannah
d 24 May 1809 ae: 6y 7m. SD
E:37
FADDER, Mrs. Elizabeth d 12
Apr 1855 ae: 68y. SD D:10
FAGAN, Mary A. d/o Joseph E. d
19 Mar 1847 ae: 3m. "Died in
Boston." GSL
FAQUNDES, Hannah d 1 Jan 1853
ae: 85y. GSL
FAIRMAN, Elizabeth d 2 Oct
1854 ae: 72y. GSL
Elizabeth d/o Robert d 2 Nov
1864 ae: 45y. GSL

FAIRMAN (continued)

Isaac s/o Robert & Martha d 19 Feb 1859 ae: 17y. A-4-7

Martha d 4 May 1874 ae: 55y. GSL

Robert d 20 Nov 1858 ae: 87y 8m. GSL

Robert s/o Robert d 10 Apr 1870 ae: 63y. GSL

FALBY, Annie F. d/o Andrew d 4 Apr 1867 ae: 6m. GSL

Edward F. s/o Andrew d 14 Feb 1864 ae: 2m. GSL

FARLEY, Abigail w/o Charles d 15 Apr 1826 ae: 32y. C:208

Sarah w/o Charles d 11 Apr 1816 ae: 22y. SBE K:106

FARMER, Florinda d/o Robert d 5 Oct 1862 ae: 3y. GSL

George s/o Robert d 15 Oct 1862 ae: 13m. GSL

FARR, Mary S. w/o J.L. d 7 May 1859 ae: 42y. GSL

Phebe d/o Daniel d 13 Apr 1849 ae: 11m. GSL

FARRINGTON, Mary S. w/o Rev. William F. d 31 Dec 1858 ae: 59y. GSL

FARWELL, Nabby w/o John F. d Dec 1803 ae: 25y. GSL

FELT, Georgietta d/o Jesse S. d 14 Dec 1860 ae: 1y 8m. GSL

FENLEY, Capt. Benjamin W. d 21 Sep 1854 ae: 28y. "Buried at sea." SBE J:134

John d 6 Dec 1857 ae: 72y 20d. GSL

Matthew d 9 Dec 1842 ae: 46y. GSL

Melinda w/o William d 7 Mar 1879 ae: 78y. J:133

Nancy d/o widow Mary d 15 Sep 1843 ae: 3y 5m. "Buried by their stone." GSL

FENNELLY, Betsy w/o John d 8 Mar 1842 ae: 55y. SBE A-17-7

Robert John s/o John d 2 May 1814 ae: 5y. SBE A-17-7

FENNO, Eleanor K. d 6 Nov 1841 ae: 16m. SD K:16

FERDINAND, Mary H. d/o Francis d 21 Aug 1846 ae: 2y. GSL

FERGUSSON, George d 13 May 1806 ae: 60y. SBE E:50

FERNALD, Abigail wid/o Peletiah d 27 July 1821 ae: 83y. I:81

Abigail wid/o Anthony d 10 Apr 1867 ae: 83y 5m. GSL

Albion s/o Joshua F. & Isabella d 14 Nov 1835 ae: 4y. SB F:98A

Annie E. d/o Anthony d 11 Sep 1882 ae: 2w. A Tomb 1

Anthony d 29 May 1843 ae: 73y. SBE I:88

Anthony H. d 4 May 1871 ae: 52yrs. GSL

Charles s/o Alfred B. d 11 July 1849 ae: 3y. GSL

Edwin s/o Anthony & Mary d 17 Sep 1803 ae: 15m. I:89

Elizabeth w/o Anthony d 19 Sep 1800 ae: 31y. I:86

Elizabeth B. d/o Anthony & Mary d 24 Sep 1807 ae: 17m. I:85

Elizabeth B. d/o Anthony & Mary d 26 July 1812 ae: 21y. I:84

Elizabeth B. d/o Anthony d 24 July 1823 ae: 7y. SD I:115

Frances d/o A. B. d 26 Aug 1851 ae: 2y. GSL

Frederick s/o Joshua F. & Isabella d 5 Nov 1832 ae: 2y 8m. SB F:98A

Dolly H. w/o Anthony H. d 21 Sep 1854 ae: 25y. GSL

Eliza E. d/o Anthony d 23 Jan 1850 ae: 21m. GSL

George P. s/o Isaac d 19 Oct 1849 ae: 6m. GSL

Isabella H. Knight wid/o Joshua F. b 23 Sep 1809 d 21 Feb 1895 F:98B

Joseph d 26 July 1865 ae: 88y. GSL

Joshua F. d 14 Apr 1856 ae: 50y. SB F:98A

Maggie L. d/o Isaac d 22 Dec 1857 ae: 6y 7m. A Tomb 66

Mary #2 w/o Anthony d 4 June 1815 ae: 32y. I:82

Mary d/o Henry B. d 21 May 1842 ae: 8y 9m. GSL

FERNALD (continued)

Mary E. d/o Anthony d 8 Aug 1853 ae: 7m 10d. "Buried in Enclosed Yard." GSL

Mercy d 16 July 1854 ae: 79y. Stone marked "My Grandmother." I:79

Peletiah b 3 Aug 1743 d 22 Feb 1816. "Born in Kittery." I:80

Rachael P. #3 w/o Anthony d 16 May 1829 ae: 46y. I:87

Susan R. d/o Isaac d 10 July 1857 ae: 18y 2m. A Tomb 66

FERRIS, Matthew d 15 Oct 1857 ae: 19y. GSL

Walter H. s/o William d 8 Dec 1857 ae: 2y 2m. GSL

FESSENDEN, Catherine d/o Dr. Hewitt d 20 Aug 1846 ae: 7m. "Buried by side of Samuel Fessenden's child." GSL

Jonathan s/o Isaac d 2 May 1866 ae: 87y. GSL

Mary D. d/o William Pitt d 9 Dec 1848 ae: 5y. Moved Evergreen Cemetery? D Tomb 73

Oliver Griswold s/o Samuel d 21 May 1851 ae: 33y. Moved Evergreen Cemetery? A Tomb 45

Oliver Griswold, Jr. s/o Oliver Griswold & M. T. d 8 Dec 1850 ae: 6m. A Tomb 45

Philip s/o Oliver G. & M. T. d 3 Feb 1849 ae: 8m. A Tomb 45

Sarah d/o Jonathan d 13 July 1857 ae: 53y. GSL

FICKETT, Albert B. s/o James H. d 7 Feb 1847 ae: 5m. A Tomb 17

Angelia w/o Simon d 11 May 1848 ae: 18y. SB D:54

David d 14 Apr 1831 ae: 35y. J:209

Elizabeth L. d 26 Sep 1875 ae: 61y. ME A Tomb 25

Capt Elliot d 26 Nov 1825 ae: 34y. B-7-17

George M. s/o Benjamin Jr. d 9 Aug 1847 ae: 15m. A Tomb 17

Isaac d 3 Mar 1877 ae: 83y. A Tomb 17

FICKETT (continued)

James H. d 29 May 1870 ae: 40y. A Tomb 17

Margaret d 25 July 1865 ae: 73y. A Tomb 17

Mary S. d/o John & Eliza d 21 July 1825 ae: 8y. B-11-22

Matilda w/o Benjamin d 7 Jan 1833 ae: 34y. B-12-13

Rhoda B. w/o Joseph H. d 1 Nov 1846. A Tomb 17

William E. s/o Luther d 24 Oct 1851 ae: 5y. GSL

FIELD, Abigail M. d/o Stephen & Abigail W. d 17 Oct 1811 ae: 9m. J:162

Abigail M. d/o Stephen & Abigail W. d 9 Apr 1814 ae: 4m. J:162

Sarah A. w/o William A. d 11 Sep 1855 ae: 22y. GSL

Tabitha d/o James & Polly S. d 14 Oct 1822 ae: 13m. SD F:71

FIELDING, Henrietta d/o Thomas d 14 Dec 1841 ae: 2y 6m. GSL

Thomas s/o Thomas d 7 May 1842 ae: 1y. GSL

FIELDS, Mary E. d/o Moses d 19 Oct 1844 ae: 1y 9m. "Buried near William Martin's fence." NS J:76

FILENER, Elizabeth d/o Patrick d 23 Dec 1869 ae: 46y. A Tomb 82

FILES, Thomas d 26 July 1847 ae: 64y. GSL

FINLEY, Harriet L. d 24 Aug 1871 ae: 64y 8m. GSL

FINNEY, Ada d/o Edward d 20 July 1853 ae: 4m. GSL

Margaret wid/o Peter d 1 Jan 1837 ae: 75y. Catholic. B-10-1

FITCH, Phebe d 6 Sep 1854 ae: 78y. SD C:166

FITZ, Elizabeth d 8 Nov 1893 ae: 85y 3m. A Tomb 31

Mehitable d 9 May 1842 ae: 76y. Widow. A Tomb 6

Rebecca d 22 Nov 1877 ae: 66y. A Tomb 31

FITZ (continued)

Rebecca B. d 22 Feb 1873 ae: 95y. A Tomb 31

FITZGERALD, George E. s/o George d 8 Oct 1858 ae: 10m. GSL

Joseph B. s/o George d 2 Feb 1870 ae: 12y. GSL

William s/o William d 19 Aug 1857 ae: 7y 4m. GSL

Willie F. s/o William d 4 July 1858 ae: 1y 7m. GSL

FLETCHER, Albert G. d Oct 1832 ae: 25y. H:153

Mary w/o Timothy d 2 Dec 1811 ae: 29y. SBE H:152

FLETT, John s/o John b Grutha, Orkneys, Scotland d 23 Mar 1760 ae: 26y. Killed in building collapse. Buried same grave as Allon McLean. Slate ledger. MD E:12

FLINT, Harriet d/o Nathaniel d 19 Apr 1843 ae: 20y. GSL

Mary d 12 Oct 1845 ae: 57y. "Buried north corner by side of fence, near the Colored Ground." GSL

FLOOD, Catherine w/o David d 27 July 1847 ae: 38y. GSL

John P. s/o David P d 2 Nov 1841 ae: 4y. GSL

Paulina A. d/o Luther & Ann b 26 Jan 1821 d 25 Oct 1821. SD I:124

FLOYD, Jeremiah s/o Hiram G. d 24 Aug 1855 ae: 8m. GSL

Joseph T. s/o Hiram & Mary A. d 13 May 1920 ae: 67y 4m 6d. NS L:17

Mary Ann w/o Hiram G. d 29 Jan 1855 ae: 23y. SB A-1-17

FOBES, Frank Mason s/o Charles d 28 June 1854 ae: 9m 10d. GSL

James d 25 Mar 1869 ae: 27y. GSL

FOGG, Charles Henry s/o Jacob & Artimesia d 15 Oct 1836 ae: 3y. A-24-25

Elizabeth E. w/o George d 23 Apr 1854 ae: 22y 7m. GSL

FOGG (continued)

Jacob d 13 Jan 1835 ae: 27y. A-24-24

Mary w/o William d 15 Dec 1827 ae: 32y. B-4-26

Robert W. s/o Enos & Experience b 18 Apr 1833 d 15 June 1851. B-13-17

Sarah Jane d/o Jacob & Artimesia d 25 May 1837 ae: 8y. A-24-25

Silas d 15 Sep 1844 ae: 40y. A-24-26

FOGLER, May d/o W. H. d 6 May 1865 ae: 7m. A Tomb 15

FOLLANSBEE, Frances d/o Thomas N. & Mary d 6 Feb 1840 ae: 2y 2m. SB K:80

Thomas N. d 28 June 1852 ae: 11y. SD K:81

FOOT, Louise Y. d/o Lendal G. L. d 2 Apr 1871 ae: 3w 4d. GSL

Mary w/o Charles d 18 Aug 1834 ae: 22y. Black. A-13-29

FOOTE, Hannah L. d/o Abner L. d 1 Sep 1864 ae: 14y 4m. GSL

FORCHEN, John s/o William d 12 June 1860 ae: 25y. "Buried at head of Rev. Freeman's lot." Black. NS A-7-24

FORD, Emma L. wid/o Robert b 1765 d 1843. MB A Tomb 22

Eunice C. d/o Timothy & Eunice d 6 Oct 1834 ae: 10m. SD I:112

Robert b 1763 d 1790. MB A Tomb 22

FORSAITH, Thomas d 22 Dec 1849 ae: 76y. A Tomb 15

FORTUNE, Diana d 18 July 1845 ae: 16y. "Buried by side of Hearse House." Black. GSL

FOSDICK, Ann d 4 Nov 1830 ae: 71y. A Tomb 45

Benjamin W. d 20 Sep 1854 ae: 44y. A Tomb 48

Henry s/o Maj. Thomas F. d Aug 1804 ae: 21y. GSL

Thomas s/o James F. d 4 Nov 1803 ae: 21y. GSL

FOSS, Charles S. s/o Alexander d

FOSS (continued)

5 Aug 1850 ae: 1y. "Buried Smith-Brown tomb." GSL

Julia A. d 30 Oct 1851 ae: 17y. GSL

FOSTER, Albert S. s/o Albert J. d 8 June 1869 ae: 29y. GSL

Arthur S. s/o Stephen & M. d 26 Apr 1819 ae: 10m. SB C:9

Caroline d/o Israel & Betsy d 6 Aug 1833 ae: 5y 8m. SBE L:82

Ellen d/o John T. & E. R. d 20 Sep 1834 ae: 15y. SD C:10

George E. s/o Charles & Martha d 29 July 1822 ae: 3m. SD B-14-8

Israel d 15 Sep 1843 ae: 47y. "Buried by his child's stone." NS L:82

Julia d/o Israel & Betsy d 31 May 1828 ae: 3y 7m. SBE L:83

Julia J. d/o Gideon & Margaret d 5 Aug 1852 ae: 22y. SBE L:84

Margaret w/o Gideon d 2 Feb 1862 ae: 65y. L:85

Martha T. d/o Stephen & M. d 14 Jan 1838 ae: 24y. SD C:6

Stephen s/o Stephen & M. b 3 Sep 1804 d 24 July 1806. SBE C:8

Stephen s/o Stephen & M. d 26 Apr 1824 ae: 42y. SB C:9

Sylvanus P. s/o Charles W. d 18 Nov 1866 ae: 1m. GSL

William W. d 2 Mar 1892 ae: 79y 7m. "Died Greely Hosp." GSL

FOWLER, Caroline d/o Philip & Dorcas b 17 Aug 1799 d 22 Feb 1804. SBE F:146

Dorcas w/o Philip d 30 Dec 1850 ae: 74y. SD F:147

Frederick Augustus d 7 Oct 1860 ae: 43y. GSL

Joseph Francis s/o Joseph & Sarah d 2 May 1831 ae: 9m. SB B-3-7

Melinda d 22 Nov 1822 ae: 6y 4m 26d. SBE F:145

Susan wid/o Clement d 9 Jan 1855 ae: 77y. GSL

FOX, Ann Hodge Jones wid/o Jabez d 9 June 1758 ae: 43y. SB F:141

Augustus s/o Daniel d 30 Jan 1868 ae: 38y. Civil War: 4th Battalion Maine Light Artillery, 2d Lt. F:96 Tomb

Betsy d/o Jabez & Ann b 17 Feb 1748 d 14 Jan 1750. GSL

Charles d 27 July 1845 ae: 63y 3m. F:96 Tomb

Charles Jr. d 16 Sep 1842 ae: 36y. F:96 Tomb

Daniel d 11 Apr 1861 ae: 80y 7m. F:96 Tomb

Elizabeth wid/o Daniel d 1 Nov 1866 ae: 74y. F:96 Tomb

Elizabeth L. d 5 Oct 1901 ae: 82y 1m 13d. F:96 Tomb

Harriet L. d/o Daniel d 16 Apr 1901 ae: 77y 2m 22d. F:96 Tomb

Jabez d 7 Apr 1755 ae: 50y. Interesting inscription. F:140

Jane McLellan wid/o Charles d 4 Apr 1864 ae: 72y. F:96 Tomb

John d 16 May 1795 ae: 46y. F:96 Tomb

John d 19 Feb 1852 ae: 67y. F:96 Tomb

Lucy A. d/o John d 21 June 1854 ae: 34y. F:96 Tomb

Sarah wid/o John d 29 Apr 1826 ae: 65y. F:96 Tomb

William s/o Jabez & Ann b 9 Nov 1754 d 19 May 1755. F:138

FRANCIS, Mrs Ann d 18 Jan 1845 ae: 40y. GSL

Hannah F. w/o William d 24 Apr 1820 ae: 38y. MB A Tomb 85

Isaac d 19 Sep 1861 ae: 24y. GSL

Joanna w/o John d 25 Dec 1859 ae: 44y. SD L:39

John R. d 27 June 1858 ae: 55y. Black. GSL

Thomas d 12 Oct 1844 ae: 17y. "Stranger." Black. GSL

FRANKLIN, Mary I. d/o widow d 12 Sep 1849 ae: 15y. Black. GSL

FRASER, Josephine d/o John S.
& Martha B. d 29 Mar 1839 ae:
3y. SD B-14-13

Martha B. d 25 Nov 1870 ae: 66y.
SBE A-22-2

William C. B. s/o John S. &
Martha B. d 17 Feb 1853 ae:
5y. SD B-14-13

FREDSON, Charlotte d 15 Apr
1850. MB B-6-7

Henrietta d 20 Mar 1860 ae: 37y.
"Died Boston, Massachu-
setts." GSL

Joseph H. d 14 Dec 1848. MB
B-6-7

FREEMAN, Anne H. w/o Daniel
d 24 Mar 1874 ae: 64y. A
Tomb 44

Annie W. d/o Daniel & Anne H.
d 4 Apr 1849 ae: 2y. A Tomb
44

Edmund B. s/o Rev. Amos N. d
14 Feb 1848 ae: 20m. Black.
GSL

Eliza w/o Capt. Joshua d 26 Oct
1830 ae: 62y. C:169

Elizabeth Jones w/o Samuel, d/o
Dr. Enoch Ilsley, wid/o Pier-
son Jones b 6 Oct 1754 d 26
Mar 1831. SB G:108

Emma d/o Andrew d 25 Nov 1859
ae: 1y 5m. "Buried in C. E.
Leonard's lot." GSL

Enoch b 19 May 1706 d 2 Sep
1788. "His wife lies near and
four children, S 17 W 4 or 5
rods from this grave." SB
G:111

Eunice d/o Capt. Daniel & Sarah
d 6 Nov 1792 ae: 17m. SB
D:151

Eunice d 16 Oct 1865 ae: 70y.
GSL

George s/o Samuel & Elizabeth
J. b 4 Mar 1796 d 27 Nov 1815.
SBE G:107

George P. s/o Capt. Jeremiah &
Lydia d 20 June 1832 ae: 27y.
SBE C:175

Harriet G. d 9 July 1850 ae: 2m.
Black. SBE A-7-23

Helen d 26 Nov 1879 ae: 41y.

FREEMAN (continued)
"Died in Boston." A Tomb 36

James #2 s/o Enoch & Mary d 5
Feb 1771 ae: 26y. F:68

Capt. Jeremiah d 7 Dec 1806 ae:
36y. SBE C:175

Joshua d 23 Sep 1770 ae: 70y.
GSL

Joshua d 2 Nov 1796 ae: 66y.
C:173

Capt. Joshua d 2 Jan 1840 ae:
76y. C:168

Lois d/o Thomas & Margaret d
13 Feb 1800 ae: 3y. C:174

Lois wid/o Joshua d 21 Mar 1813
ae: 80y. C:172

Lothrop s/o Enoch & Mary d 26
Apr 1753 ae: 1m. SD F:73

Lydia wid/o Capt. Jeremiah d 27
July 1854 ae: 86y. SBE C:175

Lydia d 31 Mar 1866 ae: 82y.
"Buried at side of Cornelius
Barnes." I:212

Lydia Ann d 10 Oct 1848 ae: 16y.
Black. SBE A-7-23

Margaret w/o Thomas d 15 Oct
1826 ae: 55y. C:171

Margaret F. d/o Rev. Amos N. &
C. d 3 Apr 1844 ae: 18m.
Black. SBE A-7-24

Mary d/o Enoch & Mary d 22 Oct
1750 ae: 4y. F:72

Mary Fowle w/o Samuel, d/o
John Fowle b 21 Nov 1749 d 7
Jan 1785. G:123

Mary Wright w/o Enoch d 19 Jan
1785. G:110

Mehitable wid/o Joshua d 12 Dec
1851 ae: 81y. GSL

Pearson s/o Joshua & Patience
Rogers b 4 Feb 1770 d 17 May
1805. "Drowned between Long
Island and Chebeague Island."
GSL

Robert W. s/o Capt. Samuel &
Hannah d 20 Dec 1804 ae: 2m.
C:176

Samuel b 15 June 1743 d 18 June
1831. SBE G:109

Samuel d 17 Sep 1831 ae: 50y.
SB G:124

Sarah d/o Joshua & Lois Pearson

FREEMAN (continued)
b 4 Jan 1751 d 5 Apr 1805. A
Tomb 84

Sarah Ann d 10 Sep 1849 ae: 7m.
Black. SBE A-7-23

Thomas d 17 Oct 1847 ae: 73y.
SB C:170

William s/o Enoch & Mary d 6
June 1765 ae: 18y. F:69

FRENCH, Benjamin B. d 25 June
1841 ae: 50y. GSL

Eunice d 30 May 1835 ae: 38y.
SBE B-3-33

FROST, Andrew d 19 Apr 1804 ae:
21y. "Died at Fort Sumner."
"Formerly of Providence,
Rhode Island." GSL

Ann d 27 Dec 1849 ae: 40y. GSL

Francis s/o late Ann d 18 Mar
1850 ae: 7y. GSL

FROTHINGHAM, Abigail Beck b
18 Jan 1799 d 15 May 1883. A
Tomb 81

Albert d 9 Feb 1872 ae: 36y. A
Tomb 81

Harriet B. d 9 July 1825 ae: 30y.
A Tomb 81

Hollis nd. SBE L:89

John d 8 Feb 1826 ae: 76y. L:88

Lewis b 28 Apr 1803 d 2 Oct
1803. SBE L:89

Martha wid/o John d 9 June
1834 ae: 71y. SB L:91

Martha d/o John b 23 Sep 1786 d
21 Oct 1806. SD L:90

Mary Allen d/o Thomas B. d 25
June 1858 ae: 10m. A Tomb
81

Mary E. Preble d/o John & Martha d 29 Oct 1814 ae: 15y.
L:88

Rylander s/o Thomas B. d 9 Aug
1867 ae: 3m 11d. GSL

Sally nd. SBE L:89

Stephen d 27 May 1857 ae: 59y.
A Tomb 81

Thomas B. s/o Stephen d 26 Nov
1868 ae: 33y. A Tomb 81

FROST, Frank F. s/o Peter B. d
9 May 1859 ae: 11y 9m.
"Buried Jonathan Stewart
tomb." GSL

FULLER, Anna A. d/o Benjamin
W. d 19 June 1856 ae: 5y 8m.
GSL

Clara d/o Sanford K. d 21 Sep
1857 ae: 14m. "Buried at head
of Simpson's grave." NS I:62

Harriet Jane d/o James H. d 27
Apr 1855 ae: 2y 6m. "Buried
in John Senter's lot." GSL

John H. s/o Benjamin C. d 24
Dec 1858 ae: 7y. GSL

Thomas s/o Collingwood d 30
Mar 1864 ae: 5y 3m. GSL

Thomas Edward s/o William d
10 Aug 1851 ae: 5y. GSL

FURBISH, Ann M. w/o James d
23 Nov 1833 ae: 23y. A Tomb
42

Annie W. d 5 Aug 1902 ae: 79y
10m 5d. "Died Boston, Massachusetts." A Tomb 66

Charles E. d 7 Aug 1881 ae: 35y.
"Died New York City." A
Tomb 66

James d 3 June 1878 ae: 82y. A
Tomb 42

James C. M. d 30 Jan 1904 ae:
70y 6m 16d. "Died Biddeford,
Maine." Civil War: 9th Reg.
Maine Inf., Adjutant. A Tomb
42

Julia A. M. d 26 May 1881 ae:
49y. A Tomb 42

FURLONG, Dana O. s/o Matthias
W. d 8 June 1853 ae: 20y.
GSL

Ellen d/o Matthias d 6 Dec 1843
ae: 10w. GSL

Harriet Eliza d/o Benjamin d 22
June 1846 ae: 21m. "Buried
by Susan Todd's grave." B-5-
28

John H. s/o Matthias d 8 Nov
1855 ae: 17y 5m. GSL

Matthias W. d 20 Sep 1864 ae:
61y. GSL

William H. s/o Matthias d 25
Oct 1863 ae: 61y. GSL

FURMAN, Christiana E. d/o John
d 31 July 1854 ae: 1y. Black.
GSL

FURNACE, Mary d 21 Apr 1842

FURNACE (continued)
ae: 38y. Widow. GSL

GAGE, Isaac d 9 May 1826 ae:
60y. War of 1812. GSL

GAMMON, Hannah w/o Ezekiel
D. d 6 Dec 1844 ae: 36y. A
Tomb 35

William E. s/o Ephraim d 15
Mar 1851 ae: 9y. GSL

GANNEN, Mary w/o Michael d 16
Feb 1807 ae: 29y. Catholic.
L:44

GARDNER, Almira w/o Andrew d
23 Aug 1845 ae: 28y. GSL

Elisha nd ae: 33y. SBE B-3-10

Israel s/o Israel & Rhoda d 3 Apr
1810 ae: 2y. B-5-25

James b 1 Sep 1764 d 20 Jan
1803. SD G:48

Jane d 23 Feb 1892 ae: 62y 1m.
"Died Greely Hospital." GSL

John D. s/o Israel & Rhoda d 20
June 1825 ae: 6m. B-5-25

Jane wid/o Elisha d 15 June
1847 ae: 86y. B-3-9 b.176 |

John B. s/o Elisha & Jane d
1812 ae: 22y. SBE B-3-10

John H. s/o Israel & Rhoda d 1
Apr 1812 ae: 2y. B-5-25

Joseph J. s/o Israel & Rhoda d
10 July 1826 ae: 3y. B-5-25

Capt. Reuben G. d 17 Jan 1823
ae: 29y. SBE B-3-8

Rhoda w/o Israel d 19 June 1842
ae: 51y. SB A-18-7 b |79 |

Sarah G. d/o Israel & Rhoda d 1
Apr 1818 ae: 1y. B-5-25

Sarah S. w/o William d 28 Oct
1841 ae: 66y. MBE G:113
Tomb

William d 19 Sep 1843 ae: 75y.
MBE G:113 Tomb

William C. s/o Elisha & Jane d
24 Oct 1831 ae: 40y. SBE B-
3-10

GARLAND, Charles A. s/o Benjamin d 22 Sep 1858 ae: 1y.
GSL

Daniel d 3 Sep 1844 ae: 63y. ME
G:43

Eleanor w/o Stephen H. d 22 Mar
1905 ae: 96y 3m 13d. "Died

GARLAND (continued)
City Home". A Tomb 14

George s/o Daniel & Phebe d 10
Aug 1804 ae: 6m. ME G:43

George W. s/o Daniel & Phebe d
19 Aug 1805 ae: 1m. ME G:43

Maria F. d/o Daniel & Phebe d
11 Apr 1807 ae: 1y. ME G:43

Phebe H. wid/o Daniel d 25 June
1858 ae: 76y. ME G:43

GATES, Frederick W. s/o Samuel
D. & Mary E. nd ae: 1y 11d.
SBE A-15-1

Samuel s/o Frederick d 25 May
1846 ae: 6y 7m. "Buried by
Philip Crandall's grave." NS
E:58

Samuel C. s/o Samuel D. & Mary
E. d 15 Aug 1850 ae: 15m.
SBE A-15-1

Samuel D. d 27 Feb 1851 ae:
31y. SBE A-15-1

GAY, Abbe M. d 4 Jan 1910 ae:
77y 9m. GSL

Alexander d 6 Sep 1847 ae: 52y.
GSL

Henrietta C. w/o Alexander d 11
July 1907 ae: 67y 3m. GSL

Mary Eliza d/o Alexander d 29
Aug 1854 ae: 19y. GSL

Rachel F. d/o Alexander & Mary
C. d 4 Apr 1900 ae: 70y. GSL

GERRISH, Alice d 16 Oct 1858
ae: 1y 10d. A Tomb 57

Barbara w/o Joseph M. d 12 Oct
1841 ae: 53y 11m. A Tomb 57

Ellen Lucretia d/o Joseph M. &
Barbara d 11 Sep 1817 ae: 1y
6m. A Tomb 57

Frederick A. s/o Joseph M. d 9
Apr 1873 ae: 49y. A Tomb 57

Joseph s/o Joseph M. & Barbara
d 26 Oct 1836 ae: 18y 10m. A
Tomb 57

Joseph Frederick Augustus s/o
Joseph M. & Barbara d 28 Sep
1813 ae: 15m. A Tomb 57

Joseph M. d 29 Apr 1853 ae: 70y.
A Tomb 57

Martha J. w/o Frederick A. d 1
Oct 1881 ae: 50y. A Tomb 57

Mary Ann d 28 Mar 1877 ae: 80y.

GERRISH (continued)
A Tomb 57
Mary Kidder d/o Joseph M. &
Barbara d 20 Oct 1831 ae: 3y.
A Tomb 57
William Morton s/o William S.
d 11 Sep 1857 ae: 9m 17d. A
Tomb 57
William Oliver s/o Joseph M. &
Barbara d 18 Oct 1831 ae: 4y
8m. A Tomb 57
GERTZ, Abby L. d/o Samuel P. d
31 July 1851 ae: 2y. GSL
Ann Maria d/o late Capt. Martin
d 1 Nov 1854. "Buried Gertz
lot." GSL
George L. s/o Capt. Samuel d 6
Mar 1849 ae: 20m. GSL
Henry d 29 Oct 1842 ae: 30y.
GSL
GIBBS, Mrs. Elizabeth d Apr 1805
ae: 34y. GSL
GIBSON, Esther w/o John d 15
Mar 1845 ae: 54y. Black.
GSL
John d 20 Nov 1859 ae: 67y.
"Died in Boston". Black.
GSL
GIDDINGS, Mary S. w/o Moses d
18 May 1851 ae: 33y. "...of
Bangor." A Tomb 11
GILBERT, inf ch/o Daniel Jr. d 4
Nov 1853 ae: 7m. A Tomb 36
Charles s/o Daniel & Nancy d 30
Dec 1811 ae: 4y. A Tomb 36
Charles H. d 17 Sep 1853 ae:
27y. A Tomb 36
Daniel d 9 Nov 1842 ae: 57y. A
Tomb 36
Daniel, J. s/o Daniel & Nancy d
28 Sep 1833 ae: 30y. A Tomb
36
Daniel W. d 12 Nov 1888 ae:
58y. "Died Chelsea, Massa-
chusetts." A Tomb 36
Eliza w/o Daniel Jr. d 5 Nov
1830 ae: 25y. A Tomb 36
Henry s/o Daniel & Nancy d 18
May 1829 ae: 20y. A Tomb 36
George s/o Daniel & Nancy d 13
Apr 1826 ae: 8m. A Tomb 36
George H. Bourne s/o Rev.

GILBERT (continued)
George d 30 Aug 1847 ae: 19m.
A Tomb 36
John s/o Daniel & Nancy d 5
July 1816 ae: 16m. A Tomb
36
John s/o Daniel & Nancy d 13
Dec 1818 ae: 1m. A Tomb 36
John s/o Daniel & Nancy d 5 Oct
1821 ae: 14m. A Tomb 36
Maria d/o Daniel & Nancy d 10
Sep 1805 ae: 10m. A Tomb 36
Nancy w/o Daniel d 27 Sep 1825
ae: 42y. A Tomb 36
Sarah #2 w/o Daniel d 28 Mar
1835 ae: 42y. A Tomb 36
GILKEY, Eliza d 6 Nov 1864 ae:
78y. A-9-4
William d 18 June 1838 ae: 22y.
SBE A-9-1
GILL, Harriet d/o Charles d 8
July 1846 ae: 18y. "Buried by
side of Dr. Coffin's tomb."
H:71
Leonard F. d 8 Apr 1864 ae: 34y.
Civil War: 13th Reg. Maine
Inf., Co. F. SD B-8-25
Lewson L. s/o Daniel & Lorinda
d 4 Mar 1849 ae: 20m. SBE
B-8-21
Louis Alexis s/o Daniel &
Lorinda d 19 Mar 1838 ae: 4y.
B-8-22
James C. s/o Daniel & Lorinda d
4 Oct 1859 ae: 8y. B-8-23
GILMAN, Jeremiah d 12 Feb
1851 ae: 65y. GSL
Samuel d 25 Mar 1852 ae: 61y.
GSL
GILSON, Lucinda w/o Bradbury d
18 Feb 1844 ae: 26y. "Buried
by Prince's stone." GSL
GLAZIER, Charles F. s/o Daniel
d 27 Aug 1850 ae: 7y. GSL
Sarah F. d/o Daniel G. d 28 Nov
1847 ae: 2y. GSL
GLEASON, Charles L. d 15 Aug
1861 ae: 37y. GSL
GODDARD, Eliza L. w/o Henry d
15 Feb 1864 ae: 75y. A Tomb
62
Mary w/o William b 27 June

GODDARD (continued)

1785 d 24 Nov 1806. SBE C:218

Mary S. d/o William & Mary b 2 Nov 1806 d 1 Jan 1807. SBE C:218

GOLDEN, inf d/o Philip d 30 Oct 1863 ae: 6w. GSL

inf d/o Philip d 30 Oct 1863 ae: 6w. GSL

Elizabeth J. d/o Philip d 20 Apr 1869 ae: 2y 9m. GSL

Frederick s/o John d 1 June 1867 ae: 5y 6m. GSL

Philip s/o Philip d 28 Aug 1855 ae: 13m. GSL

GOLDER, Mary d/o Philip E. d 28 Aug 1861 ae: 2y. GSL

GOODALE, Daniel d 20 Mar 1876 ae: 81y. A Tomb 1

Eunice w/o Daniel d 25 Mar 1877 ae: 72y. A Tomb 1

GOODHUE, Edmund Quincy b 3 Sep 1828 d 4 July 1889. Civil War: 17th Reg. Maine Inf., Co. D. C:161

Eleanor J. d/o Daniel J. d 4 Aug 1855 ae: 10w. GSL

Frederick s/o Daniel d 3 May 1859 ae: 6w. GSL

Hannah d/o Richard S. & Sarah W. d 23 Aug 1831 ae: 12y. SD C:160

Harriet F. d 10 Oct 1866 ae: 33y. GSL

Richard d 11 Oct 1820 ae: 63y. SB A-21-1

Richard d 5 Oct 1882 ae: 61y. Civil War: 10th Reg. Maine Inf., Co. C. NS A-21-1

Richard S. d 6 Dec 1856 ae: 63y. War of 1812. A-21-3

Sarah W. w/o Richard S. d 8 Nov 1851 ae: 52y. A-21-2

GOODING, A. P. Bedlow d/o Richard & Ellen C. d 2 Sep 1845 ae: 13m. GSL

Catherine J. w/o George C. d 17 Feb 1825 ae: 27y. SD J:144

Dorcas w/o Richard d 29 Jan 1820 ae: 63y. SBE H:140

Harriet d/o Lemuel & Sarah b 21

GOODING (continued)

Dec 1802 d 17 June 1849. H:142

James b 1696 d 21 Apr 1780. D:102

James d 8 Feb 1793 ae: 70y 4m. Revolutionary War. D:96

Henry s/o Henry & Elizabeth d 12 Sep 1836 ae: 17m. SBE A-7-7

Isabel d/o Lemuel Jr. d 2 Sep 1842 ae: 3m. GSL

Lemuel d 28 Sep 1865 ae: 86y. SB H:138

Mary b 1700 d 1778. D:102

Nabby C. Lewis d 29 Dec 1832 ae: 25y. SB A-7-6

Rebecca d/o Josiah & Hannah d 25 Apr 1753 ae: 23y. Interesting stone. G:137

Richard d 30 July 1831 ae: 80y 5m. Revolutionary War. SBE H:141

Sarah w/o Lemuel d 30 Sep 1861 ae: 79y. SBE H:139

GOODNOW, William b 16 Sep 1796 d 9 Sep 1863. MD A Tomb 18

GOODRICH, Frances J. d/o Capt. Simon d 14 Apr 1847 ae: 13y. SBE A-16-10

Rebecca K. R. d/o Col Thomas Baker, w/o Isaac F. d 2 Feb 1834 ae: 29y. J:103

Capt. Simon d 3 July 1845 ae: 35y. SBE A-16-10

GOODWIN, Charles d 5 Apr 1844 ae: 41y. A Tomb 36

Fear Thacher w/o John b 1 Feb 1748 d 26 Mar 1829. "...of Barnstable, Massachusetts." B-1-22

John b 18 Oct 1751 d 3 Apr 1829. "Born Plymouth, Massachusetts." Revolutionary War. B-1-23

Lucy Allen d/o Thomas & Abigail b 13 Oct 1798 d 6 Mar 1801. E:4

Mary d/o John F. & Ruth E. nd. SD I:62

Mary Jackson d/o Thomas &

GOODWIN (continued)

Abigail b 25 Mar 1800 d 5 Sep 1800. E:5

Solomon d 12 Nov 1772. "Hanged for murder." GSL

GOOKIN, Samuel d 15 Aug 1804 ae: 75y. GSL

Sarah wid/o Samuel d 16 Aug 1804 ae: 73y. GSL

GOOLD, Abigail w/o Joseph d 11 Apr 1853 ae: 73y. GSL

Apphia d/o Dr. John & Apphia d 19 Apr 1836 ae: 23y. B-5-1

Benjamin J. s/o M. d 1 Feb 1853 ae: 15m. A Tomb 72

Bethiah w/o Simon d 8 Sep 1872 ae: 94y. A Tomb 28

George F. s/o Richard d 10 Apr 1856 ae: 7y. A Tomb 72

Georgietta d/o Richard d 19 Mar 1859 ae: 17m. A Tomb 72

Harriet E. d/o William & Eliza d 20 May 1846 ae: 5y 3m. SB A-3-6

Joseph b 1752 d 1838. Revolutionary War: 15th Massachusetts Continental Line. B-10-7

Martha w/o William d 6 July 1838 ae: 32y. SBE A-3-5

Robert d 14 July 1825 ae: 42y. B-7-15

Sarah H. d/o Joseph & Abigail d 30 Aug 1823 ae: 20y. B-10-7

Seveda E. d/o R. T. & S. A. d 21 May 1847. A Tomb 72

William D. s/o William & Eliza d 15 Oct 1843 ae: 10m. SB A-3-6

William T. s/o William & Martha d 25 Nov 1831 ae: 2y 3m. SD A-3-4

William T. s/o William & Martha d 11 Oct 1836 ae: 2m. SD A-3-4

GORDON, Althea wid/o Capt. Nathaniel d 29 June 1858 ae: 93y. SBE A-19-11

Edward M. s/o Charles F. d 29 May 1861 ae: 2y. GSL

Elizabeth w/o Lewiş d 18 Mar 1843 ae: 42y. B-9-28

GORDON (continued)

Elizabeth d/o Lewis d 21 Dec 1846 ae: 23y. GSL

George J. s/o Charles F. d 5 Mar 1868 ae: 1y 6m. GSL

Hannah w/o Nathaniel d 28 June 1808 ae: 46y. H:125

Lewis d 26 May 1858 ae: 70y. GSL

Lydia Ann d/o Lewis & Elizabeth d 18 Feb 1826 ae: 7m. SB B-9-26

GORE, Richard d 7 Sep 1854 ae: 77y. GSL

Thankful d 25 Sep 1850 ae: 86y. A Tomb 55

GORHAM, Abba Louise d/o Capt. William Jr. & Martha O. d 22 Apr 1839 ae: 14m. J:149

Charles H. s/o William & Charlotte d 27 June 1826 ae: 1y. SB J:151

Charlotte B. wid/o William d 15 Dec 1867 ae: 75y. SBE J:153

John d 17 July 1843 ae: 34y. GSL

Joseph Beal s/o William & Charlotte d 27 Aug 1843 ae: 17m. J:152

Martha O. w/o Capt. William Jr. d 5 May 1843 ae: 35y. SBE J:148

Victoria d/o Capt. William Jr. & Martha O. d 26 Aug 1840 ae: 2m. SBE J:148

William b 1777 d 3 Jan 1851. SBE J:150

William Wallace s/o Capt. William Jr. & Martha O. d 22 Mar 1832 ae: 7d. J:149

GORMAN, Mary w/o Michael d 13 Dec 1846 ae: 33y. GSL

GOSSAM, William d 8 Aug 1860 ae: 39y. "Buried in G. R. Marstin's lot, near the school house." B-5-3

GOSSON, Harriet d/o John d 31 Oct 1841 ae: 1y. GSL

GOUGH, Abby L. d/o George d 2 Sep 1861 ae: 1y. GSL

GOULD, Angeline O. w/o Frederick d 1 Oct 1889 ae: 64y.

GOULD (continued)
G:35A

Aness w/o Thomas d 20 Feb 1812 ae: 56y. H:74

Charles s/o Moses & Susan d 26 July 1822 ae: 13y 7m. ME A Tomb 2

Daniel d 24 May 1866 ae: 59y 4m. ME A Tomb 2

Daniel d 27 Sep 1897 ae: 68y. ME A Tomb 2

Franklin Osgood s/o Thomas O. d 20 June 1851 ae: 5m. A Tomb 17

Frederick s/o Moses d 12 Dec 1845 ae: 3y 6m. ME A Tomb 2

Frederick R. s/o Daniel & Angeline b 4 May 1851 d 31 Dec 1904. G:35B

Hannah M. w/o Thomas O. d 19 Mar 1851 ae: 28y. A Tomb 17

James S. nd. NM A Tomb 1

Jacob d May 1804 ae: 86y. "Formerly of Weymouth, Massachusetts." GSL

Mary w/o Daniel d 20 Dec 1882 ae: 79y. ME A Tomb 2

Mary E. d/o Daniel & Mary d 5 July 1838 ae: 9m. ME A Tomb 2

Milbury M. s/o William d 21 Aug 1856 ae: 9w. GSL

Moses d 22 Nov 1839 ae: 62y 6m. ME A Tomb 2

Randolph s/o Daniel & Mary d 7 Jan 1842 ae: 2y 4m. ME A Tomb 2

Richard T. d 25 Sep 1859 ae: 37y. "Buried at side of J. Treat's grave." GSL

Susan wid/o Eleazer d 11 Jan 1855 ae: 69y. GSL

Susan w/o Moses d 8 Mar 1850 ae: 73y 3m. ME A Tomb 2

Thomas d 27 Jan 1816 ae: 60y. H:75

William s/o William d 1 Oct 1843 ae: 9m. "Buried by his stone." GSL

GOWAN, Susan d 7 Sep 1851 ae: 75y. GSL

GOWER, John d 26 Aug 1861 ae:

GOWER (continued)
71y. SD B-14-11

Sarah Clough w/o John d 7 Oct 1875 ae: 80y. SD B-14-11

GRACE, Elizabeth Mitchell wid/o James E. d 31 Aug 1846 ae: 71y. A Tomb 48

Harriet E. d/o Samuel d 2 Dec 1845 ae: 18m. GSL

GRAFFAM, Benjamin d 21 Jan 1855 ae: 38y. GSL

Charles P. d 27 Feb 1847 ae: 2y. GSL

Martha d 12 July 1853 ae: 50y. GSL

GRAHAM, Charles s/o Asa d 27 Feb 1844 ae: 7m. "Buried by Thatcher's stone." NS B-1-32

David d 16 May 1854 ae: 27y. "Native of Pictou, Nova Scotia." A-1-26

Nancy E. d/o Asa d 12 Dec 1845 ae: 9m 5d. "Buried by side of Sarah Thatcher's grave." NS B-1-31

GRANT, Ellen d/o Jotham d 23 Sep 1843 ae: 17m. "Buried at foot of Poole's stone." GSL

Harriet Elizabeth d/o William T. d 15 Aug 1861 ae: 4m. GSL

Jotham buried 26 Feb 1855 ae: 57y. "Buried at side of wife." GSL

Lydia w/o Jotham d 6 July 1854 ae: 59y. GSL

Martha d/o Jotham S. d 14 Aug 1850 ae: 1y. "Buried near Friends' Ground." GSL

William Miltimore d 29 Feb 1892 ae: 75y. "Died Greely Hospital." GSL

GRAY, George D. s/o Ira & Betsy d 22 Sep 1820 ae: 3y 8m. H:35A

Joseph d 17 Dec 1863 ae: 56y. A Tomb 6

Mary w/o Alexander d 24 Jan 1851 ae: 65y. GSL

GREELY, David d 2 Mar 1838 ae: 48y. J:30 Tomb

GREEN, ---- ch/o Capt. Daniel d

GREEN (continued)

6 May 1857 ae: 2m 5d. GSL

Abigail wid/o Daniel d 12 Jan 1835 ae: 69y. SD I:190

Daniel d 20 Jan 1833 ae: 78y. Revolutionary War: Cpl. I:189

Eben s/o Charles d 8 Jan 1844 ae: 6y. "Buried by R. Goold's stone." NS B-7-15

Emma d/o Henry & Polly d 17 June 1822 ae: 18y. C:151

George S. s/o Henry & Sarah d 12 Dec 1847 ae: 19y. SBE L:49

Henry s/o Henry & Polly d 9 Sep 1809 ae: 23y. SD A-6-10

Henry d 27 Mar 1849 ae: 52y. SBE L:49

John d 18 Apr 1845 ae: 46y. GSL

Joshua d 24 Sep 1835 ae: 36y. C:150

Henry d 24 Jan 1848 ae: 85y. Revolutionary War. C:149

Lucy d/o Daniel d 1 Nov 1843 ae: 2w. GSL

Mary d 23 May 1717. Oldest surviving stone. D:30

Mary wid/o Samuel d 31 July 1839 ae: 64y. L:48

Mary w/o Jesse d 1 July 1807 ae: 22y. L:47

Mary d/o Jesse & Mary d 28 Nov 1806 ae: 3m. SB L:46

Polly wid/o Henry b 4 Sep 1763 d 20 Oct 1857. C:148

Samuel d 20 Mar 1831 ae: 55y. SBE L:45

Mrs. Sophia d 1 Jan 1861 ae: 78y 9m. "Died in Plymouth, Massachusetts." GSL

William s/o Henry & Polly d 26 Feb 1828 ae: 27y. C:152

GREENLEAF, Caroline K. d/o Simon & Hannah b 23 July 1819 d 19 Aug 1822. F:127

Charlotte K. d/o Patrick H. & M. L. b 10 Dec 1833 d 10 Oct 1834. SD A-1-7

John s/o Simon & Hannah b 15 Dec 1824 d 15 Jan 1855. F:130

Capt. Joseph d 3 Oct 1795 ae: 59y. K:45

GREENLEAF (continued)

Sarah d 23 Oct 1852 ae: 74y. GSL

Susannah wid/o Capt. Joseph d 22 Dec 1816 ae: 78y. K:45

Theresa d/o Simon & Hannah d 20 Sep 1821 ae: 3m. F:129

Thomas Parsons b 28 Mar 1831 d 23 May 1831. A-1-6

William H. s/o Amos d 28 June 1846 ae: 2m. "Buried in James R. Mitchell family range." NS B-6-25

GREENOUGH, Ada d/o Major d 7 July 1861 ae: 1y. GSL

Hannah wid/o Parker d 31 Aug 1845 ae: 67y. GSL

GREENWOOD, Mercy w/o John d 17 Dec 1770 ae: 27y. SB C:194

Mrs. Sarah d 28 July 1773 ae: 42y. "...of Boston." C:195

Sarah wid/o Isaac, first Hollis Professor of Mathematics, Harvard College, d 23 May 1776 ae: 68y. C:196

GREER, Harriet Frances d/o John d 23 July 1859 ae: 1y 15d. GSL

GRIDLEY, Abigail d/o Deacon Richard of Boston d 9 Mar 1846 ae: 68y. A-15-15

Lydia d/o Deacon Richard, of Boston d 27 Oct 1849 ae: 87y. A-15-16

Sarah d/o Deacon Richard of Boston d 25 May 1841 ae: 79y. A-15-14

GRIFFIN, Andrew d 31 July 1810 ae: 32y. H:99

Benjamin d 29 Oct 1810 ae: 25y. SD D:6

Charles F. s/o Moses d 25 Nov 1846 ae: 15m. GSL

Ebenezer d 16 Oct 1823 ae: 62y. D:5

Edward S. d 5 Sep 1829 ae: 24y. K:39

James s/o James d 15 June 1842 ae: 5y. GSL

John F. s/o William & Eliza A. d 14 Sep 1850 ae: 18y. SB

GRIFFIN (continued)
J:160

Judith wid/o Ebenezer d 21 May 1837 ae: 77y. D:4

Laura d/o William H. d 5 Dec 1853 ae: 1y. GSL

Leonard d 28 June 1822 ae: 29y. SD D:6

William d 1 Sep 1852 ae: 43y. SBE J:161

William E. d 10 Jan 1862 ae: 14y. A Tomb 84

GRIFFITH, Eliza d 21 Dec 1874 ae: 83y. A Tomb 11

Maria P. d 15 Feb 1883 ae: 83y. A Tomb 11

Mary N. wid/o Dr. David d 4 May 1853 ae: 77y. A Tomb 11

GRINDLE, Lydia d 26 Oct 1849 ae: 87y. GSL

GRIPEY, Charles d 11 Aug 1851 ae: 51y. Black. GSL

GROHSARTH, Emma L. d/o Charles d 21 Oct 1866 ae: 4y 2m. Small stone marker. A Tomb 64

GROSS, Ralph s/o Nathaniel & Rebecca d 5 Aug 1800 ae: 11d. SB K:90

GROVER, Ann Maria d/o Thomas J. d 7 Aug 1854 ae: 1y 6d. GSL

GRUEBY, Almira L. w/o Edward L. d 20 Feb 1836 ae: 28y. A Tomb 46

Charles Harris s/o Capt. Edward L. & Mary d 20 Sep 1818 ae: 12y 8m. F:9

Henry R. s/o George H. d 16 Sep 1849 ae: 8m. A Tomb 36

Samuel Freeman s/o Capt. Edward L. & Mary d 3 May 1819 ae: 8y. F:9

GUBTAIL, Betsy w/o John d 23 Sep 1825 ae: 37y. B-11-23

GUINANS, Michael s/o Philip d 27 Nov 1841 ae: 4m. Catholic. GSL

GUINN, James B. s/o Philip d 24 June 1846 ae: 20m. Catholic. GSL

John H. d 9 Sep 1846 ae: 11m.

GUINN (continued)
GSL

GUNNISON, Betsy w/o Elihu d 28 Aug 1840 ae: 61y. B-15-11

Elihu d 23 Oct 1826 ae: 51y. B-15-11

James s/o Elihu d 3 Aug 1824 ae: 11y. B-15-11

GURLEY, Royal d 24 Aug 1824 ae: 49y. B-5-19

GUSTIN, Ebenezer d 1 Mar 1794 ae: 58y. Revolutionary War. B-3-36

Lucy wid/o Ebenezer d 28 Dec 1827 ae: 86y. B-3-37

GWYNN, James s/o George & Hannah d 24 June 1846 ae: 1y 8m. A-9-17

Sarah Hoyt wid/o Holland b 1809 d 23 Apr 1894 ae: 84y 9m. A-9-10

GWYNNE, Holland d 9 Mar 1887 ae: 80y. A-9-9

HAGERTY, John M. s/o John & Susan d 8 Feb 1828 ae: 2y 5d. B-11-4

HAGGETT, Henry s/o Samuel d 14 Jan 1844. "Buried by Swan's tomb." A Tomb 45

John d 7 Nov 1820 ae: 31y. J:217

William H. s/o John & Charlotte nd. SD J:218

HAINES, Mary d 30 Nov 1841 ae: 90y. GSL

William d 1 June 1845 ae: 68y. GSL

William L. d 19 May 1863 ae: 53y. GSL

HALE, Anne d 31 Dec 1799 ae: 29y. D:26

James Henry s/o John & Mary d 23 Apr 1820 ae: 1y. D:101

Mary w/o Samuel d 12 Mar 1871 ae: 90y 7m. SB A-1-16

Samuel d 10 July 1840 ae: 69y. SB A-1-15

William Pepperrell s/o Dr. Eliphalet & Elizabeth d 29 Jan 1738 ae: 10w. D:86

HALEY, Ann E. d/o Joseph & Mary b 11 June 1811 d 22 July

HALEY (continued)
1811. H:11
George s/o John & Sarah d 14
Jan 1814 ae: 2y. H:76
George s/o John & Sarah d 3 Oct
1816 ae: 2y. H:76
James s/o Joseph & Mary b 19
Oct 1799 d 26 Oct 1799. H:11
James E. s/o Joseph & Mary b
11 Mar 1804 d 7 Mar 1816.
H:11
Jane wid/o Joseph d 15 Apr 1848
ae: 61y. GSL
Joel d 24 Oct 1844 ae: 32y.
"Buried in Family Range."
GSL
John d 11 Apr 1818 ae: 32y.
H:76
Mary w/o Joseph d 10 Sep 1835
ae: 57y. I:128
Mary J. d/o John & Sarah d 12
Dec 1813 ae: 5y. H:76
Mehitable d/o Joseph & Mary d
26 Feb 1822 ae: 6y. SD H:10
HALL, inf d 6 Sep 1835 ae: 11m.
SD B-3-43
Aaron s/o Peter & Ann d 15 June
1828 ae: 20y. "Died at sea."
I:121
Abigail w/o Nahum d 14 May
1807 ae: 22y. SB C:35
Alice w/o Daniel d 18 Dec 1861
ae: 65y. GSL
Alice d/o George d 26 Aug 1856
ae: 15w 4d. A Tomb 44
Alice T. d/o William d 17 Sep
1857 ae: 3y 11m. GSL
Amelia L. wid/o Simeon d 21
June 1871 ae: 75y. A Tomb 44
Amos B. d 10 Aug 1850 ae: 27y.
A Tomb 7
Anna wid/o Peter b 23 Mar 1784
d 29 May 1856. A-3-9
Carroll P. N. s/o John d 3 Nov
1875 ae: 5y. A Tomb 44
Charles C. P. s/o Capt. Paul &
Sarah d 24 July 1840 ae: 11y.
A-11-12
Clark d 18 Oct 1827 ae: 23y. B-
9-42
Dorcas A. d/o Elijah d 11 Aug
1841 ae: 13y. GSL

HALL (continued)
Ebenezer d 13 Aug 1823 ae: 46y.
B-11-14
Edward s/o Charles d 20 June
1865 ae: 1y 6m. GSL
Eliza N. w/o Elijah d 20 Feb
1846 ae: 44y. "Died in Chel-
sea, Massachusetts." GSL
Elizabeth d/o Nahum d 31 Jan
1807 ae: 15m. C:37
George W. s/o Winslow & E. M.
b 1844 d 1846. SB B-5-40
Hannah d/o George d 10 Dec
1854 ae: 18m. A Tomb 44
Harriet T. w/o Simeon d 22 Dec
1823 ae: 39y. A Tomb 44
Harriet A. d/o Charles d 19 July
1855 ae: 14m 14d. GSL
Hannah Bridges w/o Deacon
Moses of Charleston, Mas-
sachusetts d 5 Mar 1843 ae:
78y. A-19-6
Harriet w/o Henry P. b 1816 d
1901. Mmt A-3-11A
Isaac s/o William W. & R. B. d
8 Aug 1855 ae: 18m 21d. SD
E:85
Joel b 1819 d 1837. "Died at
sea." Mmt A-3-11A
Joel B. s/o William W. & R. B.
d 2 Apr 1860 ae: 5w. SD E:85
John H. s/o Paul & Sarah d 5
Nov 1900 ae: 65y 3m 23d. A
Tomb 64
John Hancock s/o Rev. Stephen
& Mary b 21 Jan 1781 d 26 Feb
1841. Mmt H:55
John P. s/o Simeon & Harriet T.
d 17 Sep 1813 ae: 3m. A
Tomb 44
Joseph B. s/o Elijah d 24 May
1844 ae: 14y. GSL
Julia Augusta d/o William &
Hannah d 1 Dec 1843 ae: 4y.
Black. A-10-31
Louis s/o Simeon & Harriet T. d
5 Sep 1806 ae: 1y. A Tomb 44
Martha Cotton d/o Rev. Stephen
& Mary b 26 July 1792 d 26
Nov 1847. Mmt H:55
Mary d/o Rev. Stephen & Mary b
13 Dec 1783 d 26 Aug 1844.

HALL (continued)
Mmt H:55
Mary w/o Thomas d 27 Mar 1828
ae: 50y. C:69
Mary Ann d/o William & Hannah
d 5 Dec 1840 ae: 5y. Black.
A-10-31
Mary Cotton d/o William Cotton,
wid/o Rev. Stephen, wid/o
Moses Holt Jr. d 27 July 1808
ae: 54y. H:56
Mary F. w/o John H. d 3 Dec
1882 ae: 46y. A Tomb 64
Noah s/o Lot & Sarah d 6 Sep
1806 ae: 9m. J:73
Capt. Paul d 28 Oct 1839 ae:
37y. A-11-11
Peter b 1 June 1774 d 11 May
1835. A-3-10
Rachael B. w/o William H. d 8
June 1866 ae: 37y 2m. GSL
Rachel S. Chase w/o Charles H.
d 25 Jan 1839 ae: 26y. A-3-11
Rebecca F. w/o William N. d 22
Oct 1834 ae: 19y. SD B-3-43
Simeon b 3 May 1781 d 7 Jan
1870. A Tomb 44
Statira E. d/o Charles d 8 Aug
1861 ae: 5y. GSL
Rev. Stephen b 28 May 1743 d 13
Sep 1794. Revolutionary War:
Maj. H:57
Stephen d 12 July 1843 ae: 76y.
B-8-36
Stephen W. S. d 17 Aug 1849 ae:
9m. A Tomb 9
Stillman s/o Peter & Ann d 5
Nov 1815 ae: 5m. I:121
Stillman s/o Peter & Ann d 22
May 1834 ae: 14y. I:121
Stillman I. b&d 1815. Mmt A-
3-11A
Sumner C. s/o Peter & Ann d 5
Aug 1826 ae: 11m. I:121
Susannah wid/o Ebenezer d 1
Feb 1825 ae: 48y. B-11-15
Thomas d 5 Aug 1844 ae: 57y.
"Formerly of Newburyport,
Massachusetts." C:70
Willard s/o Rev. Stephen & Mary
b 5 June 1788 d 1818. Mmt
H:55

HALL (continued)
William d 13 Oct 1862 ae: 70y.
GSL
William Augustus s/o Rev.
Stephen & Mary b 6 Oct 1785 d
1812. Mmt H:55
William M. d 11 Oct 1864 ae:
56y. "Died in Boston." GSL
Willie s/o Charles B. d 28 May
1870 ae: 10m. GSL
HALLIDAY, Elizabeth Mussey
w/o James b 8 Jan 1784 d 5
Jan 1872. A Tomb 35
Lydia w/o Capt. James d 22 Mar
1809 ae: 24y. J:69
HALY, Joseph d 10 Apr 1866 ae:
95y. "Died in Boston." GSL
HAM, Anthony F. s/o Jacob &
Mary d 24 Mar 1817 ae: 9y 4m.
I:91
Charles H. d 1 Nov 1865 ae: 51y.
GSL
Edward W. s/o Charles H. &
Nancy d 15 Sep 1842 ae: 1y
7m. SD A-8-16
Harry E. s/o George W. d 13 Mar
1880 ae: 1y. GSL
Jacob s/o Jacob & Mary d 19 Sep
1806 ae: 1y 7m. I:91
Martha wid/o Shadrack d 16 Aug
1832 ae: 88y. I:19
Mary w/o Jacob d 6 June 1835
ae: 55y. I:90
Nancy w/o Charles d 7 Jan 1880
ae: 66y. GSL
Robert T. s/o Charles H. d 25
Dec 1861 ae: 22y. GSL
Tobias s/o Jacob & Mary d 10
Aug 1821 ae: 18y. I:91
Tobias F. s/o Jacob & Mary d 12
Sep 1803 ae: 13m. I:91
HAMBLET, Charles d 22 Dec
1843 ae: 4y 6m. A Tomb 30
Edwin s/o John D. Jr. d 21 July
1847 ae: 3y. A Tomb 30
Eunice wid/o John D. d 13 Dec
1853 ae: 67y. A Tomb 30
Franklin A. s/o Charles d 14 Sep
1857 ae: 6y 10m. A Tomb 30
Georgianna d/o George W. d 13
Sep 1848 ae: 6m. "Buried at
foot of J. Frothingham's

HAMBLET (continued)
grave". NS L:88

John D. d 29 Jan 1850 ae: 73y. A Tomb 30

Julia A. d/o Charles d 6 Sep 1849 ae: 18m. A Tomb 30

Mary w/o Charles d 27 Oct 1842 ae: 22y. A Tomb 30

Benjamin d 14 May 1859 ae: 54y 3m. A Tomb 30

Eliza d 17 Sep 1855 ae: 49y. A Tomb 30

HAMILTON, Catherine d 21 Sep 1833 ae: 52y. B-12-6

Edward s/o Thomas & Matilda d 26 Mar 1845 ae: 5m. SD I:45

Eliza wid/o James d 18 Aug 1850 ae: 36y. GSL

Harriet J. w/o Jonas d 7 Sep 1856 ae: 24y 9m. SD B-14-4

Hattie d/o Jonas & Harriet J. d 29 Apr 1856 ae: 18m. SD B-14-4

James d 10 Mar 1848 ae: 44y. GSL

James d 17 May 1862 ae: 16y 3m. GSL

Capt. John d 15 June 1847 ae: 51y. "Buried at head of Daniel S. Moody's grave." NS G:10

Mary wid/o Richard d 16 July 1858 ae: 70y. GSL

Sarah W. wid/o Capt. John d 8 Nov 1858 ae: 63y. "Died in Chelsea, Massachusetts." GSL

Susannah d/o Thomas d 5 Oct 1849 ae: 2y. GSL

Thomas nd. SD A-3-30

William d 7 Aug 1861 ae: 70y. GSL

HAMMETT, Hannah B. d/o William & C. d 8 July 1845 ae: 10y. Black. SB A-24-29

Josephine d/o William & C. d 6 Sep 1852 ae: 11y. Black. SBE A-24-30

HAMMOND, Abby d/o William d 25 Nov 1845 ae: 10w. GSL

HAMPSON, David d 9 Dec 1849 ae: 20y. Black. GSL

HANCE, Hannah d 8 Nov 1842 ae:

HANCE (continued)
86y. Widow. Black. GSL

HANNAFORD, Alonzo s/o Enoch L. d 4 Feb 1856 ae: 3m. GSL

Elizabeth wid/o Zaccheus d 28 Feb 1860 ae: 82y. GSL

Nancy L. C. d 26 Mar 1855 ae: 6y 9m. GSL

Solomon s/o Joseph d 18 Sep 1846 ae: 4y. GSL

Zaccheus d 10 Sep 1835 ae: 51y. SD H:6

HANSCOMB, Abigail wid/o Solomon d 30 Jan 1854 ae: 84y. SB J:97

HANSON, Alice G. d/o Veranus C. d 17 Oct 1864 ae: 3m. GSL

Franklin G. s/o Gardner d 16 Mar 1855 ae: 5y. GSL

Jane J. d 29 Sep 1843 ae: 38y. MBE A Tomb 56

L. A. d/o Samuel d 27 Feb 1860 ae: 50y. A Tomb 42

Mary E. w/o Moses d 26 Sep 1873 ae: 58y. "Buried Quaker Lot." GSL

Dr. Moses d 30 Mar 1866 ae: 58y 3m. SBE J:227

Nancy w/o William d 16 Jan 1814 ae: 33y. SBE K:79

Peter d 24 Aug 1853 ae: 66y. "Native of Holmestrand, Norway." B-11-28

Philip Greely s/o Samuel d 18 June 1853 ae: 4y. A Tomb 42

Statira w/o Samuel d 12 Aug 1836 ae: 39y. A Tomb 42

William B. s/o Elisha & Jane d 21 Feb 1896 ae: 63y 8m. GSL

William McLellan d 21 Feb 1896 ae: 64y. Civil War: 25th Reg. Maine Inf., Co. A. USN-USS Ohio. A Tomb 56

HARDON, Sarah wid/o Joseph d 11 June 1848 ae: 49y. GSL

HARDING, Ann wid/o Dr. Stephen b 12 Feb 1755 d 1 Jan 1826. E:55

Ariston s/o Dr. Stephen & Ann b 20 Mar 1781 d 22 Dec 1806. "Died abroad." SBE E:53

59

HARDING (continued)

Charles d 13 July 1849 ae: 49y. A Tomb 10

Charles W. d 10 May 1890 ae: 54y. A Tomb 46

Daniel s/o Dr. Stephen & Ann b 3 Jan 1790 d 11 July 1811. "Died abroad." SBE E:53

Frank A. d 24 Aug 1909 ae: 49y 2m 9d. "Died Malden, Massachusetts." F:93 Tomb

George F. s/o Charles d 10 Dec 1864 ae: 24y. Civil War: 16th Reg. Maine Inf., Co. F. F:93 Tomb

Harriet d/o Stephen & Ann b 25 Apr 1794 d 12 May 1800. E:54

Jane B. wid/o David d 14 Sep 1844 ae: 38y. A Tomb 26

Job s/o Dr. Stephen & Ann b 7 Aug 1873 d 31 Oct 1810. "Died abroad." SBE E:53

Louisa d/o Charles & Martha W. d 18 May 1835 ae: 22m. A-1-12

Maria A. d 23 Dec 1908 ae: 86y 7m 3d. F:93 Tomb

Mary E. d/o Charles W. & Maria Albina d 16 Dec 1952 ae: 88y 2m 8d. GSL

R. Augustus d 6 Aug 1846 ae: 21y. A Tomb 26

Sarah w/o Noah d 7 Apr 1809 ae: 49y. SD C:55

Stephen s/o Dr. Stephen & Ann b 1 June 1788 d 28 Aug 1819. "Died abroad." SBE E:53

Dr. Stephen b 21 Mar 1761 d 27 Aug 1823. SBE E:53

HARDY, Anna d/o John d 31 Mar 1865 ae: 1y. GSL

James L. s/o John d 16 May 1869 ae: 7m. GSL

Joseph s/o John d 5 July 1857 ae: 2y 10m. GSL

Lizzie d/o Joseph d 13 Nov 1862 ae: 6y. GSL

Mary Ann d/o John d 25 Oct 1854 ae: 1y 6m. GSL

Sarah A. d 23 Nov 1931 ae: 60y. "Died Tewksbury, Massachusetts." GSL

HARDY (continued)

William M. s/o John d 1 Aug 1864 ae: 1y 9m. GSL

HARFORD, Catherine E. w/o Hiram A. d 18 Dec 1848 ae: 32y. H:148

Sarah d/o Hiram d 10 May 1844 ae: 10y. GSL

HARLOW, Louisa d/o Edward d 7 Dec 1853 ae: 4m 20d. GSL

HARMON, Amelia D. d/o Benjamin & Mary E. nd. SBE B-6-15

Benjamin M. s/o Dominicus & Harriet d 1 Sep 1832 ae: 21y. C:191

Betsy w/o Deacon John d 3 Nov 1811 ae: 27y. SBE C:53

Charles H. s/o James H. d 18 May 1848 ae: 8m. GSL

Clarissa w/o Robert d 17 July 1819 ae: 22y. SB K:163

Emma F. d/o John H. d 22 Mar 1850 ae: 8m. GSL

Frances A. d/o Benjamin & Mary E. nd. SBE B-6-15

Frances A. d/o Benjamin & Mary E. d 26 Apr 1832. B-6-14

Georgianna W. d/o Benjamin & Mary E. nd. SBE B-6-15

James H. s/o William d 10 Feb 1868 ae: 3y 10m. GSL

Julia Foster d/o Lorenzo D. d 24 May 1855 ae: 1y. GSL

Louisa d/o John & Betsy d 24 Aug 1806 ae: 9m. SBE C:54

Louisa d/o Benjamin d 28 Sep 1843 ae: 3m. "Buried by his stone." GSL

Peletiah d 5 Nov 1856 ae: 50y. "Died Boston, Massachusetts." GSL

Rebecca C. w/o Peletiah d 23 Mar 1835 ae: 52y. SB A-1-24

Rebecca D. d/o Pelatiah & Rebecca C. d 3 May 1838 ae: 17y. SBE A-1-25

Russell S. s/o Dominicus & Harriet d 31 Dec 1841 ae: 19y. C:192

Sally w/o Francis d 25 Nov 1845 ae: 68y. B-11-6

HARMON (continued)

William d 6 July 1843 ae: 23y. GSL

HARPER, Mary d/o William & Mary d 1 Mar 1759 ae: 16m. E:72

Samuel d 20 Oct 1857 ae: 84y. I:159

Sarah w/o Samuel d 7 July 1849 ae: 74y. SBE I:158

HARRIS, Edwin Rea s/o Samuel & Abigail C. d 29 Sep 1837 ae: 8m. J:104

Elizabeth d/o Benjamin & Anne Titcomb, wid/o John d 24 Mar 1834 ae: 64y. C:224

Elizabeth wid/o William d 10 Sep 1858 ae: 79y. GSL

Elizabeth B. Capren wid/o Mary d 20 Nov 1861 ae: 78y. H:95

George s/o William & Elizabeth d 4 May 1843 ae: 24y. SBE A-8-3

John d 8 Dec 1853 ae: 76y. GSL

Josephine w/o Thomas R. d 2 Mar 1857 ae: 17y. SB A-16-11

Mary d/o William & Elizabeth d 11 Apr 1840 ae: 32y. SD A-8-2

Rachel E. d/o Thomas d 2 Sep 1846 ae: 2y 6m. GSL

Thankful M. w/o John d 25 Nov 1853 ae: 62y. GSL

William d 13 June 1844 ae: 64y. SD A-8-4

HARROD, Elizabeth w/o Joseph d 20 Apr 1842 ae: 54y. A Tomb 55

HARRY, John H. s/o John d 3 Aug 1841 ae: 6m. GSL

HART, Clara L. w/o Thomas d 22 July 1870. SBE B-12-9

Capt. Francis d 28 Mar 1816 ae: 38y. SB J:37

Francis d 4 Feb 1850 ae: 45y. GSL

Major James d 4 May 1825 ae: 78y. "Born in England." Revolutionary War: Adj-Continental Army. B-12-11

Phebe w/o Hanson M. d 22 Feb 1846 ae: 33y. A Tomb 69

Thomas d 20 Apr 1836 ae: 37y.

HART (continued)

SD B-12-10

Thomas s/o Thomas d 13 Sep 1854 ae: 29y. SD B-12-10

HARTFORD, Susan H. w/o Solomon H. d 17 Jan 1865 ae: 20y 11m. SD J:158

HARTWELL, Evelina Ann w/o Peter d 4 Dec 1846 ae: 34y. GSL

Herman d 10 Nov 1851 ae: 53y. GSL

HARWOOD, Frederick O. s/o Otis d 30 June 1841 ae: 8y. GSL

HASKELL, Abigail d 25 June 1852 ae: 46y. GSL

Adeline d/o William & Lucy d 12 May 1802 ae: 38m. SD K:148

Alexander N. b 9 Aug 1802 d 23 July 1883. MBE A-10-1

Betsy Priscilla Gray d/o John d May 1804 ae: 2y 3m. GSL

Charles F. s/o Alexander N. & Elizabeth N. d 21 Mar 1847 ae: 5y 7m. A-10-3

Charles Swett s/o Alexander N. & Elizabeth N. d 19 Sep 1841 ae: 2y. A-10-2

Cyrus W. d 14 Sep 1895 ae: 62y. Civil War: Maine Coast Guard Heavy Artillery, Co. B. NS A-5-19

Dorcas B. w/o Joshua d 4 Aug 1891 ae: 81y 6m. A Tomb 9

Elizabeth L. w/o John W. d 23 Jan 1849 ae: 58y. K:18

Elizabeth N. w/o Alexander N. b 9 Jan 1810 d 28 Sep 1889. MBE A-10-1

Forestine d/o Thomas M. d 14 Aug 1854 ae: 15m. A Tomb 9

Frank F. C. s/o John A. d 9 Nov 1849 ae: 3y 10m. GSL

Frank H. s/o John A. d 12 Sep 1853 ae: 15m. GSL

John A. d 15 July 1856 ae: 52y. "Buried near the Friends' Ground." GSL

John Swett s/o Alexander N. & Elizabeth N. d 27 Aug 1836 ae:

HASKELL (continued)
14m. A-10-2

John W. d 5 June 1849 ae: 68y.
K:17

Jonathan s/o Nathaniel of Gloucester, Massachusetts, d 1 Oct
1800 ae: 22y. K:23

Jonathan s/o William & Lucy d
18 Nov 1838 ae: 35y. K:20

Joseph B. d 6 June 1881 ae: 74y.
A Tomb 9

Lucy w/o William d 6 Dec 1838
ae: 59y. SBE K:19

Mary M. w/o Lyman d 13 Apr
1837 ae: 26y. SBE A-5-19

Mary W. d/o Alexander N. &
Elizabeth N. b 17 June 1837 d
3 Sep 1864. MBE A-10-1

Melinda w/o Joseph P. d 30 Oct
1871 ae: 61y. A Tomb 9

Nathaniel d 11 Sep 1856 ae: 90y.
GSL

Phebe M. d/o Joshua d 8 Sep
1857 ae: 14y 9m. A Tomb 9

Sarah d/o John W. & Elizabeth d
23 May 1822 ae: 2y 2m. K:22

Sarah H. d/o Joseph d 27 Dec
1855 ae: 18y. A Tomb 9

Theodore Dwight s/o Josiah d 9
Aug 1848 ae: 14m. "Buried at
head of Mrs. Levi Bolton's
grave." GSL

Thomas d 10 Feb 1785 ae: 97y.
GSL

William s/o William & Lucy d 2
Oct 1800 ae: 15m. SB K:24

William d 4 Dec 1855 ae: 83y.
A Tomb 9

William H. d 15 June 1867 ae:
58y. A Tomb 9

HASKINS, Elizabeth w/o Edward
d 15 Aug 1868 ae: 44y. GSL

Henrietta d/o Edward d 24 Apr
1868 ae: 19y. GSL

Lucy w/o Edward d 14 May 1859
ae: 75y. GSL

Philip M. d 31 Mar 1826 ae: 46y.
B-8-12

HATCH, Charles s/o Frederick d
7 Aug 1843 ae: 3m. "Buried
by side of Baker's stone."
GSL

HATCH (continued)
Crowell d 17 Oct 1859 ae: 71y.
GSL

Elizabeth d 12 May 1851 ae: 56y.
GSL

Elizabeth Jane d/o Caleb S. d 12
July 1846 ae: 16y 9m. GSL

Frederick s/o Frederick d 31
July 1846 ae: 6w. "Buried at
head of Ezekiel Patten's
grave." NS B-5-18

Lucy L. d/o David d 1 Sep 1847
ae: 3y. GSL

Martha wid/o Walter d 18 Sep
1834 ae: 65y. SB J:185

Martha G. d/o Walter & Martha d
21 May 1838 ae: 44y. SD
J:186

Sally B. b 11 May 1801 d 24 May
1802. J:183

Sarah E. wid/o Benjamin d 14
Nov 1828 ae: 31y. SBE B-1-35

Capt. Walter d 8 Mar 1811 ae:
39y. SD J:184

Walter S. b 1 Mar 1800 d 3 June
1800. J:183

William F. s/o Anthony d 10
Dec 1848 ae: 5y. "Buried by
side of James Freeman -
1771." NS F:68

HAWKINS, Elizabeth L. w/o
Charles d 23 Mar 1893 ae: 48y
5m. GSL

HAY, Ann M. w/o Oliver H. d 6
Oct 1852 ae: 26y. SBE A-21-
5

Clara J. d/o Joseph & Maria M.
d 16 Apr 1851 ae: 21y. SBE
A-21-6

Ella d/o Joseph F. d 25 Mar
1853 ae: 6m. GSL

Ellen A. d/o Joseph & Maria M.
d 6 Feb 1853 ae: 19y 10m.
SBE A-21-4

Nelly d/o Joseph & Maria M. d
25 Mar 1853 ae: 6m. SBE A-
21-4

HAYDEN, Eliza S. w/o Josiah d
12 July 1807 ae: 21y. "Drowned at Richmond's Island."
Unusual stone. L:79

Robert S. s/o Josiah & Eliza S. d

HAYDEN (continued)

12 July 1807 ae: 10m. "Drowned at Richmond's Island." Unusual stone. L:79

HAYE, Peter d 21 Feb 1869 ae: 69y. GSL

HAYES, Erastus Grenville s/o Erastus & Mary b 20 Sep 1825 d 2 June 1826. B-6-21

Mrs. Lucy d 24 Aug 1839 ae: 70y. A-7-9

Mary Barton d/o Erastus & Mary b 20 Sep 1825 d 25 Apr 1826. B-6-21

Ursula P. w/o Peter d 25 Nov 1859 ae: 57y. SD C:237

HAYNES, Abby d/o William & Ann d 20 Aug 1819 ae: 2y. B-9-13

Ann w/o William d 25 May 1829 ae: 43y. B-9-12

Mary d 28 Nov 1841 ae: 90y. B-9-14

Mary E. w/o James d 29 Oct 1869 ae: 47y. GSL

William d 1 June 1845 ae: 68y. B-9-13

HEAD, James d 30 Mar 1835 ae: 43y. Grave between A Tomb 67 & A Tomb 68. MD A:89

HEARL, Caroline E. d/o George d 3 Aug 1841 ae: 3m. GSL

HEFFORD, Edward s/o Charles d 10 July 1853 ae: 9m. GSL

HELMER, Sarah w/o John d 21 Aug 1810 ae: 51y. SB L:42

HEMPHILL, Capt. Orson d 14 Sep 1826 ae: 26y. "...of Sutton, New Hampshire. Died in this town while on a visit for his health." B-6-23

HENLEY, Eunice wid/o Col. James d 15 June 1849 ae: 65y. GSL

James d 17 Oct 1843 ae: 61y. "Murdered." GSL

HENRY, James d 27 July 1847 ae: 16m. Black. GSL

HERRICK, Dr. Martin d 15 July 1820 ae: 73y. SBE A-21-7

HERSEY, Elias d 31 May 1837 ae: 49y. A Tomb 31

HERSEY (continued)

Frederick W. s/o Joshua nd. ae: 19y. "Removed from Bangor." A Tomb 31

H. C. s/o Joshua nd. ae: 14y. "Removed from Bangor." A Tomb 31

HEWITT, Sophia Ostinelli d/o late James d 31 Aug 1845 ae: 46y. A Tomb 48

HICKEY, Dennis d 27 Nov 1841 ae: 25y. "Stranger." Catholic. GSL

HIGGINS, Frances E. d/o Simeon d 9 Dec 1841 ae: 9y. GSL

Frederick L. s/o Simeon d 24 Jan 1862 ae: 2m. GSL

Lucius M. s/o Capt. Lucius & Adaline d 16 Aug 1825 ae: 4y. B-9-24

William s/o Micha d 4 Dec 1862 ae: 5y 6m. GSL

HILL, Edward s/o George & Priscilla d 11 Nov 1820. F:109

Elizabeth d 4 Apr 1832 ae: 34y. C:96

Elizabeth H. d 13 Dec 1925 ae: 63y. A Tomb 21

Elizabeth J. d/o Abner d 1 Aug 1867 ae: 15m. GSL

George s/o George & Priscilla d 12 Feb 1820 ae: 5y. SB F:110

James d 21 Jan 1868 ae: 42y. A Tomb 21

Mary A. w/o James B., d/o Alexander & Sarah Millican d 6 Nov 1916 ae: 80y 2m. NS F:75

Minerva R. d 23 Sep 1848 ae: 11m. F:95 Tomb

Richard d 13 Sep 1861 ae: 73y. "Murdered." Black. GSL

HILLER, George d 26 Sep 1851 ae: 58y. GSL

HILLMAN, Betsy W. wid/o John d 26 June 1861 ae: 57y. GSL

Benjamin B. s/o John F. d 30 June 1857 ae: 2y. GSL

Frederick G. s/o Horace B. d 16 June 1861 ae: 14m. GSL

John P. d 24 Oct 1856 ae: 51y.

HILLMAN (continued)
"Drowned at Cape Ann." GSL

Sarah L. d/o John T. d 2 Aug 1857 ae: 4y 9m. GSL

HILTON, Thomas h/o Rachael Shaw d Dec 1793. J:106

HINDS, Ann P. w/o Elisha d 13 Oct 1831 ae: 25y. K:56

Edward s/o Elisha d 10 Aug 1842 ae: 17m. GSL

Eveline d/o Ambrose d 31 May 1863 ae: 2y 6m. GSL

John s/o John d 22 Feb 1853 ae: 4y 6m. GSL

Mary E. d/o John & Ellen d 2 Oct 1859 ae: 18y 2m. SD I:113

William s/o John d 3 Dec 1843 ae: 8d. "Buried by his stone." GSL

Edward d 8 Apr 1869 ae: 92y. GSL

HINKLEY, Charles F. s/o Noah & N. C. d 21 June 1835 ae: 16m. GSL

Edward N. s/o Noah & N. C. d 11 Oct 1884 ae: 59y. A Tomb 36

Frances E. d/o Noah & N. C. d 18 May 1833 ae: 14m. A Tomb 36

Henry C. s/o Noah & N. C. b 1837 d 1873. A Tomb 36

Mary A. d/o Noah & N. C. d 20 July 1834 ae: 20y. A Tomb 36

Noah d 30 Sep 1857 ae: 68y. A Tomb 36

HITCHCOCK, Benjamin Thaxter s/o D. G. d 21 Feb 1845 ae: 19y. A Tomb 45

HITCHINGS, Nellie S. d/o George F. d 23 July 1863 ae: 7w 5d. A Tomb 11

Frederick s/o George F. d 21 Nov 1860 ae: 18m. A Tomb 11

HOBART, John d 9 Aug 1824 ae: 67y. ME A Tomb 58

Leah adopted d/o John & Polly d 29 Jan 1822 ae: 25y. ME A Tomb 58

Polly wid/o John d 10 Mar 1841 ae: 80y. ME A Tomb 58

HOBBY, John d 4 May 1802 ae:

HOBBY (continued)
52y. Revolutionary War: Capt., Continental Army. Massachusetts Society of the Cincinnati. GSL

HOBSON, George W. s/o John d 22 Sep 1852 ae: 18m. GSL

Lewis A. s/o Almon L. d 17 Feb 1849 ae: 2y. A Tomb 9

HODGE, Elizabeth w/o Francis C. d 14 May 1841 ae: 31y. F:180

Elizabeth P. w/o Francis d 18 May 1841 ae: 31y. GSL

Joseph P. s/o William & Sarah M. d 12 May 1858 ae: 19y. SD B-1-27

Mary E. d/o William & Sarah M. d 20 Nov 1856 ae: 20y 5m. SD B-1-27

Sarah E. d/o William & Sarah M. b 25 Jan 1832 d 30 July 1850. SD B-1-25

Sarah M. w/o Joseph d 3 Jan 1860 ae: 52y 7m. "Buried in Joseph Poland's lot." NS B-1-27

William Poland s/o William & Sarah M. d 29 Aug 1831 ae: 15m. F:177

HODGES, Elizabeth d/o John R. & Susan d 31 July 1834 ae: 2y. A-1-32

Joseph P. s/o William, gr s/o Joseph Poland d 12 May 1858 ae: 19y. "Died Boston, Massachusetts." GSL

Sarah E. d/o William d 30 July 1850 ae: 18y. GSL

Thomas d 26 July 1798 ae: 36y. L:26

HODGKINS, Ellen d/o Philip d 9 Sep 1843 ae: 18m. "Buried at head of Crawford's stone." GSL

Ellen K. d/o Edward H. d 19 Dec 1848 ae: 5y. "Buried near the upper gate." GSL

George s/o Joseph d 29 Mar 1843 ae: 4y. GSL

George M. s/o Joseph E. d 13 Dec 1847 ae: 9m. GSL

HODGKINS (continued)

Henry s/o Walter d 30 Aug 1874 ae: 4w. GSL

Mary F. d/o Joseph E. d 5 Aug 1845 ae: 4m. GSL

Nathaniel K. d 6 Oct 1825 ae: 29y. I:2

Olive d 31 Dec 1846 ae: 63y. Widow. GSL

Priscilla w/o Thomas d 27 Aug 1821 ae: 48y. I:3

Priscilla K. d/o Nathaniel K. & Susan d 18 June 1825 ae: 3y. I:4

Susan J. d/o Nathaniel K. & Susan d 28 Sep 1826 ae: 9m. I:4

HODSDEN, Asa s/o David d 11 Aug 1843 ae: 14m. A Tomb 16

Mary Ann d/o David d 2 Aug 1844 ae: 4w. A Tomb 16

HOFFMAN, Caroline w/o James d 18 Feb 1892 ae: 36y 1m. GSL

HOGAN, Willie s/o James d 27 July 1873 ae: 10m. A Tomb 30

HOIT, Charles s/o William & H. G. d 6 May 1847 ae: 16y. SB A-9-7

Fanny d/o John M. & Caroline d 26 Feb 1821 ae: 31y. SD C:210

Greenwood s/o William Jr. nd. SD A-9-16

Huldah nd. SD A-9-16

Sarah d/o John T. & Betsy d 24 June 1812 ae: 1y. SD C:211

William s/o John M. & Caroline d 22 June 1821 ae: 31y. SD C:210

William d 13 May 1838 ae: 63y. A-9-16

HOLBROOK, Harriet d/o Salvin & Rachel d 9 Nov 1825 ae: 2y. SD B-7-18

HOLDEN, Amos d 22 Nov 1842 ae: 26y. "Foreigner." GSL

Charles s/o William & Jane d 7 Jan 1802 ae: 8m. SBE K:75

Elizabeth w/o Charles d 4 Jan 1851 ae: 45y. A Tomb 2

HOLDEN (continued)

Henry s/o William & Jane d 12 Nov 1833 ae: 33y. SBE K:73

Henry Sampson s/o George H. d 18 Oct 1862 ae: 8y 3m. GSL

Jane d/o William & Jane d 8 Sep 1807 ae: 15m. SBE K:75

William d 9 Oct 1827 ae: 50y. SBE K:74

HOLLAND, John d 2 May 1837 ae: 37y. Black. Catholic. SBE A-11-19

Julia Ann d/o Mary Ann d 14 Feb 1839 ae: 11y. Black. Catholic. A-11-20

Mary Ann d 16 Apr 1844 ae: 52y. Black. Catholic. GSL

William s/o Capt. William & Elizabeth b 22 Aug 1768 d 23 Aug 1770. C:193

HOLM, Elvira w/o Gustavus d 11 Apr 1841 ae: 54y. SB A-9-6

Jane P. d/o Gustavus & Elvira d 3 Feb 1838 ae: 23y. SBE A-9-5

HOLMES, Augustus d 23 Jan 1855. GSL

James d 12 May 1832 ae: 62y. B-10-16

John d 17 May 1846 ae: 36y. GSL

Margaret w/o James Jr. d 1 Oct 1826 ae: 16y 4m. B-10-15

HOLT, Amanda S. d/o Joseph T. d 4 May 1847 ae: 2y. "Buried near the gate." GSL

Moses d 26 June 1772 ae: 28y. H:27

HOMER, Henry d 28 Sep 1851 ae: 38y. SB H:67

Samuel d 1 May 1814 ae: 55y. F:105 Tomb

Sarah wid/o Samuel d 30 June 1858 ae: 93y. F:105 Tomb

HOMMELL, Joseph s/o William d 16 Sep 1852 ae: 14y. Black. GSL

HOOD, Daniel d Oct 1866. A Tomb 73

Harriet E. w/o Daniel d 16 Dec 1826 ae: 25y. A Tomb 73

HOOLE, Hannah wid/o Capt.

HOOLE (continued)

William d 11 May 1830 ae: 76y. SB E:89

Huldah F. w/o Joseph d 2 May 1860 ae: 70y. A Tomb 38

Joseph d 9 Apr 1868 ae: 84y. A Tomb 38

Sarah d/o William & Hannah b 1794 d 12 Mar 1880. A Tomb 38

Capt. William d 21 May 1828 ae: 83y. SB E:88

HOOPER, Henry A. s/o James d 28 Sep 1846 ae: 22m. "Buried by side of Mrs. Robinson's grave near the fence." GSL

John s/o John K. d 16 May 1843 ae: 16y. GSL

Matilda H. d 4 Aug 1883 ae: 75y. "Buried in Gould tomb." GSL

Sarah W. b 29 Oct 1797 d 11 Dec 1878. SD C:26

William A. s/o John K. d 23 Mar 1843 ae: 18y. GSL

HOPE, Robert A. s/o Robert & Ann d 1802. Unusual stone. I:25

William I. s/o Robert & Ann d 1806. Unusual stone. I:25

HOPKINS, Dorcas w/o James D. d/o Daniel & Lydia Tucker d 17 June 1816 ae: 29y. F:17

Elizabeth d 4 June 1849 ae: 74y. SBE I:52

James D. d 17 June 1840 ae: 68y. F:16

Louisa H. d 27 Oct 1848 ae: 52y. F:15

Mary w/o James D. d/o John & Mary Bagley d 9 Mar 1802 ae: 24y. F:17

HORR, Anna w/o John d 8 Nov 1849 ae: 74y. GSL

HORTON, Abigail d 23 Sep 1871 ae: 99y 4m. SD K:179

Isabella W. d/o Rufus & Abigail d 18 Sep 1836 ae: 24y. SD K:178

Judith d/o Rev. Jothan & Judith b 21 Feb 1832 d 15 Mar 1832. SD I:135

Rufus d 6 Sep 1840 ae: 81y.

HORTON (continued)

Revolutionary War. SD K:180

HOSSACK, Charles d 9 Oct 1807 ae: 52y. Revolutionary War. SBE J:98

Elijah s/o Charles & Elizabeth d Sep 1818 ae: 30y. SBE J:98

Elizabeth w/o Charles d 2 May 1805 ae: 45y. SBE J:98

HOVEY, Capt. Aaron d 2 Feb 1816 ae: 45y. I:165

Eunice b 16 Aug 1790 d 14 Feb 1858. I:161

Deliverance wid/o Samuel d 18 Sep 1835 ae: 75y. SD I:166

Jane w/o Thomas b 2 Nov 1772 d 20 Oct 1799. SBE C:103

Margaret b 2 Sep 1792 d 20 Apr 1852. I:163

Nathaniel d 12 June 1821 ae: 26y. I:162

Samuel d 13 Sep 1822 ae: 65y. SD I:164

Sophia w/o Thomas d 24 Mar 1832 ae: 56y. SD C:101

Thomas s/o Thomas & Jane b 12 Apr 1799 d 19 Oct 1799. SBE C:103

Thomas d 13 Mar 1830 ae: 68y. SBE C:102

HOW, Abigail w/o Daniel d 6 Sep 1837 ae: 68y. A Tomb 71

Daniel d 16 Sep 1819 ae: 57y. A Tomb 71

Daniel Jr. b 1795 d 18 May 1847. A Tomb 71

Eliza w/o Daniel Jr. d 18 Feb 1874 ae: 80y. A Tomb 71

Harriet E. d/o Daniel b 1825 d 21 Sep 1843. A Tomb 71

John d 26 Jan 1859 ae: 66y. A Tomb 71

Joseph d 1 Aug 1820 ae: 29y. A Tomb 71

Joseph b 1820 d 1870. A Tomb 71

Leonard Gates s/o John & Susan d 11 Apr 1829 ae: 6y. A Tomb 71

Maria W. b 1830 d 1836. A Tomb 71

Sarah T. b 1829 d 1844. A Tomb

71
Woodbury s/o Nathan d 18 Oct 1843 ae: 17y. "Buried by side of C. French's stone." GSL

HOWARD, Willie F. s/o Edward B. d 23 Dec 1859 ae: 3m. GSL

HOWE, Abba Eliza w/o William d 17 Oct 1847 ae: 28y. "Died in Lowell, Massachusetts." A Tomb 53

George d 11 July 1844 ae: 41y. A Tomb 9

George M. d 3 Mar 1887 ae: 64y. F:105 Tomb

Hattie L. d/o John M. d 3 Oct 1861. GSL

John T. s/o John M. d 23 Sep 1861 ae: 2y. GSL

Mary w/o Edward d 11 Sep 1810 ae: 28y. F:105 Tomb

Mary w/o Lysander d 27 Oct 1845 ae: 39y. GSL

Mary T. d 16 Sep 1810 ae: 7w. F:105 Tomb

Nathan d 14 Jan 1859 ae: 78y. GSL

S. w/o Edward d 19 May 1864 ae: 74y. F:105 Tomb

HOWELL, Emily d/o Benjamin & Rebecca d 19 July 1840 ae: 30y. A-1-22

Loruhamah w/o Silas d 7 Jan 1811 ae: 60y. J:67

Mary R. d/o Benjamin & Rebecca d 4 Nov 1838 ae: 22y. SB A-1-21

Rebecca w/o Capt. Benjamin d 22 Feb 1835 ae: 44y. SB A-1-20

Silas d 7 May 1846 ae: 101y. "Buried beside his wife." NS J:67

HOYT, Albert s/o William d 15 Nov 1857 ae: 7y 10m. GSL

Mrs. Eliza d 25 Apr 1860 ae: 57y. GSL

Harriet M. wid/o Joseph A. d 25 Jan 1896 ae: 77y 1m. SD A-18-6

Jane w/o Reuben d 5 June 1869 ae: 61y. A-14-7

Joseph A. d 30 July 1853 ae: 41y. SB A-18-6

Lemuel T. s/o Reuben & Jane d 1 Apr 1865 ae: 26y. Civil War: 16th Reg. Maine Inf., Co. H. SBE A-14-8

Mehitable wid/o William d 19 Feb 1849 ae: 70y. GSL

Reuben d 13 Sep 1885 ae: 84y. SBE A-14-6

William F. s/o Reuben & Jane d 20 Apr 1849 ae: 13y. SBE A-14-9

HUBBS, Capt. Daniel G. d 10 Apr 1827 ae: 31y. I:1

Frances d/o Moses & Mary L. d 24 Oct 1823 ae: 2y 7m. K:50

Lucy Gage wid/o Alexander d 10 Nov 1844 ae: 88y. A-8-6

HUDSON, Daniel D. s/o John B. & Harriet b 29 July 1823 d 20 Jan 1824. SD K:38

Harriet w/o Benjamin b 21 Oct 1790 d 23 May 1849. SBE C:65

Joseph s/o Joseph d 24 Oct 1842 ae: 16y. GSL

HUGHES, William H. s/o Henry d 28 June 1857 ae: 3y 5m. Black. GSL

William M. d 18 Sep 1859 ae: 1m 7d. Black. GSL

HUMPHREY, Ebenezer d 25 Dec 1807 ae: 45y. I:171

Hannah d 8 June 1883 ae: 85y. SD B-4-5

Lucinda w/o Milo d 14 Dec 1852 ae: 29y. "Died in Boston." GSL

Octavius D. s/o A. M. & Caroline d 13 Sep 1824 ae: 1y 4d. SBE F:11

Olive H. d/o A. M. & Caroline d 16 Apr 1827 ae: 1y 4m 17d. SBE F:11

HUMPHRIES, Maria d/o Archibald b Feb 1798 d 31 July 1863. SBE A-10-8

Mary wid/o Archibald b Feb 1776 d 14 Oct 1860. "Born Armagh, Ireland." A-10-8

HUNKINS, Dr. Seth d 15 May 1867. Mmt & ledger. A Tomb 50

HUNNEWELL, Abba d 17 Mar 1844 ae: 82y. Widow. ME A Tomb 76

HUNNEWILL, Lucy d/o Elijah d 27 Nov 1813 ae: 29y. "...of Windham." I:118

HUNT, Virginia E. d/o Woodman & Eunice d 21 Aug 1846 ae: 6y 6m. SBE B-5-16

HUNTLEY, Gertie d/o J. W. d 3 May 1886 ae: 2y. A Tomb 1

HUNTRESS, Anna w/o James d 3 Mar 1861 ae: 71y. SD I:207

Frederick C. d 23 Dec 1839 ae: 34y. A-1-4

James d 3 Sep 1821 ae: 35y. SD I:207

Mary E. d/o Silas B. & S. J. nd. SD B-9-10

HURD, William s/o George d 16 Apr 1842 ae: 10m. GSL

HURDY, William s/o John d 29 Aug 1852 ae: 8m. GSL

HUSE, Emeline d/o James & Lydia L. b 17 Oct 1804 d 7 Oct 1843. MD A-15-9

Harry Pennell s/o William d 27 Jan 1862 ae: 1y 7m. GSL

James b 19 Sep 1779 d 9 Jan 1864. MD A-15-9

James b 30 Sep 1808 d 9 Aug 1827. MD A-15-9

Lydia E. d/o William d 14 Oct 1856 ae: 18y. "Buried beside mother's grave." NS J:119

Lydia Lowell w/o James b 24 June 1779 d 16 May 1858. MD A-15-9

Lydia L. b 16 Aug 1806 d 23 Oct 1834. MD A-15-9

Mary Jane w/o William b 6 Nov 1815 d 7 Oct 1852. SB J:119

Mary L. d/o William & Mary J. b 4 Mar 1837 d 20 Sep 1837. J:118B

HUSSEY, Amanda d/o Henry d 24 June 1852 ae: 17y. GSL

Amos d 14 Mar 1846 ae: 40y. "...of Rhode Island." Black.

HUSSEY (continued)
GSL

Erastus B. d 17 Apr 1864 ae: 28y. A-15-11

Frederick d 11 June 1854 ae: 23y. GSL

Henry d 27 May 1844 ae: 59y. SBE A-15-13

Miriam d/o Samuel F. & Thankful d 4 Dec 1844 ae: 54y. "Buried Friends' Ground." SB K:176

Samuel F. d 1837. "Friends' Ground." SB K:174

Sarah wid/o Henry d 27 Feb 1845 ae: 49y. SBE A-15-12

Thankful wid/o Samuel F. d 25 Mar 1851 ae: 92y. "Friends' Ground." SBE K:175

HUSTON, Abigail w/o Samuel d 15 June 1841 ae: 30y. GSL

Annie M. d/o William Blake d 29 Jan 1894 ae: 76y 5m. GSL

Charles A. s/o Paul & Delphina P. d 15 Feb 1851 ae: 1y 11m. SBE A-13-18

Charles W. s/o Paul d 15 Jan 1851 ae: 20m. GSL

Delphina d/o Alden Crooker d 26 Aug 1895 ae: 75y 6m. SD A-13-16

Dora Louisa d/o Paul & Delphina P. d 7 Sep 1899 ae: 48y 7m. A-13-17

Frank E. s/o Paul & Delphina P. d 21 June 1868 ae: 7y 3m. A-13-17A

George F. s/o Paul & Delphina P. d 19 Dec 1850 ae: 4y 2m. SBE A-13-19

Mrs. Nancy d 3 Mar 1846 ae: 89y. A Tomb 62

Paul d 18 Nov 1871 ae: 66y 3m 28d. SBE A-13-16

Mary d 2 Mar 1848 ae: 64y. Widow. GSL

HUTCHINS, Albert J. d 25 Sep 1909 ae: 65y 11m 19d. NS A-10-26

Annie R. w/o Samuel d 30 Apr 1865 ae: 83y. SBE A-10-25

Caroline Augusta d/o Lewis S. d

HUTCHINS (continued)
6 Sep 1841 ae: 3w. SBE A-10-24

Benjamin d 26 July 1828 ae: 22y. "Drowned at Peaks Island." SBE A-10-23

Caroline F. d/o Seth C. d 6 Sep 1858 ae: 7m 18d. GSL

Horace s/o Lewis C. & Louisa C. d 28 Sep 1842 ae: 8w. SBE A-10-24

John s/o Joseph B. d 4 Sep 1864 ae: 2m 15d. GSL

John C. s/o Lewis S. & Louisa C. d 31 Jan 1859 ae: 4y 11m. SBE A-10-24

Lewis S. d 5 May 1900 ae: 84y 9m 2d. NS A-10-26

Louisa Corey w/o Lewis S. d 16 Aug 1872 ae: 56y. SBE A-10-26

Nathaniel R. s/o Lewis S. & Louisa C. d 18 Nov 1827 ae: 17y. SBE A-10-23

Sarah B. wid/o Lewis S. d 30 June 1913 ae: 81y. SD A-10-24

Selden M. s/o James d 26 Dec 1847 ae: 6m. GSL

HUTCHINSON, Charles s/o Stephen & Susan d 27 May 1831 ae: 6m. SB C:71

William d 15 Apr 1820. Revolutionary War. GSL

ILSLEY, ch/o Isaac & Augusta d Sep 1807 ae: 3y. A Tomb 77

Mrs. Abigail d 11 Apr 1842 ae: 88y. SB C:204

Ann M. d/o Nathaniel & Judith d 22 May 1826 ae: 14m. B-9-20

Augusta w/o Isaac d 31 Sep 1851 ae: 76y. A Tomb 77

Deacon Benjamin J. b 11 Aug 1772 d 21 June 1856. A Tomb 72

Benjamin Jr. b 10 Jan 1795 d 8 June 1880. A Tomb 72

Betsy w/o Nathan d 21 Feb 1846 ae: 43y. A Tomb 72

Betsy D. wid/o Deacon Benjamin J. b 1 June 1774 d 18 Nov 1859. A Tomb 72

ILSLEY (continued)
Caleb s/o Benjamin & Betsy D. d 28 Aug 1817 ae: 17d. A Tomb 72

Caroline d/o Parker & Phebe d 6 Jan 1822 ae: 24y. J:125

Caroline d/o Nathan & Betsy d 1 Sep 1840 ae: 15y. A Tomb 72

Charles s/o Parker & Phebe nd. J:125

Charles P. s/o Charles & Phebe nd. J:125

Charlotte A. d/o Isaac & Augusta d 8 Oct 1819 ae: 16y. A Tomb 77

Daniel d 10 May 1813 ae: 73y. Revolutionary War: Maj., Massachusetts Milita, Muster Master. C:234

Daniel d 26 Sep 1889 ae: 76y. A Tomb 86

Edner R. d/o Benjamin & Nancy d 2 July 1826 ae: 19m. A Tomb 72

Elizabeth d/o Nathan & Betsy d 1 Sep 1840 ae: 13y. A Tomb 72

Ellen M. d/o Jeremiah d 29 Nov 1866 ae: 2m. GSL

Enoch d 10 Nov 1811 ae: 81y. Rev/War. SBE C:203

Frances d/o Frederick d 16 Apr 1842 ae: 3y 3m. "Buried in Arthur Mack tomb." GSL

Grace E. d/o Jeremiah d 28 Sep 1875 ae: 13y. A Tomb 72

Harriet d/o Hosea & Lucy d 20 Sep 1788 ae: 19m. J:129

Henry S. s/o Henry d 25 June 1847 ae: 27y. A Tomb 72

Hosea d 18 Sep 1826 ae: 63y. B-4-25

Isaac d 15 Apr 1781 ae: 78y. GSL

Isaac d 17 Oct 1853 ae: 89y. A Tomb 77

Isaac s/o Benjamin & Betsy D. b 1804 d 28 May 1856. A Tomb 72

Isabella w/o Ferdinand I. d 17 Sep 1837 ae: 34y. SBE I:12

James C. s/o Joseph & Sally N.

ILSLEY (continued)

d 10 July 1812 ae: 15y. A Tomb 72

Jane w/o Robert d 26 Jan 1817 ae: 44y. A Tomb 79

Joseph s/o Joseph & Sally N. d 20 Aug 1805 ae: 10y. A Tomb 72

Joseph b 1770 d 11 Nov 1819. A Tomb 72

Joseph b 1806 d 1886. A Tomb 72

Judith w/o Nathaniel d 11 Aug 1854 ae: 69y. SBE I:11

Leonard s/o Benjamin Jr. & Nancy C. b 1829 d 26 July 1875. A Tomb 72

Rev. Leonard d 7 July 1903 ae: 84y 6m 28d. "Died Seguin, Texas." A Tomb 72

Lucy d 6 Oct 1878. "Died of old age." GSL

Lucy wid/o Hosea d 23 May 1838 ae: 73y. B-4-24

Luther s/o Benjamin Jr. & Nancy C. b 1822 d 1 Apr 1852. A Tomb 72

Mary w/o Daniel d 10 Aug 1812 ae: 71y. C:235

Mary M. d/o Charles & Phebe nd. J:125

Matilda L. w/o Francis L. d 11 May 1829 ae: 26y. SBE D:62

Moses s/o Charles & Phebe nd. J:125

Nancy Clough w/o Benjamin Jr. b 1797 d 3 Dec 1859. A Tomb 72

Nathan b 1800 d 19 Oct 1870. A Tomb 72

Nathaniel b 10 Mar 1781 d 19 Oct 1870. SBE I:10

Robert d 9 Apr 1823 ae: 55y. A Tomb 77

Rovena d/o Charles & Phebe d 23 Dec 1820 ae: 13y. J:125

Sally N. wid/o Joseph b 1771 d 1825. A Tomb 72

Sarah I. w/o Joseph d 31 Dec 1849 ae: 33y. A Tomb 72

Rev. Silas b 1809 d 1886. A Tomb 72

ILSLEY (continued)

Sarah d 1 May 1846 ae: 86y. A Tomb 35

William s/o Daniel & Mary d Sep 1806 ae: 37y. C:236

William d 9 Apr 1873 ae: 66y. GSL

INGERSOLL, Ann d/o Isaac d 18 Oct 1843 ae: 2y 6m. GSL

Lydia d/o Josiah d 28 May 1804 ae: 14y. SD J:95

Mary w/o Benjamin d 10 May 1733 ae: 42y 4m. D:81

INGRAHAM, Abigail Milk w/o Joseph H. d 17 May 1785. E:6 Tomb

Ann B. d/o George T. d 22 July 1848 ae: 18y 8m. E:6 Tomb

Ann Tate w/o Joseph H. d 25 Mar 1844 ae: 77y. E:6 Tomb

Edward s/o Joseph H. & Abigail d 30 June 1777 ae: 19m. E:6 Tomb

Edward s/o Joseph H. & Abigail d 17 Aug 1779 ae: 17m. E:6 Tomb

Eleanor d/o Amy d 13 May 1904 ae: 3y 4m. E:6 Tomb

Eliza d 13 Mar 1880 ae: 88y. E:6 Tomb

Frances E. d/o Thomas & Mary d 1 Sep 1840 ae: 16y. "Drowned in Casco Bay." A-13-13

George C. s/o George W. d 21 Mar 1851 ae: 1y. GSL

George T. d 30 Dec 1875 ae: 80y. E:6 Tomb

George T. s/o George T. & Martha d 4 Sep 1911 ae: 76y. E:6 Tomb

James M. d 2 June 1856 ae: 75y. "Died Biddeford, Maine." E:6 Tomb

Joseph H. d 11 Feb 1818. E:6 Tomb

Joseph H. d 3 Nov 1841 ae: 90y. E:6 Tomb

Julia A. P. d/o James R. d 22 Mar 1847 ae: 22y. E:6 Tomb

Martha wid/o George T. d 2 May 1890 ae: 88y 2m. E:6 Tomb

Mary d/o Thomas & Mary d 14

INGRAHAM (continued)

Apr 1827 ae: 5y. SB I:70

Mary wid/o Thomas d 4 Aug 1877 ae: 77y 4m. SBE A-13-12

Mary Adams wid/o Samuel Parkman b 15 Oct 1798 d 4 Feb 1876. E:6 Tomb

Mary C. d/o Thomas & Mary d 16 Aug 1847 ae: 16y. A-13-14

Mary K. wid/o William d 12 Jan 1867 ae: 71y. GSL

Philip H. s/o Edward d 1 Sep 1853 ae: 22y 7m. E:6 Tomb

Samuel Parkman s/o Joseph Holt & Ann Tate b 22 Nov 1796 d 25 June 1863. E:6 Tomb

Sarah w/o William d 24 Sep 1803 ae: 40y. F:57

Sarah A. w/o William H. d 29 Aug 1856 ae: 38y. GSL

INGALLS, John C. s/o Nathaniel d 31 Aug 1854 ae: 10m. GSL

IRISH, John Hamlin d 23 May 1847 ae: 32y. GSL

JACK, Bella R. d/o Benjamin & Sarah Bell w/o William B. d 18 Dec 1859 ae: 25y. B-13-9

JACKSON, Adaline w/o Valentine d 12 Oct 1858 ae: 17y 7m. "Buried in Jacob Riggs' lot." GSL

Ann d 19 Dec 1845 ae: 60y. Black. GSL

Frances E. d/o John M. d 11 Aug 1893 ae: 2y 20m. GSL

Frederick s/o William d 12 Apr 1864 ae: 3w. GSL

Josephine Foster d/o Alden d 6 Sep 1845 ae: 22m. GSL

Marcus Quincy s/o Alden & Mehitable Q. d 31 May 1828 ae: 23m 26d. K:159

Mary d/o Alden d 20 Sep 1843 ae: 2y. GSL

Rachel d 30 Nov 1848 ae: 77y. Black. GSL

JACOBS, Abigail B. w/o Elias d 19 Mar 1853 ae: 68y. B-11-17

Elias d 11 Nov 1828 ae: 44y. B-11-19

JAMES, Catherine d/o Robert d

JAMES (continued)

20 Aug 1852 ae: 7m. Catholic. GSL

JAMESON, Mrs. Ann d 3 June 1847 ae: 69y. "Buried John Anderson tomb." A Tomb 68

James d 16 Mar 1850 ae: 31y. "Died at Marine Hospital." GSL

William C. s/o Capt. J. & Jane b 16 Jan 1808 d 23 Sep 1810. G:29

JENKINS, Rev. Charles b Barre, Massachusetts 28 Aug 1786 d Portland, Maine 29 Dec 1831. "Installed Pastor of Third Congregational Church, Portland 9 Nov 1825." Mmt between A Tomb 82 & A Tomb 83. A:87

Deborah wid/o Isaac d 12 Jan 1854 ae: 72y. GSL

JENKS, John d Dec 1858 ae: 32y. GSL

Nancy d/o William d 23 Oct 1859 ae: 71y. SBE F:148

Deacon William nd. "...and family." Revolutionary War. F:149

JERRIS, Abigail w/o Peter d 16 Nov 1860 ae: 65y 7m. GSL

Angie w/o William H. d 9 Feb 1862 ae: 33y. GSL

Ansel Curtis s/o William H. d 26 Apr 1862 ae: 2m 17d. GSL

Catherine d/o William H. d 5 Sep 1849 ae: 3m. GSL

Charles Freeman s/o William H. d 18 Aug 1857 ae: 9m 20d. GSL

Ellen d/o William H. d 1 Aug 1855 ae: 1y 5m 20d. GSL

Peter d 20 Aug 1855 ae: 76y. "Buried in Wm. Jerris' lot." GSL

JEWELL, Frances S. w/o Ezra d 29 Oct 1839 ae: 26y. A-11-13

JEWETT, Eleanor d/o James & Ruby d 12 Sep 1806 ae: 13m. SB H:185

Franklin H. s/o Jedediah d 15 Feb 1850 ae: 19m. F:96 Tomb

JEWETT (continued)

Hamilton Parker s/o Jedediah d 27 May 1859 ae: 8y. F:96 Tomb

Deacon James b 28 May 1758 d 16 Sep 1843. "Born in Newburyport, Massachusetts." SBE A-19-3

Jedediah d 10 Oct 1863 ae: 56y. Mayor - Portland. F:96 Tomb

Louisa A. w/o Albert d 18 May 1839 ae: 30y. SBE A-10-22

Polly d 1799. SB H:183

Ruby B. w/o Deacon James d 31 Dec 1850 ae: 79y 8m. SBE A-19-4

Ruth d 8 May 1848 ae: 91y 10m. Widow. A Tomb 77

JOHNSON, Theodore d 6 Sep 1860 ae: 3d. GSL

Amelia w/o Samuel d 11 July 1857 ae: 64y. A Tomb 8

Caleb d 12 Apr 1806 ae: 26y. K:85B

Caleb d 5 July 1852 ae: 80y. Black. GSL

Caroline A. d 27 Mar 1901 ae: 21y 9m. "Died Waltham, Massachusetts." GSL

Charles s/o Isaac d 23 June 1850 ae: 3m. Black. GSL

Charles F. s/o Peter & Sally M. d 25 Jan 1849 ae: 11y. SBE A-14-12

Charles H. s/o John H. d 20 Jan 1883 ae: 3y. "Buried Gould tomb." GSL

Charlotte Brown d/o Peter d 3 Apr 1850 ae: 18m. Black. GSL

Daniel M. s/o Peter & Sally M. d 27 June 1854 ae: 19y. SBE A-14-12

Edward s/o Daniel & Mary G. d 4 Nov 1805 ae: 14m 12d. K:34

Elizabeth A. d/o Peter & Sarah d 17 Oct 1840 ae: 10y. A-14-10

Elizabeth D. d 2 Dec 1837 ae: 42y. I:96

Frederick s/o Daniel & Mary G. nd. SB K:33

George K. d 15 Oct 1847 ae: 5y. GSL

JOHNSON (continued)

Horatio s/o Daniel & Mary G. nd. SB K:33

Isaac d 17 Apr 1863 ae: 69y. Black. GSL

Isabella P. d 8 July 1898 ae: 74y 7m. GSL

Israel d 14 June 1854. "...of New York." GSL

John d 20 Nov 1853 ae: 45y. "Died Marine Hospital." GSL

John s/o Elbridge d 5 Nov 1841 ae: 6y. GSL

John s/o Isaac d 4 June 1842 ae: 2y 10m. Black. GSL

John M. d 8 July 1848 ae: 26y. "Died Charlestown, Massachusetts." Black. GSL

Josie M. d/o Joseph & Johanna Mason, w/o Samuel d 8 Oct 1913 ae: 65y 6m 28d. "Died Yarmouth, Maine." A Tomb 8

Leonard s/o Leonard d 14 Oct 1841 ae: 2y. GSL

Lorenzo F. s/o Peter & Sarah d 14 Sep 1843 ae: 16m. A-14-11

Lucy d/o Daniel & Mary G. nd. SB K:33

Mrs. Lydia d 21 Aug 1860 ae: 79y. Black. GSL

Mary d 22 Feb 1866 ae: 83y. A Tomb 72

Mary C. d/o Isaac d 26 Dec 1847 ae: 9y. Black. GSL

Mary J. d/o Thomas d 29 May 1854 ae: 9y. GSL

Moses s/o Samuel & R. d 5 Oct 1773 ae: 22y 7m 24d. Unusual inscription. D:107

Peter d 4 Apr 1853 ae: 80y. Black. GSL

Samuel d 3 May 1825 ae: 38y. B-1-17

Sarah w/o Andrew d 1 Nov 1868 ae: 78y 5m. SB C:142

Sarah A. d 5 May 1857 ae: 94y. "Buried side of Dorcas Beeman's grave." NS I:55

Sarah N. d 5 May 1757 ae: 93y. SD F:111

W. d 26 Dec 1849 ae: 26y. Black. GSL

JOICE, Clarissa Eliza d/o William F. & Sarah d 29 Jan 1844 ae: 18y. SBE A-8-20

Sarah wid/o William F. d 8 Nov 1868 ae: 74y 8m. SB A-8-23

Sarah J. d/o William P. d 8 July 1858 ae: 35y. SBE A-8-24

Sarah Jane d 2 Sep 1820 ae: 2y. SBE A-8-20

William F. d 26 Mar 1850 ae: 58y. SB A-8-22

William J. s/o William F. & Sarah d 4 Jan 1848 ae: 27y. SB A-8-21

JONES, Abigail d 23 Nov 1853 ae: 81y. "Buried 6' from Prince Shapley's grave." Black. GSL

Albert H. s/o Bartholomew d 22 Feb 1849 ae: 5m. GSL

David s/o Capt. David & Elizabeth d 30 Aug 1891 ae: 63y. NS D:102C

Capt. David d 19 July 1860 ae: 74y. SD D:102A

Dorcas wid/o John d 10 Jan 1850 ae: 79y. GSL

Elizabeth wid/o Capt. David d 28 Aug 1885 ae: 88y 10m. SD D:102B

Elizabeth D. d/o Bartholomew & Mary d 14 Sep 1834 ae: 15m. SBE G:50

Elizabeth S. d/o William J. d 16 Mar 1849 ae: 6m. Black. GSL

Elizabeth T. d/o William J. d 4 Aug 1848 ae: 2y. Black. GSL

Ephraim d 16 Dec 1785 ae: 71y. C:207

Esther w/o William d 7 Apr 1860 ae: 30y. "Buried beside Nathaniel Aiken's grave." GSL

Frances d/o Pearson & Betsy d 26 Sep 1774 ae: 1m 9d. C:190

Hannah w/o Jonas d 29 May 1749 ae: 27y. GSL

Harriet P. d/o William J. & Mary E. d 25 Oct 1846 ae: 8m. Black. A-10-29

Helen d/o Henry d 8 Feb 1844 ae: 4y 6m. "Buried beside his stone." GSL

Henrietta T. d/o Henry A. &

JONES (continued)

Eliza L. d 25 Jan 1838 ae: 6y. J:127

Hodassah w/o S. P. d 7 May 1855 ae: 28y 5m. GSL

Isaac s/o William d 6 Apr 1850 ae: 12d. GSL

James d 14 Oct 1834 ae: 33y. "Formerly of England." I:42

James C. s/o Bartholomew & Mary d 3 Jan 1832 ae: 5m. SBE G:50

Josiah s/o Josiah E. d 28 Feb 1847 ae: 1y 8m. Black. SD A-7-26

Levi d 3 Dec 1850 ae: 45y. Black. GSL

Louisa C. d/o Bartholomew & Mary d 11 May 1830 ae: 3w. SBE G:50

Mary d/o Pearson & Betsy d 22 Sep 1773 ae: 11m. C:189

Mary w/o Ephraim d 19 Sep 1775 ae: 55y. C:206

Mary w/o Capt. John d 26 Apr 1795 ae: 32y 6m. SD K:170

Mary w/o Rowland d 21 Jan 1819 ae: 50y. H:177

Mary w/o Bartholomew d 2 Nov 1842 ae: 43y. SB G:51

Mary F. d/o Bartholomew & Mary d 26 Mar 1851 ae: 25y. SB G:52

Pearson d Jan 1781 ae: 32y. GSL

Phebe A. d/o William H. & Annett G. d 22 Feb 1847 ae: 3y. Black. A-11-21

Phineas d 5 Nov 1743 ae: 39y. F:139

Rebecca Louisa d/o William H. d 30 Mar 1850 ae: 17m 7d. Black. GSL

Rhoda d 5 Apr 1859 ae: 55y. GSL

Ruth C. d/o William H. & Annett G. d 26 Sep 1842 ae: 17m. Black. A-11-21

Samuel A. s/o William H. d 16 Apr 1855 ae: 12y. Black. GSL

Sarah d/o S. P. buried 24 July 1855 ae: 1y. "Died East Cambridge, Massachusetts." GSL

William s/o William H. d 27

JONES (continued)
Sep 1841 ae: 2 1/2y. Black.
GSL
William D. s/o William d 2 Aug
1851 ae: 15m. Black. GSL
William H. s/o Allinson d 14
Dec 1846 ae: 2y 5m. Black.
GSL
William J. s/o William J. &
Mary E. d 15 Apr 1848 ae: 18d.
Black. SBE A-10-29
JORDAN, ---- d/o Josiah d 13
Aug 1855 ae: 8w. "Buried in
David Chandler's lot." GSL
Abigail #2 w/o James d 10 Feb
1791 ae: 38y. J:7
Edward s/o James d 23 Feb 1868
ae: 67y 7m. GSL
Eliza d 10 Nov 1882 ae: 82y. A
Tomb 40
Frances wid/o Morgan d 3 Jan
1860 ae: 63y. A Tomb 77
George Montgomery s/o Asa &
Mercy d 12 May 1851 ae: 10m
10d. K:89
Harriet Ann d/o David R. &
Joanna W. d 5 Dec 1854 ae:
2y. "Buried in mother's
grave." A Tomb 52
James s/o James & Mary d 16
Sep 1791 ae: 4y. J:11
James d 8 Sep 1820 ae: 67y.
Revolutionary War: Cpl. J:12
Joanna W. w/o David R. d 10
Sep 1854 ae: 37y. A Tomb 52
Joanna wid/o Lemuel d 16 Dec
1855 ae: 78y. C:58
Luther d 7 Nov 1827 ae: 40y. B-
5-36
Lydia d/o James & Abigail d 21
Dec 1790 ae: 9m. J:8
Lydia d 5 Aug 1854 ae: 84y. GSL
Lydia Barnes wid/o James d 5
Aug 1854 ae: 85y. SB J:12
Margaret w/o Luther d 15 Mar
1827 ae: 46y. B-5-37
Mary #1 w/o James d 3 Sep 1788
ae: 33y. SD J:10
Mary E. d/o William & Tamson
d 15 Aug 1853 ae: 5y. SBE
J:197
Mary T. d/o William, 2nd d 15

JORDAN (continued)
Sep 1847 ae: 3w. GSL
Nancy Hunnewell d/o Asa &
Theodotia d 31 Oct 1819 ae:
11y. K:88
Orren d 12 Sep 1843 ae: 20y. A
Tomb 40
Rebecca C. w/o Josiah d 15 May
1856 ae: 28y. GSL
Sarah w/o David d 12 Apr 1836
ae: 63y. B-5-35
Susannah d/o James & Mary d 31
Aug 1790 ae: 10y. J:9
William d 19 Sep 1843 ae: 75y.
A Tomb 39
William C. s/o Josiah d 3 Jan
1857 ae: 6y. GSL
JOY, Benjamin d 4 July 1824 ae:
34y. SBE K:83
Loice w/o Benjamin d 1 July
1827 ae: 40y. SBE K:83
JUNKINS, Deborah w/o Isaac d 11
Jan 1851 ae: 71y. SBE G:57
Hannah d/o Isaac & Deborah d 6
June 1821 ae: 14y. SBE G:58
Isaac d 23 Oct 1824 ae: 44y.
SBE G:60
James d 28 Feb 1842 ae: 37y.
G:59
Samuel d 13 June 1826 ae: 27y.
B-6-22
KEATING, Mary d 9 Dec 1841 ae:
48y. GSL
KELLERAN, Capt. Edward d 5
Oct 1846 ae: 69y. A-9-15
Edward Jr. d 29 Mar 1838 ae: 11y
5m. A-9-12
Lucy Reed w/o Edward d 16 Apr
1843 ae: 63y. A-9-14
Mary P. d 12 July 1817 ae: 7w.
SBE A-9-13
KELLEY, Amelia C. d/o Samuel
& Mary d 18 Sep 1829 ae: 5m.
A-24-5
James Harrison s/o Joseph L. &
Elizabeth S. d 20 Apr 1833 ae:
4y. A-24-7
Joseph C. s/o Samuel & Mary d
29 Jan 1828 ae: 3y 2m. A-24-5
Richard A. d 28 Oct 1828 ae:
20y. B-9-27
Samuel d 6 Apr 1829 ae: 41y.

KELLEY (continued)
"For several years the/
Teacher of one of the/Moni-
torial Schools in/this town."
A-24-6

KELLY, Dennis s/o John d 16
Jan 1849 ae: 3m. GSL

John s/o John d 23 June 1848 ae:
6y. "Buried at foot of Mary
Barbour's grave." Catholic.
GSL

Lucy d/o John d 5 Nov 1850 ae:
4y. Catholic. GSL

Mary w/o George d 30 Nov 1842
ae: 24y. GSL

Capt. Richard d 23 Jan 1810 ae:
30y. C:84

KELSEY, Martha w/o Samuel d
16 Aug 1837 ae: 37y. SB B-
10-8

Samuel d 6 June 1848 ae: 46y.
SB B-10-8

Samuel R. s/o Samuel & Martha
d 4 Mar 1853 ae: 24y. SB B-
10-8

KEMP, Henry d 18 May 1858 ae:
40y. "Native of St. Johns,
New Brunswick." "Died on
board the steamer *Admiral*."
GSL

KENDALL, Asaph d 2 Oct 1851
ae: 84y. GSL

George H. d 31 Dec 1842 ae: 29y.
A-19-12

Hannah wid/o Asaph d 3 Dec
1853 ae: 75y. GSL

KENNARD, Adelaide A. d/o R.
W. d 15 Aug 1850 ae: 7m.
GSL

Adelaide M. d/o Richard W. d 26
Apr 1846 ae: 6d. GSL

KENNEY, William A. s/o George
d 31 Oct 1856 ae: 7y 4m. NS
B-8-34

KENSEY, James d 19 Nov 1856
ae: 50y. "Died in the Watch
House." GSL

KENT, Benjamin s/o John &
Mary d 17 Oct 1775 ae: 17m.
C:22

Charles Edward s/o Reuben Jr. d
10 July 1847 ae: 3y 6m. GSL

KENT (continued)
Ellen d/o Reuben Jr. d 4 July
1847 ae: 1y. GSL

John d 22 Aug 1803 ae: 59y. C:20

Justin d 16 Apr 1850 ae: 82y. SB
A-12-7

Mary w/o John d 11 Apr 1803 ae:
58y. C:21

Lucy d/o Justin & Lucy d 27 Sep
1849 ae: 55y. SB A-12-8

Lucy w/o Justin d 13 Jan 1840
ae: 82y. SBE A-12-6

Rebecca d 23 Oct 1842 ae: 29y.
GSL

KEYES, Adelaine G. w/o Deane
W. d 28 Jan 1857. SB G:53

KIEL, Mary d/o James d 20 Aug
1858 ae: 3y 9m. GSL

KIMBALL, Achsah s/o David &
M. d 12 Nov 1828 ae: 24y 8m.
B-5-39

Alford D. s/o William C. d 29
Nov 1849 ae: 2y. GSL

Charles d 5 Jan 1862 ae: 71y. A
Tomb 52

Elizabeth Maria d/o John &
Nancy d 12 May 1816 ae: 6y.
L:31

Elizabeth P. d/o John & Nancy d
1 Apr 1809 ae: 9m. SD L:29

Francis s/o William C. d 13 Jan
1849 ae: 3m. "Buried beside
Moses Smith's grave." GSL

Georgianna A. d/o George R. d
18 Jan 1851 ae: 4m. A Tomb
21

Giles M. d 26 Sep 1805 ae: 20m.
SD J:193

Jennie A. d/o Jeremiah d 11 Apr
1864 ae: 15y 8m. GSL

Jeremiah d 16 Oct 1848 ae: 46y.
GSL

Jeremiah d 19 May 1849 ae: 29y.
GSL

Leando G. s/o George R. d 27
Jan 1851 ae: 5y. A Tomb 21

Lois d 19 Sep 1833 ae: 30y. SB
B-8-16

Lucy M. d/o Jotham d 11 Apr
1864 ae: 59y 10m. A Tomb 40

Mary w/o Jeremiah d 20 July
1852 ae: 57y. GSL

KIMBALL (continued)

Mehitable b 21 Sep 1823 d 9 July 1825. B-8-17

KINGSBURY, Harriet w/o John d 28 Nov 1871 ae: 61y. A Tomb 15

KINSMAN, Dr. Aaron d 11 May 1808 ae: 41y. SB H:143

Eleanor b 19 Aug 1804 d 5 Sep 1804. H:58

Eliza D. d/o Nathan K. b 21 Oct 1803 d 28 Aug 1804. H:58

KNAPP, Anthony d 4 Dec 1851 ae: 72y. GSL

Anthony d 11 Oct 1854 ae: 38y. GSL

Harriet E. w/o Jonathan M. d 22 Aug 1835 ae: 20y. SD I:59

Margaret A. w/o Anthony d 5 May 1847 ae: 32y. "Buried James Crie tomb." GSL

Samuel b 22 May 1835 d 2 Aug 1835. SD I:59

Sarah D. d/o Anthony & Dolly d 10 Feb 1824 ae: 9y. B-9-18

KNIGHT, Amelia d/o Capt. Benjamin & Mary b 17 Oct 1820 d 29 Oct 1820. A-2-10

Anthony s/o Anthony & Marcy d 14 Oct 1804 ae: 11m. F:124

Capt. Benjamin d 14 Dec 1860 ae: 81y. SB A-2-6

Benjamin s/o Capt. Benjamin & Mary b 25 Jan 181- d 4 Apr 181-. A-2-10

Benjamin d 12 Oct 1881 ae: 73y. A Tomb 41

Betsy d/o Benjamin & Mary b 6 Jan 1777 d 6 Oct 1786. F:106

Betsy d/o Benjamin & Mary b 29 June 1792 d 17 Dec 1810. SD F:112

Caroline d/o W. H. d 7 Feb 1844 ae: 3m. GSL

Charles s/o Anthony & Marcy d 22 Aug 1802 ae: 3m. F:124

Charles W. s/o Robert H. & Sarah d 29 Mar 1847 ae: 5y 3m. SD A-2-13

Charles W. s/o William H. d 5 May 1847 ae: 5m. "Buried at foot of William Knight's

KNIGHT (continued)

grave." GSL

Daniel O. K. s/o late J. d 4 Nov 1857 ae: 19m 28d. "Buried in grave with his father." GSL

Edward s/o Jonathan & Roseanna d 21 Nov 1826 ae: 13m. B-1-34

Edward d 19 Dec 1847 ae: 45y. A Tomb 82

Edward L. s/o Stephen d 3 Oct 1847 ae: 9w. GSL

Elizabeth d 26 Jan 1857 ae: 25y. "Buried NW side of Matthew Finley's grave." GSL

Elizabeth w/o Reuben b 22 Oct 1791 d 9 May 1876. SBE A-19-16

Elizabeth A. d/o William & Emily d 21 Aug 1864 ae: 40y. SBE B-3-29

Emily w/o William d 9 Feb 1850 ae: 50y. SBE B-3-27

Emily C. d/o William & Emily d 12 May 1833 ae: 11y. B-3-28

Eunice M. d/o Reuben & Elizabeth d 18 Feb 1843 ae: 22y. SBE A-19-13

Fitz Henry s/o Capt. Isaac d 28 July 1858 ae: 21y. A Tomb 66

Frances P. d 16 Mar 1867 ae: 40y 8m. A-19-17

Fannie P. d/o Capt. Benjamin & Mary d 13 Oct 1858 ae: 35y. SB A-2-5

Frederick E. s/o Benjamin d 4 Nov 1857 ae: 9y. A Tomb 66

Frederick O. s/o Robert H. d 22 Aug 1845 ae: 1y. SD A-2-13

George s/o Robert d 29 Mar 1847 ae: 5y. GSL

Henry s/o Isaac d 31 Mar 1870 ae: 57y. Civil War: USN. A Tomb 66

Henry H. s/o Henry & Sarah d 29 Dec 1887 ae: 35y. A Tomb 66

Isaac d 29 Jan 1761 ae: 45y. SD C:231

Isaac s/o Benjamin & Mary b 16 Feb 1786 d 6 Dec 1787. SB F:107

Capt. Isaac d 10 May 1846 ae:

58y 5m. A Tomb 66

Capt. Jacob Jr. d 3 Feb 1821 ae: 25y. SBE H:1

Jacob d 10 May 1841 ae: 66y. A Tomb 41

James s/o Edward d 27 June 1843 ae: 1y. A Tomb 41

Joseph s/o Isaac d 14 Nov 1843 ae: 5m. A Tomb 66

Joshua M. d 23 Sep 1840 ae: 3y. SBE A-17-17

Capt. Joshua d 1 Nov 1848 ae: 75y. War of 1812. SBE A-17-17

Julia d/o Capt. Benjamin & Mary b 2 Sep 1818 d 20 Sep 1818. A-2-10

Marcy w/o Anthony d 17 Aug 1824 ae: 53y. F:124

Mary w/o Capt. Joshua M. nd ae: 67y. SBE A-17-16

Mary d 29 July 1842 ae: 92y. Widow. A Tomb 41

Mary wid/o Jacob d 16 Sep 1857 ae: 83y. A Tomb 41

Mary wid/o Capt. Benjamin d 15 Nov 1861 ae: 78y. A-2-7

Mary Ann d/o late Capt. Joshua d 7 Aug 1851 ae: 53y. GSL

Mary H. d/o Capt. Benjamin & Mary b 9 Oct 1806 d 17 Nov 1806. A-2-10

Nabby d/o Benjamin & Mary b 15 Dec 1789 d 16 Oct 1798. F:108

Nabby w/o Cat. Isaac d 4 Aug 1857 ae: 67y. A Tomb 66

Nancy d 24 Dec 1863 ae: 70y. SB H:72

Olive #2 w/o Anthony, wid/o John C. Hill d 18 July 1826 ae: 43y. F:125

Rebecca w/o Samuel d Dec 1804 ae: 49y. GSL

Reuben s/o Anthony & Marcy d 12 Aug 1797 ae: 6m. F:124

Reuben s/o Anthony & Marcy d 11 June 1819 ae: 20y. F:124

Reuben d 17 July 1862 ae: 69y 5m. SB A-19-15

Robert H. s/o Capt. Benjamin d 4 Jan 1859 ae: 45y 5m. SD

A-2-13

Ruth Gertrude d/o Henry & Sarah d 6 Feb 1878 ae: 18y. A Tomb 66

Sally B. d 1 Feb 1844 ae: 45y. A Tomb 85

Samuel d 18 Oct 1851 ae: 74y. SBE B-8-18

Sarah M. wid/o Henry d 1 Nov 1896 ae: 76y 3m. "Died South Paris, Maine." A Tomb 66

Stephen d 4 Feb 1870 ae: 77y. A Tomb 41

Susan d/o Daniel d 8 Jan 1855 ae: 13m. GSL

Thomas R. s/o Reuben & Elizabeth d 14 June 1844 ae: 26y. SB A-19-14

William d 10 Feb 1830 ae: 35y. B-3-31

Capt. William d 13 Jan 1852 ae: 55y. GSL

William F. s/o Samuel & Abigail d 8 Jan 1826 ae: 22m. B-8-19

William F. s/o William & F. A. d 2 Mar 1850 ae: 2y 3m. SBE A-23-3

William W. s/o Benjamin & Mary d 15 May 1806 ae: 24y. "Died on his passage from St. Bartholomew's to Portland." F:113

Capt. William W. s/o Capt. Benjamin & Mary d 31 Mar 1832 ae: 24y. "Drowned on his passage from Portland to Havana." A-2-11

William W. s/o Robert H. & Sarah d 29 July 1838 ae: 10m. SD A-2-12

Willie R. s/o Robert H. & Sarah d 6 Feb 1860 ae: 1y 9m. SD A-2-13

KNOX, Eliza w/o Amos P. d 25 Sep 1826 ae: 27y. B-5-32

James E. s/o Charles H. & Harriet d 4 Oct 1838 ae: 2y 8m. B-1-18

KOTZSCHMAR, Mary Ann d/o Midian & Mary Ann Griffin

KOTZSCHMAR (continued)

Torrey, wid/o Herman b Sacramento, California, 16 Dec 1853 d Cambridge, Massachusetts, 16 May 1937. A Tomb 34

LABOY, James s/o Rudolph d 2 July 1862 ae: 2y 7m. GSL

Rudolph s/o Rudolph d 19 Mar 1866 ae: 3y 3m. GSL

LAMBERT, Abba A. d/o Samuel d 16 Sep 1856 ae: 1y. GSL

Ann Maria d 2 Feb 1847. Black. A Tomb 62

LANCASTER, John P. L. s/o Sewell & Judith d 4 Feb 1814 ae: 3y 5m. SD H:109

Maj. Sewell d 24 Dec 1812 ae: 34y. SBE H:108

Rev. Thomas d 27 Jan 1831 ae: 89y. Born Rowley, Massachusetts. Minister: 1st Congregational Church, Scarboro. Revolutionary War: Chaplain. GSL

LANCEY, John d 11 Dec 1842 ae: 80y. Black. GSL

LANDERS, Richard s/o John d 9 Oct 1842 ae: 5y. Catholic. GSL

LANE, Amos C. s/o Capt. Joseph & Gratey d 15 July 1819 ae: 9y. K:142

Daniel s/o Daniel & Julia d 19 Apr 1816 ae: 1y 22d. F:12

Gratey w/o Capt. Joseph d 11 Dec 1818 ae: 38y. K:143

John G. d 12 July 1827 ae: 21y. SD B-1-41

Joseph s/o Capt. Joseph & Gratey d 6 Aug 1813 ae: 15m. K:142

Lucretia w/o Col. Daniel d 27 May 1862 ae: 77y 6m. A Tomb 74

Theophilus d 11 July 1848 ae: 71y. GSL

William s/o Charles B. d 30 May 1866 ae: 1d. GSL

LANG, Rosetta H. d/o Samuel W. d 30 Dec 1844 ae: 15y. A Tomb 9

LAROQUE, Martha d/o Henry & Elizabeth d 4 June 1805 ae: 16m. J:20

LARRABEE, Benjamin d 3 Dec 1809 ae: 75y. C:147

Ellen G. d/o William D. d 28 July 1849 ae: 5y. GSL

Joseph s/o William d 17 Jan 1833 ae: 8y. F:94

Lois D. w/o Joseph d 1 July 1830 ae: 36y. F:58

Lydia w/o William d 18 Aug 1872 ae: 87y. GSL

Mary d 28 Mar 1829 ae: 22y. B-4-13

Nabby w/o Philip d 25 Sep 1849 ae: 67y. B-8-35

Sarah wid/o Benjamin d 25 Oct 1819 ae: 85y. C:146

Stephen d 1 Mar 1718 ae: 66y. Unusual stone. E:90

Stephen d 7 Jan 1851 ae: 42y. GSL

William d 21 June 1844 ae: 59y. F:94

LARUE, Dorcas w/o John d 12 Dec 1845 ae: 42y. "Froze to death while intoxicated." GSL

LATHAM, Clifford s/o Hartley W. d 15 Mar 1893 ae: 3h. GSL

LAWRENCE, Frances d/o Nathaniel J. d 29 Aug 1849 ae: 3y. Black. GSL

Joseph d 26 Nov 1847 ae: 8m. Black. GSL

LEACH, Deborah w/o William B. d 6 Nov 1870 ae: 68y 6m. SD D:24

Fanny S. d/o Robert S. & Nancy d 1 Jan 1827 ae: 2y. SD B-13-7

Hannah d 22 Mar 1843 ae: 53y. Widow. GSL

Hannah W. d/o John & Hannah d 10 Apr 1819 ae: 3y 4m 12d. SBE B-4-11

Henry B. d 28 Dec 1842 ae: 38y. GSL

John d 5 Oct 1836 ae: 61y 6m 15d. GSL

Joseph P. s/o John & Hannah d 13 Sep 1823 ae: 3y 6m. SB

LEACH (continued)

B-4-10

Robert S. d 28 Nov 1826 ae: 28y. B-13-6

LEAVIS, Elizabeth d 3 Apr 1828 ae: 36y. J:77

Mary d 28 May 1802 ae: 4y. J:76

Thomas Jr. d 6 Aug 1824 ae: 31y. J:75

LEAVITT, Abigail w/o Benjamin d 11 Oct 1819. H:37

Benjamin d 30 Aug 1821 ae: 57y. H:36

Charles P. s/o William d 2 June 1844 ae: 10m. A Tomb 75

Hannah w/o Capt. Job d 19 Dec 1816 ae: 32y. SD E:86

Hattie Ellen d/o Daniel d 10 Nov 1861 ae: 8m. A Tomb 38

Joshua s/o Joshua & Sally d 28 July 1828 ae: 9y 2m. SD K:149

Mary H. w/o Eli d 11 Apr 1823 ae: 27y. G:27

Sarah d 18 Apr 1861 ae: 78y. GSL

Susan d/o Joseph d 21 Dec 1842 ae: 2y. GSL

LEE, Jane d/o Stephen & Hannah d 26 Apr 1809 ae: 3y. D:122

Joseph s/o Stephen & Hannah d 19 Apr 1813 ae: 21y 6m. D:124

LEFAVOR, Elizabeth d/o Nathaniel & Hannah d 13 Apr 1830 ae: 16y. I:120

Hannah w/o Nathaniel d 23 Oct 1819 ae: 41y. SBE I:119

Nathaniel d 28 Feb 1842 ae: 64y. GSL

LEIGHTON, Franklin B. s/o James G. & E. A. d 1 July 1853 ae: 3m 15d. SD A-10-19

Lizzie d/o William d 11 Aug 1859 ae: 2w. "Buried near DeSanchez." NS B-12-1

Margaret d/o Jeremiah d 4 Sep 1842 ae: 22m. GSL

LELAND, Loanis M. d/o Leonard & Chloe d 25 Apr 1832 ae: 6y. B-8-24

Lovice R. d/o Leonard & Chloe d

LELAND (continued)

15 Apr 1832. B-8-26

LEMANS, Alfred d 26 Jan 1853 ae: 22y. GSL

LEMONT, William T. s/o Samuel S. d 10 Feb 1867 ae: 31y 7m. F:95 Tomb

LENHAM, Ellen Ann d/o James d 29 Apr 1846 ae: 9m. "Buried at foot of Lucy Moody's grave." NS G:21

Frances d/o James d 29 Nov 1846 ae: 3y 6m. GSL

LEONARD, Abigail C. wid/o Rev. George d 7 Apr 1843 ae: 41y. Eroded monument between A Tomb 82 & A Tomb 83. A:88

Alice E. d/o Levi A. d 18 Aug 1860 ae: 10m. GSL

Charles E. s/o Levi A. d 15 Mar 1857 ae: 2d. GSL

Rev. George d 11 Aug 1831 ae: 29y. "Pastor of First Baptist Church." Eroded monument between A Tomb 82 & A Tomb 83. A:88

Jacob d 14 July 1843 ae: 63y. GSL

Nancy w/o Abraham d 9 Oct 1807 ae: 24y. K:105

LEOPOLD, Elizabeth A. w/o John H. d 7 Oct 1854 ae: 27y. SBE J:225

Elizabeth E. d/o John H. & Elizabeth A. d 29 Oct 1854 ae: 2m 6d. SBE J:225

LEWEY, John d 11 June 1852 ae: 77y. Black. GSL

Mary A. F. d 9 Sep 1854 ae: 70y. Black. GSL

LEWIS, Ada Jane d/o William d 28 July 1853. "Died Boston, Massachusetts." GSL

Capt. Ansel d 11 Mar 1844 ae: 48y. A Tomb 4

Burton L. s/o Albert S. & Clara d 1 Dec 1898 ae: 9d. Ledger. A Tomb 59

Charles G. s/o Albert S. Jr. & Myra B. d 22 Aug 1909 ae: 7m 3d. Ledger. A Tomb 59

Clara J. d/o George W. d 28 Sep

LEWIS (continued)

1855 ae: 9m. Ledger. A Tomb 59

Comfort wid/o Ansel d 4 May 1865 ae: 88y 9m. A Tomb 4

Elijah P. d 15 Feb 1870 ae: 36y. Ledger. A Tomb 59

Elijah P. s/o John d 16 Feb 1870 ae: 3y 8m. Ledger. A Tomb 59

Eliza d/o Ansel & Comfort d 28 Sep 1800 ae: 11m. G:16

Eliza P. d/o Ansel & Jane d 18 Dec 1916 ae: 90y. A Tomb 4

Capt. Enoch H. d 30 June 1824 ae: 62y. C:72

Fanny Thurlo w/o Thomas d 16 July 1827 ae: 43y. F:86

George Thurlo s/o Thomas & Fanny T. d 17 Sep 1825 ae: 11y 3m. F:86

George W. s/o Capt. George d 22 Apr 1857 ae: 23y 5m. Ledger. A Tomb 59

Harriet w/o Capt. Joseph d 26 Aug 1855 ae: 23y. Ledger. A Tomb 59

Jame M. w/o Ansel d 7 Jan 1874 ae: 81y. A Tomb 4

John d 6 Sep 1858 ae: 28y. GSL

John d 19 June 1874 ae: 67y. Ledger. A Tomb 59

Capt. John Lindsey d 21 Jan 1825 ae: 52y. F:165'

Julia Ann d/o Albert S. & Alice d 30 Apr 1916 ae: 24d. Ledger. A Tomb 59

Julia L. d/o late George W. d 5 July 1857 ae: 9m. Ledger. A Tomb 59

Lydia w/o Stephen d 14 Oct 1852 ae: 79y. SBE A-7-21

Mary wid/o Capt. John L. d 8 May 1844 ae: 63y. "Buried Family Range." SBE F:164

Mary Jane d/o Stephen L. & Jane R. d 9 Mar 1841 ae: 21y. J:155

Minnie L. d/o Albert S. d 2 Nov 1886 ae: 1y 8m. Ledger. A Tomb 59

Rebecca w/o Capt. John L. d 9

LEWIS (continued)

Dec 1804 ae: 27y. SD F:167

Sabrina H. wid/o John b 7 July 1809 d 24 Sep 1889. Ledger. A Tomb 59

Sarah E. d 24 Oct 1879 ae: 35y. A Tomb 36

Sarah G. w/o George W., d/o David & Tryphena Williams d 13 Mar 1829 ae: 25y. D:80

Shuah wid/o Capt. Enoch H. d 8 Aug 1829 ae: 58y. C:72

Stephen d 26 June 1844 ae: 75y. "Buried 10 feet from hearse house." SBE A-7-20

LIBBEY, Elliot d 10 Apr 1825 ae: 42y. H:144

Nancy wid/o Elliot d 30 May 1840 ae: 56y. H:145

LIBBY, Ann M. d 10 Aug 1882 ae: 32y. GSL

Caleb d 31 May 1837 ae: 51y. A-8-10

Edward T. s/o Joseph d 17 June 1865 ae: 1y 10m. GSL

Emily H. d 4 July 1835 ae: 12y. A Tomb 44

Francis A. s/o J. d 14 Aug 1848 ae: 24y. "Killed on the cars at Kennebunk." A Tomb 74

Horatio d 23 Aug 1818 ae: 15d. A Tomb 14

Joseph d 28 Dec 1815 ae: 51y. "Died at Gray, Maine." H:68

Joseph d 12 Aug 1822 ae: 32y. E:87

Lendall W. s/o Zenas d 18 Mar 1871 ae: 39y. A Tomb 14

Mary w/o Joseph d 28 Sep 1839 ae: 73y. H:68

Miriam d 11 Sep 1822 ae: 3y. A Tomb 14

Phebe w/o Jacob d 29 Sep 1824 ae: 30y. SD B-11-16

Samuel d 27 Mar 1820 ae: 22y. G:26

Sarah wid/o Caleb d 18 Aug 1854 ae: 60y 6m. A-8-10

Sarah W. d 30 July 1838 ae: 20y. A-8-11

Zenas d 8 Nov 1848 ae: 56y. A Tomb 14

LIGHT, Nancy d 20 Dec 1848 ae: 75y. Widow. "Buried beside Mrs. Motley's grave stone." GSL

LINCOLN, Harriet w/o Royal d 24 Sep 1847 ae: 69y. A Tomb 56

Jane R. w/o Samuel d 1 Oct 1872 ae: 72y. SB J:156

Mary d/o Royal & Harriet d Jan 1824 ae: 7y 10m. A Tomb 56

Melzar d 24 Sep 1805 ae: 29y. K:162

Royal d 5 Sep 1865 ae: 85y 10m. A Tomb 56

Samuel d 18 Sep 1880 ae: 83y. SBE J:157

LINDSEY, Samuel s/o Mary, widow d 19 Sep 1842 ae: 10y. GSL

LISCOMB, Betsy, w/o Capt. John d 15 Apr 1860 ae: 64y. SBE A-2-18

Elizabeth B. d 10 Nov 1888 ae: 62y 7m. "Died Old Ladies Home." GSL

Hattie E. d/o John J. d 24 May 1866 ae: 11y 6m. GSL

Mary Jane d/o John G. d 19 June 1849 ae: 4y. GSL

LITTLE, Amanda d/o William D. d 22 Aug 1847 ae: 1y. GSL

Elizabeth wid/o Dr. Timothy d 20 Nov 1853 ae: 76y. GSL

Emily Shaw d/o William D. d 17 Apr 1844 ae: 3y. GSL

James S. s/o William H. d 25 Aug 1854 ae: 8w. A Tomb 42

Jane E. d/o Haller d 24 June 1850 ae: 13y. "Buried near the Friends' Ground." GSL

Rebecca w/o Stephen d 23 Sep 1847 ae: 71y. MB A Tomb 23

Timothy, M.D. d 27 Nov 1849 ae: 73y. GSL

LITTLEFIELD, Mary d/o William & Mary F. d 23 Aug 1842 ae: 2y 5m. SD A-4-1

LITTLEJOHN, Charles L. d 14 Apr 1858 ae: 76y 3m. GSL

Clement d 22 Feb 1898 ae: 72y. "Died Boston, Massachusetts." GSL

LITTLEJOHN (continued)
Enoch s/o Charles & Sarah d 21 Nov 1842 ae: 27y. A-12-10

Mary d/o Charles & Sarah d 1 Mar 1840 ae: 18y. A-12-9

Sarah w/o Charles d 27 Aug 1855 ae: 78y. GSL

LLOYD, Nancy d 11 July 1800 ae: 23y. SD L:2

William R. d 24 Mar 1819 ae: 23y. Lt., Royal Navy. "Native Portsmouth, England." Unusual stone. K:13

LOCKE, Frank Homer s/o Worthington S. d 31 Aug 1862 ae: 3w. A Tomb 8

LOMBARD, Ellen M. d/o Jane d 15 Dec 1841. GSL

LON, Benjamin d 7 Sep 1826 ae: 46y. B-15-18

LONG, Alice M. d/o John F. & Elizabeth d 26 July 1857 ae: 14m. SD L:41

Alonzo E. s/o Eliakim d 16 Oct 1864 ae: 31y. Civil War: 25th Reg. Maine Inf., Co. B. NS L:41

Charles s/o Eliakim d 24 May 1852 ae: 21y. GSL

Eddie s/o John F. & Elizabeth d 29 July 1857 ae: 9d. SD L:41

Edward s/o John F. d 28 July 1854 ae: 2m. GSL

Eliakim s/o John E. d 18 Nov 1846 ae: 22m. "Buried at foot of Mrs. Bradbury's grave stone." GSL

James E. s/o Alonzo d 30 Dec 1857 ae: 7w. "Buried east of Francis Plummer'a grave." GSL

John Anderson s/o Eliakim d 30 Mar 1851 ae: 3m. GSL

Mary Esther d/o Eliakim d 13 Oct 1851 ae: 9y. GSL

Rheuby d/o Eliakim d 23 July 1852 ae: 5m. GSL

Sarah E. d/o Eliakim d 18 Oct 1847 ae: 11m. GSL

Sarah W. w/o Nathaniel C. d 25 Nov 1854 ae: 43y. GSL

LONGFELLOW, Abigail d/o Ste-

LONGFELLOW (continued)

phen & Tabitha d 21 Sep 1756 ae: 7m 18d. F:31

Stephen d 1 May 1790 ae: 68y. F:32

Tabitha Bragdon w/o Stephen d 11 Jan 1777 ae: 54y. F:33

LORD, Betsy J. wid/o William d 5 Mar 1873 ae: 86y. SBE E:24

Caroline W. d/o Joseph & Mary A. d 28 Sep 1846 ae: 10y. SBE F:152

Charles Tebbets s/o Joseph & Mary Ann b 3 Nov 1829 d 15 Oct 1830. F:151

Eliza C. w/o William C. d 25 Dec 1887 ae: 71y. GSL

Elizabeth A. d/o William & Betsy d 28 Nov 1841 ae: 29y. E:23

John d 18 Feb 1825 ae: 50y. SD F:150

John T. s/o Samuel & Almira b 8 Nov 1808 d 13 July 1813. J:78

Joseph d 25 Mar 1857 ae: 52y. GSL

Martha d/o William & Betsy d 10 Apr 1836 ae: 25y. "Died at Ipswich, Massachusetts." E:22

Nathaniel s/o John & Sarah nd. ae: 9y. F:150

Sally w/o Samuel d 19 May 1802 ae: 24y. J:43

Sally w/o William d 28 Sep 1803 ae: 18y. GSL

Samuel s/o Samuel & Almira b 7 Aug 1806 d 21 Aug 1806. J:78

Samuel d 7 Apr 1811 ae: 31y. J:39

Sarah w/o John d 1 Oct 1855 ae: 78y. SD F:150

Tryphene wid/o Capt. Samuel d 8 Nov 1851 ae: 90y. "...of Ipswich, Massachusetts." GSL

William b 22 Aug 1776 d 12 Sep 1854. E:25

Windsor d 28 Sep 1856 ae: 59y. "Died Boston, Massachusetts." GSL

LORETTE, Antonio d 12 June

LORETTE (continued)

1844 ae: 49y. GSL

LORING, Abigail wid/o Capt. Ignatius d 6 Oct 1835 ae: 77y. A-4-3

Alfred s/o J. Hayes nd. SD G:128

Ann Rebecca d/o J. Hayes nd. SD G:128

Charles s/o George & Lucy d 1 Sep 1829 ae: 2y. L:65

Elizabeth wid/o Nicholas d 5 Dec 1860 ae: 84y. GSL

Eunice d/o George & Lucy d 19 May 1820 ae: 11m. L:65

Eunice d/o George & Lucy d 15 May 1827 ae: 2y. L:65

Frances L. d/o Elizabeth d 13 Sep 1841 ae: 16m. GSL

Capt. Ignatius d 7 Aug 1805 ae: 49y. "Died in Grenada." A-4-3

Isaac d 2 Apr 1844 ae: 46y. "Buried beside A. Loring." GSL

J. Hayes d 18 Sep 1851 ae: 47y. SD G:128

Jane d/o George & Lucy d 30 Aug 1820 ae: 13m. L:65

Lucretia C. d/o Horace & Sarah d 26 Oct 1831 ae: 9m. SB J:174

Rhoda w/o Friend d 26 Oct 1824 ae: 38y. B-14-21

Capt. Samuel d 7 Jan 1826 ae: 28y. G:115

Sarah P. w/o Horace d 2 Mar 1863 ae: 54y. SB J:175

Sophia Tobey d/o George & Lucy d 4 Feb 1830 ae: 15y. L:64

Sylvester d 15 July 1855. GSL

William Shaw s/o George & Lucy d 27 Apr 1817 ae: 3d. L:65

LOVE, Alice M. d/o William H. & Rhoda J. d 13 Mar 1861 ae: 10m 23d. SD C:73

Elizabeth d 17 Sep 1844 ae: 74y. GSL

Mary F. d/o William H. & Rhoda J. d 8 Dec 1856 ae: 10m 12d. SD C:73

Rhoda J. w/o William Henry d

LOVE (continued)
27 Aug 1861 ae: 28y 10m. SD
C:74

William Henry d 18 Dec 1902 ae:
84y 2m 2d. "Died York,
Maine." Civil War: 10th Reg.
Maine Inf., Co. C. NS C:73

LOVETT, Harriet E. d/o John d
15 July 1856 ae: 2y. "Buried
at head of James Jordan's
wife's grave." NS J:10

Mary E. d/o John d 22 Dec 1862
ae: 12y. "Buried near James
Jordan." NS J:12

LOVIS, Jane d 4 Nov 1841 ae:
49y. GSL

Jeanett D. S. d 12 June 1823 ae:
57y. SBE B-5-5

Jeanett D. S. b 24 June 1792 d 2
Nov 1841. SBE B-5-6

LOW, Clarence H. d 28 June 1824
ae: 14y. SD B-7-25

James d 20 Aug 1844 ae: 49y.
Black. GSL

James d 18 Jan 1863 ae: 69y.
"Native of Bath, Maine."
Black. GSL

Mary w/o John d 29 Nov 1856 ae:
69y. SBE B-7-27

LOWE, George B. s/o William
A. d 18 Nov 1880 ae: 9y. GSL

Mary A. w/o Isaac M. d 20 May
1857 ae: 23y. "Buried near
head of Hancock St., at head of
John Brooks." GSL

LOWELL, Capt. Abner d 30 Sep
1828 ae: 88y. Revolutionary
War. K:52

Albert Bailey s/o Emma d 26
June 1817 ae: 5y. J:123

Amos Gilman s/o Amos & Caroline P. d 5 June 1849 ae: 10m.
SBE I:111

Anna d/o Abner d 23 Dec 1842
ae: 10m. GSL

Annie E. d 3 Nov 1876 ae: 72y.
GSL

Caroline w/o Aaron D. d 11 Sep
1842 ae: 34y. SBE E:21

Carrie L. d 18 Dec 1861 ae: 4w.
GSL

Catherine A. d 17 Nov 1872 ae:

LOWELL (continued)
64y. A Tomb 15

Capt. Daniel d 28 Apr 1809 ae:
34y. K:44

Edward H. d 2 June 1862 ae: 38y.
GSL

Elizabeth w/o Abner d 21 July
1843 ae: 27y. GSL

Elizabeth wid/o Capt. William d
19 Sep 1858 ae: 78y 7m. GSL

Emma d 11 Mar 1844. "Buried
beside her son's stone." NS
J:123

Enoch d 11 July 1832 ae: 66y.
Revolutionary War. K:49

Eunice w/o Enoch d 7 June 1874
ae: 74y. A Tomb 15

Capt. John d 18 June 1825 ae:
39y. "Killed while building
navigation monument on Stage
Island, at mouth of Saco
River." K:46

Joseph H. d 28 May 1833 ae:
33y. "Drowned on his passage
from Matanzas to Boston."
K:49

Lucy A. d/o George W. d 4 Dec
1846 ae: 20m. GSL

Mary w/o Capt. Daniel d 26 Dec
1801 ae: 21y. K:43

Mary wid/o Enoch d 18 Aug 1845
ae: 75y. K:48

Mercy Paine w/o Capt. Abner d 9
Dec 1807 ae: 64y. K:51

Sally w/o John d 28 Sep 1812 ae:
24y. K:47

William s/o Enoch & Mary d 20
Oct 1800 ae: 5m. SD K:42

William s/o Enoch & Mary d Oct
1835 ae: 28y. "Died at Port
Mahon." K:48

Capt. William d 22 Mar 1853 ae:
84y. GSL

LOWTHER, Dr. John d 1794 ae:
54y. GSL

Mary Burnham d/o Dr. John d 26
Dec 1840 ae: 65y. A-14-14

LUDKINS, Anna d 24 Feb 1867
ae: 23y. GSL

LUFKIN, Adalia d/o Richard d 28
July 1853 ae: 14y. Black.
GSL

83

LUFKIN (continued)

Eunice M. d/o Samuel S. d 27 Jan 1846 ae: 7m. A Tomb 30

Samuel S. s/o Samuel S. d 7 Jan 1849 ae: 2y. A Tomb 30

Sarah d 10 Dec 1858 ae: 25y. Black. GSL

LUNT, Benjamin F. b 26 June 1832 d 23 July 1889. A Tomb 44

Daniel s/o Samuel & Sarah b 19 Nov 1749 d 29 Nov 1823. Revolutionary War: Capt., Continental Inf., Massachusetts Society of the Cincinnati. GSL

Deborah T. wid/o Dr. Moses D. d 1885 ae: 75y. B-2-22

James d 21 Aug 1800 ae: 50y. GSL

Capt. James d 7 Aug 1849 ae: 74y. A Tomb 44

Joseph d 15 Sep 1804 ae: 48y. GSL

Mary d 5 June 1856 ae: 67y. SB D:61

Molly Starbuck w/o Daniel d 25 Dec 1787. GSL

Rebecca w/o Noah d 20 Dec 1851 ae: 24y. GSL

Sarah d 6 Aug 1846 ae: 93y. Widow. "Buried near the pathway." GSL

Sarah wid/o James d 24 Nov 1849 ae: 53y. A Tomb 44

Susan w/o Dr. Moses d 15 May 1841 ae: 32y. GSL

LYFORD, Frederick W. s/o Gideon C. & H. E. d 31 July 1823 ae: 8m. SBE B-5-7

LYMAN, Caroline B. d 14 Mar 1840 ae: 30y. A Tomb 81

Edward W. s/o S. R. d 5 Jan 1863 ae: 5y. A Tomb 81

LYNCH, Alice d/o John d 30 Nov 1849 ae: 10m. GSL

Catherine w/o Patrick d 25 June 1831 ae: 42y. Catholic. B-10-6

John B. s/o Rev. Benjamin d 28 Nov 1855 ae: 19y. Black. GSL

MACDONALD, Rebecca M. w/o Rev. William d 11 May 1853 ae: 32y. GSL

MACK, Andrew d 10 Jan 1838 ae: 52y. H:60

Ann M. B. d/o Andrew & Nancy W. d 6 Dec 1843 ae: 24y. SBE H:60

Annie A. d/o Charles d 20 Aug 1861 ae: 1y. GSL

Emma Ella d/o Charles F. d 20 Dec 1861 ae: 4y. GSL

John H. d 10 Apr 1855 ae: 28y. SD H:62

Nancy W. w/o Andrew d 9 Oct 1856 ae: 67y. H:60

Simon S. s/o Andrew & Nancy W. d 19 Jan 1833 ae: 8y. SD H:61

Capt. William McLean s/o Andrew & Nancy W. d 4 Mar 1856 ae: 24y. SBE H:60

MACKAY, James s/o Alexander d 30 Dec 1857 ae: 2y 1m. "Buried at head of Thomas Oxnard's grave." NS H:130

John s/o Alexander d 30 Dec 1857 ae: 3y 5m. "Buried at head of Thomas Oxnard's grave." NS H:130

MACKIE, Andrew b 8 Feb 1773 d 30 Sep 1827. "Native of Scotland." ME A Tomb 25

Andrew Jr. d 28 Aug 1813 ae: 10m. ME A Tomb 25

Deborah d 17 Sep 1819 ae: 10m. ME A Tomb 25

Deborah w/o Andrew d 6 Sep 1876 ae: 83y. ME A Tomb 25

Deborah S. d 10 June 1810 ae: 20y. ME A Tomb 25

George s/o George d 17 Oct 1859 ae: 2y. ME A Tomb 25

Isabella H. d 28 Mar 1810 ae: 17y. ME A Tomb 25

Joseph S. d 6 Jan 1837 ae: 19y. ME A Tomb 25

MACKIN, Adda J. d/o Joseph d 16 Apr 1865 ae: 9m. GSL

MACKINDO, John C. d 2 May 1852 ae: 34y. Black. SB L:18

MACON, Mary Jane d/o Edward C. d 15 Oct 1853 ae: 5m. GSL

MACY, Harriet L. d/o Thomas F.

MACY (continued)
d 24 Apr 1845 ae: 4y 9m.
"Buried at head of Elizabeth
Noyes' grave." NS C:99
MADDOX, Mary d 4 Nov 1834 ae:
20y. SBE A-3-7
Mrs. Rebecca d 17 Jan 1848 ae:
63y. SB A-3-8
MAHAN, inf ch/o J. T. d 14 Dec
1856 ae: 8w. "Buried beside
Bolles' child's grave near cor-
ner." GSL
John s/o late John d 28 Apr 1846
ae: 28y. NM A Tomb 67
William s/o James d 17 May
1857 ae: 16m. GSL
William M. s/o Michael d 19
Feb 1850 ae: 13m. GSL
MAHONEY, Mary Ann d/o Moses
d 15 Aug 1847 ae: 24y. GSL
William d 28 Feb 1853 ae: 67y.
Catholic. GSL
MALCOM, Eunice H. w/o James
R. d 13 Dec 1835 ae: 28y.
SBE J:137
Joseph s/o William & Mary b 10
Nov 1815 d 28 July 1818.
J:141
MALONEY, Mary E. d/o James d
19 Oct 1855 ae: 17m. GSL
MANLY, Catherine F. d/o Daniel
& Mehitable d 13 Aug 1813 ae:
6y. SB E:51
Daniel d 5 Oct 1837 ae: 63y.
Portland's first bank robber –
1818. SBE E:47
Emily C. F. b 1809 d 12 Oct
1887. E:46
Mehitable w/o Daniel d 29 May
1818 ae: 35y. SBE E:48
MANN, Christopher d 21 Sep 1845
ae: 67y. "Buried beside wife's
grave." NS B-8-4
Mary w/o Christopher d 24 Dec
1822 ae: 28y. B-8-4
Rebecca wid/o Christopher d 18
June 1865 ae: 76y 10m. GSL
MANNING, Louis A. d 20 Feb
1905 ae: 1y 8m. NS F:18
Mary Wood d/o Alfred d 10 Feb
1898 ae: 3w 1d. GSL
MANSFIELD, Charles F. s/o Ed-

MANSFIELD (continued)
ward & Ann d 5 Sep 1826 ae:
16m. SBE B-2-20
Charles M. s/o Edward & Ann d
9 Sep 1843 ae: 2y 1m. SBE
B-2-20
Dorcas C. d/o Edward & Ann d
11 Feb 1834 ae: 17m. SBE
B-2-20
Edward G. s/o Edward & Ann d
19 Oct 1822 ae: 3y 6m. SBE
B-2-20
Edward Pierce s/o Edward & Ann
d 24 Jan 1851 ae: 22y. B-2-18
Joseph s/o Edward d 14 Sep 1850
ae: 14y. GSL
Joseph P. s/o Edward & Ann d
14 Sep 1850 ae: 14y 6m. SBE
B-2-19
Justina d/o L. S. d 10 Apr 1846
ae: 10m. "Buried beside Dea-
con John Phillips grave." NS
B-2-23
Mary W. d/o Edward & Ann d 17
July 1823 ae: 14m. SBE B-2-
20
Pierce s/o Edward d 22 Jan 1851
ae: 23y. GSL
Rebecca F. d/o Edward & Ann d
1 Sep 1832 ae: 20m. SBE B-
2-20
MANTINE, Augustus H. d 13 Jan
1893 ae: 76y. NS B-10-17
Henry A. s/o Lory d 27 Sep 1850
ae: 1y. GSL
Lemuel N. R. s/o Augustus d 11
Jan 1893 ae: 42y 4m. NS B-
10-17
MANUEL, Amos C. s/o Chris-
topher C. & Sophia d 22 June
1827 ae: 6y. Black. A-13-33
Calvin D. s/o Christopher d 17
Oct 1854 ae: 34y. Black. GSL
Christopher C. d 22 Dec 1845 ae:
63y. Black. GSL
Christopher L. s/o late Chris-
topher d 16 Aug 1861 ae: 23y.
Black. GSL
Edwin R. s/o Christopher C. &
Sophia d 13 Oct 1835 ae: 13m.
Black. A-13-32
Foster s/o Luther d 25 Dec 1861

MANUEL (continued)
ae: 8y 8m. Black. GSL

George D. s/o Christopher C. & Sophia A. d 30 Nov 1864 ae: 28y. Black. A-13-31

Henry M. s/o Christopher C. d 21 Oct 1845 ae: 19y. Black. GSL

Joseph s/o Philip d 15 Dec 1847 ae: 2y. Black. GSL

Julia Ann d/o Christopher C. & Sophia d 30 June 1837 ae: 14y. Black. A-13-32

Luther J. d 2 Dec 1862 ae: 42y. Black. GSL

Mary Ann d/o Philip d 21 Apr 1848 ae: 8m. Black. GSL

Nancy w/o Christopher C. d 6 May 1815 ae: 22y. Black. L:11

Philip s/o Philip d 30 Jan 1843 ae: 2m. Black. GSL

Sophia L. w/o Christopher d 24 May 1875. "...and their children." Black. A-11-22

Thomas A. D. s/o Christopher C. d 3 July 1841 ae: 12y. Black. GSL

Walter T. s/o Luther T. d 1 Mar 1857 ae: 11m 18d. Black. GSL

MARBLE, Stephen M. d 26 Apr 1860 ae: 57y 4m. A Tomb 13

MARCH, Caroline B. w/o Charles R. d 26 Feb 1856 ae: 19y. A Tomb 69

Caroline Zereda d/o Charles R. & Caroline B. d 24 Feb 1857 ae: 1y 9m. A Tomb 69

Capt. Charles B. d 21 Jan 1864 ae: 33y. A Tomb 69

Charles F. d 28 July 1861 ae: 53y. A Tomb 69

Edmund d 25 Mar 1811 ae: 44y. J:2

Sabrina W. d 17 Nov 1845 ae: 22y. SD D:110

MARINER, Edward H. s/o Joseph & Susan b 11 Apr 1817 d 4 Oct 1821. E:91

MARK, John H. s/o Gabriel d 6 Aug 1841 ae: 23m. GSL

Rhoda w/o Godfrey d 10 Oct 1835

MARK (continued)
ae: 22y. A-4-4

MARKELL, Moses s/o N. d 9 Sep 1842 ae: 4y. GSL

MARRETT, ---- d 2 Jan 1853 ae: 76y. Widow. GSL

James H. s/o James H. d 14 Jan 1868 ae: 8m. GSL

MARSH, Julia d/o Abraham d 26 Mar 1844 ae: 11y. Black. GSL

MARSHALL, James d 8 Jan 1844 ae: 66y. "Buried beside F. Woods' stone." NS A-16-7

Martha w/o Francis d 21 Oct 1762 ae: 76y. E:80

Samuel B. s/o Samuel B. d 1 Oct 1845 ae: 2y 2m. GSL

William H. s/o A. P. d 23 May 1856 ae: 5w. GSL

William H. s/o Samuel B. d 30 Apr 1851 ae: 5y 6m. GSL

MARSTIN, Sarah w/o George R. d 30 Mar 1833 ae: 24y. SD B-5-3

MARSTON, Belinda d 6 Feb 1859 ae: 48y. H:34

Fred W. s/o Jeremiah & Medora d 16 Aug 1919 ae: 41y 5m. A Tomb 42

Harriet w/o Joseph d 28 June 1846 ae: 50y. GSL

John J. d 3 Nov 1898 ae: 52y. "Died Natick, Massachusetts." A Tomb 42

Lucy d/o Zachariah & Sarah b 27 Dec 1803 d 11 Sep 1805. H:30

Lucy d 26 Nov 1841 ae: 70y. Widow. GSL

Lucy S. wid/o Jonathan b 27 Oct 1788 d 3 Jan 1861. I:160

Medora M. w/o John J. d 18 Sep 1902 ae: 52y. GSL

Sarah w/o Zachariah d 30 Oct 1806 ae: 27y. H:31

Sarah wid/o Zachariah d 22 Nov 1841 ae: 60y. H:33

Zachariah d 13 Nov 1813 ae: 34y. H:32

MARTIN, Elizabeth P. d 3 Aug 1885 ae: 85y 8m. A-4-9

Francis d 21 Feb 1836 ae: 64y. Black. Catholic. A-10-34

MARTIN (continued)

Hannah d 18 Feb 1822 ae: 61y. "Formerly of Gorham." B-13-1

Hannah d 17 Dec 1863 ae: 71y. A Tomb 45

Harriet Frances d/o Jeremiah & Elizabeth P. d 19 Nov 1835 ae: 19m 5d. A-4-8

Jeremiah d 31 Jan 1842 ae: 42y. SD A-4-9

Mary w/o Francis d 1 Feb 1822 ae: 42y. Black. Catholic. SD L:1

Sophia w/o William d 25 Apr 1828 ae: 27y. J:76

MARWICK, Andrew S. d 7 Jan 1833 ae: 42y. B-9-7

Hannah w/o Capt. Atwood d 19 Nov 1864 ae: 79y. A Tomb 15

Lydia d 22 Mar 1844 ae: 85y. Widow. "Buried beside Newball's stone." NS B-9-5

Sarah d 12 May 1843 ae: 23y. GSL

MASON, Abijah d 6 Mar 1825 ae: 30y. "Formerly of Dedham." B-6-8

Alonzo s/o James S. d 1 Jan 1857 ae: 19y 4m. GSL

Charles A. s/o Charles & Temperance P. b 20 Dec 1823 d 1 Sep 1825. B-5-22

Henry s/o John & Loiza d 27 Dec 1822 ae: 6w. SD B-12-2

John d 19 Mar 1826 ae: 36y. B-12-3

Levi Lockhart d 11 Apr 1845 ae: 61y. GSL

Lucy wid/o John d 23 Mar 1854 ae: 96y. GSL

Margaret A. d/o Seth E. d 19 Sep 1847 ae: 5m. GSL

Munroe C. s/o Andrew B. & G. W. d 16 June 1825 ae: 16y. SBE A-1-5

Seth d 19 Aug 1848 ae: 38y. A Tomb 69

Temperance P. w/o Charles d 30 Dec 1831 ae: 33y. SBE B-5-23

William F. s/o Charles & Temperance P. b 20 Dec 1823 d 27

MASON (continued)

Aug 1825. B-5-21

MAUGER, John DeJ., Jr. s/o late John DeJersey d 20 Oct 1858 ae: 18m. A Tomb 58

John DeJersey d 4 Mar 1858 ae: 34y. "Native of Matanzas." A Tomb 58

MAXFIELD, Susan W. d 30 Nov 1841 ae: 38y. SBE A-16-12

MAXWELL, Deborah w/o Joseph d 3 Apr 1858 ae: 66y. SD I:154

Ernesto M. s/o William & Carmen d 25 Oct 1861 ae: 5m 7d. SD C:78

James d 14 Feb 1850 ae: 39y. GSL

MAY, Rufus L. s/o Silas & Pamelia d 8 Sep 1826 ae: 13m. B-5-31

MAYLAND, John d Mar 1804 ae: 19y. "Native of Ireland." GSL

MAYNARD, Mary Frances d/o Cornelius D. d 1 Nov 1844 ae: 19y. A Tomb 32

MAYO, Apphia d/o Simeon & Martha b 12 Jan 1785 d 17 Apr 1839. SBE J:33

Charles A. s/o Alphonso d 23 Dec 1856 ae: 2y. A Tomb 70

Charles Edward s/o Alphonso d 4 Sep 1859 ae: 9 1/2m. A Tomb 70

Ebenezer nd. H:71 Tomb

Eliza d/o Simeon & Martha b 1 Aug 1795 d 7 Sep 1847. SBE J:31

Ephraim d 12 July 1885 ae: 78y. GSL

Maria d/o Simeon & Martha b 23 Nov 1788 d 16 Jan 1840. SBE J:32

Martha d 19 Sep 1831 ae: 75y. SBE J:34

Mary d/o Simeon & Martha b 16 May 1798 d 24 Dec 1853. SBE J:21

Nancy w/o Ephraim d 5 Nov 1855 ae: 50y. GSL

Richard Derby s/o Eben & Jane d Sep 1803 ae: 2y. GSL

MAYO (continued)

Richard Derby s/o Eben & Jane d 7 Sep 1806 ae: 22m. A-19-11A

Sarah M. d/o Simeon & Martha b 1 Apr 1793 d 4 Dec 1876. SBE J:25

Sarah S. d 26 Sep 1837 ae: 26y. SBE K:69

Thomas d 11 Nov 1839 ae: 24y. SBE K:68

MCALLISTER, Albert D. s/o Stephen H. & Mary J. d 23 July 1860 ae: 13y 6m. A-13-2

MCANELLEY, Henry s/o Patrick & Margaret d 20 Aug 1839 ae: 3y. Catholic. SD B-9-3

Margaret w/o Patrick d 7 July 1838 ae: 28y. Catholic. B-9-4

Patrick d 6 Jan 1845 ae: 36y. "Buried beside his wife's grave stone." Catholic. NS B-9-4

MCCANN, Bridget d/o Daniel d 26 Aug 1852 ae: 7m. Catholic. GSL

Catherine d/o Daniel d 17 Sep 1854 ae: 13m. Catholic. GSL

Elizabeth w/o John d 14 May 1841 ae: 68y. GSL

MCCARTER, Elizabeth d/o William d 26 July 1866 ae: 10m. A Tomb 20

MCCARTY, Filene s/o Timothy & Sarah d 14 May 1826 ae: 15m. Catholic. SD B-14-6

Patrick d 10 Sep 1849 ae: 87y. Catholic. GSL

MCDONNELL, Agnes d 20 Aug 1859 ae: 35y. Catholic. GSL

MCDOWELL, George d 24 July 1832 ae: 28y. B-13-5

Margaret w/o William d 29 Aug 1882 ae: 73y. GSL

Nancy d 24 Aug 1878. "Died Portsmouth, New Hampshire." GSL

William H. d 27 June 1882 ae: 81y. GSL

MCDUFFIE, Charles R. d 26 Sep 1869 ae: 6m. GSL

MCGERHAN, Rosanna d/o Pat-

MCGERHAN (continued)

rick d 16 Oct 1842 ae: 3y. GSL

MCGIVEN, Carrie w/o Patrick d 23 May 1881. Catholic. GSL

Caroline d/o David & Nancy Archibald d 15 Jan 1881. I:208

MCGOWAN, Anna Bella w/o Samuel d 4 June 1857 ae: 33y 6m. " Buried at head of Nelson Burns' lot." GSL

MCGREGOR, Eddie A. s/o Edward & Rose d 3 Mar 1886 ae: 5y. GSL

MCINTOSH, Eben d 30 Apr 1859 ae: 84y. A Tomb 86

Eliza wid/o Charles d 15 Nov 1894 ae: 84y 2m. GSL

George Henry s/o John d 13 Feb 1849 ae: 6w. GSL

Patience w/o Capt. Ebenezer d 18 July 1841 ae: 54y. A Tomb 86

MCKENNEY, Caroline E. d/o William Hartshorn, w/o Alendo d 28 Jan 1859 ae: 24y. GSL

David d 28 July 1864 ae: 73y. GSL

Edwin F. s/o James H. & Sarah R. d 30 June 1847 ae: 4y 5m. SD K:171

Lucy M. d/o David & Mary G. d 16 Sep 1817 ae: 8m 2d. SD K:172

Mary G. wid/o David d 21 Dec 1866 ae: 76y. GSL

MCKENZIE, David d 1 Jan 1847 ae: 41y. "Buried beside ladder house." GSL

John Anderson s/o John d 24 July 1855 ae: 9m. GSL

MCKER, John A. s/o Robert d 19 Sep 1860 ae: 1y. GSL

MCKEYE, John s/o John d 25 July 1847 ae: 18y. GSL

MCLANLIN, Thomas d 11 Mar 1853 ae: 6m. Black. GSL

MCLEA, Daniel d 3 Apr 1851 ae: 47y. GSL

MCLEAN, Allon b Orkneys, Scotland, d 23 Mar 1760 ae: 26y. Deputy Collector: Royal Customs. Killed in building

MCLEAN (continued)

collapse. Buried in same grave with John Flett. Slate ledger: Destroyed. E:12

MCLELLAN, Albert d 21 Oct 1819 ae: 2y 8m. A Tomb 56

Anna C. wid/o William d 11 Oct 1851 ae: 69y. A Tomb 56

Betty #4 w/o Capt. William d 7 June 1798 ae: 53y. SBE H:178

Caroline w/o Thomas d 18 Apr 1900 ae: 82y 7m 17d. A Tomb 29

Charlotte w/o Stephen d 22 Sep 1802 ae: 39y. F:95 Tomb

Cornelia d 10 May 1843 ae: 45y. F:95 Tomb

Eben s/o Thomas d 11 Nov 1864 ae: 54y. A Tomb 86

Elizabeth w/o Bryce d 1 Sep 1770 ae: 78y. GSL

Elizabeth d/o John & Sally d 2 Dec 1796 ae: 22m. H:188

Elizabeth W. d 26 May 1856 ae: 36y. A Tomb 86

Ellen w/o William d 29 Oct 1856 ae: 35y. Black. GSL

Enoch d 15 Dec 1841 ae: 40y. Black. GSL

Enoch s/o Enoch d 14 Sep 1856 ae: 13m. Black. GSL

Frederick A. d 20 Sep 1848 ae: 28y. A Tomb 56

George s/o Capt. William d 22 Feb 1801 ae: 19y. "Died in Surinam." H:181

Hannah d/o Capt. George d 20 Sep 1803 ae: 17m. GSL

Hannah d 26 Apr 1836 ae: 65y. F:95 Tomb

Maj. Hugh d 7 Feb 1823. Revolutionary War - War of 1812. A Tomb 86

Jane #3 w/o Capt. William d 13 July 1788 ae: 45y. H:182

Jane w/o Arthur d 19 Feb 1811 ae: 54y. A Tomb 86

Jane w/o Thomas d 5 Dec 1849 ae: 64y. A Tomb 86

Jane R. d 8 May 1892 ae: 74y. "Died Boston, Massachusetts." A Tomb 86

MCLELLAN (continued)

Capt. John d 17 Mar 1849 ae: 82y. SBE H:187

John Lancaster s/o John & Sally d 3 June 1790 ae: 21m. H:188

John R. s/o Capt. Thomas d 10 Apr 1846 ae: 27y. A Tomb 86

John Ross s/o Eben d 24 Apr 1859 ae: 12y. A Tomb 86

Lydia d/o Capt. John & Sally d 3 June 1807 ae: 14y 4m. H:111

Martha wid/o Enoch d 19 Sep 1845 ae: 51y. Black. GSL

Mary w/o Capt. William d 24 Feb 1764 ae: 24y. H:179

Mary w/o Isaac d 6 Nov 1801 ae: 22y. MBE G:113 Tomb

Mary w/o Capt. Joseph d Oct 1804 ae: 66y. GSL

Mary #2 w/o Capt. William d 28 July 1813 ae: 79y. H:180

Mary #2 w/o Arthur d 15 June 1825 ae: 59y. A Tomb 86

Mary A. d 26 July 1831 ae: 27y. F:95 Tomb

Mary Ann w/o William d 2 Jan 1846 ae: 48y. "Buried east corner Friends' Ground." GSL

Capt. Samuel d 14 May 1854 ae: 59y. "Suicide." A Tomb 86

Sarah Indacot d/o John & Sally d 26 Sep 1791 ae: 16m. H:188

Sally w/o John d 29 Apr 1797 ae: 29y. SBE H:186

Stephen d 25 Oct 1823 ae: 58y. Revolutionary War. F:95 Tomb

Capt. Thomas d 21 May 1861 ae: 80y. A Tomb 86

Thomas T. s/o Thomas & Jane d 18 Aug 1827 ae: 13y. A Tomb 86

Mehitable Griffin Davis w/o John, wid/o Ebenezer Davis d 21 Apr 1823 ae: 55y. A Tomb 84

Capt. William d 28 July 1813 ae: 79y. Revolutionary War. H:181

William d 2 June 1844 ae: 67y. A Tomb 56

MCMANNUS, Harriet E. w/o Robert, d/o Capt. Benjamin & Mary Knight d 10 June 1832

MCMANNUS (continued)
ae: 21y. A-2-9

MCNAB, Nelly d/o James d 12 May 1857 ae: 2y 5m. A Tomb 15

MCNAMARA, Fred Howard s/o A. d 17 July 1860 ae: 2w. GSL

MEANS, Frances C. Colby w/o George C. b 1827 d 1855. Mmt G:4

George W. C. b 1822 d 1852. Mmt G:4

MEAYBRY, Margaret b 13 June 1733 d 25 Dec 1799. D:147

MEEHAN, George W. s/o George d 7 Sep 1858 ae: 10m. GSL

MEGGUIRE, James d 3 Oct 1848 ae: 38y. GSL

James H. d 10 Feb 1820 ae: 37y. SBE B-1-30

Rebecca w/o James H. d 29 Oct 1846 ae: 64y 7m. SBE B-1-30

Sarah J. w/o James d 23 July 1838 ae: 33y. SBE A-9-18

MELLEN, Bridget d/o Lawrence & Catherine Mullen d 1831 ae: 7m. Catholic. B-14-2

John s/o John d 15 Sep 1843 ae: 4m. "Buried at foot of J. Dean's stone." GSL

Susan d/o Lawrence & Catherine Mullen d 1831 ae: 10m. Catholic. B-14-2

MERCY, Walter H. s/o George L. & Sarah H. d 3 June 1856 ae: 9m. SBE K:124

MERRILL, Abbie L. d/o Joseph L. & Abigail Churchill d 10 Apr 1904 ae: 64y 7m. "Died Greely Hospital." GSL

Alford d 12 Sep 1843 ae: 32y. A Tomb 7

Charles C. s/o Peter & Sarah d 31 Dec 1832 ae: 18m. SBE B-2-7

Dolly d 2 Apr 1862 ae: 69y 10m. F:95 Tomb

Dorcas E. d/o Joseph d 30 Oct 1845 ae: 15y. GSL

Eben B. d 4 Oct 1836 ae: 34y. SBE B-1-5

MERRILL (continued)
Edith d/o late James d 27 Feb 1859 ae: 4m 8d. A Tomb 7

Edward d 3 Dec 1848 ae: 28y. "Died East Thomaston." GSL

Elias d 21 Oct 1824 ae: 63y. SBE B-1-6

Eliza w/o James M. d 30 May 1846 ae: 33y. A Tomb 7

Elizabeth wid/o Elias d 31 Mar 1850 ae: 86y. SBE B-1-7

Eunice wid/o Nathaniel d 20 May 1865 ae: 82y. GSL

George W. d 16 Dec 1837 ae: 15m. F:95 Tomb

Harriet Louisa d/o Winthrop S. d 19 May 1848 ae: 10m. "Buried beside James Jordan - 1820." NS J:12

James d 6 Feb 1859 ae: 36y. A Tomb 7

James B. d 8 Apr 1860 ae: 17m. GSL

Lorenzo s/o Edward d 27 May 1841 ae: 2y. GSL

Lucy d 3 Mar 1851 ae: 67y. F:95 Tomb

Lydia d 21 Apr 1858 ae: 53y. GSL

Mandana d 28 Oct 1874 ae: 85y. A-18-4

Margaret Ann d/o Paul & Eleanor d 20 Sep 1835 ae: 17y. SBE A-3-19

Margaret R. w/o Capt. Joseph B., d/o Robert & Mary York d 13 Jan 1837 ae: 25y. A-3-36

Maria L. d/o Winthrop d 24 Aug 1845 ae: 5m. GSL

Martha wid/o John d 24 Feb 1852 ae: 75y. GSL

Mary w/o Peter d 14 Dec 1823 ae: 31y. B-2-6

Peter d 1 Nov 1846 ae: 58y. GSL

Seward d 2 Apr 1862 ae: 69y 10m. GSL

Seward d 23 July 1867 ae: 77y. F:95 Tomb

Seward H. s/o Seward & Dolly d 31 Aug 1825 ae: 17m. SBE B-2-5

Seward H. d 12 Oct 1848 ae: 22y.

MERRILL (continued)

F:95 Tomb

Susan T. d 23 Dec 1845 ae: 58y. SBE A-18-5

Thomas d 14 Aug 1852 ae: 70y. A Tomb 7

Winthrop S. s/o W. S. d 22 Aug 1849 ae: 18m. GSL

MERRY, Abbie E. w/o John d 26 Feb 1891 ae: 78y 5m 26d. GSL

Adrianna d/o John & Abba E. d 20 Feb 1847 ae: 2y. J:1

John d 20 Mar 1891 ae: 81y 3m. GSL

MERRYMAN, Joseph Baker s/o Jacob d 14 June 1846 ae: 4y. C:128

MESERVE, Abby L. d/o John L. & Abby L. d 7 Jan 1832 ae: 4m. A Tomb 29

Abby L. w/o John L. d 7 Feb 1832 ae: 25y. A Tomb 29

Francis I. s/o Curtis & Olive b 11 Sep 1823 d 15 Sep 1824. B-9-19

John d 18 Mar 1860 ae: 68y. GSL

John Albert s/o John d 26 Aug 1854 ae: 8m. GSL

John L. d 4 Feb 1865 ae: 59y. A Tomb 29

Lydia E. d/o Francis M. d 23 Aug 1863 ae: 6y 5m. GSL

Mary L. d/o John L. & Abby L. d 12 July 1840. A Tomb 29

MESERVEY, Olive w/o Curtis d 17 May 1851 ae: 56y. GSL

MESSENGER, inf ch/o J. d 25 Dec 1860 ae: 2d. GSL

MIERS, John d 2 Nov 1805 ae: 38y. L:69

MILK, Anna Dunn Deering w/o Deacon James d 7 Sep 1769 ae: 58y. E:75

Deacon James b Jan 1710 d 19 Nov 1772. Colonial Wars. Ledger: Broken - eroded. E:73

James s/o Deacon James & Sarah Brown d 12 Apr 1773 ae: 29y. GSL

Lydia Hall d 20 Apr 1771 ae: 1y 2m. E:77

MILK (continued)

Sarah d/o Deacon James & Sarah Brown d 18 Nov 1760 ae: 22y 9m. E:78

Sarah Brown w/o Deacon James d 29 Apr 1761 ae: 40y 10m. E:74

MILLER, Anna Belle d/o W. O. d 8 Apr 1885 ae: 2y 4m. GSL

Elizabeth W. d/o J. S. d 27 May 1855 ae: 1y 9m. F:95 Tomb

John d 25 Nov 1831 ae: 52y. B-6-19

Margaret w/o John d 26 Mar 1822 ae: 32y. I:102

Margaret J. d/o Robert d 24 Oct 1869 ae: 27y. GSL

Mary Elizabeth d/o John & Betsy d 11 Feb 1830 ae: 6y. B-6-19

Samuel A. s/o Augustus A. d 2 Sep 1848 ae: 6m. MB A Tomb 22

Sarah W. d/o John & Margaret d 25 Oct 1821 ae: 2y. I:102

MILLETT, Francis Albert s/o Nathaniel S. d 14 July 1854 ae: 11y. GSL

Judith E. d/o Nathaniel S. d 12 July 1863 ae: 24y. GSL

Lucretia G. w/o Thomas R. d 23 Dec 1858 ae: 25y 9m. GSL

Nathaniel S. d 21 June 1845 ae: 55y. "Buried at foot of Henry Titcomb's grave." NS C:215

MILLIKEN, ---- s/o John F. d 4 Oct 1842 ae: 7y. GSL

Albert s/o James J. d 17 Aug 1843 ae: 10m. "Buried beside C. Blake's stone." GSL

Capt. Alexander d 9 Nov 1873 ae: 74y. MB A Tomb 21

Caroline d/o Charles & Eunice d 22 Oct 1840 ae: 10y 8m. SD B-3-20

Charles A. s/o Capt. Alexander & Sarah d 20 Oct 1849 ae: 18y. MB A Tomb 21

Charles I. s/o Capt. Alexander & Sarah d 29 Jan 1867 ae: 4y. MB A Tomb 21

Frank E. s/o W. H. d 12 June 1861 ae: 10m. A Tomb 17

MILLIKEN (continued)

George W. s/o Charles d 26 Aug 1853 ae: 16m. GSL

James Hill s/o Capt. Alexander & Sarah d 22 Jan 1868 ae: 42y. MB A Tomb 21

John s/o John F. d 23 Sep 1842 ae: 5m. GSL

John Alger s/o Capt. Alexander & Sarah d 9 Oct 1862 ae: 19y 2m. MB A Tomb 21

Julia A. d/o Capt. Alexander & Sarah nd. MB A Tomb 21

Sarah w/o Isaac d 10 Oct 1839 ae: 52y. A-11-10

Sarah w/o Capt. Alexander d 10 Mar 1878 ae: 77y. MB A Tomb 21

Sarah M. W. d/o Capt. Alexander & Sarah nd. MB A Tomb 21

Sophronia d/o Charles & Eunice d 12 Nov 1832 ae: 6y 6m. B-3-19

Susan S. d/o John & Jemima d 9 Oct 1843 ae: 1y. E:8

MILLIONS, Juliet d/o Thomas & Mary d 19 Mar 1822 ae: 5m. I:48

Mary w/o Thomas d 30 Mar 1832 ae: 33y. I:49

Thomas d 13 Mar 1834 ae: 35y. I:50

MILLS, ---- d/o Elisha & Sally d 1 Oct 1803 ae: 17m. SD K:164

Edward A. s/o William H. & S. A. d 9 May 1833 ae: 4y. SBE A-3-12

Jonas d 24 July 1825 ae: 49y. SD K:166

Sally w/o Jonas d 10 Mar 1805 ae: 28y. SBE K:165

William s/o Robert d 5 Dec 1850 ae: 3w. GSL

MILNER, George s/o Daniel d 22 July 1846 ae: 2m. "Buried at foot of Benj. Crockett's child's grave." GSL

MINOT, Betsy d 19 Oct 1849 ae: 59y. GSL

Clarissa w/o Capt. Thomas d 10 Dec 1837 ae: 64y. F:21

MINOT (continued)

Edward M. d 22 Oct 1847 ae: 40y. GSL

George C. s/o Thomas & Clarissa d 19 Jan 1855 ae: 56y. F:22

Jane R. d 12 Aug 1849 ae: 38y. "Buried near Elder's tomb." A Tomb 39

Margaret wid/o George d 30 Jan 1858 ae: 78y. "Buried in Thomas Minot's lot." NS F:22

Sarah d 18 Dec 1857 ae: 53y. "Died in Yarmouth." Black. GSL

Stephen s/o Rev. Timothy & Mary d 3 Sep 1759 ae: 28y. Unusual inscription. D:103

Thomas b 20 Mar 1769 d 7 Feb 1808. F:23

MITCHELL, Ann Maria d/o Rev. Mirabar d 25 Sep 1847 ae: 20y. ME A Tomb 27

Anna d/o Joseph d 7 Oct 1859 ae: 2m. GSL

Annie L. w/o E. L. d 14 May 1866 ae: 36y. SBE A-10-21

Catherine w/o Benjamin F. d 13 Jan 1846 ae: 20y. SB A-8-9

Charles C. d 7 Nov 1849 ae: 62y. ME A Tomb 27

Charles M. d 18 June 1826 ae: 4y. ME A Tomb 27

Dorcas d 6 Aug 1842 ae: 67y. Widow. GSL

Elbridge K., M.D. b 1819 d 12 May 1850. A Tomb 38

Eliza P. w/o Reuben d 21 Aug 1874 ae: 78y. A Tomb 48

Francis B. d 4 Jan 1852 ae: 39y. A Tomb 27

Frank A. d 21 June 1864 ae: 44y 10m. KIA - Petersburg, Virginia, Civil War: 39th Reg. Massachusetts Inf., Co. B. D:69

Gryza d/o James R. & Susan d 1 Apr 1828 ae: 4y. B-6-25

Hannah H. wid/o Elbridge K., d/o William & Mary Woodbury b 1820 d 30 Mar 1854. A Tomb 38

MITCHELL (continued)

Henry s/o Reuben d 20 Aug 1873 ae: 76y. GSL

Isaac s/o Alexander d 21 May 1864 ae: 14y. GSL

Jerusha w/o Benjamin d 17 May 1846 ae: 58y. GSL

Joseph Titcomb s/o Reuben & Eliza P. d 25 Oct 1859 ae: 39y. A Tomb 48

Joshua d 25 Mar 1845 ae: 65y. SD D:70

Joshua Jr. d 27 Nov 1865 ae: 50y. Civil War: 12th Reg. Maine Inf., Co. I. SB D:69

Joshua B. s/o Robert Jr. & Esther b 16 Dec 1803 d 19 Nov 1806. SD H:26

Julia W. d/o Silvanus & Lucia W. d 14 Oct 1827 ae: 17m. H:155

Lizzie N. w/o Robert d 13 Nov 1868 ae: 43y. SBE I:139

Lucia W. d/o Silvanus & Lucia W. d 19 Aug 1821 ae: 4m. H:154

Lucy Ellen d/o James R. & Susan d 21 Mar 1834 ae: 7m. B-6-27

Mary wid/o Richard d 1 Sep 1850 ae: 90y. H:84

Mary d/o E. d 15 Oct 1857 ae: 1y 9m. GSL

Mary w/o Joshua d 9 Nov 1879 ae: 88y. GSL

Mary wid/o Robert d 1 Sep 1850 ae: 89y. "Died in Boston." GSL

Mary D. d/o Joshua d 18 July 1848 ae: 17y. SD D:70

Octavia d/o Reuben & Eliza P. d 11 Nov 1832 ae: 8y. A Tomb 48

Mrs. Rebecca d 13 Nov 1820 ae: 70y. "Died at Grand Manan, New Brunswick." C:79

Reuben d 11 Nov 1858 ae: 58y. A Tomb 48

Robert d 3 Feb 1820 ae: 69y. H:85

Sally T. wid/o William C. d 13 Dec 1868 ae: 71y. ME A

MITCHELL (continued)

Tomb 27

Samuel d 26 Mar 1813 ae: 21y. SD H:12

Samuel s/o Joshua d 18 Aug 1830 ae: 17y. SD D:70

Susan d/o Benjamin d 28 June 1843 ae: 18y. GSL

Susan J. d/o James R. & Susan d 3 Dec 1826 ae: 5m. B-6-26

Susan R. w/o James R. d 11 June 1853 ae: 55y. SBE B-6-28

William C. d 10 Apr 1865 ae: 75y. ME A Tomb 27

William G. d 1 Nov 1874 ae: 56y. ME A Tomb 27

William H. s/o Robert d 9 Oct 1849 ae: 20m. GSL

MONROE, William s/o John d 9 July 1856 ae: 2y 6m. GSL

MONTAIN, Anna C. d/o Charles d 3 Oct 1863 ae: 11m. GSL

MONTGOMERY, Eliza wid/o Dr. Nathaniel d 3 July 1857 ae: 72y. A-24-22

Hannah W. d/o Nathaniel & Eliza d 29 Aug 1843 ae: 23y. SB A-24-20

James M. s/o Nathaniel & Eliza d 29 Sep 1859 ae: 47y. SB A-24-20

John s/o Nathaniel & Eliza d 10 Aug 1810 ae: 2y 6m. SBE I:76

John A. b 1817 d Sep 1884. A-24-22A

Mary Dennison wid/o John A. d 7 Sep 1895 ae: 80y 3m. A-24-22A

Nathaniel s/o Nathaniel & Eliza d 24 May 1838 ae: 34y. SB A-24-20

Dr. Nathaniel b 14 Nov 1779 d 21 Jan 1857. SBE A-24-21

Sarah L. d/o Nathaniel & Eliza d 28 Apr 1834 ae: 6y. SBE A-24-19

Thomas J. s/o Nathaniel & Eliza d 22 Nov 1854 ae: 30y. SBE A-24-21

William b 8 May 1805 d 5 Aug

MONTGOMERY (continued)
1830. SB I:75
MOODY, inf d/o Enoch nd ae:
5m. SBE G:21
Ann S. w/o Enoch b 11 Sep 1783
d 9 July 1866. SBE G:21
Ann Weeks #2 w/o Enoch d 9
Jan 1795 ae: 62y. E:69
Benjamin d 8 May 1816 ae: 63y.
Revolutionary War. G:2
Daniel S. s/o Samuel & Mary d
14 July 1821 ae: 21y. "Died at
Havana." G:10
Desiah H. wid/o William d 9
June 1850 ae: 57y. B-4-7
Dorcas d 20 Aug 1849 ae: 85y. A
Tomb 60
Dorcas Cox w/o Enoch d 7 Sep
1743 ae: 22y. SB E:71
Edward s/o William & Rachael d
27 Aug 1823 ae: 17y. G:19
Emma d 23 May 1847 ae: 48y. A
Tomb 60
Emma wid/o Capt. Lemuel d 22
Sep 1849 ae: 80y. A Tomb 60
Enoch d 10 Feb 1777 ae: 63y.
Revolutionary War. SB E:70
Enoch s/o Enoch & Ann Weeks d
19 Dec 1812 ae: 61y. E:66
Enoch b 10 Jan 1787 d 30 Nov
1851. SD G:22
Eunice d 24 Oct 1789 ae: 7m. 2d.
G:13
Francis d 27 Sep 1821 ae: 27m.
SBE G:20
Franklin b 26 Feb 1814 d 9 May
1877. Civil War: USN, 2nd
Asst. Engineer. A Tomb 60
George s/o Samuel & Emma nd.
SB G:12
George d 4 Jan 1804. G:11
Harriet d/o William & Rachel d
19 Apr 1805 ae: 4m. G:17
Harriet d/o William & Molly d 5
Oct 1799 ae: 9m. G:14
Henry s/o Enoch & Lucy d 11
Aug 1813 ae: 4d. SBE G:20
Henry Franklin s/o Franklin &
Lucy S. d 20 Aug 1848 ae: 6m.
A Tomb 60
Henry W. d 10 June 1803 ae: 1y.
G:11

MOODY (continued)
John d 26 Aug 1818 ae: 29y. SD
F:123
John W. d 6 Feb 1840 ae: 29y.
A Tomb 60
Joshua d 20 Feb 1748 ae: 51y.
GSL
Capt. Lemuel d 11 Aug 1846 ae:
79y. Revolutionary War. A
Tomb 60
Lemuel s/o Benjamin & Sally d
12 Sep 1855 ae: 63y. SD G:1
Lucy w/o Enoch b 29 Apr 1791 d
11 Jan 1822. SD G:21
Lucy Crosby d/o Franklin &
Lucy S. d 24 Aug 1846 ae: 5m.
A Tomb 60
Lucy Shaw w/o Franklin C. d 7
Dec 1859 ae: 44y. A Tomb 60
Mary d/o Samuel & Mary d 22
Oct 1808. G:9
Mary wid/o Samuel d 6 Nov 1847
ae: 73y. A Tomb 60
Molly w/o William d 5 Aug 1799
ae: 41y. G:15
Nancy d/o William & Molly d 29
July 1807 ae: 23y. G:18
Nancy Elizabeth d/o William d
17 Sep 1826 ae: 3y 3m. B-4-6
Capt. Nathaniel d 7 May 1815 ae:
57y. G:5
Polly d 14 June 1789 ae: 2m 23d.
G:13
Polly d/o Benjamin & Sally d 13
Aug 1855 ae: 65y. SD G:1
Sally Richards w/o Benjamin d
15 Aug 1815 ae: 59y. G:3
Samuel d 5 Apr 1729 ae: 62y.
Colonial Wars. Interesting
stone. D:27
Samuel s/o Samuel & Esther d
22 Sep 1758 ae: 59y. GSL
Samuel d 1 Aug 1844 ae: 75y. A
Tomb 60
William b 16 Feb 1756 d 16 Feb
1821. Revolutionary War.
G:19
William d 22 July 1835 ae: 40y.
SB B-4-7
MOORE, Ann M. d 22 Apr 1858
ae: 34y 8m. SB B-4-20
Charles s/o Elijah & Sally b 31

MOORE (continued)

Oct 1807 d 22 Feb 1808. G:138

Ephraim d 14 Mar 1869 ae: 69y. SBE A-7-22

George F. d/o James B. & Sally d 19 Aug 1829 ae: 1y. SD J:163

Julia A. d/o James B. & Sally d 20 Oct 1817 ae: 2m. SD J:163

Mary d 30 Nov 1842 ae: 40y. Widow. GSL

Mary P. wid/o Ephraim d 23 Jan 1887 ae: 86y 5m. GSL

Sally w/o Capt. Elijah d 30 May 1811 ae: 27y. SD G:130

Sally d/o Capt. Elijah & Sally d 14 Sep 1811 ae: 6m 17d. SBE G:131

William s/o Elijah & Sally b 17 Aug 1805 d 24 Apr 1806. G:136

William d 20 Oct 1850 ae: 42y. GSL

William E. d 22 Mar 1843 ae: 33y. GSL

William H. s/o late William d 20 Nov 1847 ae: 6y. "Buried Strangers' Ground." GSL

MORGAN, Frederick C. H. s/o John d 11 Aug 1841 ae: 19m. GSL

George E. s/o A. P. d 6 Apr 1859 ae: 1y. GSL

John d 3 Jan 1855 ae: 91y. GSL

Lilly d/o Theophilas B. d 25 Nov 1861 ae: 17m. GSL

Mary d 28 Apr 1866 ae: 93y. GSL

Mary M. d/o James d 15 Sep 1867 ae: 5m. A Tomb 30

Rosanna d/o Theophilus d 17 June 1846 ae: 13m. "Buried beside Simeon Alexander." NS H:168

Sarah A. d/o Jacob L. d 9 June 1858 ae: 16y. GSL

MORRILL, Charles S. d 10 Aug 1849 ae: 38y. GSL

Charles S. s/o late Charles S. d 19 Aug 1849 ae: 5y. GSL

Clara C. d/o A. W. d 30 Sep 1857 ae: 1y 9m. "Buried at

MORRILL (continued)

head of O. Everett's wife's grave." NS E:40

Mary wid/o Capt. Asa d 1 Sep 1835 ae: 57y. B-2-16

Nancy d 25 Sep 1847 ae: 24y. GSL

MORRIS, Hester d/o William d 21 Sep 1851 ae: 5y. Black. GSL

George H. d 13 Oct 1863 ae: 31y 10m. GSL

Martha F. d/o George d 19 Mar 1864 ae: 16m. GSL

William d 19 Jan 1862 ae: 54y. Black. GSL

MORRISON, Charles J. s/o Daniel d 11 Dec 1870 ae: 42y 5m. GSL

Daniel d 1 Feb 1870 ae: 85y. GSL

Francis A. d/o Daniel Jr. d 24 Dec 1852 ae: 11m. GSL

Julia M. d/o Daniel d 24 Mar 1847 ae: 10m. "Buried at head of Samuel Allen's child's grave." NS B-10-20

MORSE, Calvin S. d 18 Aug 1841 ae: 37y. GSL

Charles A. s/o John R. & Harriet A. d 29 June 1923 ae: 74y 11m 25d. I:142A

Elisha d 3 Sep 1845 ae: 76y. SBE A-19-1

Elizabeth w/o Elisha d 11 May 1845 ae: 72y. A-19-2

George s/o John & Ann b 19 Aug 1804 d 7 Sep 1804. SB I:21

Harriet A. Murch w/o John R. b 5 Dec 1826 d 18 Apr 1907. I:142B

John R. d 20 Sep 1897 ae: 73y 10m 6d. I:142C

John S. s/o John R. & Harriet A. b 23 Feb 1854 d 6 May 1905. I:137B

Lizzie Markly d/o John R. d 4 Oct 1860 ae: 1y 11m. I:137B

Moses L. s/o John & Ann b 19 Nov 1800 d 8 June 1805. SB I:21

Stephen C. d 8 Oct 1861 ae: 26y

MOSES, Henry d 15 July 1842 ae: 55y. SBE

Margaret F d/o Rufus & Margaret W d 7 Oct 1840 ae: 12y 15d. SB C:167

Mary M w/o TB Jr d 21 Nov 1843 ae: 25y. H:104

MOSLEY, Blanche d/o Charles B d 12 June 1867 ae: 6m. GSL

MOSLICH, William d 19 Dec 1847 ae: 36y. GSL

MOTLEY, Anna L d/o Richard & Sally nd. ae: 6m. SD H:173

Edward d 21 Jan 1860 ae: 24y. GSL

Edward s/o Thomas & Emma d 27 Feb 1857 ae: 73y. H:167

Emma Waite wid/o Thomas d/o John Waite d 19 Jan 1830 ae: 85y. H:168

Nancy Marble w/o Capt. Robert d/o Daniel & Ann b 7 May 1777 d 23 Jan 1804. H:170

Sally Weeks w/o Richard d/o Lemuel Weeks d 30 Dec 1809 ae: 27y. H:172

Thomas d 27 Dec 1808 ae: 63y. H:169

William Henry s/o Richard & Sally nd. ae: 10m. H:171

MOULTON, Charles s/o William Jr & Hannah b 18 Apr 1798 d 30 June 1799. I:64

Edward d 19 Apr 1867 ae: 62y. GSL

Capt Elias d 7 May 1845 ae: 66y 6m. A-13-2

George Lowther s/o William Jr & Hannah b 11 Feb 1796 d 9 May 1800. I:63

Mary, wid/Capt. Elias d Dec 1854 ae: 73y 5m. "Died Windham." SB A-13-3

Mercy Ann w/o Levi Q d 12 Sep 1854 ae: 33y. GSL

Thomas s/o William Jr & Hannah d 13 Oct 1809 ae: 16y. SB I:65

MOUNTFORT, Annie C d/o James d 21 Mar 1893 ae: 64y 1m. GSL

Cynthia w/o Samuel d 26 Dec

MOUNTFORT (continued) 1837 ae: 76y. SB D:31

Capt Daniel b 25 July 1794 d 23 Dec 1839. A Tomb 35

Daniel d 23 Dec 1839 ae: 45y. SBE D:35

Daniel d 9 Jan 1822 ae: 60y. Rev/War. D:36

Daniel E s/o Elias d 7 Apr 1862 ae: 22y. Civ/War: 10th Reg Maine Inf Co B d typhoid fever, Harper's Ferry, VA. A Tomb 35

Daniel W s/o Joseph d 14 Aug 1854 ae: 20m. GSL

Edmund d 21 Nov 1737 ae: 43y. SB D:31

Edmund s/o Edmund & Mary d 29 Apr 1806 ae: 74y. SB D:31

Elizabeth d 29 Dec 1818 ae: 89y. D:29

Elizabeth I d/o Daniel & Elizabeth d 17 Dec 1876 ae: 70y. SB D:39

Elizabeth wid/o Daniel d 6 Jan 1852 ae: 84y. SBE D:35

Hannah Caswell wid/o Edmund d 1 Dec 1813 ae: 83y. SB D:31

Isaac s/o Daniel & Elizabeth d 5 Oct 1809 ae: 21y. "Died at Havana." D:38

James d 26 Apr 1873 ae: 81y. A Tomb 35

Jane d/o Daniel & Elizabeth d 7 May 1868 ae: 64y. SB D:39

Jennie P d/o Capt Joseph d 31 Aug 1858 ae: 15m. GSL

John d 1815 ae: 19y. "Lost on the Dash." D:35

Joseph d 3 Sep 1881 ae: 69y. GSL

Joseph s/o Daniel & Elizabeth d 14 Sep 1809 ae: 20y. D:33

Mary D w/o Joseph d 20 Aug 1888 ae: 63y 10m. GSL

Mary d/o Edmund & Hannah d 1 Mar 1825 ae: 71y. SB D:31

Mary d/o Samuel & Cynthia d 2 Jan 1828 ae: 44y. SB D:31

Mary Moody wid/o Edmund d 1751 ae: 50y. SB D:31

Mary Mussey wid/o Capt Daniel

MOUNTFORT (continued)
b 1O Jan 1791 d 15 June 1851. A Tomb 35

Mary S w/o James d 21 Nov 1877 ae: 85y. A Tomb 35

Samuel d 21 Oct 1819 ae: 83y. D:28

Samuel s/o Edmund & Hannah d 5 Aug 1828 ae: 73y. SB D:31

William s/o Daniel & Elizabeth d 1O Feb 1824 ae: 24y. D:38

MOXEY, Ezra d 4 Sep 1852 ae: 38y. GSL

MUGFORD, Adaline w/o Peter d 1O Nov 1834 ae: 26y. A-2-20

Horace M s/o Peter d 1 June 1863 ae: 25y 8m 22d. GSL

John Bisbee s/o Peter & Adaline d 24 Dec 1835 ae: 6y. SBE A-2-21

MULHERN, Edward W s/o Edward d 14 Mar 1866 ae: 8m. GSL

MUNSELL, Hannah d 29 Sep 1858 ae: 89y 1Om. "Buried in Capt JB Coyle's lot." GSL

MURCH, Albert N d 30 Dec 1857 ae: 34y. L:58

Almira w/o Josiah d 30 Sep 1881 ae: 83y 4m. I:140

Ann widow d 14 May 1843 ae: 87y. GSL

Charles J s/o Josiah & Almira d 7 Sep 1855 ae: 22y 7m. SBE I:138

Charles S s/o Sumner C d 7 June 1857 ae: 4w. NS I:141A

Edwin F s/o Josiah d 16 June 1859 ae: 21y. GSL

Eliza A d/o John & Elizabeth b 12 Apr 1820 d 5 Nov 1821. SD L:54

Elizabeth T d/o John & Elizabeth nd. ae: 14y. L:52

Elizabeth w/o John d 18 Mar 1863 ae: 69y. SB L:60

George d 14 Aug 1861 ae: 73y. GSL

George Washington s/o Josiah & Almira d 7 Aug 1825 ae: 22m. SD G:125

Harriet d/o Josiah & Almira b 5

MURCH (continued)
Feb 1820 d 1O Sep 1820. SD G:126

Harriet T d 5 Mar 1858 ae: 29y. L:57

John d 14 Feb 1849 ae: 58y. L:59

Josiah b 3 Jan 1798 d 9 Oct 1883. SBE I:141

Mary Ann d/o John & Elizabeth b 1 Nov 1825 d 21 Sep 1831. L:55

Sarah Ann d/o John & Elizabeth b 4 Mar 1817 d 3 May 1819. L:53

Sumner Cummings s/o John & Elizabeth d 2 Aug 1832. L:56

Thomas s/o Josiah & Almira b 18 Aug 1822 d 1O Feb 1823. SD G:127

MURDOCK, Alice A w/o Rev Thomas J d 1O Feb 1820 ae: 23y. SBE H:2

MURPHY, Margaret d/o John d 8 Mar 1853 ae: 1y. Catholic. GSL

William d 22 July 1850 ae: 20y. GSL

MURRAY, Cornelius s/o Silas P & Margaret d 16 June 1825 ae: 25d. B-12-8

Ebenezer R d 1 Feb 1847 ae: 33y. Black. GSL

George M d 23 May 1844 ae: 24y. "Died in Cambridge." Black. GSL

MUSSEY, Betsy wid/o Capt Daniel d 26 Nov 1835 ae: 77y. SBE C:134

Charles s/o John & Abby d 29 Mar 1836 ae: 2y 2m. SD K:66

Capt Daniel d 31 Aug 1828 ae: 73y. SBE C:133

John s/o B & M d 23 May 1837 ae: 29y 9m. K:65

Mary B w/o Daniel d 25 Oct 1852 ae: 51y. B-5-13

NASH, Elizabeth w/o Andrew d 19 Mar 1849 ae: 23y. A Tomb 30

George E s/o Andrew T d 3 Mar 1849 ae: 3m. A Tomb 30

NASON, Abba Ann w/o Elisha P d

NASON (continued)

16 Oct 1847 ae: 21y. GSL

Capt Albert G d 28 Mar 1847 ae: 35y. "Drowned from the barque *Cactus*." GSL

Dolly wid/o Capt John d 6 May 1858 ae: 73y. SD I:150

Maria d 21 Jan 1844 ae: 25y. "Buried beside C French's stone." GSL

Price B L d 26 Dec 1846 ae: 18y. GSL

Susan d 23 Jan 1855 ae: 88y. GSL

NEAL, Caleb H d 12 May 1852 ae: 27y. Black. GSL

Gilbert Stacy s/o MH d 14 Aug 1858 ae: 9m. GSL

John d 7 Dec 1798 ae: 53y. K:154

Sarah Wadsworth, wid/o John d/o "Dr John Wadsworth of Duxbury, Massachusetts & s/o John Wadsworth, tutor at Cambridge College in 1775." d 26 Dec 1830 ae: 86y. K:153

NELSON, Elinore d/o Andrew d 18 Jan 1862 ae: 11m. GSL

Eliza Ann d 15 Aug 1845 ae: 19y. GSL

Julius J s/o Peter d 15 Oct 1850 ae: 2y.

NEPTUNE, John d 22 May 1853 ae: 31y. Black. GSL

NEVENNS, William H s/o William H & Clarissa J d 4 Nov 1855 ae: 9y 7m. B-13-2

NEWALL, John H s/o James B d 1O Sep 1849 ae: 15m. GSL

NEWBALL, George N s/o Albert & Susan d 22 Aug 1800 ae: 1Om 9d. SB D:105

Nancy Marwick d 25 July 1815 ae: 27y. SBE B-9-5

William d 8 July 1814 ae: 35y. SBE B-9-5

NEWCOMB, Betsy Loring w/o William d 29 June 1895 ae: 88y. "Died Emporia, VA." NS G:128

NEWELL, Almira E w/o James B d 11 Dec 1866 ae: 56y. GSL

Eliza Jane d/o James B d 27

NEWELL (continued)

July 1847 ae: 1y. GSL

John s/o James B d 3 May 1846 ae: 20m. GSL

Lillian C d 12 Dec 1857 ae: 6y 7m 7d. GSL

Lucretia d/o James B & Almira d 26 Jan 1840. J:211

Lucretia E d/o James B & Almira d 11 Oct 1841 ae: 1y. GSL

NEWHALL, Albert d 17 Mar 1853 ae: 81y. "Buried Newhall tomb." GSL

NEWINGHOUSE, Cornelius d 28 Jan 1805 ae: 22y. "Crewman, ship *Richmond*." GSL

NEWMAN, Bethiah w/o Thomas d 5 Aug 1801 ae: 53y. G:73

Chester Howard s/o John C d 1O Feb 1895 ae: 3y. A Tomb 24

Daniel d 20 Apr 1823 ae: 51y. G:69

Elizabeth w/o Cornelius d 6 Aug 1798 ae: 21y. G:74

Hannah w/o Samuel d 23 Aug 1855 ae: 75y. GSL

John W d 24 July 1890 ae: 78y 8m. A Tomb 24

Lucy E d/o John W & Lucy H d 12 Oct 1813 ae: 3m. SBE K:21

Lydia d/o Thomas & Anna d 1 May 1813 ae: 23y. G:70

Lydia d/o Thomas & Lydia d 8 May 1789 ae: 20y. G:76

Margaret d/o Cornelius & Elizabeth d 26 Oct 1801 ae: 3y 5m. G:75

Marian w/o John C d 11 Mar 1896 ae: 33y 2m 15d. A Tomb 24

Martha d 9 Oct 1847 ae: 62y. GSL

Nancy d/o Cornelius & Catherine b 11 Jan d 11 Aug 1806. SD

Samuel d 25 Oct 1864 ae: 81y 6m. GSL

Sewall C s/o John C & Marian d 13 July 1891 ae: 4m. A Tomb 24

Thomas d 28 Nov 1801 ae: 65y. G:72

NEWTON, Eliza d 25 Feb 1869 ae: 64y. GSL

NICHOLS, Ann d 31 Dec 1813 ae: 24y. SD E:43

Anna w/o Amos d 11 July 1824 ae: 31y. SBE B-1-4

Arabella M d 30 Apr 1855 ae: 56y. A Tomb 17

Charles s/o Rev Ichabod & Dorothea T d 6 May 1819 ae: 24d. A Tomb 84

Col Martin d 27 Oct 1814 ae: 36y. SBE C:34

Dorothea T w/o Rev Ichabod d 17 Apr 1831 ae: 46y. A Tomb 84

Ellen M d/o late Thomas d 28 Dec 1854. A Tomb 17

Eunice wid/o Martin d 24 Aug 1829 ae: 50y. SBE C:30

Frances Ellen w/o Charles E d 24 Apr 1848 ae: 25y. d/o Capt John & Catherine Williams "Died New York." MmtE A Tomb 14

Harriet W d/o Herbert J & Mary A d 11 Mar 1851 ae: 18y. SB C:44

Herbert s/o Herbert J & Mary A d 8 Aug 1858 ae: 18y 8m. SB C:43

John d 1 Sep 1844 ae: 22y. "Stranger, sailor" "Buried Strangers' Ground near hearse house door." GSL

John d 22 May 1819 ae: 36y. E:42

John Taylor Gilman s/o Rev Ichabod & Dorothea T d 4 Jan 1814 ae: 17m. A Tomb 84

Lucy Milk d/o John & Elizabeth d 31 July 1819 ae: 6y. E:41

Mary A A d/o Amos & Anna d 28 July 1824 ae: 13w 4d. SBE B-1-4

Theodore s/o Francis & Hannah D d 13 May 1850 ae: 2y 6m. SD E:10

William Wallace s/o Charles E & Frances E d 19 Oct 1848 ae: 21m. MmtBE A Tomb 14

NILES, Abraham W s/o Abraham W d 10 Feb 1859 ae: 18y 8m.

NILES (continued) Black. GSL

Ebenezer D d 6 Apr 1835 ae: 35y. B-11-21

Eugene Francis s/o Charles W d 14 May 1854 ae: 2y. GSL

Eugene Frank s/o Charles W d 3 July 1861 ae: 5y. GSL

Harriet Elizabeth d/o Abraham W d 2 Jan 1846 ae: 14y 4m. Black. GSL

Isaac R s/o Abraham W d 16 June 1845 ae: 2 1/2y. Black. GSL

Judith d 28 Apr 1847 ae: 85y. Black. GSL

Lanath w/o Stephen d 9 Dec 1852 ae: 60y. GSL

Sarah d/o Charles W d 4 Mar 1859 ae: 11m. GSL

Stephen d 18 Dec 1863 ae: 69y. GSL

NOBLE, Abigail w/o Webber d 6 July 1846 ae: 38y. "Buried in Abigail Brackett's grave." NS I:192

Catherine d/o John & Jane d 9 Sep 1902 ae: 83y 4m 8d. "Died Greely Hosp." NS A-7-14

Ellen d 30 Dec 1866 ae: 78y. GSL

Franklin S s/o Robert d 6 Sep 1848 ae: 5m. GSL

Jane w/o John d 15 Apr 1875 ae: 80y. SBE A-7-15

John d 10 Feb 1837 ae: 44y. SB A-7-14

Robert d 20 May 1852 ae: 37y. GSL

Sarah w/o Webber d 18 Apr 1837 ae: 38y. SD I:191

NOLCINI, Charles Murray s/o PC & Mary A d 7 Apr 1827 ae: 9w. B-13-20

NORRIS, Albert L s/o Capt William d 27 Oct 1845 ae: 16y. GSL

Betsy d/o Ezekiel G d 24 Feb 1846 ae: 2y. "Buried at head of Priscilla Washburn's grave." NS B-3-41

NORTH, Anna W d/o John W d 6

NORTH (continued)

July 1854 ae: 11y 5m. GSL

Harriet D d/o John W & HR d 15 Aug 1852 ae: 6y. GSL

John d 22 July 1863 ae: 82y 9m. GSL

Mary d/o John d 1 Apr 1844 ae: 1y. Black. GSL

NORTON, Abigail w/o Rufus d 23 Sep 1871 ae: 99y 4m. "Buried Quaker Ground." GSL

Anna K d/o George L d 15 Dec 1862 ae: 3m. GSL

Asa d 26 Aug 1882 ae: 79y. GSL

Cordelia d/o Jabez d 30 Sep 1846 ae: 12y. GSL

Henry D d 3 Dec 1895 ae: 57y 11m. GSL

Josiah d 24 July 1831 ae: 56y. "Erected by Asa H & Aaron Norton." B-10-18

Nancy d 11 Oct 1884 ae: 77y. "Died Cleveland, Ohio." GSL

Sarah B w/o Aaron d 27 Jan 1844 ae: 33y. A-9-21

NORWOOD, John s/o Joshua & Lydia b 18 Oct 1813 d 2 Mar 1814. SD K:141

NOWELL, Betty w/o Zacheriah d 12 Sep 1823 ae: 62y. F:172

Charles H s/o Henry & Mary d 24 Aug 1825 ae: 11m. B-1-19

Moses d 10 Apr 1853 ae: 89y. War/1812. GSL

Moses s/o Zacheriah & Elizabeth d 5 Oct 1798 ae: 6y 7m. F:171

Zacheriah b1751 d1836 Rev/War: Sgt 15th Reg Massachusetts Cont Line. SB F:173

NOXON, Peter S d 28 July 1853. "Died Lexington, Kentucky." GSL

NOYES, Anna M d/o John H d 15 Aug 1862 ae: 3y 7m. GSL

Charles Holden s/o Osgood & Mary Ann d 27 Jan 1836 ae: 2y. D:137

David d 24 Oct 1845 ae: 80y. A Tomb 52

Dorcas C d 2 Apr 1847 ae: 53y. A Tomb 52

NOYES (continued)

Dorcas d 21 Nov 1840 ae: 64y. J:164

Dorcas w/o Capt Nathaniel d 11 Oct 1809 ae: 27y 8m. D:123

Ebenezer d 1 Nov 1848 ae: 74y. GSL

Edward F d 16 Feb 1857 ae: 54y. GSL

Elizabeth w/o David d 15 Mar 1804 ae: 65y. C:99

Eunice d 25 Mar 1842 ae: 58y. GSL

Ferdinand s/o Abial T & M d 3 June 1846 ae: 16m. SD C:100

Ferdinand s/o Abial T & M d 22 Oct 1850 ae: 4y. GSL

George Henry s/o Robert & Elizabeth b 3 Aug 1840 d 22 Dec 1840. J:164

Hannah w/o Newman d 3 Jan 1843 ae: 61y. "Buried Smith tomb." F:105 Tomb

Harriet G w/o Stephen d 29 Nov 1865 ae: 73y 5m. H:147A

Harriet T d/o Charles d 27 Oct 1847 ae: 1y. GSL

Mrs Hepsibah d 30 Sep 1845 ae: 76y. GSL

Horatio s/o Jacob d 25 Dec 1821 ae: 14y. Died of injuries received in falling from belfry of "Old Noyes, Jerusalem." D:60

Hosea I d 3 Nov 1904 ae: 76y 10m. H:97A

Jacob d 30 June 1820 ae: 52y. D:60

James W s/o James d 14 Aug 1855 ae: 13m. "Buried in E Walsh's lot." NS F:51

James W s/o William & Mary d 20 Aug 1846 ae: 1y 11m. "Buried Strangers' Ground." A-5-23

John d 3 Aug 1824 ae: 53y. SBE J:165

Joseph d 13 Oct 1795 ae: 55y. Rev/War. D:22

Joseph d 14 Feb 1755 ae: 66y. GSL

Judith D w/o George N d 13 Sep

NOYES (continued)
1831 ae: 36y. J:171

Louisa F w/o Ward d 29 Aug 1852 ae: 40y. GSL

Louisa H b1822 d1915. H:97A

Lucinda P w/o Daniel P d 24 Mar 1859 ae: 37y. A Tomb 44

Martha C d/o Prince B d 8 June 1863 ae: 4y 2m. A-12-1A

Mary d 17 Aug 1882 ae: 64y. H:147C

Mary E d/o Pierce B & SS d 23 Feb 1851 ae: 2y. SBE A-12-1

Mary J w/o John d 30 Aug 1849 ae: 46y. GSL

Mary w/o Joseph d 3 Aug 1772 ae: 33y. D:20

Mary w/o William d 14 Aug 1846 ae: 33y. "Buried Strangers' Ground." SBE A-5-24

Newman d 29 Sep 1849 ae: 77y. F:105 Tomb

Noah d 14 June 1800 ae: 68y. SD J:131

Pierce B b 10 Sep 1814 d 12 Nov 1876. A-12-1

Sarah E d 8 Nov 1892 ae: 72y 8m. "Died Quincy, MA." SD A-12-2

Sarah G L d/o John d 24 Sep 1849 ae: 18y. GSL

Sarah Prentiss wid/o Pierce B b 1821 d 1892. A-12-1 1/2

Silas s/o Enoch & Margaret d 7 Oct 1801 ae: 1y 3m. SD J:89

Stephen d 14 Apr 1870 ae: 80y. H:147B

Stephen Jr d 18 Oct 1901 ae: 71y 6m. Civ/War: 10th Rgt Maine Inf Co B. H:147D

Susan C d 4 Oct 1848 ae: 30y. GSL

Susannah w/o Noah d 11 July 1799 ae: 57y. J:130

Susannah C d/o John & Dorcas d 3 Oct 1848 ae: 31y. SBE J:167

William s/o Jacob & Ann d 29 Apr 1802. SD D:25

William M d 3 May 1853 ae: 25y. GSL

OBEAR, William R d 4 Aug 1855 ae: 63y. SBE C:77

O'BRION, James d 19 June 1851 ae: 43y. GSL

O'DONNELL, Mary w/o James d 7 June 1844 ae: 31y. F:96 Tomb

O'FRIELL, John s/o B & E d 22 Nov 1834 ae: 15y. Catholic. C:89

OLIVER, Frank Hector s/o Andrew d 9 Sep 1881 ae: 12y. "Died Berlin Falls, NH." A Tomb 1

OLNEY, Rev Gideon W d 18 Feb 1838 ae: 45y. A Tomb 83

ORCUTT, Edwin d 29 June 1850 ae: 41y. A Tomb 58

ORDWAY, Emily N d/o Reuben d 20 Nov 1851 ae: 23y. A Tomb 57

Frances A E d/o Joseph M Gerrish d 20 Aug 1895 ae: 84y 10m 7d. A Tomb 57

Reuben d 21 June 1856 ae: 55y. A Tomb 57

O'RILEY, Martin d 14 June 1843 ae: 47y. "Native of Ireland, County Tipperary, Parish of Anacarty" "Buried with four children." Catholic. B-14-9

ORMSBEE, H Elizabeth d/o Marcus d 5 Apr 1849 ae: 14y. GSL

ORMSBY, Frederick d 24 Mar 1858 ae: 61y. GSL

John H Jan 1793-13 Apr 1841. "Born in Europe." MmtE E:93

OSBORN, John O s/o William d 27 Apr 1845 ae: 8y. "Buried beside Mary Pote." Black. NS J:93

OSBORNE, George S s/o Woodbridge C d 27 Aug 1849 ae: 10y. GSL

Lucy A S w/o A O d 22 Oct 1892 ae: 72y. "Died Boston, Maine." F:95 Tomb

Mamie E d/o A P d 19 June 1877 ae: 19y. "Died Boston, MA." A Tomb 7

Mary A d/o Thomas d 8 Oct 1850 ae: 2y. GSL

OSGOOD, Abby L d/o late Capt Francis d 8 Apr 1862 ae: 15y.

OSGOOD (continued)
A Tomb 17

Abraham b Amesbury, England 1729 d 23 Dec 1816. Rev/War. C:12

Cornelia C d/o Abraham Jr d 22 May 1849 ae: 2y. A Tomb 82

Eunice w/o Gen Francis B d 18 Sep 1854 ae: 77y. SD C:14

Gen Francis B d 6 Sep 1817 ae: 40y. C:13

Georgetta d/o Abraham Jr d 3 Apr 1849 ae: 5y. A Tomb 82

Lydia w/o Thomas d 26 Oct 1848 ae: 55y. GSL

Mary w/o Abraham d 17 May 1841 ae: 50y. A Tomb 82

Sarah w/o Timothy d 16 Nov 1838 ae: 73y. A Tomb 45

Sarah d/o Thomas d 24 Apr 1866 ae: 55y. GSL

Timothy d 22 Aug 1839 ae: 80y. A Tomb 45

William E d 27 Oct 1837 ae: 30y. C:15

OSWALD, Sylvia d 28 Aug 1852 ae: 53y 8m. Black. GSL

OWEN, Abigail b 17 Oct 1800 d 23 Aug 1802. A Tomb 39

Abigail d/o Ebenezer & Abigail d 13 Jan 1820 ae: 55y. SBE H:47

Abigail Cotton w/o Ebenezer d/o Deacon William & Sarah Cotton d 26 May 1798 ae: 56y. SB H:45

Abigail C d/o Joseph & Sarah d 23 Aug 1802 ae: 2y. H:46

Ebenezer d 26 Aug 1817 ae: 79y. Rev/War. H:44

James A s/o William S d 4 Dec 1859 ae: 31y. GSL

John d 24 Nov 1842 ae: 67y. GSL

Joseph b 24 Oct 1769 d 24 Feb 1836. A Tomb 39

Martha b 14 Mar 1804 d 14 Apr 1804. A Tomb 39

Martha O d/o Joseph & Sarah d 14 Apr 1804 ae: 1m. H:46

Mary d 15 May 1838 ae: 72y. A Tomb 39

Mary d 27 June 1871 ae: 83y.

OWEN (continued)
SBE C:138

Sarah, wid/o Joseph d 31 Jan 1849 ae: 82y. A Tomb 39

Susan B w/o William S d 8 Sep 1859 ae: 58y. GSL

William S d 28 May 1861 ae: 68y. GSL

OXNARD, Caroline G d/o Edward & Martha b 10 Feb 1828 d 2 Sep 1829. H:135

Edward s/o Thomas & Sarah b 30 July 1747 d 2 July 1803. Rev/War: Loyalist. H:132

Henry s/o Edward & Rebekah d 27 Sep 1807 ae: 13m 19d. H:103

Martha Preble d/o Jedediah Preble wid/o Thomas d 16 Oct 1824 ae: 70y. SB H:134

Mary Fox wid/o Edward d/o Jabez Fox d 22 Aug 1835 ae: 81y. H:129

Thomas s/o Thomas & Sarah d 20 May 1799 ae: 59y. Rev/War: Loyalist. H:130

PAGE, Daniel s/o Richard d 27 June 1858 ae: 3w. GSL

Julia A w/o William SC d 4 July 1905 ae: 83y 10m 11d. GSL

Sarah d 29 June 1841 ae: 60y. GSL

PAINE, ---- wid/o Jonathan buried 31 Apr 1850 ae: 51y. "Moved from Work House tomb to side of husband's grave stone." GSL

Alexander s/o Capt Jonathan & Dorcas d 18 Sep 1818 ae: 29y. "Died in Demarara." G:42

Alma G d/o JS d 28 Aug 1849 ae: 7y. "Buried near turn of the road." GSL

Arabella d 1 Aug 1823 ae: 9m. B-14-15

Charles C s/o David & CAS b 1841 d 30 Sep 1843. MmtE A Tomb 36

Daniel M b 4 Feb 1826 d 25 Oct 1845. B-3-2

Dorcas d/o Capt Jonathan & Dorcas d 13 Nov 1806 ae: 39y. G:44

PAINE (continued)

Eliza W S d/o David & CAS b 1840 d 1843. MmtE A Tomb 36

Emily d 21 July 1837 ae: 28y. B-2-15

Franklin s/o David & CAS b&d 1857. MmtE A Tomb 36

George B s/o John S d 6 Sep 1851 ae: 1y. MmtE A Tomb 36

Dr James d 11 Feb 1822 ae: 63y. SBE I:178

Jane d/o David d 3 Sep 1843 ae: 2y. MmtE A Tomb 36

Jane wid/o John KH d 17 Mar 1863 ae: 72y. B-3-3

John B s/o John KH & Jane d 17 Apr 1830 ae: 9y. B-3-3

John K H b 1787 d 28 Aug 1835. B-3-4

Jonathan d 11 Aug 1823 ae: 51y. SD B-14-16

Jonathan d 2 May 1859 ae: 60y. MmtE A Tomb 36

Josiah d 21 Jan 1825 ae: 65y. NMmt A Tomb 51

Sarah W d 13 Nov 1838 ae: 78y. SBE I:177

Thomas d 24 Jan 1802 ae: 77y. Rev/War. MmtB MmtE I:179

Thomas d 22 Dec 1861 ae: 22y. Civ/War: "Brevet in cavalry battery." GSL

William d 30 Aug 1861 ae: 64y. GSL

PALMER, Isaiah H s/o Henry & J d 5 June 1848 ae: 3y. Black. A-7-27

Joseph E s/o Joseph d 29 Nov 1850 ae: 2y. A Tomb 21

Thomas L d 30 Jan 1850 ae: 28y. Black. GSL

PARIS, Sally wid/o d 7 Oct 1842 ae: 49y. GSL

PARKER, Caroline E wid/o Nathaniel d 23 Feb 1856 ae: 26y. GSL

Ellen A d/o William W & Mary A d 15 Oct 1849 ae: 16m 15d. I:149

George d 23 Aug 1853 ae: 19y. "...of Bangor" "Died Marine Hospital." GSL

PARKER (continued)

Hannibal d 29 Sep 1849 ae: 31y. SBE J:82

John H T s/o Isaac & Rebecca d 27 Sep 1804 ae: 2y. J:198

Joseph H s/o Isaac & Rebecca d 27 Sep 1800 ae: 9m. J:199

Louisa A d/o William & Sarah d 3 June 1822 ae: 8m. I:145

Mary wid/o d 17 Aug 1847 ae: 43y. GSL

Mary A w/o Joseph d 24 Aug 1838 ae: 42y. I:5

Mary Ann d/o William & Sarah d 13 Apr 1811 ae: 6m. I:146

Mary E w/o Irvino W d 6 Feb 1892 ae: 57y. GSL

Mary Kent d/o William & Sarah d 21 May 1816 ae: 2y 6m. I:147

Sarah w/o William d 10 Aug 1827 ae: 36y. SBE I:144

William d 4 Mar 1841 ae: 58y. SBE I:143

William S s/o William W & Mary A d 2 Apr 1850 ae: 9y 2m. SD I:148

PARKHURST, Franklin s/o William C d 13 Apr 1848 ae: 3y 3m. A Tomb 30

PARKS, Susan d/o Joseph & Elizabeth d 6 Sep 1825 ae: 1y 10m. B-11-2

PARRS, Charles L s/o John & Rebecca R d 20 Nov 1837 ae: 5m. Black. SD A-13-26

Priscilla d/o John d 6 Nov 1852 ae: 15m. Black. GSL

Rebecca R w/o John d 22 Nov 1837 ae: 32y. Black. SBE A-13-26

PARSONS, ---- s/o Nathaniel d 14 Apr 1853 ae: 29y. GSL

Ann w/o Samuel d 15 Sep 1856 ae: 29y. "Died Westbrook, Maine." GSL

Betsy d/o George W & Ann I d 19 Nov 1838 ae: 15m. SB B-4-14

Edwin MD d 29 Apr 1860 ae: 53y. A Tomb 68

Elizabeth w/o Thomas B d 25

PARSONS (continued)

Nov 1843 ae: 59y. SD H:73

George A s/o Benjamin d 8 Sep 1857 ae: 16m. GSL

George Anderson s/o George W & Ann I d 13 Oct 1842 ae: 24y. A-14-13

George J d 12 Oct 1842 ae: 24y. GSL

George R B s/o Richard & Huldah d 2 Feb 1853 ae: 20m. K:59

Hannah w/o Josiah d 13 Sep 1847 ae: 55y. "Buried south of alley to Hancock Street." GSL

Henry B s/o Peter & Nancy d 13 Feb 1823 ae: 16y. D:119

Jane w/o Capt Samuel d 17 Dec 1851 ae: 43y 5m. K:78

John R s/o Richard & Huldah d 2 Mar 1847 ae: 4d. K:59

Capt Josiah d 31 Aug 1826 ae: 68y. B-4-15

Julia H Bragdon w/o Richard b 26 Dec 1822 d 24 Nov 1868. "Born Durham, Maine." K:58

Richard d 3 July 1883 ae: 69y. K:57

Robert s/o George W & Ann I d 5 Sep 1827 ae: 13m. SB B-4-14

William F s/o William d 9 May 1846 ae: 16m. GSL

William H d 28 May 1832 ae: 23y. SBE K:76

PASCAL, Amy d/o John d 26 Aug 1847 ae: 7m. "Buried near the hearse house." GSL

Emily w/o John d 19 June 1854 ae: 53y. SBE J:224

George H s/o George d 12 Sep 1847 ae: 8m. GSL

Madeline M d/o John & Emily d 23 Nov 1853 ae: 16y. SBE J:224

Sarah G d/o John & Emily d 19 Oct 1854 ae: 19y. SBE J:224

PATCH, Mrs Margaret d 19 Aug 1852 ae: 74y. GSL

Nehemiah d 29 May 1846 ae: 79y. "Buried beside son." GSL

PATRICK, Esther w/o Stephen d 9 July 1841 ae: 48y. GSL

PATRICK (continued)

Frances A d/o Stephen d 15 June 1841 ae: 6y. GSL

PARTRIDGE, Elizabeth w/o William P d May 1804 ae: 41y. GSL

PATTEN, Charles S b 1809 d 23 Feb 1881. A Tomb 33

Charles S Interred 11 Aug 1938. A Tomb 33

Ezekiel d 24 Dec 1822 ae: 31y. SBE B-5-18

Horace Ward d 26 Apr 1865 ae: 4y 5m. GSL

John d 20 Feb 1834 ae: 46y. A Tomb 33

John E d 25 Apr 1838 ae: 24y. A Tomb 33

Olive L d 8 Aug 1838 ae: 20y. A Tomb 33

Olive L wid/o John d 11 Feb 1864 ae: 74y. A Tomb 33

Stephen d 18 Feb 1855 ae: 90y. GSL

Susan w/o Stephen b 3 Dec 1781 d 5 Jan 1810. SBE I:51

Susannah wid/o Robert d 4 May 1841 ae: 77y. A Tomb 33

PATTERSON, Elizabeth d 29 Sep 1842 ae: 33y. GSL

John d 3 Aug 1858 ae: 38y. "Born Lisbon, Portugal" "Died at the hospital." GSL

John H s/o Louisa d 8 Feb 1864 ae: 13y. GSL

Margaret wid/o Capt William d 2 Apr 1835 ae: 67y. SBE B-12-12

Margaret, d/o Simon d 22 Mar 1842 ae: 35y. GSL

Mary L d/o William d 27 May 1849 ae: 1y. Black. GSL

PAUL, James d 1 Nov 1869 ae: 83y. GSL

PEARCE, Charles H s/o Eben d 15 Mar 1846 ae: 3y. GSL

Lucinda C adopted d/o JK & Sarah S d 29 Aug 1848 ae: 19y. L:51

PEARSON, Abby T d/o Joseph L d 13 Oct 1859 ae: 6m. GSL

Albert s/o George d 18 June 1842

PEARSON (continued)

ae: 6m. GSL

Albert R s/o John & Ann d 11 Nov 1831 ae: 1y. SBE F:4

Ann w/o John d 4 Feb 1838 ae: 31y. SBE F:4

Ann L d/o John d 2 May 1852 ae: 18y. GSL

Anna w/o Samuel d 15 Sep 1856 ae: 59y. SD J:208

Charles d 1 Nov 1830 ae: 41y. B-7-2

Clarina Jenks d/o Henry & Dolly d 2 Aug 1819 ae: 11m 16d. F:126

Dolly w/o Henry d 5 Oct 1842 ae: 49y. GSL

Elizabeth d 21 Mar 1851 ae: 70y. GSL

Ellen Marie d/o John d 11 Mar 1855 ae: 9y. GSL

Freddie s/o Moses d 3 Nov 1858 ae: 6w. GSL

Georgianna Haskell wid/o Charles B d/o Alexander N & Elizabeth Haskell b 11 Dec 1849 d 12 Apr 1930. A-10-3

Hannah Mason w/o John d 10 May 1848 ae: 35y. SBE F:7

Harriet d 3 Apr 1832 ae: 19y. B-2-13

Harriet d/o John d 17 Oct 1841 ae: 16m. GSL

Henry S d 31 Aug 1878 ae: 89y. A Tomb 57

John d 27 Jan 1883 ae: 79y. GSL

John H s/o John D & Mary C b 1 June 1828 d 1 July 1828. B-6-29

Josiah d 13 June 1849 ae: 74y. GSL

Loring A s/o Benjamin d 2 Sep 1858 ae: 6y. GSL

Mary d 20 Mar 1865 ae: 65y. GSL

Mary s/o William d 26 Nov 1845 ae: 60y. GSL

Moses d 5 June 1778 ae: 82y. Sheriff: Cumberland County Col/Wars. C:186

Samuel d 18 Nov 1856 ae: 73y. "D. Westbrook, ME" NS J:209

PEARSON (continued)

Sarah w/o Moses d/o William Titcomb d 2 Nov 1766 ae: 73y. C:185

William S s/o John d 31 Aug 1845 ae: 9m. GSL

PECK, Henry d 23 Dec 1839 ae: 29y. Black. A-10-33

Mary J d/o Rev Benjamin D d 27 Oct 1857 ae: 18y 7m. A Tomb 68

PENNELL, ---- w/o John d 8 Oct 1854 ae: 33y. GSL

Anna d/o Thomas d 25 Jan 1857 ae: 9m. GSL

Charles H s/o Jonathan & Margaret d 20 Mar 1825 ae: 3m. SBE D:56

Clara d/o widow d 3 Oct 1842 ae: 16y. GSL

Clarissa w/o John d 13 Apr 1861 ae: 34y 9m. GSL

Edward s/o Leonard d 10 Nov 1842 ae: 3y 6m. GSL

Eliza T d/o Horace W d 6 Feb 1845 ae: 15m. "Buried beside Joel Haley." GSL

George F s/o Josiah d 14 July 1848 ae: 21y. GSL

Harriet E d/o Jonathan & Margaret d 22 Sep 1831 ae: 11m. SBE D:56

Harriet W wid/o John d 30 May 1860 ae: 49y 4m. "Buried in same grave with J Pennell." GSL

Henrietta d/o Horace W d 3 June 1849 ae: 1y. GSL

Horace W d 20 July 1861 ae: 50y. GSL

Jane B d/o William L d 19 Sep 1850 ae: 10m. GSL

John s/o Jonathan & Margaret d 10 Mar 1836 ae: 9m. SBE D:56

John d 4 May 1854 ae: 75y. GSL

John N s/o Thomas d 25 July 1864 ae: 35y 5m. GSL

Jonathan d 4 Mar 1866 ae: 65y. SD D:57

Margaret w/o Jonathan d 26 Jan 1852 ae: 47y 5m. SBE D:56

PENNELL (continued)

Margaret A d/o Jonathan & Margaret d 14 Nov 1848 ae: 23y. SB D:55

Martha D w/o John N d 24 Aug 1854 ae: 25y. GSL

Mary J Knight w/o John d 28 July 1863 ae: 54y 8m. GSL

Samuel E B s/o Jonathan & Margaret d 26 June 1855 ae: 18y 5m. SD D:58

Sarah d/o Charles d 15 May 1843 ae: 21y. GSL

Mrs Sarah A K d 31 Aug 1852 ae: 22y. GSL

William H s/o Clement d 28 Apr 1845 ae: 12y. A Tomb 30

PERAGIN, Frances A d/o David d 27 Oct 1849 ae: 3m. Black. GSL

PERRY, Harriet C d/o John d 17 Aug 1848 ae: 10m. GSL

Mary Ann J w/o John d 21 Apr 1849 ae: 35y. GSL

PETERS, Ann d 17 Apr 1856 ae: 76y. "Died Work House." GSL

Ann Christianna d/o William B & Mary b 30 Dec 1806 d 1 Oct 1812. H:164

Elizabeth P 2nd w/o William B d 30 Sep 1849 ae: 62y. H:162

H s/o Barnett & Sophia d 1832 ae: 6m. G:15A

H P s/o Barnett & Sophia nd. ae: 6m. SD H:165

John s/o John d 7 June 1843 ae: 6w. GSL

Mary w/o William B b 6 Sep 1770 d 19 Oct 1825. H:161

W B d 1832 ae: 3y 6m. G:15A

William B s/o Barnett & Sophia d 1832 ae: 3y 6m. SD H:165

William B s/o Barnett & Sophia d 23 July 1835 ae: 14m. SD H:166

William B d 3 Oct 1837 ae: 62y. H:160

PETERSON, Africa H d 16 Apr 1825 ae: 29y. B-14-22

Caroline d/o Manuel d 12 Aug 1851 ae: 2y. GSL

Capt Daniel d 26 Oct 1856 ae:

PETERSON (continued)

73y. SBE B-8-31

Frederick s/o John d 9 Oct 1866 ae: 6y. GSL

Hewett W s/o Capt Daniel & Sarah d 10 Mar 1842 ae: 23y. "Lost at sea." SBE B-8-31

John b 16 Oct 1800 d 21 July 1846. Black. SBE A-10-30

John A s/o Daniel & Sarah d 24 Sep 1826 ae: 1y 8m. SD B-8-8

Joseph H s/o Manuel d 26 June 1858 ae: 7y 6m. GSL

Sarah d/o Daniel & Sarah nd. SD B-8-29

Sarah M w/o Capt Daniel d 2 May 1873 ae: 78y. B-8-30

William s/o John d 20 Nov 1857 ae: 2y. GSL

PETTENGILL, Charles B s/o David & Mehitable d 14 Sep 1858 ae: 37y. MmtB A Tomb 21

PETTINGILL, Daniel d 1 Jan 1805 ae: 67y. F:75

Daniel s/o Daniel & Mehitable d 16 Aug 1896 ae: 86y. MmtB A Tomb 21

David d 7 Mar 1847 ae: 74y. MmtB A Tomb 21

Dorcas d/o David & Mehitable d 7 May 1881 ae: 66y. MmtB A Tomb 21

Harriet d/o David & Mehitable d 3 Feb 1848 ae: 42y. MmtB A Tomb 21

Julia A d/o Daniel & Martha A d 25 Mar 1932 ae: 89y 6m 7d. MmtB A Tomb 21

Martha A w/o Daniel d 20 Sep 1894 ae: 76y. MmtB A Tomb 21

PETTES, Georgianna d/o Horatio Q d 26 Aug 1845 ae: 1y. GSL

Georgianna M d/o Horatio Q d 5 Jan 1851 ae: 5y. GSL

Horatio Q s/o Horatio Q d 17 Apr 1850 ae: 17m. GSL

Josephine d/o Horatio Q d 13 May 1851 ae: 3y. GSL

Nancy wid/o Stephen d 19 July 1859 ae: 55y. GSL

PETTES (continued)

William O s/o Horatio Q d 28 Apr 1844 ae: 18m. "Buried Family Range." GSL

PHAGINS, Mary Adelaide d/o Joseph E & Sarah L d 19 Mar 1847 ae: 3m. I:175

Sarah Josephine d/o Joseph E & Sarah L d 24 Mar 1847 ae: 4y 3m. I:175

PHENE, Capt George d 16 Sep 1842 ae: 33y. SD H:77

Helen M d/o George & Elizabeth d 10 Jan 1843 ae: 6m. SD H:77

PHILBROOK, Daniel d 20 Feb 1833 ae: 41y. G:66

Emily Jane d/o Daniel & Rachel C b 1818 d 1 Sep 1846. G:68

Hannah d/o Daniel & Rachel C b 1829 d 4 Aug 1849. G:67

Harriet Newall d/o Daniel & Rachel C b 1820 d 1903. G:68

Rachel C w/o Daniel d 31 May 1878 ae: 82y. G:66

PHILLIPS, Fourteen infant children of William & Elizabeth. H:23

Three infant children nd. I:44

Charles B s/o Warren d 8 May 1853 ae: 3m. GSL

Elizabeth w/o William d 9 Sep 1833 ae: 38y. H:23

Elizabeth D d/o Warren d 7 June 1852. GSL

Frances W d 4 July 1848 ae: 3m. SD J:83

Harriet d 2 Nov 1805 ae: 18m 13d. I:44

Jane d 8 June 1860 ae: 61y 5m. Black. SD L:27

John d 29 Nov 1792 ae: 14m 10d. I:44

Deacon John d 19 Apr 1826 ae: 64y. B-2-23

Margaret wid/o Deacon John d 9 Oct 1856 ae: 85y. B-2-24

Mary E d/o Humphrey d 27 Nov 1846 ae: 3y. GSL

Mary Louisa d 8 Apr 1844 ae: 14y. GSL

Mary A w/o Warren d 28 Nov 1857 ae: 43y. GSL

PHILLIPS (continued)

Nathaniel d 5 Apr 1851 ae: 58y. GSL

Osgood P s/o Warren & Mary A d 25 July 1845 ae: 5w. SD J:83

Rebecca widow d 29 Oct 1844 ae: 85y. "Buried beside s/o Wm Phillips." GSL

William d 23 June 1844 ae: 54y. "Buried Family Range." GSL

PHINNEY, Capt George d 17 Sep 1842 ae: 36y. GSL

Joanna wid/o Rev Clement d 8 Jan 1859 ae: 73y 6m. GSL

PICKARD, Abigail d/o Mrs Ruth d 28 Apr 1827 ae: 17y. SD B-2-32

Ruth d 28 May 1868 ae: 81y. GSL

PIDGEON, Hannah w/o William d 4 Mar 1843 ae: 64y. GSL

Rev William d 8 Feb 1848 ae: 77y. GSL

PIERCE, Lucinda C d/o Jesse K d 28 Aug 1848 ae: 20y. "Died in Boston." GSL

Lucy w/o Eli d 31 Oct 1802 ae: 30y. H:98

Margaret E d 5 Feb 1851 ae: 23y. Black. GSL

Octavia O d/o RN d 4 Sep 1857 ae: 8m. A Tomb 53

Samuel d Jan 1805 ae: 70y. GSL

Susan A d 11 Aug 1845 ae: 14y. F:96 Tomb

PIERRE, Elizabeth d 6 Dec 1854 ae: 68y. Black. GSL

Peter d 21 Aug 1854 ae: 95y 10m 7d. Black. GSL

PINGREE, Justina E d/o Aaron d 24 Feb 1855 ae: 16m. GSL

PITMAN, Rachel wid/o Joshua d 17 Nov 1847 ae: 81y. GSL

PITTEE, Laura S d/o Francis H Cross d 3 Dec 1896 ae: 53y. "Died Augusta - insane." A Tomb 73

Mabel Alice d/o Charles T d 18 Aug 1889 ae: 13y 6m 27d. A Tomb 73

PLUMLEY, Walt. Brad. s/o Burton B d 7 Feb 1894 ae: 28y GSL

PLUMMER, ---- w/o John d 5 Oct 1814 ae: 35y. SBE C:67

Abigail wid/o Moses b 9 Apr 1780 d 6 Oct 1860. C:60

Albert Crockett s/o Moses d 2 Dec 1862 ae: 24y. GSL

Albion M s/o HG d 6 Feb 1857 ae: 7m. GSL

Asa d 12 Mar 1828 ae: 65y. D:78

Edmund S d July 1832 ae: 26y. C:60

Elias s/o Moses & Abigail nd. C:60

Eliza d/o Moses & Abigail nd. C:60

Eliza A w/o William d 9 Aug 1860 ae: 24y 6m. SBE J:159

Else wid/o Asa d 12 Feb 1843 ae: 79y. D:79

Erastus d 22 Sep 1834 ae: 68y. F:50

Esther w/o Moses d 20 July 1815 ae: 70y. SB C:66

Fanny w/o Moses I d 2 Feb 1827 ae: 31y. F:114

George s/o Moses & Abigail nd. C:60

John d 8 Mar 1816 ae: 39y. SB C:68

John W S s/o Moses & Abigail d Oct 1824 ae: 14y. C:60

Joseph b 5 Sep 1770 d 9 Aug 1802. F:49

Mary w/o Moses I d 21 Mar 1859 ae: 53y. SBE D:77

Mary d 21 Sep 1841 ae: 31y. GSL

Mary E w/o Edwin d/o Thomas Norton d 13 Jan 1848 ae: 24y. A Tomb 57

Moses b 3 Jan 1772 d 13 Dec 1847. C:62

Moses d 17 Oct 1824 ae: 84y. C:64

Moses I d 23 Mar 1867 ae: 78y. SBE D:76

Moses J d 14 Nov 1861 ae: 29y. "Died in Matansas." GSL

Samuel s/o Moses & Abigail nd. C:60

Capt Samuel M s/o Moses & Abigail d 17 Oct 1851 ae: 39y. C:60

PLUMMER (continued)

William d 1 Feb 1808 ae: 33y. C:59

William C s/o Moses J d 23 Oct 1841 ae: 3w. GSL

POICE, William d 27 Mar 1850 ae: 55y. GSL

POLAND, Benjamin d 8 Dec 1817 ae: 66y. A Tomb 30

Betsy w/o Stephen d 2 Sep 1807 ae: 27y. I:197

Joseph d 3 Nov 1851 ae: 66y. SD B-1-26

Marian wid/o Stephen d 1 Mar 1858 ae: 75y. B-4-8

Mary w/o William C d 25 May 1832 ae: 21y. F:178

Martha H w/o William C d 18 May 1841 ae: 28y. F:179

Mary Louisa d/o William C & Mary d 14 Aug 1831 ae: 16m. F:176

Stephen d 16 May 1823 ae: 44y. B-4-9

POLLARD, George s/o Sarah d 16 Feb 1855 ae: 1y. GSL

POLLEYS, Elcy w/o William d 13 Nov 1830 ae: 65y. SBE B-7-8

Frederick d 3 Aug 1823 ae: 21y. SBE B-7-6

Frederick R s/o Samuel & Sarah B d19 Aug 1829 ae: 7m. B-7-5

Mary W w/o Capt William d 3 Jan 1846 ae: 50y. GSL

Sarah B D w/o Samuel d 18 Nov 1829 ae: 23y. SBE B-7-4

William d 19 Mar 1830 ae: 68y. Rev/War: Sgt. SBE B-7-7

POLLIS, Mary d/o Woodbury d 10 Nov 1843 ae: 3m. "Buried beside J M Waterhouse stone." GSL

POLLOCK, William C s/o George W d 10 Dec 1854 ae: 4m. "Buried 2nd grave south of Vernon stone." GSL

POMEROY, Mrs Ann Quincy b 5 Apr 1802 d 24 Feb 1866. MmtD A Tomb 18

Phebe d 23 Apr 1828 ae: 40y. B-2-23

POND, Clara wid/o Caleb d 5 Aug 1864 ae: 74y. A Tomb 36

POOLE, Abigail d 24 Aug 1855 ae: 68y. GSL

Abijah d 9 May 1820 ae: 80y. Rev.War. MmtB C:126

Abijah Jr d 24 Aug 1855 ae: 68y. MmtB C:126

Albert W b 1813 d 1865. Mmt A-4-10

Ariadne d/o Calvin d 23 Dec 1860 ae: 10m 5d. GSL

Caroline d/o James Jr & Patience d 8 Aug 1813 ae: 18m. SD K:157

Diana w/o Nathaniel d 21 Jan 1859 ae: 23y. GSL

Dorcas Tucker wid/o Abijah d 10 Mar 1824 ae: 67y. MmtB C:126

Eunice wid/o James d 11 Oct 1854 ae: 88y. GSL

Frederick M s/o Nathaniel d 30 Jan 1861 ae: 3y. GSL

George W d 5 Oct 1821 ae: 27y. MmtB C:126

James b1786 d1868. Mmt A-4-10

James M b 1823 d 1853. "Lost at sea." Mmt A-4-10

Joanna d 15 Aug 1864 ae: 69y. MmtB C:126

Marcy R d/o James Jr & Patience d 6 Jan 1817 ae: 13d. SD K:158

Marcy w/o James d 9 Oct 1798 ae: 34y. K:155

Marjorie Ida d/o HA d 1 Feb 1893 ae: 4d. "Died Boston, Massachusetts." GSL

Mary Swanton w/o Abijah Jr d 1 Feb 1833 ae: 36y. MmtB C:126

Patience H w/o James b 1790 d 1837. Mmt A-4-10

Samuel d 28 Aug 1793 ae: 2y. MmtB C:126

Samuel d 1 Oct 1802 ae: 6y. MmtB C:126

Sarah w/o James b 1801 d 1864. Mmt A-4-10

William d 29 Sep 1807 ae: 18y. MmtB C:126

POOR, Charles H s/o Henry & Eliza d 13 Sep 1827 ae: 13m. SBE J:64

Eliza P d 19 Sep 1828 ae: 2m. SBE J:64

Eliza P w/o Henry d 19 June 1828 ae: 22y. SBE J:63

Emily Goodwin w/o Daniel A d 19 Dec 1836 ae: 46y. B-1-24

Lucy d 30 Dec 1849 ae: 82y. GSL

Mary A P w/o Henry d 4 Mar 1830 ae: 21y. SBE J:65

POPE, Abiah B C w/o Charles d 8 Mar 1841 ae: 27y. SBE J:58

Abiah d/o Charles & Abiah BC d 30 Apr 1841 ae: 4m 14d. SBE J:58

Caroline d/o Joseph & Hannah d 13 Nov 1836 ae: 18y. SBE J:59

Charles s/o Joseph & Caroline b 6 Dec 1815 d 28 Apr 1816. F:122

Edward Charles s/o Joseph & Caroline b 20 May 1817 d 29 Aug 1819. F:121

Frances d/o Joseph & Hannah d 29 June 1841 ae: 19y. J:57

Hannah d/o Joseph & Hannah b 3 Apr 1828 d 27 June 1828. F:119

Hannah w/o Joseph d 16 May 1828 ae: 30y. F:119

Hannah wid/o Joseph d 8 Oct 1828 ae: 17y. SB J:60

Harriet T d/o Joseph & Hannah nd. SBE J:62

Helen Maria d/o Joseph & Hannah d 8 Oct 1828 ae: 17y. SBE J:61

Joseph b 14 July 1778 d 7 Apr 1852. SBE F:118

Lucretia d/o Joseph & Hannah b 11 May 1824 d 28 Mar 1825. F:120

PORTER, Dr Aaron d 30 June 1837 ae: 85y. B-1-13

Emma Elizabeth w/o Richard King d 26 Oct 1827 ae: 31y. B-1-12

Henry C s/o Capt Seward & Eliza

PORTER (continued)
d 23 Aug 1809 ae: 18m. SBE F:62

Mary C w/o Richard King d 15 June 1847 ae: 58y. B-1-11

Mary K d/o Richard King d 27 Aug 1850 ae: 33y. SBE B-2-11

Paulina w/o Dr Aaron d 26 Feb 1832 ae: 74y. SBE B-1-14

Richard King d 25 July 1859 ae: 75y. SB B-2-10

Capt Seward d 29 Mar 1838 ae: 54y. SBE F:67

Thomas R s/o Capt Seward & Eliza d 27 Mar 1825 ae: 18y 9d. SBE F:66

William H s/o Capt Seward & Eliza d 3 Oct 1810 ae: 9m. SBE F:63

POTE, Mary Irish w/o Gamlial d 25 Nov 1804 ae: 53y. J:93

POTTER, Elizabeth d/o Ebenezer d 8 Oct 1801 ae: 26y. I:100

Harriet E d/o George d 8 July 1850 ae: 2m. Black. GSL

Lydia Ann d/o George d 16 Oct 1848 ae: 16y. Black. GSL

Sarah A d/o George d 23 Sep 1849 ae: 7m. Black. GSL

William d 24 Nov 1858 ae: 18y. Black. GSL

POWELL, John b 13 Aug 1778 d 3 Feb 1829. "Born in Liverpool, England" B-3-35

John W s/o John & Sarah d 22 June 1839 ae: 22y. SB B-3-34

Sarah wid/o John d 3 Feb 1851 ae: 72y. GSL

Susan B Colby w/o Jesse d 28 Dec 1884 ae: 79y. A-11-3

POWERS, Darius d 7 July 1847 ae: 22y. "Drowned in Portland Harbor." GSL

Julia A d 6 Oct 1849 ae: 5m. Black. GSL

PRATT, Mary Ella d/o Alvin P d 26 Apr 1858 ae: 12y 8m. A Tomb 52

Mary Griggs d/o John & Eliza d 13 Oct 1811 ae: 9m. J:139

William s/o Simeon & Sarah d 4 Dec 1820 ae: 4m. SD J:140

PRAY, George H s/o George E d 9 Feb 1863 ae: 3y. GSL

PREBLE, Charles s/o Ebenezer & Mary d 28 Apr 1791 ae: 6y. I:95

Dorcas w/o Ebenezer b 30 May 1759 d 20 Feb 1784. C:202

Commodore Edward d 25 Aug 1807 ae: 46y. Rev/War Barbary War. Mmt A Tomb 65

Mary d/o Edward Deering & Sophia Wattles b 10 Sep 1834 d 15 Sep 1835. Mmt A Tomb 65

Mary w/o Ebenezer d 15 Mar 1794 ae: 31y. Interesting stone. I:94

Mary wid/o Edward d 26 May 1851 ae: 81y. Mmt A Tomb 65

PRENTISS, Abba w/o Thomas M d 14 Mar 1804 ae: 22y. H:14

Abigail w/o Artemus d 6 Apr 1865 ae: 86y 6m. GSL

Artemus d 3 Sep 1868 ae: 85y 6m. GSL

Caroline d/o William E & Abigail b 29 Dec 1805 d 6 May 1810. J:176

Eliza A s/o Artemus & Eunice b 10 May 1825 d 11 Sep 1839. SD J:26

Elizabeth E d/o James d 13 July 1855 ae: 13m. GSL

George M s/o Artemus d 24 Jan 1895 ae: 75y. SD A-2-22

Julia A w/o James d 1 Sep 1846 ae: 26y. A-2-22

Mary S s/o Artemus & Eunice b 8 May 1814 d 26 Sep 1836. SD J:26

Mary w/o Artemus d 13 Nov 1852 ae: 74y. SD B-9-11

Sarah A w/o George M d 23 Feb 1903 ae: 73y 19d. NS A-2-22

William S s/o Artemus & Eunice b 16 Jan 1817 d 24 Mar 1836. SD J:26

PRICE, David d 19 May 1872 ae: 79y. GSL

Sarah wid/o John d 5 Aug 1824 ae: 94y. C:137

PRICHARD, Capt John d 20 Jan

PRICHARD (continued)
1823 ae: 51y. B-4-3

Margaret wid/o Capt John d 21 Jan 1846 ae: 80y. B-4-4

PRIDHAM, Charles s/o James d 14 Aug 1847 ae: 15m. "Buried at head of Ingraham tomb." NS E:6

James R s/o James H d 7 Apr 1868 ae: 1y 6m. GSL

Mary d/o James d 11 Aug 1843 ae: 13m. GSL

PRIME, Anna wid/o Samuel d 27 July 1865 ae: 73y. GSL

PRINCE, Deacon Caleb d 27 Sep 1826 ae: 64y. D:66

Caleb d 27 Oct 1831 ae: 33y. D:67

Charles E s/o Ebenezer & Matilda L d 17 June 1825 ae: 14m. SD D:125

Dorcas d/o John d 11 May 1847 ae: 18y. GSL

Capt Ebenezer d 23 June 1860 ae: 68y. GSL

Ebenezer F s/o Capt Ebenezer & Matilda L d 19 Jan 1841 ae: 20y 9m. A-15-2

Edward C d 28 Nov 1849 ae: 28y. F:95 Tomb

Edward C s/o Charles d 23 Nov 1851 ae: 11m. GSL

Eunice d 7 Oct 1850 ae: 60y. F:95 Tomb

Frederick s/o AD d 23 Oct 1854 ae: 19m. GSL

Isaac d 2 July 1843 ae: 85y. SB B-3-25

Julia d/o Ebenezer d 27 Aug 1842 ae: 14m. GSL

Martha w/o Deacon Caleb d 5 Sep 1821 ae: 59y. "...of Candia, New Hampshire." D:65

Mary H w/o Joseph B d 28 July 1833 ae: 38y. SBE D:64

Matilda L w/o Capt Ebenezer d 22 Nov 1841 ae: 42y. A-15-3

Phebe M w/o Capt Daniel C d 6 May 1847 ae: 35y. A Tomb 9

Sarah w/o Isaac d 5 Nov 1831 ae: 67y. B-3-24

PROCTOR, Abba A d/o Capt Ben.

PROCTOR (continued)
& Lucinda d 2 Sep 1841 ae: 14y. GSL

Benjamin F d 14 Dec 1854 ae: 24y. SB A-1-11

Charles J s/o Jeremiah d 1 Mar 1842 ae: 1y. GSL

Esther wid/o John d 26 Aug 1848 ae: 90y. SBE D:37

Lucinda wid/o Capt Benjamin d 28 Feb 1862 ae: 57y. SB A-1-10

Richard s/o Benjamin & Sary d 20 Sep 1748 ae: 2y 8m. SBE D:26

Samuel d 16 Mar 1765 ae: 85y. GSL

Sary d/o Benjamin & Sary d 11 July 1741 ae: 7d. SBE E:26

Thomas s/o Benjamin & Sary d 5 Mar 1747 ae: 9y. SBE E:26

PUDOR, Rudolph A s/o Clementine Ferdinand d 11 Sep 1857 ae: 3m. A Tomb 57

PURINTON, Alonzo d/o Nathaniel L & Melinda d 12 June 1844 ae: 2y 7m. I:54

Diana wid/o Amos d 19 May 1866 ae: 77y. GSL

George E s/o Robert H d 30 Mar 1870 ae: 3y 9m. GSL

Henrietta L d/o Nathaniel L & Melinda d 6 Apr 1840 ae: 8m. I:53

John d 29 May 1866 ae: 78y 7m. GSL

John L s/o John d 17 Oct 1856 ae: 28y. GSL

Joshua R s/o John & Mary R d 2 Sep 1846 ae: 21y. A-2-15

Mary R w/o John d 30 Mar 1862 ae: 52y. SB A-2-16

Simeon H d 14 June 1845 ae: 39y. GSL

William H s/o John & Mary R d 16 June 1833 ae: 6y. SBE A-2-14

PURKILL, Ann Christianna b 12 Aug 1727 d 2 Jan 1812. H:163

PUTNEY, Caleb Augustus s/o Alexander H & Mary W d 26 June 1835. A-1-28

PUTNEY (continued)

Frederick H s/o Alexander H d 8 Sep 1848 ae: 3m. GSL

Mary W w/o Alexander H d 12 May 1836 ae: 29y. A-1-28

PYCOTT, Elizabeth North w/o William d 5 Feb 1849 ae: 72y. "Formerly of England." B-14-31

William d 9 July 1850 ae: 80y. B-14-30

QUICK, Andrew s/o Peter d 28 Dec 1866 ae: 6y 7m. GSL

QUIMBY, Elizabeth H d/o widow d 1 Nov 1841. GSL

Mary Alice d/o Albus R d 18 Aug 1858 ae: 5y 8m. GSL

Thomas R d 14 Dec 1855 ae: 42y. GSL

QUINBY, Charlotte R d/o Joseph & Eliza d 15 Feb 1822 ae: 2m. GSL C:2

David d 9 May 1854 ae: 84y. SD D:127

John d 21 Aug 1863 ae: 45y. A Tomb 66

Joseph B s/o Joseph & Eliza d 23 Oct 1822 ae: 9y. C:1

Olive J Woodman w/o John d 29 Feb 1864 ae: 43y. A Tomb 66

Susan w/o David d 12 Jan 1854 ae: 77y. GSL

QUINCY, Ann B wid/o Jacob b 26 Nov 1773 d 1 Sep 1863. MmtD A Tomb 18

Caroline M d/o Samuel M & Sarah d 19 Jan 1869 ae: 66y. SBE C:158

Charles E b 25 Feb 1805 d 9 Feb 1856. MmtD A Tomb 18

Elizabeth d/o Marcus & Mehitable d 15 Apr 1832 ae: 19y. K:161

Enoch s/o Marcus & Mehitable d 6 June 1804 ae: 6w. SB K:160

Faustina S d/o Albert Y d 6 Jan 1857 ae: 6m 10m. GSL

Frederick s/o Horatio G d 1 June 1854. GSL

Helen M W d/o Samuel M & Sarah d 19 Dec 1869 ae: 63y. SBE C:159

QUINCY (continued)

Horatio G s/o HG d 20 Apr 1854 ae: 20y. GSL

Jacob d 20 Oct 1829 ae: 68y. A Tomb 18

John J s/o Jacob & Ann d 5 Dec 1826 ae: 16y. MmtD A Tomb 18

Marcus Edward s/o Marcus & Mehitable d 18 Feb 1821 ae: 16m. SB K:160

Mary d 20 Feb 1883 ae: 80y. GSL

Sally w/o William S d 1 Oct 1833 ae: 65y. SD A-3-1

Samuel M b 25 Nov 1809 d 2 Apr 1810. SBE C:156

Samuel M d 8 June 1852 ae: 81y. SBE C:157

Samuel M III d 7 Mar 1821 ae: 3w. SBE C:156

Sarah A d 5 Oct 1899 ae: 88y 24d. "Died New York City." GSL

Sarah wid/o Samuel M d 22 Feb 1821 ae: 41y. SBE C:156

William J s/o Jacob & Ann d 28 Jan 1840 ae: 39y. MmtD A Tomb 18

William S d 3 Oct 1833 ae: 66y. SD A-3-1

QUINN, John A d 30 Dec 1887 ae: 82y. GSL

RACKLEFF, Alfred H s/o James B d 10 Feb 1864 ae: 6y. GSL

Azalia d 11 Aug 1853 ae: 22y. "Buried James Rackleff's yard." NS K:94

Benjamin d 22 Oct 1863 ae: 53y. GSL

Chandler s/o Capt James & Olive d 10 Sep 1810 ae: 5y. K:100

Charles d 23 Nov 1844 ae: 37y. SBE K:103

Edward d 19 May 1826 ae: 28y. SB K:98

Ellen M d/o Charles & Mary b 5 Aug 1833 d 30 Nov 1835. SBE K:104

Frances E d/o James & Harriet d 13 Oct 1855 ae: 9m. SBE K:94

RACHLEFF (continued)

George s/o Capt James & Olive d Mar 1811 ae: 1y 6m. K:101

Harriet d/o Nelson & H d 22 June 1822 ae: 4y 10m. SBE B-8-1

Infant s/o Capt James & Olive d Jan 1812 ae: 12d. K:102

Capt James d 21 Apr 1880 ae: 100y 5m 15d. SBE K:97

Capt James Jr d 30 July 1855 ae: 38y. SBE K:94

James H s/o James B d 8 Oct 1852 ae: 16m. GSL

Capt John d 2 Feb 1805 ae: 26y. K:99

Nelson d 1 Jan 1855 ae: 69y. "Died Portsmouth, New Hampshire." GSL

Olive d 9 Oct 1866 ae: 83y. K:96

Stephen N s/o Nelson & H d 10 Sep 1846 ae: 20y. SB B-8-2

RACKLYFT, Benjamin d 25 July 1851 ae: 67y. GSL

Benjamin d 25 June 1854 ae: 70y. GSL

Charles d 25 Mar 1850 ae: 30y. GSL

Emily C d/o Benjamin & Sally d 11 Oct 1844 ae: 19y. SBE C:130

Harriet T d/o late Charles d 17 May 1850 ae: 11m. "Died in Bangor." GSL

Sally d 22 Jan 1871 ae: 83y. GSL

Samuel d 12 Sep 1857 ae: 32y. "Native of Rockland, Maine." GSL

RADFORD, Benjamin d May 1820 ae: 73y. A Tomb 29

Benjamin Jr d 21 Dec 1862 ae: 87y 9m. A Tomb 29

Daniel d 11 July 1836 ae: 50y. SBE A-5-10

Daniel s/o Daniel & Dorcas d 29 Dec 1846 ae: 25y. SBE A-5-12

Dorcas, wid/Daniel d 12 June 1889 ae: 96y 8m. SD A-5-11

Eben L s/o Benjamin Jr & Mary d 7 Sep 1800 ae: 17m. A Tomb 29

Eben L s/o Benjamin Jr & Mary

RADFORD (continued)

d 12 Aug 1805 ae: 4y. A Tomb 29

Frances Ellen d/o Daniel & Dorcas d 20 Aug 1821 ae: 23m. SBE A-5-10

Frank s/o Lincoln & Priscilla d 30 Nov 1850 ae: 15m. A Tomb 29

Harriet d 18 Sep 1887 ae: 68y 8m. A Tomb 29

James E B s/o Daniel & Dorcas d 26 Nov 1846 ae: 21y. SBE A-5-12

Joseph B s/o Daniel & Dorcas d 11 June 1833 ae: 18y. "Died at sea." SBE A-5-10

Lincoln d 1 Oct 1863 ae: 53y 11m. A Tomb 29

Margaret M w/o Lincoln d 27 May 1854 ae: 38y. A Tomb 29

Mary d 25 Feb 1876 ae: 71y 8m. A Tomb 29

Mary d/o William d 25 Sep 1853 ae: 46y. GSL

Mary w/o Benjamin Jr d 30 Aug 1848 ae: 72y. A Tomb 29

Priscilla w/o Lincoln d 29 Nov 1850 ae: 29y. A Tomb 29

Sarah w/o William d 22 Aug 1826 ae: 16y. B-9-37

RAMSDELL, Lorenzo d 11 Apr 1853 ae: 21y. "Died Marine Hospital." GSL

RAMSEY, Ann Louisa Payson s/o John M & Martha d 15 Mar 1842 ae: 14y. A-17-11

Charles F s/o John & Martha b 9 May 1808 d 5 June 1808. "Died in Harpswell." K:30

Charles F s/o John & Martha b 31 Dec 1811 d 29 Nov 1813. K:30

Clarissa d/o William d 20 Nov 1842 ae: 2y 5m. GSL

Capt John M d 25 Aug 1846 ae: 75y. SBE A-17-14

Joseph B s/o John M & Martha d 1 May 1897 ae: 76y 6m 4d. GSL

Martha w/o Capt John M d 23 Sep 1845 ae: 63y SBE A-17-13

RAMSEY (continued)

Mary B w/o Joseph B d 26 Sep 1900 ae: 76y 6m 2d. GSL

Sarah w/o Beza d 11 June 1842 ae: 31y. SBE A-17-12

William s/o John M & Martha d 1 May 1819 ae: 18y. "Died in Port-au-Prince." A-17-11

RAND, George W s/o Samuel d 22 Aug 1856 ae: 18m. "Buried at foot of John Clough's grave." NS B-14-10

John J s/o Samuel & Nancy d 16 Aug 1837 ae: 6m. A-13-23

John s/o Christopher & Eunice d 12 Oct 1823 ae: 2y. A-2-4

Mary C d/o Samuel & Nancy d 6 Oct 1846 ae: 16m. SBE A-13-23

Mary C d/o Samuel d 1 Oct 1850 ae: 5y. GSL

Nancy w/o Samuel d 28 Dec 1877 ae: 65y 2m. A-13-22

Rev Samuel d 10 Oct 1830 ae: 46y. GSL

Samuel d 29 Dec 1886 ae: 80y. A-13-21

Sarah d/o Samuel d 1 Apr 1845 ae: 10y 5m. "Buried in Abner Briggs' range." NS G:100

RANDALL, Asa C d 8 Sep 1808 ae: 8y. A Tomb 83

Catherine M d/o Orrin d 25 Oct 1847 ae: 4m. GSL

Edward P d 4 Dec 1857 ae: 38y. GSL

Elizabeth d/o Kinecum d 2 May 1844 ae: 22y. GSL

Job d 11 Nov 1839 ae: 60y 9m. A-11-15

Kinecum d 24 May 1842 ae: 57y. GSL

Mary A d/o Nathaniel & Elly d 24 June 1806 ae: 6m 13d. SD K:61

Mary E d/o Charles d 16 Feb 1842 ae: 2y 7m. A Tomb 17

Mary R w/o Thomas d 25 June 1844 ae: 31y. A Tomb 57

Nancy wid Kinecum d 17 Dec 1845 ae: 65y. GSL

Polly w/o Caleb d 13 May 1804

RANDALL (continued)

ae: 96y. SD J:96

Sarah wid/o Job d 11 Feb 1866 ae: 84y 11m. A-11-16

William d 9 Sep 1858 ae: 45y. GSL

RAY, George nd. Lot with wooden fence - destroyed. C:90

James A s/o John G & Margaret E d 29 June 1849 ae: 21y 12d. F:161

Margaret Elizabeth J w/o John G d 24 Apr 1902 ae: 81y 2m 2d. "Died Everett, Massachusetts." F:161

RAYMOND, Elizabeth B #2 w/o Samuel L d 30 Sep 1815 ae: 22y. I:186

Martha L d/o Samuel & Elizabeth d 6 Mar 1817 ae: 3y 4m. I:185

Mary E d/o Samuel L & Elizabeth R d 1 July 1822 ae: 15m. I:187

RAYNES, Mary A w/o Solomon d 3 Dec 1823 ae: 24y. SB H:5

REA, Abba F d/o Isaac d 2 June 1846 ae: 14y. "Buried beside John Frothingham." NS L:88 Monument-L:92

Albus MD d 14 Oct 1848 ae: 54y. A-5-3

Dorcas Moody b 6 Oct 1808 d 5 May 1885. SB A-5-4

Eleanor T d/o David d 13 Sep 1849 ae: 16m. A Tomb 82

Nancy M B w/o Albus MD d 19 Apr 1836 ae: 36y. A-5-1

Samuel Hahneman s/o Dr Albus & Dorcas d 14 Nov 1845 ae: 18m. A-5-2

READ, Jane d 19 Feb 1849 ae: 5y. "Member of the Orphan Asylum." GSL

REDLON, Charles L s/o Benjamin M d 30 July 1861 ae: 6y. "Died in Rockland, Maine." GSL

REED, George s/o Philemon P d 22 Oct 1844 ae: 3m. GSL

Mrs Hannah d 16 Mar 1785 ae: 24y. GSL

114

REED (continued)

Mary d 31 July 1848 ae: 63y. "Died in the Alms House" "Buried at foot of Mrs. Rea's grave." NS A-5-1

REESE, Rev William I b 25 Dec 1798 d 6 Sep 1834. "Died Buffalo, New York." Large marble monument A-2-1

REEVES, John F d 12 June 1849 ae: 50y. A Tomb 81

RELHAN, Mary d 30 Nov 1856 ae: 75y. "Buried beside husband." GSL

Richard d 29 Oct 1841 ae: 49y. "Native of Porto Rico." GSL

REMICK, George W s/o Capt John & Dorcas d 16 July 1821 ae: 9m. I:200

RENTON, Mary d/o Thomas & Isabella d 4 Feb 1832 ae: 12y 3m. SBE B-8-34

William s/o Thomas & Isabella d 25 Sep 1850 ae: 6w. SBE B-8-34

REVERE, John Frederick s/o Dr John & Lydia d 2 June 1818 ae: 2y 10m. SD K:144

REYNOLDS, ---- d 1 Jan ---- ae: 29y. MmtB B-6-7

Elizabeth wid/o Thomas d 1 July 1854 ae: 69y. MmtB B-6-7

Capt James d 1 Jan 1837 ae: 26y. "Died in New Orleans." MmtB B-6-7

Jane d 20 Mar 1850 ae: 29y. MmtB B-6-7

Martha D w/o JE d/o B Dearborn d 11 Mar 1849 ae: 25y. "...of Bangor" MmtB A Tomb 23

Mary wid/o William d 28 Feb 1855 ae: 48y. SBE B-8-32

Thomas d 12 July 1846 ae: 85y. Rev/War. MmtB B-6-7

RHODES, Cornelius d 13 Aug 1846 ae: 76y. GSL

RICE, Abraham P d 17 May 1848 ae: 54y. "Death by drowning" "Buried Strangers' Ground" "...of Roxbury, Maine, a dockee." GSL

Catherine A d/o Lemuel & C d

RICE (continued)

16 Sep 1854 ae: 27y. B-3-6

George Harris s/o Sarah d 8 May 1841 ae: 8y. GSL

Martha Hatch d/o Lemuel & C b 20 July 1825 d 3 Sep 1825. B-3-5

Mary w/o Simeon T d 19 Nov 1854 ae: 52y. A Tomb 40

Sarah R d 23 Sep 1869 ae: 49y. GSL

Susan w/o David d 29 Apr 1854 ae: 58y. GSL

Thomas d 22 Apr 1857 ae: 33y. "Died at Marine Hospital" "Buried at head of S Whittier's grave" "Native of Baltimore, Maryland." GSL

RICH, Arthur F s/o Ebenezer d 20 Feb 1891 ae: 33y 4m. GSL

Catherine wid/o Ebenezer d 17 Feb 1891 ae: 63y 7m. GSL

Ebenezer d 9 Aug 1890 ae: 83y. SD A-5-5

Elizabeth w/o Ebenezer b 5 Mar 1774 d 20 Feb 1812. G:45

Esther d 12 June 1869 ae: 90y. MmtE A Tomb 25

Florence d/o Marshall A d 22 Dec 1861 ae: 16m. GSL

Samuel d 7 Sep 1831 ae: 58y. GSL

Willie L s/o Andrew J d 24 Feb 1859 ae: 7m. GSL

RICHARDS, Adelaide d/o Joshua d 13 Jan 1847 ae: 16m. GSL

Benjamin d 9 Aug 1854 ae: 58y. GSL

Edward d 8 May 1864 ae: 68y. SBE E:17

George P d 31 July 1849 ae: 17y 9m. "Died at sea." SBE A-16-6

John d 10 Oct 1804. "Accidentially run over by his own truck." GSL

John K d 15 Aug 1837 ae: 30y. SBE A-6-5

Mary d/o John d 18 June 1894 ae: 93y 9m. GSL

Mary Frances Dana d/o Thomas T & Mary Jane d 13 Feb 1845

RICHARDS (continued)
ae: 4y 10m. A-9-20

Mary Louisa d/o JF d 28 Dec 1848 ae: 10m. GSL

Richard d 19 Feb 1823 ae: 43y. Black. SD L:8

Sarah F d/o Willard d 13 Mar 1842. GSL

Sarah Jane d/o John K d 1 Apr 1850 ae: 14y 8m. "Died in Boston." SBE A-16-6

Sarah w/o Edward d 27 Apr 1854 ae: 50y. SBE E:18

Sophia W w/o Willard d 9 Dec 1847 ae: 59y. GSL

Willard d 24 Sep 1851 ae: 63y. GSL

RICHARDSON, Adelaide d/o PW d 22 Apr 1846 ae: 2y 4m. "Buried at head of Mehitable Preble's grave stone." GSL

Ann H d/o Joshua & Ann d 21 Sep 1820 ae: 20m. SD H:70

Ann w/o Joshua d 19 Oct 1850 ae: 63y. A Tomb 58

Clara M d/o PW d 8 Jan 1852 ae: 2m. GSL

Eunice w/o Joshua d 24 Mar 1804 ae: 26y. SBE H:69

Frank O s/o Charles d 8 Jan 1850 ae: 11m. A Tomb 58

George s/o Jacob d 25 Jan 1862 ae: 7y. Black. GSL

Georgianna d/o Charles d 28 Apr 1849 ae: 16m. A Tomb 58

Isaac d 15 Dec 1848 ae: 86y. Black. GSL

Joshua s/o NP d 27 Sep 1856 ae: 1y 8m. A Tomb 58

Marcy w/o Convers d 4 June 1802 ae: 67y. K:156

Rosanna d 5 Sep 1858 ae: 68y. Black. GSL

Sarah d 29 Nov 1854 ae: 92y. GSL

William d 16 May 1845 ae: 87y. Black. GSL

RICHMOND, Silas M d 25 Oct 1811 ae: 29y. K:146

RICKER, Huldah d 28 Jan 1850 ae: 60y. A Tomb 16

Mary E w/o Albert d 23 July

RICKER (continued)
1857 ae: 24y. GSL

RICKERSON, Harriet F d/o Thomas F d 2 June 1847 ae: 20m. "Buried at foot of Henry Titcomb's grave." NS C:215

RIDEOUT, Lina F d 14 Sep 1857 ae: 13m. GSL

RIELLY, Mary wid/o Simeon d 23 May 1837 ae: 53y. A-8-8

RIGGS, Clara A d/o Jacob d 26 Aug 1866 ae: 26y. GSL

Clinton s/o John H d 3 Oct 1863 ae: 3y 5m. GSL

Ella F d/o John H d 6 July 1856 ae: 20m 16d. GSL

George E d 8 Sep 1882 ae: 1w. GSL

Jacob d 7 Nov 1858 ae: 61y. GSL

John L d 10 June 1833 ae: 39y. A-3-13

Margaret d/o Stephen & Margaret d 9 May 1796 ae: 25y. K:169

Mary d 13 May 1806 ae: 73y. I:188

RILEY, John d 3 June 1861 ae: 32y. GSL

Martin d 14 June 1843 ae: 47y. GSL

Michael s/o Michael d 27 Sep 1841 ae: 1y 11m. GSL

Stephen G s/o Benjamin F & Susan d 13 June 1850 ae: 2y. SD F:134

RINGLES, William d 20 Dec 1842 ae: 43y. Black. GSL

RIPLEY, Martha M w/o Thomas B b 16 May 1798 d 1 May 1836. SBE J:22

Thomas Baldwin d 4 May 1876 ae: 81y. J:24

Thomas Henry d 6 June 1852 ae: 23y. J:23

William M b 3 Jan 1834 d 6 Jan 1835. J:22

ROACH, Hannah L wid/o Thomas L d 27 Oct 1831 ae: 79y. SBE K:5

James H L d 20 Mar 1860 ae: 69y. SD K:4

Mary Gordon d/o James H &

ROACH (continued)

Tabitha d 22 Dec 1829 ae: 7y. K:2

Tabitha S L w/o James L d 1 Aug 1875 ae: 80y. "Died Boston, Massachusetts." GSL

Capt Thomas L d 19 Mar 1820 ae: 55y. SBE K:5

ROBBINS, George s/o Edward A d 9 Oct 1862 ae: 14m. GSL

John d 2 June 1855 ae: 22y. "Sailor - killed in Rum Riot" "Buried at head of John Noble's grave stone" NS A-7-14

Sarah H d/o William d 10 Mar 1849 ae: 7m. "Buried beside Benjamin Adams'- 1805 grave stone." NS I:105

ROBERTS, Betsy wid/o Joshua d 28 Feb 1848 ae: 83y. GSL

Clara d/o Henry d 8 Dec 1841 ae: 9m. GSL

Deborah d 5 Nov 1821 ae: 51y. D:116

George d 1 Feb 1815 ae: 42y. "Lost in the Dash." SD A-13-5

George L s/o Stillman d 24 July 1841 ae: 9y. GSL

Hannah wid/o George d 4 Aug 1855 ae: 83y. SD A-13-5

Henry D d 29 Nov 1846 ae: 38y. GSL

John H s/o HS & Clarissa P d 3 Nov 1837 ae: 2y 7m. SB F:8

John Jr d 2 Nov 1732 ae: 33y 6m 16d. SB I:176

John L d 5 Jan 1844 ae: 42y. SBE A-2-23

Mary Caroline d/o George & Hannah d 16 Apr 1848 ae: 47y. A-13-4

Mary Ellen d/o John G d 23 June 1849 ae: 3y. GSL

Mary wid/o John d 12 July 1849 ae: 77y. GSL

Melville C s/o William H d 18 Feb 1849 ae: 4m. "Buried at head of Nolcini's child's grave." NS B-13-20

Reuben d 27 Oct 1851 ae: 52y. GSL

ROBERTS (continued)

Sally d 4 Nov 1821 ae: 22y. D:117

William F s/o Charles W d 14 May 1855 ae: 15m. GSL

ROBINSON, Albert s/o Daniel & Isabella d 13 May 1815 ae: 3y 6m. J:6

Anson L s/o late Thomas d 8 May 1844 ae: 26y. GSL

Betsy K w/o Capt Ebenezer d 8 Apr 1832 ae: 27y. A-24-9

Catherine d/o Capt Ebenezer & Hannah d 5 Apr 1835 ae: 14y. SBE A-24-11

Charles P s/o late Samuel d 2 June 1861. "Died Mobile, Alabama." GSL

Charlotta F d/o Capt Joshua d 11 Sep 1816 ae: 2y 4m. SD D:115

Capt Ebenezer d 5 Dec 1835 ae: 48y. SBE A-24-12

Edward d 23 Oct 1837 ae: 62y. H:86

Edward s/o Edward & Elizabeth B d 18 Apr 1812 ae: 11y. H:86

Eliza A d/o Daniel & Saphrona d 23 Nov 1838 ae: 4m. SBE F:10

Elizabeth B wid/o Edward d 12 Dec 1849 ae: 69y. H:87

Elizabeth P d/o Capt Ebenezer & Betsy K d 2 May 1832 ae: 1y 9m. SBE A-24-10

Hannah d/o Capt Joshua & Hannah d 9 Apr 1865 ae: 74y. SD D:113

Hannah w/o Capt Ebenezer d 5 Oct 1827 ae: 35y SBE A-24-11

Hannah wid/o Joshua d 22 July 1841 ae: 76y. SD D:113

Infant ch/o Thomas F d 24 Dec 1861. SD C:165

James D s/o Hosea d 8 Sep 1846 ae: 1y. A Tomb 27

John d 6 Feb 1775 ae: 60y 1m 8d. SB I:180

John Thomas s/o Edward & Elizabeth B d 2 Mar 1804 ae: 1m. H:86

Capt Joshua d 1 Dec 1820 ae: 63y. Rev/War. SD D:113

ROBINSON (continued)

Capt Joshua d 7 Mar 1816 ae: 31y. SD D:115

Lorenzo s/o Thomas d 2 Dec 1863 ae: 11m. GSL

Lucy Ellen d/o William & Sophronia d 22 Mar 1831 ae: 18y. G:102

Lucy I d/o Capt Ebenezer & Hannah d 17 Oct 1825 ae: 18m. SBE A-24-11

Lucy Nichols d/o Samuel & Harriet d 16 Jan 1820 ae: 6m. J:128

Martha d/o Capt Joshua & Hannah d 23 Feb 1811 ae: 2y. SD D:113

Mary E w/o Joseph M d 5 Mar 1893 ae: 45y 11m 5d. GSL

Mehitable d/o Joshua & Hannah d 24 Dec 1850 ae: 40y. SD D:113

Olivia M d/o Daniel Jr d 7 Jan 1848 ae: 5y. A Tomb 5

Stephenira d/o Capt Joshua & Hannah d 26 Oct 1810 ae: 17y. SD D:113

Susan R w/o George D d 27 Jan 1866 ae: 33y. A Tomb 69

Thomas d 2 June 1868 ae: 48y. GSL

Thomas F d 2 June 1856 ae: 48y 2m. "...with four of his children." SD C:165

William d 29 Dec 1820 ae: 54y. G:103

ROBISON, Anson S d 9 May 1844 ae: 26y. A Tomb 79

Elizabeth C d 11 Nov 1816 ae: 3y 8m. A tomb 79

Elizabeth d 8 Aug 1829 ae: 29y. A Tomb 79

Elizabeth wid/o Capt Thomas d 24 Mar 1866 ae: 82y. A Tomb 79

Jane N d/o Robert I & Jane S d 2 Aug 1846 ae: 3y 6m A Tomb 79

Janes S wid/o Robert I d 17 Feb 1891 ae: 77y. A Tomb 79

Mary d 23 Nov 1835 ae: 21y. A Tomb 79

ROBISON (continued)

Mary L s/o Robert I & Jane S d 12 Oct 1860 ae: 15y 3m 17d. A Tomb 79

Robert Ilsley s/o Thomas & Eliza d 13 June 1878 ae: 70y 5m. A Tomb 79

Sarah J d 21 Dec 1852 ae: 42y. A Tomb 79

Capt Thomas d 25 Aug 1823 ae: 45y. A Tomb 79

Thomas d 24 Sep 1851 ae: 48y. A Tomb 79

ROGERS, ---- w/o George d 7 Oct 1854. GSL

Ann Pickering d/o John & Mary d 11 Nov 1829 ae: 9m. E:33

Caroline G d/o John E d 9 July 1853 ae: 4y 6m. "Buried Rogers' tomb." GSL

Catherine G d/o Charles & Mary d 8 Feb 1858 ae: 23y. SD F:70

Charles d 22 July 1840 ae: 72y. A Tomb 46

Cornelia d/o Charles & Hannah b 13 Aug 1799 d 10 May 1801. Unusual stone. J:40

Cyrus d 19 Jan 1855 ae: 24y. "Casualty by Rail Road." GSL

Esther J w/o Gershom d 11 Feb 1756 ae: 20y. SBE D:32

George W d 19 Sep 1856 ae: 59y. GSL

Rogers, Hannah T wid/o Charles d 29 Sep 1860 ae: 85y. A Tomb 46

Capt Joshua d 25 Oct 1823 ae: 65y. D:3

Maria C w/o Charles Jr b 15 May 1804 d 29 May 1827. A Tomb 46

Mary H b 23 Mar 1813 d 17 Feb 1824. A Tomb 46

Mary wid/o Capt Joshua d 5 Jan 1847 ae: 87y. D:2

Moses d 2 Nov 1856 ae: 72y. "Died Marine Hospital" "Native Bristol, Maine." GSL

William d 20 Aug 1803 ae: 29y. K:41

ROLF, Benjamin d 29 Aug 1860 ae: 82y 8m. GSL

ROLF (continued)

Cornelia C d/o Joseph M d 23 Nov 1864 ae: 1y 3m. A Tomb 20

Harriet d/o Samuel & Anna d 7 Oct 1811 ae: 11m. SD C:163

ROLFE, Benjamin s/o Benjamin d 21 Sep 1843 ae: 7w. GSL

Charles N s/o Charles H d 27 May 1866 ae: 7m. GSL

David S d 21 Mar 1842 ae: 44y. A-14-16

Rebecca S wid/o Jacob d 21 Sep 1843 ae: 72y. A-14-15

ROLLINS, Samuel d 8 Apr 1783 ae: 40y. "Killed by bursting of cannon, celebrating end of Revolutionary War." GSL

ROPES, Charles F s/o George & CR b 7 Apr 1837 d 15 Mar 1842. SBE A-10-13

Frederick s/o George & CR b 4 Oct 1841 d 5 Nov 1843. SBE A-10-12

George b 13 Jan 1809 d 6 Dec 1842. SBE A-10-14

ROSCOE, Laura J d 2 Nov 1881 ae: 46y. "Died Wakefield, Massachusetts." Black. GSL

ROSS, Capt Alexander b 19 Oct 1717 d 24 Nov 1763. "Born Stroma, Orkneys." Ledger – MmtB&E E:13

Ann M d/o William d 20 July 1848 ae: 1y. A Tomb 82

Benjamin d 5 Aug 1848 ae: 66y. A Tomb 82

Clara d/o William d 19 Jan 1855 ae: 6w. GSL

David b 14 Mar 1751 d 29 Dec 1841. "Born Ft. Augustus, Invernesshire, Scotland" "Immigrated to this place 1774.) A Tomb 82

Duncan M s/o Duncan M d 8 Aug 1846 ae: 16m. A Tomb 82

Elisa J M d/o William d 20 June 1854 ae: 19y. A Tomb 82

Elizabeth Duguid wid/o Capt Alexander b 1 Jan 1721 d1 Mar 1798. "Born Stroma, Orkneys." Ledger-MmtB&E E:13

ROSS (continued)

Emma Jane d/o John H d 5 Dec 1863 ae: 2y 5m 15d. A Tomb 82

Emma w/o David d 25 May 1824 ae: 52y. A Tomb 82

Grizzy wid/o Capt William d 13 July 1835 ae: 65y. "...of Grand Manan, N.B." C:82

James M s/o James M d 12 Mar 1855 ae: 17m. GSL

John C s/o John M d 16 Mar 1848 ae: 14m. A Tomb 82

Mary Ann d/o William d 5 May 1847. A Tomb 82

Mary Jane d/o John d 19 Nov 1841 ae: 2y. GSL

Mary T d/o William d 19 Mar 1844 ae: 2y. A Tomb 82

Nancy wid/o Benjamin D d 21 Mar 1837 ae: 54y. I:20

Walter D s/o David Jr d 18 Feb 1846 ae: 5m. A Tomb 82

William d 25 Nov 1848 ae: 38y. "Died in Eastport." A Tomb 82

ROUNDY, Benjamin s/o Benjamin d 16 Jan 1844 ae: 6m. GSL

ROWE, Anna M d/o James d 29 Aug 1863 ae: 9y 1m. GSL

Charles B d 13 June 1901 ae: 69y. "Died Bridgewater, Massachusetts." A Tomb 39

Clara M d 28 Oct 1904 ae: 71y 11m 19d. A Tomb 39

Isaac d 24 Apr 1855 ae: 77y. A Tomb 39

Isaac s/o Isaac d 12 Nov 1866 ae: 41y. A Tomb 39

James W s/o Frank d 22 Sep 1857 ae: 6d. "Buried near head Hancock Street." GSL

John C s/o James d 7 Apr 1857 ae: 16m. GSL

Johnson d 28 Nov 1860 ae: 2y. "Buried near head Hancock Street." GSL

Lucy d/o James Abbott d 26 June 1870 ae: 80y 4m. GSL

Lucy Jane d/o Henry H d 18 Feb 1855 ae: 4d. A Tomb 39

ROWE (continued)

Mrs Sarah d 23 Sep 1852 ae: 61y GSL

Sarah Elizabeth d/o Isaac Jr d 1 Feb 1849 ae: 7y. A Tomb 39

ROYCE, William H s/o Bailey d 5 Oct 1848 ae: 6w. GSL

RUBY, Janett C w/o Reuben d 21 Oct 1827 ae: 22y. Black. A-11-24

William A s/o Reuben & Janett d 29 Oct 1828 ae: 3y. A-11-23

RUNNELLS, Emily J d/o Samuel D & Jane d 13 Feb 1835 ae: 6w. C:162

Jane w/o Samuel D d 29 Nov 1835 ae: 26y. SBE C:164

Ransom d 19 May 1854 ae: 45y. "Died Marine Hospital." GSL

Samuel s/o Samuel D & Jane d 17 Jan 1832 ae: 2m. SD C:162

Sarah E d 23 Sep 1840 ae: 21y. SBE A-14-1

Thomas d 12 July 1846 ae: 85y. GSL

Thomas s/o Thomas & Sally b 8 May 1810 d 31 Aug 1811. G:90

Two infants d/o's Thomas & Sally nd. G:90

Walter H d 4 July 1845 ae: 27y. SBE A-14-3

RUSSELL, Albion d 21 Jan 1848 ae: 27y. GSL

Alice M d/o Moses d 27 Aug 1845 ae: 13m. GSL

Hannah A w/o John H d 13 Aug 1864 ae: 38y. SB A-7-16

Harriet d/o Joseph d 18 Feb 1844 ae: 13y. GSL

Jeremiah d 27 Mar 1883 ae: 67y. GSL

Joseph R d 7 May 1862 ae: 46y. GSL

Maria R w/o John H d 27 Sep 1863 ae: 25y. A Tomb 69

Mary E d 3 May 1863 ae: 54y. GSL

RUSSWURM, John d 26 Apr 1815 ae: 54y. "Formerly resident of Port Antonio, Island of Jamaica" "D. in Westbrook." SD I:193

RYDER, Hattie d/o John d 6 Sep 1867 ae: 6m. A Tomb 20

Hattie M d/o John d 14 Oct 1866 ae: 2y 6m. "Died in New York." A Tomb 20

RYERSON, Ebenezer d 29 Apr 1849. GSL

SAFFORD, Esther w/o Jeremiah d 28 Aug 1863 ae: 59y. GSL

SALVADORE, Adelaide d/o Joseph d 27 Nov 1851 ae: 7m. GSL

Annis d 20 Feb 1852 ae: 3y. GSL

Annis D d/o wid/o Annis d 12 Mar 1845 ae: 29y. "Buried Family Range." GSL

Annis w/o John d 1 Nov 1860 ae: 70y. GSL

Emma S d/o Joseph d 23 Nov 1857 ae: 2y 7m. GSL

Frederick E s/o Joseph d 7 Feb 1859 ae: 2y. GSL

Margaret d/o Joseph d 30 Jan 1852 ae: 7y. GSL

SAMPLES, George s/o James d 19 Dec 1855 ae: 22y 6m. Black. GSL

James H d 17 Oct 1876 ae: 99y. Died: "Good old age" Black. GSL

Peter s/o James d 24 Jan 1844 ae: 6y. Black. GSL

Sophia w/o James d 15 Aug 1859 ae: 52y 4m. Black. GSL

SAMPSON, Abigail w/o Col John d 3 Apr 1858 ae: 66y. SD I:155

Amelia M w/o Thomas R d 19 Sep 1840 ae: 25y. A-13-15

David d 26 Feb 1848 ae: 56y. Black. SD L:21

John d 28 Aug 1832 ae: 44y. I:156

Micah d 21 Sep 1821 ae: 81y. I:157

SAMUEL, Elizabeth A d 10 Nov 1851 ae: 25y 6m. Black. SBE L:14

Margaret d/o Edward & Margaret d 3 May 1854 ae: 15y 9m. SBE L:16

Margaret w/o Edward d 22 Apr 1850 ae: 52y. Black. SBE L:15

SANBORN, Olive d/o Simeon & Anna b 3 Apr 1804 d 27 Aug 1806. SD K:31

SANDFORD, Capt Thomas d 18 Feb 1811. GSL

SANDS, Charles P s/o Porter & Priscilla d 10 May 1824. SD B-2-8

SANFRANCISCO, Antonio d 9 July 1858 ae: 20y. "Died at Marine Hospital" "Native of Campeachy, Mexico" "Buried at head of Samuel Whittier." GSL

SARGENT, Adah, #2 w/o Nathan d 20 Mar 1822 ae: 55y. C:119

Alice d/o Eli d 4 Jan 1855 ae: 3y 8m. GSL

Betsy d/o Nathan & Adah d 19 June 1807 ae: 17m. C:120

Caroline F wid/o Deacon Charles F d 17 June 1858 ae: 31y. GSL

Charles F d 27 Mar 1858 ae: 40y 2m. SD B-8-7

David d 18 Oct 1836 ae: 63y. SB A-5-9

Capt Eli d 10 July 1860 ae: 54y. A-21-8

Eli s/o Capt Eli d 1 May 1846 ae: 86y. "Buried in Miss Herrick's yard." GSL

Eliza B d 21 Sep 1844 ae: 35y. GSL

Elmira K Hood wid/o Capt Eli b 1815 d 22 Jan 1907. A-21-8

Franklin T d 17 Nov 1852 ae: 28y. SBE F:53

George E s/o John & Rebekah b 24 Jan 1837 d 7 Apr 1857. SD C:122

Hannah D d/o David & Mary d 20 Apr 1829 ae: 17y. A-5-7

Henry A s/o John & Rebekah b 8 Sep 1840 d 12 Dec 1859. SD C:123

John b 17 Jan 1803 d 17 Sep 1864. SD C:124

John Collins s/o John & Rebekah d 25 Mar 1836 ae: 1y. C:121

John W s/o widow Mary d 17 May 1851 ae: 19y. SD F:54

Josiah H s/o Ebenezer d 17 Dec

SARGENT (continued)
1845 ae: 9y. GSL

Julia A d 4 June 1854. GSL

Mary C w/o David d 15 Sep 1857 ae: 81y. SB A-5-8

Mary E d 29 June 1853 ae: 23y. SBE F:52

Mary E d/o Gilman & Mary d 6 Aug 1825 ae: 9m. B-2-14

Nathan b 7 Mar 1763 d 30 Nov 1841. SBE C:118

Rebecca C wid/o John d 8 June 1889 ae: 79y 8m. "Died Rumford, Maine." GSL

Rufus G s/o Gilman & Mary d 28 Aug 1821 ae: 20m. B-2-14

Sarah D d 6 Dec 1853 ae: 53y. SB A-5-6

Solomon d 14 Nov 1862 ae: 70y. GSL

SARSTROFF, ---- s/o Henry d 7 Aug 1843 ae: 10d. GSL

Francea adopted d/o Henry d 21 Aug 1850 ae: 5w. GSL

SATTER, Mary d/o late John d 27 Apr 1856 ae: 57y. "Buried at head of A Fernald's grave." NS I:88

SAVILLE, Judith w/o James d 30 Dec 1839 ae: 36y. A-11-6

SAWYER, Abigail wid/o Capt Ephraim d 11 Nov 1851 ae: 77y. SD A-17-1

Agnes M d/o James d 4 Dec 1841 ae: 13m. GSL

Charles C d 27 Sep 1864 ae: 45y 5m. GSL

Charles F s/o Edward W d 8 Aug 1871 ae: 8m 26d. GSL

David Tilden s/o Reuben d 26 July 1859 ae: 8y. A Tomb 56

Edward R d 10 June 1889 ae: 80y. "Died Alms House - insanity." GSL

Edwin A s/o Edwin & Emily A d 12 Dec 1851 ae: 17y. SD A-17-3

Eliza w/o Capt James d 7 Aug 1855 ae: 77y. SD A-3-33

Emily E d 14 June 1845 ae: 4m. SD A-17-4

Frank H s/o Charles d 18 June

SAWYER (continued)

1870 ae: 3m. GSL

George W s/o John M d 24 Aug 1864 ae: 2y. GSL

Hannah w/o John d 9 Mar 1865 ae: 77y. A Tomb 5

Capt James d 14 Mar 1845 ae: 81y. A-3-32

Jane Ilsley d/o Reuben & Phebe b 18 July 1818 d 19 July 1818. D:120

Capt John d 20 Dec 1831 ae: 48y. "Perished at sea." A-11-14

John G d 31 Oct 1863 ae: 48y. A Tomb 5

John M s/o John H d 20 Aug 1864 ae: 32y 10m. GSL

John s/o Capt John d 7 Dec 1839 ae: 33y. A-11-14

Joseph A s/o Edwin & Emily A d 22 Jan 1860 ae: 16y 6m. SD A-17-2

Lydia W d/o Capt James & Eliza d 13 Nov 1838 ae: 19y. SBE A-3-31

Lydia wid/o Richard C d 6 Dec 1846 ae: 59y. SB B-2-28

Maria w/o Edward d 6 June 1878 ae: 72y. GSL

Mary w/o James d 13 Aug 1863 ae: 84y. SD I:17

Nathan d 8 Sep 1824 ae: 30y. D:112

Nathan d 9 Dec 1841 ae: 79y. GSL

Phebe d 15 Aug 1821 ae: 28y. SB D:114

Phebe Newman d/o Reuben & Phebe b 2 Jan 1820 d 15 Aug 1820. D:118

Rebecca B d 6 Oct 1848 ae: 33y. GSL

Reuben d 23 Dec 1822 ae: 31y. SB D:114

Richard C d 23 Mar 1844 ae: 65y. SD B-2-29

Sally d 20 June 1873 ae: 82y. SBE C:247

Susan d/o Reuben & Phebe b 18 July 1818 d 19 July 1818. D:121

Susan wid/o Porter d 5 Mar 1861

SAWYER (continued)

ae: 84y 4m. "Buried in A Osgood's lot." NS C:12

Willie s/o Moses H & Anna M nd. ae: 9m. SD K:53

SCHOENECK, Vera Elsa d/o Lewis N d 10 Oct 1891 ae: 9m. 18d. A Tomb 9

SCOTT, Capt Andrew d 24 Sep 1825 ae: 61y. Rev/War. SBE B-1-21

Catherine w/o John B d 17 May 1876 ae: 73y. "Died Boston, Massachusetts." GSL

Charles A s/o John B & Catherine d 1 Oct 1826 ae: 20m. H:83

Eleanor w/o John d 25 Nov 1841 ae: 36y. Black. GSL

Eliza w/o John B d 8 Apr 1823 ae: 25y. H:81

Joseph s/o Lloyd d 16 Jan 1844 ae: 1y. Black. GSL

Martha E w/o Rev James R Pastor First Baptist Church b 17 Mar 1813 d 9 July 1851. MmtE between A Tomb 82 & A Tomb 83 A:88

Martha V F d/o Rev James R & Martha E d 11 Mar 1858 ae: 8y. MmtE between A Tomb 82 & A Tomb 83 A:88

Mary E d/o John B & Eliza d 1 Oct 1831 ae: 12y. SD H:80

Mary wid/o Capt Andrew d 15 Sep 1831 ae: 62y. SB B-1-20

Rufus S d 17 Jan 1846 ae: 24y. SD H:82

SCRIBNER, Daniel W d 7 Feb 1892 ae: 57y. GSL

SCUDDER, Zenas s/o James d 3 Aug 1855 ae: 10m. "Buried west of Bryant's stone." GSL

SEAVER, Albion W s/o Horace & Sylvia d 25 Oct 1823 ae: 1y 2d. SD J:226

SEAVEY, Charles F s/o James D d 17 July 1849 ae: 5w. GSL

Emma R wid/o James d 26 Apr 1876 ae: 61y. A Tomb 82

James d 1 Nov 1831 ae: 41y. A Tomb 82

SEDGLEY, Mary d/o Joseph & Abigail d 25 Apr 1812 ae: 20y. "...of Bowdoinham" D:108

SEELEY, Hattie Ellen d/o Capt Edward d 9 Sep 1861 ae: 1y. GSL

SENNETT, Mary J w/o John d 6 Sep 1854 ae: 37y. GSL

SENTER, Henry C d 8 Feb 1844 ae: 30y. "Buried beside S Clark's stone" GSL

SEWALL, Betsy d 20 Dec 1819 ae: 25y. A Tom 73

John E s/o Ezra d 21 May 1847 ae: 12y. A Tomb 35

Mary Ann d 1 Apr 1860 ae: 55y 9m. Black. GSL

SHACKFORD, Ebenezer s/o Ebenezer & Eliza d 31 July 1819 ae: 15d. SD J:188

Eliza w/o Ebenezer d 19 July 1819 ae: 26y. SD J:187

SHAPLEIGH, Eunice H d 28 Oct 1869 ae: 76y 3d. Black. SD L:9

Prince W d 28 Apr 1843 ae: 44y. Black. SD L:9

SHATTUCK, Betty d 24 Dec 1856 ae: 61y. A Tomb 35

Molly d Oct 1804 ae: 19y. GSL

SHAW, Benjamin d 8 Feb 1823 ae: 74y. "Died at Baliz, Honduras" H:35

Capt Benjamin Jr d 17 Oct 1814 ae: 34y. G:132

Charles F d 2 Dec 1832. A Tomb 69

Capt David A d 22 Jan 1829 ae: 28y. B-9-41

Edgar d 10 Jan 1879 ae: 17y. GSL

Edvardus d Aug 1803 ae: 21y. H:35

Eliza E wid/o Joshua S d 27 Mar 1877 ae: 68y. A Tomb 69

Esther #2 w/o Capt Benjamin d June 1802 ae: 35y. H:35

Esther w/o David P d 5 Nov 1829 ae: 26y. G:101

Eunice C d/o Capt Benjamin Jr & Eunice d 23 Apr 1838 ae: 29y. G:132

SHAW (continued)

Eunice w/o Capt Benjamin Jr d 23 Aug 1819 ae: 30y. G:132

Frances Ellen d/o Nathaniel & Nancy d 24 Jan 1831 ae: 13m. J:4

Franklin D s/o John L d 15 Oct 1865 ae: 16m 12d. A Tomb 69

George F M s/o Joshua S d 11 Apr 1848 ae: 4m. A Tomb 69

George Webster s/o Nathaniel & Eliza H d 5 Apr 1833 ae: 4m. K:129

Hannah d 26 Sep 1848 ae: 54y. GSL

Hepzebeth w/o Neal b 4 Apr 1773 d 15 July 1812. D:34

Jane M d/o Nathaniel & Nancy d 9 Jan 1833 ae: 18y. K:129

John d Apr 1812 ae: 17y. H:35

John s/o Capt Benjamin Jr & Eunice d 19 July 1837 ae: 24y. "Died at Demarara." G:132

Joshua S d 31 Jan 1876 ae: 72y 3m. A Tomb 69

Josiah d Nov 1804 ae: 53y. GSL

Lucy w/o Benjamin d Apr 1788 ae: 36y. H:35

Mary d 27 Jan 1876 ae: 74y. SB C:245

Mary d/o Capt Benjamin & Lucy d Nov 1798 ae: 19y. H:35

Nancy w/o Nathaniel Jr d 6 Dec 1830 ae: 40y. J:4

Nathaniel d 16 Aug 1831 ae: 71y. Rev/War: Cpl. I:198

Polly wid/o Nathaniel d 14 Nov 1841 ae: 79y. I:199

Rachael w/o Samuel d 16 Oct 1849 ae: 79y. I:106

Samuel d June 1818. J:106

Samuel s/o Capt Benjamin & Esther Lost at sea Jan 1815 ae: 20y. H:35

Sarah Ann d/o Nathaniel & Nancy d 27 May 1818 ae: 11m. J:4

Sarah d 22 Jan 1849 ae: 63y 7m. SB K:130

Sarah E w/o Luther d 5 Sep 1848 ae: 30y. "Child 3m old buried in same grave." GSL

William d Aug 1798 ae: 13y H:35

SHAW (continued)

William H d 24 Sep 1875 ae: 55y. Civ/War: 29th Reg Maine Inf Co E. J:5

William March s/o Nathaniel & Nancy d 2 Feb 1820 ae: 14m. J:4

William s/o John C d 7 July 1841 ae: 7m. GSL

William s/o Nathaniel d 24 Sep 1875 ae: 55y. "Died Dover, New Hampshire." GSL

SHEA, Edward s/o Nicholas & Barbara d 5 Aug 1824 ae: 4y. B-10-5

Eleanor d 3 Aug 1807 ae: 9m. B-10-4

Job d 12 Apr 1848 ae: 35y. Black. GSL

Nicholas d 3 Dec 1875 ae: 57y. SBE B-10-3

Nicholas d 31 Oct 1813 ae: 16m. B-10-4

Nicholas d 4 Mar 1824 ae: 48y. SD B-10-2

SHEAFE, John s/o William & Mary d 7 Sep 1838 ae: 29y. "Lost from the brig *Alna*, on the Florida coast." C:94

Mary w/o William d 17 May 1831 ae: 55y. C:94

William d 19 Sep 1848 ae: 41y. GSL

William d 23 Apr 1844 ae: 67y. C:95

SHEAL, Eliza w/o William d 3 June 1888 ae: 78y. G:62

William d 15 Aug 1887 ae: 92y. "Died Greely Hospital." G:61

SHED, Ann w/o Capt James d 14 July 1809 ae: 21y. L:34

Hepzibah w/o Thomas d 22 Sep 1799 ae: 46y. L:35

Thomas d 17 Feb 1806 ae: 60y. L:36

SHEPARD, Frances d 19 Nov 1814 ae: 19y 10m. SBE D:139

James M s/o John M & S M d 23 Mar 1856 ae: 3m. SBE C:36

SHEPHERD, Elizabeth Ruby wid/o Lewis d 3 Apr 1839 ae: 83y. Black. SD L:20

SHEPHERD (continued)

Lewis d 22 Dec 1833 ae: 82y. "Soldier of the Revolution." Black. A-24-27

Rushworth s/o Lewis & Elizabeth d 20 Apr 1831 ae: 33y. Black. GSL

Sarah wid/o Capt Joseph d 10 Dec 1846 ae: 80y. Black. GSL

SHEPLEY, Mary d/o Leonard D d 29 Sep 1858 ae: 17m. F:105 Tomb

SHERIDAN, Daniel d 21 July 1851 ae: 19y. "Killed on board steamer *Boston*, on trip from Bangor, by being crushed to death in the crank pit, where he had fallen." Catholic. GSL

Elizabeth wid/o John d 21 Aug 1865 ae: 41y. GSL

Thomas d 4 Dec 1850 ae: 20y. Catholic. GSL

SHERREDON, Ann d 18 Mar 1825 ae: 3y. Catholic. C:116

Dennis d 15 Mar 1825 ae: 1y. Catholic. C:116

John d 27 Sep 1837 ae: 42y. Catholic. C:116

SHIELDS, Charles R s/o Charles H d 20 Oct 1861 ae: 18m. A Tomb 6

Edward d 28 Mar 1854 ae: 55y. "Died in Boston" A Tomb 6

John s/o Capt Edward d 7 Mar 1848 ae: 21y. A Tomb 6

Mary d 23 Jan 1851 ae: 19y. A Tomb 6

Woodward d 20 May 1862 ae: 19y 3m. A Tomb 6

SHIRLEY, Arthur d 21 Jan 1864 ae: 82y. A Tomb 11

Arthur s/o Arthur d 5 Mar 1844 ae: 21y. A Tomb 11

Clara C d/o George H d 23 Aug 1849 ae: 24d. A Tomb 11

George H b 13 Sep 1816 d 14 Mar 1904. A Tomb 11

Joshua d 13 Apr 1819 ae: 30y. "Printer" I:43

Martha E d/o George H & Mary M d 4 Nov 1852 ae: 8y 9m. A Tomb 11

SHIRLEY (continued)

Mary E d 9 Mar 1913 ae: 62y 3m 9d. "Died Brooklyn, New York" A Tomb 11

Mary M w/o George H b 17 June 1810 d 31 Mar 1890 "Died Brooklyn, New York" A Tomb 11

Ruth w/o Arthur d 25 Nov 1851 ae: 62y. A Tomb 11

SIFTIN, Mary T w/o Nicholas d 11 May 1848 ae: 38y. "Buried beside Andrew Mack" NS H:60

SIGGS, John d 8 June 1858 ae: 77y. Black. GSL

Margaret Jane d/o John d 28 Nov 1855 ae: 14y. Black. GSL

Mary w/o John d 26 May 1835. Black. A-7-25

SILSBY, Thomas d 13 Sep 1838 ae: 30y. SBE B-11-1

SIMMONS, Alphonso R. s/o Edward d 18 Mar 1848 ae: 6m. GSL

Catherine d 19 Sep 1868 ae: 93y. GSL

Francis H s/o Edward W d 2 Dec 1847 ae: 5y. GSL

Kezia wid/o William d 17 Nov 1823 ae: 82y. E:62

Mary d 30 Dec 1857 ae: 79y. GSL

William d 29 Sep 1780 ae: 40y. "Died in Halifax - native of London" E:62

Capt William s/o William & Kezia nd. ae: 24y. "Died at sea." E:62

SIMONDS, Edward d 27 Apr 1869 ae: 68y. GSL

SIMONTON, Amanda d/o Timothy & Mary d 25 Oct 1827 ae: 2y 1m. SB J:13

Ellen d/o John d 31 Oct 1841 ae: 8m. GSL

Frances d/o Timothy & Mary d 1 Sep 1827 ae: 3w 3d. SB J:14

James d 24 Nov 1877 ae: 87y. Mmt A Tomb 5

Louisa E d/o James d 3 Oct 1847 ae: 19y. Mmt A Tomb 5

Lucy d 11 July 1883 ae: 90y.

SIMONTON (continued)

"...and their family" Mmt A Tomb 5

Mary wid/o Thomas d 6 Mar 1825 ae: 59y. I:145

Mary d 17 Aug 1876 ae: 81y. Mmt A Tomb 5

Mary wid/o Thomas d 20 June 1850 ae: 86y. Mmt A Tomb 5

Mary Allen d/o Timothy & Mary d 4 Sep 1827 ae: 3w. SB J:14

Nellie M d/o Albert H d 9 Aug 1865 ae: 7m 15d. Mmt A Tomb 5

Phebe L d/o James & Lucy d 3 Apr 1900 ae: 84y 10m 11d. Mmt A Tomb 5

Ruth w/o Thomas, d/o Capt Thomas Dodge d 15 Aug 1810 ae: 30y. J:180

Thomas d 23 Sep 1812 ae: 34y. J:181

Capt Thomas d 6 Mar 1813 ae: 26y. I:145

Thomas D s/o Thomas & Ruth d 16 Feb 1820 ae: 19y. SB J:182

William s/o Thomas & Ruth b 1 Mar 1806 d 16 Oct 1806. SB J:179

William D d 19 Sep 1811 ae: 2y 9m. J:181

William P s/o William d 30 Oct 1848 ae: 8y. Mmt A Tomb 5

SIMPSON, Abraham Henderson s/o John A d 12 Nov 1862 ae: 2y. GSL

Ada d 4 May 1860 ae: 4m. GSL

Alexander s/o Alexander d 5 Sep 1858 ae: 2y. GSL

Isabella w/o Robert d 17 Sep 1855 ae: 67y. I:62

John d 1 Sep 1861 ae: 44y 4m 18d. SBE I:61

Mark d 25 Aug 1849 ae: 60y. GSL

Robert d 28 Feb 1858 ae: 71y. "Buried beside wife's grave" NS I:62

SIMS, Almira W w/o Hugh W d 22 May 1849 ae: 32y 6m. K:107

SKILLINGS, Anna w/o Titus d 26 Aug 1824 ae: 38y. Black. L:19

SKILLINGS (continued)

Daniel d 10 Nov 1846 ae: 72y. SBE K:114

Eben d 8 Apr 1868 ae: 58y. "Moved from Alms House Yard 19 June 1868." GSL

Elizabeth w/o John d 21 Mar 1806 ae: 25y. K:117

George s/o John & Margaret d 12 Sep 1826 ae: 17y. SB K:121

Georgianna d/o George W & Margaret P d 25 Nov 1842 ae: 2y 5m. SD C:105

Frederick d 14 Aug 1847 ae: 6m. GSL

George W s/o Joseph d 26 Jan 1846 ae: 7m. "Buried beside William Hoyt's grave." NS A-9-16

Capt John d 20 Mar 1829 ae: 52y. K:116

John H s/o John M & Mary d 16 June 1846 ae: 13m. SD K:72

Louisa D w/o Eben d 14 Aug 1863 ae: 48y. GSL

Margaret w/o Capt John d 21 Apr 1846 ae: 65y. K:118

Mark s/o John & Elizabeth d 13 Sep 1901 ae: 6m. SBE K:119

Mary w/o Daniel d 8 July 1831 ae: 49y. SBE K:115

Mary Ann w/o Charles d 22 Feb 1848 ae: 31y. GSL

Mary C H w/o John M b 20 Oct 1811 d 27 Dec 1873 SD K:71

Otis H d 4 Mar 1887 ae: 37y. GSL

Sally D d/o John & Elizabeth d 4 Mar 1808 ae: 5y 5m. K:120

Samuel E s/o Eben d 15 Apr 1850 ae: 3y 8m. GSL

Sarah wid/o William d 20 Sep 1854 ae: 68y. GSL

Susan d 25 June 1864 ae: 64y. SB K:113

Titus d 27 Feb 1842 ae: 66y. Black. GSL

William d 3 July 1842 ae: 65y. GSL

SKINNER, Lydia d 5 Apr 1853 ae: 84y. GSL

SLADE, James P d 27 Mar 1867

SLADE (continued)
ae: 40y. A Tomb 1

SLATER, Betsy wid/o James d 8 Mar 1863 ae: 70y 9m. SB A-13-7

Daniel M s/o James & Betsy d 11 Aug 1855 ae: 22y 7m. SBE A-13-8

Isabella d/o James & Betsy d 26 May 1832 ae: 3y 3m. SBE A-13-9

Isabella d/o James & Betsy d 6 Nov 1836 ae: 2y 9m. SBE A-13-9

James b 18 Jan 1773 d 10 Apr 1853 SBE A-13-6

James s/o James & Betsy d 1 Sep 1825 ae: 11y 9m. SBE A-13-9

Capt John M d 31 Mar 1871 ae: 52y. SBE A-13-8

Priscilla w/o James d 26 May 1806 ae: 22y. Interesting Stone F:174

SLEEPER, Sarah H w/o James P d 13 Feb 1853 ae: 40y. A Tomb 16

SMALL, Arthur s/o Arthur M d 20 July 1841 ae: 4y 11m. GSL

Charles s/o James d 8 Apr 1846 ae: 4m. "Buried beside Elliot Fickett's grave" NS B-7-17

Daniel d 18 Mar 1815. War/1812 GSL

Ephraim d 19 Apr 1850 ae: 82y. "For a number of years laborer with N L Dana" Black. GSL

Frances A d/o William & Sarah B d 4 Feb 1825 ae: 10m. SB H:89

Frances E d/o wid Sarah d 1 Feb 1848 ae: 19y. GSL

Capt Henry d 4 Oct 1825 ae: 55y. SD B-11-11

Howard M s/o William & Sarah B d 8 July 1841 ae: 11y. SBE A-14-2

James F s/o Thomas d 31 Jan 1848 ae: 6y. GSL

John H s/o Benjamin d 16 May 1845 ae: 4m. "Buried beside Tim. Boston's grave" NS K:12

SMALL (continued)

Joseph d 5 June 1843 ae: 63y. GSL

Josephine d/o Charles J d 2 Apr 1869 ae: 15m. GSL

Mary d 11 Mar 1878 ae: 79y. A Tomb 1

Mary Susan d/o Samuel d 25 Apr 1847 ae: 21y. A Tomb 36

Melvin W s/o William & Sarah B d 8 July 1841 ae: 8y. SBE A-14-2

Sarah B d 28 July 1887 ae: 84y. SBE A-14-5

Sarah S wid/o Edward d 5 Apr 1866 ae: 77y 5m. GSL

Sarah W wid/o Capt Henry d 27 May 1871 ae: 81y. A-11-11

Timothy d 27 Feb 1818 ae: 75y. C:11

William d 15 Jan 1879 ae: 82y. War/1812 A-14-4

William B d 20 Feb 1870 ae: 46y. GSL

William H s/o Anthony & Dorcas b 11 May 1811 d 9 Jan 1812 SD I:34

Willlam H #2 s/o Anthony & Dorcas b 23 Oct 1812 d 23 Dec 1814 SD I:34

SMART, Mrs Nancy d 3 July 1845 ae: 82y. GSL

SMELLAGE, Almira E d/o George W d 19 Feb 1860 ae: 5m 9d. GSL

Frederick W s/o George W d 16 Oct 1865 ae: 8y 2m. A Tomb 9

SMITH, ---- wid/o Joseph H d 19 Feb 1851 ae: 62y. MmtE A Tomb 25

---- ch/o Richard d 8 July 1853 ae: 7w. GSL

Ada d/o Francis O J d 14 Sep 1842 ae: 19y. A Tomb 32

Amasa G s/o Gilman d 14 Dec 1863 ae: 6y 7m. GSL

Anne wid/o Eliphalet d 31 July 1836 ae: 73y. SBE A-2-3

Arixene w/o Henry d 6 Dec 1820 ae: 27y. SBE F:163

Benjamin s/o Henry & Elizabeth d 11 Sep 1804 ae: 24y. "Born

SMITH (continued)

in Dedham" SB K:86

Charles d 6 June 1848 ae: 62y. "Seaman - buried at foot of Samuel S Beckett's grave" GSL

Claude s/o Charles M d 9 May 1853 ae: 11w. GSL

Corwin s/o Robert & Mercy d 2 Aug 1733 ae: 4mos. SD D:84

Capt David d 30 July 1822 ae: 80y. F:105 Tomb

David b1822 d1870 SD H:65

Elizabeth w/o Capt David d 11 Aug 1805 ae: 58y. F:105 Tomb

Elizabeth d/o Nathan M d 4 Dec 1858 ae: 4y 10m. GSL

Elizabeth H wid/o Rev Thomas d 16 Mar 1799 ae: 83y. Slate Ledger D:87

Eliphalet d 21 Apr 1825 ae: 65y. SD A-2-2

Ella A d/o Charles d 12 Feb 1856 ae: 2y 6m. GSL

Ellen E d/o John d 15 Mar 1846 ae: 3y 6m. GSL

Francis P s/o William H d 8 Sep 1853 ae: 23y. GSL

Frederick Southgate s/o Henry & Arixene d 14 Feb 1814 ae: 8w. F:116

George A b 1 Jan 1818 d 8 Dec 1883 SBE B-6-11

George Albert B s/o Lucy E d 4 Nov 1848 ae: 4y 4m. GSL

Hagar d 14 Dec 1848 ae: 88y, Black. GSL

Harriet d 28 Aug 1856 ae: 22y 3m. GSL

Harriet w/o Thomas d 18 Nov 1900 ae: 85y 1m 9d. GSL

Hattie d/o Joseph d 25 Nov 1862 ae: 1y. "Died in Boston" "Buried under the hill" GSL

Henrietta d/o George W d 13 Dec 1848 ae: 3y. "Buried at foot of Thos. Freeman's grave" GSL

Ida Vesta d/o Moses C d 9 Dec 1860 ae: 7m 17d. GSL

J F d/o Charles W d 9 Nov 1862 ae: 5y 8m. GSL

SMITH (continued)

James H s/o James d 11 Dec 1856 ae: 3y. "Buried in John Alexander's grave" NS I:194

Dr John s/o Rev Thomas & Sarah Tyng d 25 Dec 1773 ae: 35y. Slate Ledger D:87

John d 7 June 1821 ae: 65y. Black. SB L:5

John s/o William d 27 Aug 1853 ae: 14w. GSL

John Coit s/o Henry & Arixene d 4 Feb 1820 ae: 17m. F:117

Gen John Kilby b 17 Dec 1753 d 7 Aug 1842 Rev/War Con Infantry War/1812 Massachusetts Soc/o the Cincinnati A-5-20

John R d 31 Dec 1863 ae: 23y. Civ/War 19th Reg Maine Inf Co D GSL

John W d 27 Oct 1856 ae: 11y. GSL

Joseph E s/o Joseph d 4 Sep 1846 ae: 2y. "Buried at head of Mrs Clarke's grave" NS C:155

Joseph H d 28 Aug 1818 ae: 24y. A Tomb 25

Julia A w/o Robert E d 4 Jan 1853 ae: 19y. SD C:240

Juliaetta d/o Robert & Julia A d 29 July 1856 ae: 3y 6m. SD C:239

Laura A d/o George A & Charlotte A d 23 July 1856 ae: 17m. SBE B-6-13

Capt Lendal d 13 Mar 1804 ae: 33y. F:105 Tomb

Marcy d/o Capt David & Elizabeth d 6 May 1789 ae: 19y. G:77

Margaret b1856 d1872 SD H:65

Mrs Mary A d 11 Apr 1860 ae: 66y. "Buried in Thomas Dodge's lot" NS I:130

Mary C w/o John D d 21 Feb 1848 ae: 34y. Black. GSL

Mary E d/o William d 21 Sep 1848 ae: 5m. GSL

Mary F d/o Francis & Martha d 26 Mar 1828 SD I:46

Mary G w/o Capt William d 22

SMITH (continued)

Jan 1823 ae: 33y. J:3

Mary K d/o Francis O J d 1 May 1864 ae: 2y. "Died Brooklyn, New York." A Tomb 32

Michael d 16 Aug 1809 ae: 31y. SB K:87

Moses d 14 Aug 1843 ae: 53y. GSL

Olive Plaisted Jordan w/o Rev Thomas b 1 May 1698 d 3 Jan 1763 Slate ledger D:87

Rachel R d/o David d 20 Jan 1860 ae: 19y. SB A-8-15

Richard E s/o Richard & Sarah d 8 July 1853 ae: 7w. SBE B-3-15

Rolvin s/o Seba & Elizabeth Oakes d 6 May 1832 ae: 7y. SBE B-2-12

Sally w/o Joseph d 29 Aug 1826 ae: 48y. I-92

Sally w/o Gen John K d 2 Feb 1837 ae: 77y. A-5-21

Sally w/o Robert H d 3 Sep 1839 ae: 63y. A-2-17

Sarah nd. MmtE A Tomb 25

Sarah, widow d 5 Aug 1843 ae: 78y. "Buried J Poole Tomb" GSL

Sarah w/o Richard d 13 Apr 1854. GSL

Sarah b1851 d1857 SD H:65

Sarah G w/o William d 6 Apr 1847 ae: 36y. A Tomb 73

Sarah Tyng w/o Rev Thomas d 1 Oct 1742 Slate Ledger D:87

Seward A s/o George A d 23 July 1856 ae: 17m. "Buried east of A Harmon's child's grave" GSL

Seymour W s/o Samuel d 6 May 1856 ae: 6w. GSL

Susan d 28 Feb 1846 ae: 41y. Black. GSL

Susan A w/o John E d 17 Nov 1850 ae: 28y 10m. A-2-25

Thomas s/o Rev Thomas & Sarah Tyng b 19 Sep 1729 d 28 Feb 1733 SD D:85

Thomas s/o Rev Thomas & Sarah Tyng d 10 Feb 1776 ae:

SMITH (continued)
40y. Slate Ledger D:87

Rev Thomas d 23 May 1795 ae: 94y. "A slab, facsimile of the original/ was erected by the First Parish in/ Portland formerly Falmouth Nov 1870/ Replaced by the First Parish Feb 1934." Slate Ledger D:87

Thomas M d 6 Sep 1864 ae: 67y. A Tomb 58

William d 3 Feb 1858 ae: 42y. GSL

William s/o William d 17 Aug 1853 ae: 15m. GSL

William A s/o William d 25 Apr 1852 ae: 11m. GSL

William R d 14 Apr 1821 ae: 21y. SBE H:3

William S s/o William T d 27 Oct 1848 ae: 5m. GSL

William Tyng d 10 Mar 1854 ae: 50y. "Buried Anderson tomb" A Tomb 68

SNIDER, William s/o William d 13 June 1845 ae: 9m. Black. GSL

SNOW, Caroline d 22 Jan 1815 ae: 21y. C:7

Ebenezer d 7 July 1803 ae: 66y. H:146

Sarah W d/o Lemuel & A d 12 Feb 1839 ae: 19y. SBE A-10-10

SOMERBY, George F s/o BC d 11 Mar 1849 ae: 2y. "Buried in Lewis Stetson's grave" NS K:63

SOPHER, Susan L b 26 July 1835 d 22 May 1838 A-3-28

SOULE, Bertha Hobart d/o Stillman d 8 Oct 1856 ae: 4y 2m. GSL

Eunice w/o Samuel d 9 Dec 1840 ae: 79y. SBE B-4-23

Frances E d/o Solomon & Cordelia d 28 Jan 1849 ae: 1y 8m. SD H:64

Henrietta d/o TS & Nancy d 24 Aug 1826 ae: 2y 7m. SD B-4-22

James W s/o Charles d 21 Mar

SOULE (continued)
1865 ae: 34y. GSL

Jesse L d 6 Oct 1858 ae: 55y. "...formerly of Yarmouth." Stone at D:102 C:76

Lois D w/o Jesse L d 31 Mar 1886 ae: 85y 7m. SD C:75

Sarah J d/o Solomon & Cordelia d 4 July 1846 ae: 1y 9m. SD H:64

SOUTHER, Dolly w/o Edward B d 18 Sep 1807 ae: 25y. K:110

Dolly d/o Edward B & Dorothy b 28 Oct 1806 d 30 Aug 1807 K:108

Edward B d 2 Aug 1824 ae: 47y. SB K:111

Margaret d/o Edward B & Dorothy b 10 July 1806 d 3 Sep 1806 K:109

SOUTHGATE, Edward P s/o Horatio d 24 Jan 1846 ae: 18y. A Tomb 61

Elizabeth B w/o Horatio Jr d 10 Aug 1850 ae: 36y. A Tomb 61

Ellen d/o Horatio d 26 Nov 1852 ae: 23y. "Died in Boston" A Tomb 61

Henry M s/o Horatio d 30 Dec 1852 ae: 17y. A Tomb 61

Robert s/o Horatio & Nabby d 25 July 1807 ae: 10m 25d. F:115

SPAULDING, Margaret C d 15 Nov 1878 ae: 65y. GSL

SPEAR, Elisa w/o James d 24 Sep 1863 ae: 52y. GSL

Frances E d 5 May 1893 ae: 54y 4m. SD B-9-39

James d 15 Sep 1873 ae: 77y. GSL

Jane w/o James d 11 Dec 1844 ae: 48y. "Buried next to the ladder house" GSL

Lucretia B w/o Frank d 3 Oct 1901 ae: 28y 2m 21d. GSL

Matilda d/o James d 19 Aug 1850 ae: 9m. GSL

Capt Pearl S b1812 d 3 Feb 1899 B-9-39

William s/o James d 11 Sep 1849 ae: 17m. "Buried beside of City Tomb." GSL

SPEAR (continued)

William H s/o Pearl S & Frances E d 15 Oct 1860 ae: 1y 7m. SD B-9-39

SPEED, John T d 22 July 1860 ae: 83y. A Tomb 32

SPENCER, Elizabeth w/o Joseph d 6 May 1862 ae: 40y. Black. A-24-28

Lavina E J d 14 July 1849 ae: 1y. Black. GSL

SPINES, Celia Newell d/o John d 5 Aug 1861 ae: 2m. GSL

SPOFFORD, John H s/o John d 12 July 1862 ae: 4d. GSL

Sarah F d/o Josiah d 9 Oct 1845 ae: 13m. GSL

SPOONER, Martha d 12 May 1843 ae: 28y. A Tomb 79

SPRING, "Mother, Father, Baby" nd. Mmt F:162

Edith nd. Mmt F:162

Edith d/o John d 3 Sep 1858 ae: 8m. "Buried in Daniel Crockett's lot." GSL

Emily A nd. Mmt F:162

Emma A d/o John d 2 Apr 1876 ae: 21y. GSL

Isaac A nd. Mmt F:162

Mary b1821 d1863 "Erected by her daughter Eliza S Smith" Mmt F:162

Zella L nd. Mmt F:162

SPRINGER, Eliza O w/o Thomas d 1 Nov 1845 ae: 25y. SBE A-16-16

Francis A s/o Rev Moses & Matilda d 21 Nov 1841 ae: 11y. A-12-13

Matilda w/o Rev Moses d 6 Dec 1839 ae: 38y 6m. SD A-12-12

Rev Moses d 21 Dec 1865 ae: 69y 10m 27d. SBE A-12-12

Samuel d 30 Oct 1826 ae: 49y. B-5-29

Sarah B d 23 Aug 1841 ae: 22y. GSL

Thomas d 12 Dec 1847 ae: 28y. GSL

STACKPOLE, Franklin s/o Winslow & Sarah d 30 Jan 1836 ae: 6y. SBE B-4-28

STACKPOLE (continued)

Katherine b1831 d1902 Mmt A-17-6

STACY, Catherine E w/o William d 1 Jan 1871 ae: 64y. SD A-5-13

Deborah d 21 Mar 1843 ae: 43y. GSL

Martha w/o William d 8 May 1842 ae: 32y. A-6-16

STALLARD, George A B s/o Thomas & Mary d 27 Apr 1827 ae: 9y. SD B-13-15

Mary wid/o Capt Thomas d 22 Aug 1855 ae: 76y. SBE B-13-16

Capt Thomas d 3 June 1852 ae: 73y. SBE B-13-14

STANFORD, Joseph s/o Robert d 30 Mar 1845 ae: 23y. GSL

Mary w/o Robert d 25 Sep 1853 ae: 63y. "Buried east of Andrew Bradbury's wife" NS A-7-12

Mary Ann d/o Robert d 30 Oct 1846 ae: 22y. GSL

STANLEY, Ellen w/o James d 11 Dec 1856 ae: 40y. GSL

Eunice M w/o Ephraim d 2 Oct 1852 ae: 56y. GSL

James d 2 Nov 1887 ae: 68y. "Died Greely Hospital" GSL

Joseph H s/o John & Alice d 7 Sep 1887 ae: 3m. GSL

Nancy w/o Jabez d 8 Feb 1848 ae: 61y. A Tomb 2

STANORTH, Casper S d 7 Nov 1850 ae: 49y. A-20-8

George s/o Joseph d 8 Aug 1858 ae: 2y. "Buried in Capt Stanorth's lot." NS A-20-8

John s/o Simon d 2 May 1869 ae: 39y. GSL

John A d 2 May 1869 ae: 39y. Civ/War 29th Rgt Maine Inf Co D SBE A-20-7

Julia F d 13 Aug 1875 ae: 35y. GSL

Lydia J wid/o Simon C d 18 May 1883 ae: 80y. GSL

Simon d 7 Nov 1850 ae: 49y. GSL

STANWOOD, David d 10 Jan 1841
ae: 75y. SD B-9-25

Capt David Jr d 6 Nov 1839 ae:
41y. SB B-9-23

Ruth d 6 Jan 1840 ae: 68y. SD
B-9-25

Capt William d 17 Feb 1829 ae:
29y. SD C:213

Capt Winthrop d 2 Aug 1820 ae:
26y. SBE C:212

STAPLES, Carroll d 5 Feb 1852
ae: 66y. SD C:233

Carroll Jr s/o Carroll & Charlotte
d 30 Sep 1845 ae: 24y. SD
C:232

Charles E s/o Richard d 7 Dec
1865 ae: 1y 3m. GSL

Charlotte d/o Carroll & Charlotte
d 22 Mar 1818 ae: 2y. SD
C:232

Charlotte d/o Carroll & Charlotte
d 17 Apr 1829 ae: 4y. SD
C:232

Charlotte d 8 Sep 1869 ae: 76y.
GSL

Ellen M d/o Carroll & Charlotte
d 17 Aug 1843 ae: 14y. SD
C:232

Franklin s/o Cyrus d 16 Feb
1847 ae: 6y. "Buried at head of
Mrs Jonas Mills' grave." NS
K:165

George A s/o Jotham & Mary d
10 Feb 1851 ae: 28y. SBE
L:81

Henrietta w/o Frank d 15 Mar
1855 ae: 19y. GSL

Henrietta C d/o Ai & Ann C d 17
Oct 1834 ae: 10y. SBE A-1-23

Leonard F s/o Jotham & Mary d
23 Dec 1853 ae: 23y. SBE L:81

Lucy w/o Charles d 2 Jan 1859
ae: 78y 4m. GSL

Maria d/o Carroll d 16 Aug 1843
ae: 14y. GSL

Robert B s/o Samuel d 25 July
1846 ae: 11m. A Tomb 63

Samuel d 12 Apr 1846 ae: 51y. A
Tomb 63

STARBIRD & Huston nd. SD A-
24-24

STARBIRD (continued)
John d 25 Jan 1839 ae: 42y. A-
23-1

STARBOARD, Cloie w/o Capt
John d 3 Mar 1822 ae: 59y.
K:123

George s/o Samuel & Eunice d
22 Sep 1806 ae: 1y. SD D:95

STARR, Eliza M d 21 June 1851
ae: 45y. GSL

STATEN, Hannah B d/o Capt
Amos d 25 Nov 1845 ae: 4m.
"Buried at head of Moses
Smith's grave" GSL

Josephine d/o Amos d 25 Aug
1848 ae: 1y. GSL

STEARNS, Ida May d/o William
P d 25 Oct 1878 ae: 5d.
"Buried Gould tomb" GSL

STEELE, David d 5 July 1837 ae:
70y. K:151

Elizabeth w/o David d 28 Dec
1815 ae: 41y. K:150

Capt Joseph d 18 Jun 1824 ae:
48y. A-1-2

Samuel d 5 Feb 1845 ae: 54y.
GSL

STENCHFIELD, Fanny w/o John
d 26 May 1821 ae: 22y. H:106

STEPHENSON, Henry s/o Stephen & Harriet b&d 17 June
1807 F:36

Capt John d 6 Dec 1817 ae: 76y.
SBE F:38

John Jr d 12 Feb 1791 ae: 18y.
F:35

Tabitha d/o John & Tabitha d 16
Feb 1777 ae: 5y 3d. F:34

Tabitha Longfellow w/o Capt
John d 23 May 1817 ae: 62y.
SBE F:37

STERLING, Nancy d 4 Feb 1880
ae: 74y. SB B-5-14

STETSON, Betsy w/o John d 1
June 1819 ae: 46y. SBE K:62

George s/o James B d 20 Apr
1849 ae: 44y. "Died in Boston"
GSL

Lewis s/o Lewis & Betsy b 18
Dec 1806 d 9 July 1813 K:63

STEVENS, inf ch/o Richard d 27
Apr 1853 ae: 11m. Black. GSL

STEVENS (continued)

Amelia Melverda d 31 Aug 1887 ae: 47y 9m. GSL

Angelia A w/o Eben S b1825 d 18 May 1850 A Tomb 27

Angelia C d/o Eben S & Angelia A b1849 d 12 June 1850 A Tomb 27

Anna d/o Samuel & Elizabeth d 26 Dec 1861 ae: 79y 6m. SB I:28

Benjamin d 13 Dec 1871 ae: 77y 4m. SD A-18-3

Betsy wid/o Jonathan d 13 Nov 1838 ae: 66y. A Tomb 73

Charles s/o William & Mary b 30 Apr 1799 d 29 Oct 1800 J:38

Clara Ellen d/o Eben S & Angelia A b1853 d 23 Aug 1854 A Tomb 27

Cornelia B d 18 Apr 1835 ae: 18y. A Tomb 40

Eben S b1826 d 17 Jan 1879 A Tomb 27

Ebenezer C b 21 Jan 1794 d 3 July 1865 MmtE A Tomb 27

Edmond s/o Isaac d 13 Oct 1862 ae: 1y. GSL

Edward P d 28 Mar 1842 ae: 4y. A Tomb 27

Edwin T s/o late Capt Joseph d 5 Dec 1848 ae: 19y. GSL

Eliza M widow d/o Henry & Elizabeth Burgess d 1 Feb 1930 ae: 91y 5m 8d. "Died City Hospital" NS A-8-5 1/2

Elizabeth d/o Samuel & Elizabeth d 22 Nov 1818 ae: 43y. I:32

Elizabeth w/o James d 17 Jan 1839 ae: 51y. J:111

Elizabeth d/o Benjamin & Sarah d 30 Aug 1842 ae: 18y. SD A-18-1

Elizabeth wid/o Samuel d 1 Apr 1850 ae: 97y 6m. SBE I:29

Elizabeth F w/o Jeremiah b 7 Jan 1801 d 22 July 1862 SBE I:7

Emily E d/o John M & Eunice d 28 Nov 1852 ae: 3m. GSL

STEVENS (continued)

Esther d/o Samuel & Elizabeth d 23 Jan 1840 ae: 49y. SBE I:33

Eunice wid/o Ebenezer d 10 Jan 1892 ae: 93y 2m 11d. A Tomb 27

Eunice C d 31 Jan 1833 ae: 17m. A Tomb 27

Eunice C d/o Eben S & Angelia A b1846 d1847 A Tomb 27

Eunice M d/o Ebenezer & Eunice d 19 Aug 1825 ae: 13m. A Tomb 27

George W d 6 May 1891 ae: 62y 6m. "Died New Gloucester, Maine" A Tomb 27

Georgiana d/o Joshua d 24 Mar 1860 ae: 16y. A Tomb 40

Harriet A d/o Jabez d 12 Nov 1856 ae: 18y 10m. A Tomb 27

Harriet H w/o Albert H d 21 May 1829 ae: 28y. A Tomb 73

Henrietta C w/o Charles H d 19 Feb 1892 ae: 45y. GSL

Jabez M d 9 Nov 1847 ae: 27y. GSL

Capt James d 2 Jan 1844 ae: 65y. "Buried beside his wife's stone." NS J:111

Jeremiah b 20 Jan 1788 d 8 Aug 1844 SB I:8

Jonathan d 18 May 1818 ae: 54y. A Tomb 73

Jonathan s/o Nathaniel & Ann d 5 Sep 1841 ae: 6y. SD I:47

Jonathan d 5 Nov 1857 ae: 83y. A Tomb 40

Capt Joseph d 28 Sep 1848 ae: 74y. GSL

Luther G d 12 Nov 1863 ae: 62y. SB G:36

Margaret wid/o William d 10 Feb 1850 ae: 89y. "Buried Butsey tomb" A Tomb 27

Margaret w/o late William d 14 Apr 1861 ae: 93y. "Buried at foot of E Oxnard's grave" NS H:132

Margaret I wid/o Jabez M d 12 Dec 1858 ae: 36y. GSL

Martha O d 19 Feb 1893 ae: about 45y. GSL

STEVENS (continued)

Mary wid/o Jonathan b 17 Nov 1753 d 8 Mar 1850 SD I:6

Mary d/o Samuel & Elizabeth d 19 Nov 1803 ae: 19y 8m. I:30

Mary, widow d 15 Nov 1854 ae: 81y. "...of Castine" "Buried 3 paces west of Jacob Noyes' stone." NS D:60

Mary Ann d/o William & Mary b 30 Jan 1801 d 29 Apr 1802 J:38

Nancy W w/o Luther G d 22 Dec 1858 ae: 58y. SBE G:37

Nellie C d/o Eben S & Angelia A b1855 d1874 A Tomb 27

Polly w/o Joshua d 31 May 1811 ae: 36y. G:54

Sarah w/o Benjamin d 23 June 1861 ae: 68y. SD A-18-2

Sarah W d/o James & Elizabeth d 6 Sep 1818 ae: 11m. SD I:38

Tabitha w/o Jonathan d 27 Mar 1856 ae: 78y. A Tomb 40

Thomas C s/o Edward & Sarah E d 18 Mar 1853 ae: 2y 4m. A Tomb 27

William Boutelle s/o W & Mersylvia d 3 Oct 1835 ae: 6m 18d. A-5-26

William Samuel s/o Samuel & Elizabeth d 27 Aug 1804 ae: 27y 10m. I:31

STEVENSON, Clarissa d/o Robert d 14 Nov 1844 ae: 8y. GSL

Ellen d/o Alexander & Louisa d 2 Apr 1841 ae: 14y. Black. A-14-20

STEWART, John d 24 Mar 1849 ae: 40y. "Buried at head of Susan Todd's grave" B-5-28

Maria L w/o William d 3 Feb 1847 ae: 28y. A Tomb 27

Matthew D d 12 Aug 1837 ae: 34y. "Formerly of Machias" A-2-26

William C d 8 Nov 1848 ae: 3y. A Tomb 27

STICKNEY, George E s/o Joseph H d 27 Aug 1855 ae: 13m. MmtB A Tomb 23

Capt Jacob d 26 Dec 1764 ae:

STICKNEY (continued)

28y. D:21

Sarah H w/o Henry R d 25 June 1827 ae: 24y. MmtE A Tomb 23

Sarah H d/o Henry R & Sarah H d 6 Sep 1827 ae: 3m. MmtE A Tomb 23

Capt Thomas d 4 Nov 1767 ae: 28y 2d. SD D:19

STIDWORTHY, Andrew J s/o John & Elizabeth d 28 May 1833 ae: 5m. B-13-19

Elizabeth w/o John d 19 Nov 1859 ae: 69y. SD B-13-18

Robert S s/o John & Elizabeth d 10 Feb 1833 ae: 3y. B-13-19

William S s/o John & Elizabeth d 26 Mar 1831 ae: 16d. B-13-19

STILLSON, Rebecca wid/o Joseph d 11 Jan 1860 ae: 83y. GSL

STIMPSON, Alexander d 17 May 1858 ae: 43y. "Buried at foot of Wm Waterhouse's grave." GSL

STIMSON, Jane d 17 Jan 1849 ae: 70y. GSL

STINSON, Alonzo P KIA 21 July 1861 ae: 19y. Civ/War: Sgt 5th Rgt Maine Inf Co H 1st Portland man to fall in battle. Mem A-14-23

Jane d 20 Feb 1849 ae: 63y. SBE G:106

STOCKBRIDGE, Joseph s/o David & Deborah d 5 Apr 1761 ae: 24y. Unusual portrait stone D:104

STOCKMAN, Caroline H Cressy w/o John B d 19 Dec 1844 ae: 32y. A Tomb 29

Dolly wid/o Capt John d 30 Aug 1866 ae: 79y. A Tomb 29

Emeline d/o Capt John & Dolly d 6 June 1825. A Tomb 29

Frederick D s/o John B & Caroline H d 1 Sep 1845 ae: 8m. A Tomb 29

John s/o Capt John & Dolly d 30 Oct 1810 ae: 1y. A Tomb 29

STOCKMAN (continued)

John d 9 June 1860 ae: 26y 4m. A Tomb 29

Capt John d 11 Oct 1833 ae: 58y. A Tomb 29

John B d Nov 1870 ae: 57y. A Tomb 29

Martha J d/o Capt John & Dolly d 4 Aug 1861 ae: 40y. A Tomb 29

Mary A d/o Capt John & Dolly d 14 May 1832 ae: 26y. A Tomb 29

William H s/o Capt John & Dolly d 3 Aug 1827 ae: 10m. A Tomb 29

STODDART, Martha wid/o David d 18 Dec 1816 ae: 73y. J:135

STODDER, Mary T d/o Enoch d 18 June 1851 ae: 1y. GSL

Col William P d 31 Mar 1860. GSL

STONE, Joseph McLellan s/o Benjamin & Betsy d 31 Jan 1801 ae: 2y 9m. SD H:110

Susan d 27 Aug 1827 ae: 20y. SBE B-5-38

Susan wid/o Daniel d 22 Apr 1866 ae: 87y 7m. GSL

STONEHOUSE, Mary w/o Capt Robert d 12 July 1807 ae: 62y. "Drowned from the Portland Packet at Richmond's Island" Unusual stone L:80

STORER, Anne w/o Woodbury d 3 Nov 1788 ae: 25y 6d. C:223

Catherine d/o Ebenezer & Catherine d 27 Aug 1802 ae: 19d. SD C:184

Elizabeth d/o Woodbury & Anne b 30 Sep 1787 d 29 Dec 1797 C:222

Ebenezer Jr s/o Ebenezer & Eunice d 14 Sep 1793 ae: 20d. C:178

Elizabeth d/o Samuel & Mary d 23 Oct 1818 ae: 23y. SBE G:65

Eunice d/o Ebenezer & Eunice d 10 Dec 1792 ae: 6m. C:179

Eunice w/o Ebenezer d 13 Nov 1798 ae: 30y. C:220

STORER (continued)

Frances Elizabeth d/o Woodbury & Margaret b 12 Jan 1798 d 4 Mar 1798 C:181

Mary B w/o Woodbury d 9 Oct 1871 ae: 80y. SD J:29

Samuel s/o Woodbury & Margaret b 6 Feb 1799 d 18 Feb 1799 C:180

Samuel d 30 Oct 1815 ae: 63y. SBE G:64

Woodbury b 12 July 1783 d 24 June 1860 SBE J:27

Woodbury d 12 July 1825 ae: 64y. SBE J:28

STOREY, Susannah w/o William d 5 Jan 1861 ae: 88y. B-14-32

William d 20 Aug 1853 ae: 77y. B-14-32

STOVER, Anne P d/o Capt Theophilus & Jane d 18 Aug 1814 ae: 20m. SBE E:30

Eliza G d/o Capt Theophilus & Jane d 27 July 1828 ae: 17y. E:31

Jane d/o Capt Theophilus & Jane d 4 Aug 1834 ae: 27y. E:32

Jane wid/o Capt Theophilus d 21 Oct 1854 ae: 72y. SD E:34

Robert d 15 Feb 1853 ae: 79y. GSL

Susan w/o Robert d 25 Apr 1847 ae: 50y. GSL

STOW, Ann d 23 May 1841 ae: 40y. Black. GSL

STREETER, Clarinda w/o Rev Russell d 28 Dec 1821 ae: 30y. SBE B-11-18

STRINGER, Thomas L s/o William d 17 Feb 1842 ae: 18m. "... of Raleigh, North Carolina." GSL

STRONG, Jane W w/o Daniel d 24 Dec 1869 ae: 72y. GSL

John d 5 July 1834 ae: 37y. B-10-9

Rebeckah wid/o Robert d 8 Feb 1858 ae: 89y. SB K:167

Robert d 28 May 1817 ae: 43y. SB K:167

STROUT, Emeline H d/o Charles W d 22 Aug 1845 ae: 1y. GSL

STROUT (continued)

George S s/o Levi & R d 17 Sep 1827 ae: 2y. B-9-40

James W s/o Edwin d 22 Sep 1849 ae: 1y. GSL

Mary A d/o Joseph d 31 Oct 1841 ae: 2y. GSL

STUART, Charles s/o Jonathan & Mary b 9 May 1798 d 28 May 1802 I:101

James s/o Charles d 29 June 1856 ae: 1y 10m. "Interred with Ann Wheeler." GSL

Jonathan d 30 June 1833 ae: 60y. SBE I:97

Mary w/o Jonathan d 8 Dec 1826 ae: 53y. SBE I:99

Mary E d/o Jonathan & Mary d 19 May 1828 ae: 23y. SBE I:98

STURDIVANT, Sarah C d/o Dr Joseph d 1 Oct 1856 ae: 11m. GSL

STURTEVANT, Cyrus H s/o Capt Cyrus d 27 Mar 1846 ae: 9m. "Buried Cyrus Sturtevant tomb" GSL

SULLIVAN, Daniel d 14 Feb 1886. "Died Marine Hospital" Catholic. GSL

John d 14 Jan 1852 ae: 26y. Catholic. GSL

SUMNER, George d 8 Aug 1859 ae: 54y. GSL

Harriet E d/o George & Anna C d 25 Nov 1840 ae: 3y. SD I:57

John d 20 June 1839 ae: 57y. SD I:60

John L d 24 Dec 1846 ae: 30y. GSL

Samuel d 23 July 1833 ae: 60y. SD I:58

Susan wid/o Samuel d 12 Aug 1850 ae: 75y. SD I:56

SWAIN, Elizabeth wid/o John d 8 Dec 1830 ae: 70y. B 6-18

SWAN, Mary wid/o William d 19 Jan 1854 ae: 72y. A Tomb 45

William d 18 Sep 1853 ae: 71y. A Tomb 45

SWEATT, William H d 15 May 1822 ae: 4y. B-9-1

SWEETSER, Bethuel b 25 Feb 1807 d 8 June 1872 SBE A-15-18

Bethuel s/o Bethuel & Leah d 20 Nov 1846 ae: 11m. SBE A-15-20

Cornelia d/o S & A d 6 Oct 1826 ae: 15m. B-5-34

Cyrus d 22 Feb 1857 ae: 54y. GSL

Eliza d/o Charles d 7 Oct 1843 ae: 6d. "Buried at head of Josiah Norton's stone." NS B-10-18

Ellen d/o Bethuel d 10 Sep 1842 ae: 14m. GSL

Frederick s/o Bethuel & Leah d 15 Apr 1856 ae: 1y 5m. SBE A-15-20

Freddie W s/o Bethuel & Leah d 13 Apr 1859 ae: 4m. SBE A-15-20

Helen L d/o Bethuel & Leah d 11 Sep 1842 ae: 4m. SBE A-15-20

Leah S w/o Bethuel d 24 May 1870 ae: 52y. A-15-19

William d 24 Mar 1769 ae: 45y 3m. SD D:98

SWETT, Elizabeth widow d 9 May 1845 ae: 83y. GSL

Hannah wid/o Stephen d 12 Oct 1847 ae: 73y. SBE C:230

Helen d/o George L d 19 May 1877 ae: 7w. A Tomb 66

Joseph d Sep 1817 ae: 76y. D:94

Lewis d 1 Apr 1850 ae: 45y. "Buried near the gate." GSL

Mary d/o Rufus d 23 Oct 1842 ae: 16m. GSL

Mehitable d 17 Oct 1836 ae: 87y. D:94

Rev Samuel d 6 Jan 1845 ae: 80y. GSL

Sarah B w/o Hiram D d 15 Nov 1855 ae: 26y. GSL

Stephen d 9 Mar 1849 ae: 69y. GSL

Stephen d 21 Jan 1870 ae: 58y. GSL

William d 20 Mar 1846 ae: 64y. GSL

SWIFT, Maria T d/o Joseph d 17 Apr 1845 ae: 29y. A Tomb 75

SYLVESTER, Abner d 17 Apr 1871 ae: 77y. SD C:242

Daniel B s/o Abner & Elizabeth d 18 Aug 1843 ae: 20y. SD C:241

Elizabeth wid/o Abner d 5 Feb 1885 ae: 87y. GSL

Mary A d/o Abner & Elizabeth d 24 June 1850 ae: 19y. SD C:241

SYMMES, William d 7 Jan 1807 ae: 45y. GSL

SYMONDS, William L & Joseph d 18 Jan 1862 ae: 28y. A Tomb 68

SYMS, Edward Smith b&d 24 Oct 1824 Black. SD A-11-17

Henry Smith d 24 Sep 1825 ae: 11m. Black. SD A-11-17

Louisa Dwight d 3 Feb 1830 ae: 3m. Black. SD A-11-17

Louisa Dwight d 23 Dec 1839 ae: 6m. Black. SD A-11-17

Mary Ann d 8 July 1848 ae: 47y. Catholic. Black. SBE A-11-18

TABER, Elizabeth d 1814. SBE J:53

Freeborn nd ae: 21y. J:52

John d 1811 J:55

Martha R nd. J:56

S Boyce d 1817 J:54

TANNER, Mary E d/o Eben & Harriet d 27 Feb 1839 ae: 2y 9m. SBE K:6

TAPE, Catherine d/o William d 24 Aug 1856 ae: 13m. "Buried east of Sarah P. Deane's grave." GSL

Elisa J d/o John d 22 Aug 1856 ae: 5m. GSL

TATEY, George H s/o George A d 23 Sep 1855 ae: 4w. GSL

TATTNALL, Charlotte d 8 Sep 1871 ae: 48y. GSL

TAYLOR, Abigail Jane d/o John & M d 6 Sep 1828 ae: 18m. B-8-33

Barzillai D s/o Joshua & Hannah d 9 Apr 1814 ae: 2y 2m. SD K:28

TAYLOR (continued)
David S d 5 July 1830 ae: 23y. F:105 Tomb

Dolly w/o Rev Joshua d 29 Sep 1807 ae: 25y. F:105 Tomb

Elmira Wilson d 4 Mar 1870 ae: 18y 6m. GSL

Jane w/o Robert d 19 Jan 1843 ae: 29y. GSL

John F s/o George E d 19 Nov 1852 ae: 2y 6m. GSL

Rev Joshua d 20 Mar 1861 ae: 93y. F:105 Tomb

Thomas s/o Thomas & Harriet A d 22 Aug 1849 ae: 22m. A-16-17

TEAGUE, Everett Stetson s/o Samuel d 23 July 1857 ae: 2y. GSL

TEBBETTS, Charles d 21 Dec 1883 ae: 83y. H:93

Eliza Ann C w/o Charles d 21 Aug 1846 ae: 42y. H:93

TENNEY, Emily w/o James A d 13 Sep 1857 ae: 28y. GSL

Sophia A w/o James A, d/o James R Mitchell d 17 May 1853 ae: 23y 4m. SBE B-6-24

TEWKSBURY, Amos B s/o Jonathan d 5 Feb 1861 ae: 46y. A Tomb 43

Edward D s/o Enoch D d 8 Nov 1849 ae: 8w. GSL

Herbert E s/o Amos B & May d 16 Apr 1870 ae: 10y 7m. A Tomb 43

John b 25 Jan 1781 d Apr 1866 Civ/War: 1st Rgt Maine Cav Co F A Tomb 43

Mary Ann w/o J M d 8 Jan 1871 ae: 38y 6m. A Tomb 43

THATCHER, James W d 27 June 1848 ae: 3y 8m. SD B-1-32

Sarah w/o William d 10 Sep 1826 ae: 49y. B-1-31

William d 26 Nov 1848 ae: 34y 6m. SD B-1-32

THAXTER, Charles E s/o Edward C d 11 Sep 1858 ae: 10y 1m. "Buried beside Jacob Riggs' child." GSL

Ellen M d/o JB d 16 Mar 1845

THAXTER (continued)

ae: 18m. "Buried beside John A Brown." NS A-7-19

Joseph d 25 Dec 1844 ae: 44y. A Tomb 13

Joseph d 6 Nov 1844 ae: 69y. A Tomb 13

Joshua d 3 Oct 1827 ae: 78y. B-7-31

Louisa d/o Joseph & Lucy b 2 Oct 1818 d 22 Sep 1820 B-7-32

Louisa w/o Edward d 15 Nov 1853 ae: 29y. "Buried in Jacob Riggs' lot." GSL

Lucy wid/o Joseph d 21 Dec 1856 ae: 82y. A Tomb 13

M Ella d/o Rufus W d 13 Nov 1897 ae: 46y. A Tomb 45

Martha E d/o Rufus S d 18 Jan 1917 ae: 94y 10m. A Tomb 45

Mary wid/o Martin d 21 July 1860 ae: 81y 1m. GSL

THAYER, Frederick L s/o Ludo d 28 May 1855 ae: 17y. F:95 Tomb

Sarah B d/o Abijah W & Susan d 3 July 1826 ae: 9m. SBE B-1-28

Solomon d 22 Dec 1857 ae: 68y. A Tomb 11

THOMAS, inf ch/o John d 4 Mar 1862 ae: 11d. Black. GSL

---- "Five/children of/Dr Stephen Thomas/were interr'd/ here/1810" C:5

Abigail w/o John d 13 May 1809 ae: 32y. SD L:3

Betsy b 16 Dec 1773 d 11 Feb 1870 A Tomb 46

Charlotte C d/o Edward d 7 Aug 1852 ae: 10m. Black. GSL

Charlotte Julia d/o Elias & Elizabeth Widgery b 20 May 1822 d 10 Nov 1920 A Tomb 62

Charles Widgery MD s/o Elias & Elizabeth Widgery b 14 Feb 1816 d 28 Mar 1866 Civ/War: 25th Rgt Maine Inf Co K A Tomb 62

Charles Widgery s/o Edward H & Charlotte A DuBois d 17 Nov

THOMAS (continued)

1893 ae: 33y 5m. "Died Tucson, Arizona." A Tomb 62

Edward H s/o Elias & Elizabeth Widgery b 1 Jan 1812 d 24 Feb 1896. A Tomb 62

Elias s/o Elias & Elizabeth Widgery b 7 Nov 1803 d 3 Jan 1822. A Tomb 62

Elias s/o Peter & Kerenhappuck (Happy) Cox b 13 Jan 1772 d 5 Aug 1872. A Tomb 62

Elizabeth Ann d/o late Capt William d 14 Dec 1846 ae: 6y. GSL

Elizabeth Widgery w/o Elias, d/o William & Elizabeth R b1779 d 2 July 1861. A Tomb 62

Ellen w/o John d 1 Mar 1862 ae: 31y. Black. GSL

Emma J M d/o John & Ellen S d 24 Aug 1861 ae: 3y 9m. Black. SD A-14-21

Francis s/o Peter & Happy d 9 Sep 1793 ae: 2y 2m. SD J:41

Frederick s/o Elias & Elizabeth Widgery b 16 Sep 1819 d 4 Oct 1819. A Tomb 62

George A s/o Elias & Elizabeth W b 24 Feb 1807 d 31 Oct 1809. A Tomb 62

George Albert s/o Elias & Elizabeth Widgery b 16 Sep 1819 d 20 Dec 1907. A Tomb 62

Hannah widow d 17 Apr 1854 ae: 88y. Black. GSL

Hannah M d/o Anthony & Dolly Knapp, w/o Capt Charles d 22 Apr 1832 ae: 22y. B-9-17

Happy Cox wid/o Peter b 11 June 1749 d 28 Oct 1838. A Tomb 62

Harriet Elizabeth d/o William & Harriet L d 31 Mar 1832 ae: 3m. A-24-23

James s/o John d 24 Aug 1861 ae: 3y. GSL

John d 15 Apr 1858 ae: 35y. Black. GSL

THOMAS (continued)

John d 23 May 1868 ae: 47y. Civ/War: USN GSL

John Widgery s/o Elias & Elizabeth Widgery b 10 June 1806 d 15 Jan 1872. A Tomb 62

Josiah Lord d 21 Nov 1859 ae: 50y. A Tomb 46

Mary wid/o John d 29 Aug 1824 ae: 71y. SD L:4

Mary Goddard d/o William W & Elizabeth G d 14 Apr 1863 ae: 6y 7m. A Tomb 62

Peter b1746 d 18 Aug 1797 Rev/War. A Tomb 62

Peter d 18 Aug 1807 ae: 51y. SB J:42

Peter d 3 Nov 1811 ae: 31y. J:79

Samuel S s/o Rev D F d 2 Dec 1869 ae: 2y 10m. GSL

William d 17 Apr 1850 ae: 49y. "Died in the Burying Ground of intemperance." GSL

William Widgery s/o Elias & Elizabeth Widgery b 7 Nov 1803 d 21 Nov 1896. A Tomb 62

THOMES, Benjamin d 22 Nov 1809 ae: 45y. GSL

Elizabeth w/o Joseph d 22 Jan 1829 ae: 71y. SBE C:140

Elizabeth d/o William & Mary d 19 Sep 1847 ae: 29y. SBE C:139

Joseph d 13 May 1835 ae: 75y. Rev/War SBE C:141

William d 26 Mar 1768 ae: 26y. A Tomb 39

THOMPSON, Andrew d 7 Mar 1805 ae: 45y. "Killed by fall of hogshead of fish." GSL

Annie E d 12 June 1949 ae: 75y. (cremated) "Died Boston, Massachusetts." A Tomb 33

Anna Clark d/o William & Mary E d 22 Sep 1870 ae: 8w. GSL

Charles d 7 July 1841 ae: 18y. GSL

Charles E s/o George C & Hannah d 6 Mar 1846 ae: 1y 6m. SBE A-14-17

THOMPSON (continued)

Charles R s/o J R d 18 Oct 1849 ae: 4y 10m. A Tomb 46

Clara M d 30 June 1873 ae: 3y 11m. Mmt A Tomb 25

Clement d 25 Feb 1829 ae: 64y. Black. SD A-14-22

Edward P d 17 Feb 1853 ae: 34y. A Tomb 9

Elizabeth d/o Hugh d 20 Mar 1855 ae: 3m. GSL

Elizabeth d 6 May 1861 ae: 89y. GSL

Esther w/o James d 25 July 1850 ae: 62y. GSL

Isabella M d 10 May 1872 ae: 30y. MmtE A tomb 25

Joseph d 16 Feb 1877 ae: 71y. A-1-18

Mary wid/o Joseph d 29 Oct 1885 ae: 90y. A-1-19

Rebecca d 25 Dec 1857 ae: 73y. "Died Windham, Maine" GSL

Thomas d 1 Jan 1846 ae: 87y. GSL

THORNDIKE, John S s/o Joseph d 12 Feb 1851 ae: 6y. GSL

Lucy d 21 Apr 1872 ae: 85y. MmtD A Tomb 19

Thankful, widow d 11 Sep 1846 ae: 78y. GSL

THORNTON, Betsy wid/o Joshua d 3 May 1859. GSL

THORP, ---- s/o Stillman d 3 May 1854 ae: 21y. A Tomb 16

Edward D s/o Orange P & Sarah A d 26 Oct 1834 ae: 10m. SBE A-3-15

Francis M s/o Orange P & Sarah A d 19 Dec 1840 ae: 9m. SBE A-3-16

Henry P s/o Orange P & Sarah A d 24 Sep 1833 ae: 16m. SBE A-3-14

Julia Willis d/o Orange P & Sarah A d 12 Feb 1843 ae: 15m. SBE A-3-17

Lily C d/o Orange P & Sarah A d 11 Sep 1853 ae: 10m. GSL

Mary Lee w/o Stillman d 1 Aug 1857 ae: 47y. A Tomb 16

Orange Parsons d 16 Feb 1875

ae: 70y. "Died West Roxbury, Massachusetts" GSL

THRASHER, Benjamin s/o Benjamin & Loruhama d 27 Oct 1773 ae: 14m 7d. G:85

Benjamin d 9 Nov 1855 ae: 64y. "Died Havana" D:47

Benjamin F s/o Joseph & Lucy d 22 Feb 1827 ae: 15y. SD B-13-12

Benjamin Franklin s/o Benjamin & Frances d 8 Dec 1860 ae: 40y. "Died Havana." D:46

Ezra B s/o Joseph & Harriet d 25 Sep 1827 ae: 13d. B-13-11

Harriet w/o Joseph d 24 Sep 1827 ae: 37y. B-13-11

Harriet d 14 Dec 1891 ae: 74y. NS B-13-13B

Deacon John d 11 July 1811 ae: 63y. MmtE A Tomb 23

Joseph d 16 July 1853 ae: 71y. SB B-13-10

Judith w/o Deacon John d 15 Jan 1795 ae: 46y. MmtE A Tomb 23

Phebe d 19 June 1825 ae: 35y. B-13-13A

Sidney d 21 May 1827 ae: 5y. D:45

THURINGTON, Ann Maria w/o John d 29 Aug 1837 ae: 29y. Black. A-13-28

THURLO, Betsy d 26 Oct 1839 ae: 69y. SBE F:87

Hannah d 15 Nov 1870 ae: 95y 1m 5d. GSL

Capt John d 17 Apr 1805 ae: 67y. F:92

Rebecca Waite w/o Capt John d 19 June 1798 ae: 55y. F:89

Miss Tamsin d 28 Mar 1820 ae: 85y. F:90

THURLOW, Edmund d 16 June 1823 ae: 33y. "... formerly of Newbury." B-6-9

THURSTON, Carrie E d/o Samuel d 1 Aug 1856 ae: 6w 3d. A Tomb 54

Charles A s/o Samuel d 25 Jan 1893 ae: 40y 11m. A Tomb 54

THURSTON (continued)
Hannah M d 28 July 1854 ae: 83y. GSL

Helen F d/o Daniel M d 3 Sep 1847 ae: 5y. GSL

Henry B s/o Samuel d 23 Sep 1853 ae: 5m. A Tomb 54

Lorenzo D s/o Daniel M d 1 Aug 1841 ae: 18m. GSL

Louisa B d/o Samuel d 23 Sep 1856 ae: 1y 6m. A Tomb 54

Lucretia H w/o Samuel d 7 Sep 1856 ae: 28y. "Died Standish, Maine." A Tomb 54

Nathaniel s/o John d 29 Apr 1842 ae: 2y 5m. GSL

Samuel d 25 Sep 1841 ae: 39y. GSL

Sarah F d/o Daniel M d 17 Sep 1847 ae: 3y. GSL

William s/o Daniel M d 20 Mar 1844 ae: 5y. "Buried by G Chase's stone." NS J:215

William s/o Daniel M d 5 Sep 1847 ae: 3m. GSL

TIBBETTS, Eliza Ann w/o Charles d 24 Aug 1846 ae: 42y. GSL

Mariah J d/o George d 2 Oct 1855 ae: 9m. GSL

TILDEN, Betsy P d 23 Nov 1871 ae: 56y. SD I:110

Henry B d 5 Apr 1870 ae: 69y 9m. SD I:109

TILLOTSON, ---- ch/o widow d 27 Nov 1841 ae: 1y. Black. GSL

TINKHAM, Abial W d 19 Dec 1830 ae: 37y. F:105 Tomb

Franklin B s/o Franklin & Jane Brooks d 31 Dec 1826 ae: 3m. A Tomb 75

Jane Brooks w/o Franklin d 6 Jan 1827 ae: 27y. A Tomb 75

Joseph W s/o Abiel W d 28 Jan 1859 ae: 29y. "Died in San Francisco, California." F:105 Tomb

TITCOMB, Anne d/o Joseph & Eunice d 19 Mar 1814 ae: 26y. C:198

TITCOMB (continued)

Anne Pearson wid/o Deacon Benjamin d 8 July 1800 ae: 72y. C:219

Deacon Benjamin d 15 Oct 1798 ae: 72y. Rev/War SD C:221

Eunice d/o Benjamin & Mary d 5 Sep 1800 ae: 10m. SD C:183

Eunice J w/o Joseph d 12 Aug 1842 ae: 87y. A Tomb 48

Henry s/o Benjamin & Mary d 16 Oct 1798 ae: 2y 11m. C:182

Henry d 17 May 1829 ae: 63y. SBE C:215

Jeremiah s/o Deacon Benjamin & Anna d 9 Aug 1777 ae: 5y. C:177

Joseph d 20 Aug 1836 ae: 80y. Rev/War A Tomb 48

Joshua s/o Benjamin & Anna d 14 Nov 1776 ae: 2y. SD C:188

Mary d/o Benjamin & Anna d 5 Apr 1769 ae: 5m. C:187

Sophia d/o Joseph & Eunice d 13 June 1810 ae: 25y. C:199

William #5 s/o Benjamin & Anna d 8 Apr 1786 ae: 18y. C:200

TOBEY, Celia w/o John d 5 Apr 1864 ae: 37y. GSL

Enoch d 6 Aug 1845 ae: 40y. "Buried near Edward Griffin's grave." NS K:39

George F s/o George W d 14 Sep 1848 ae: 15m. GSL

Lucy G w/o Dr C C d 1 Jan 1846 ae: 38y. GSL

Margaret wid/o John d 26 Sep 1868 ae: 94y. GSL

Nabby w/o Samuel d 23 Oct 1813 ae: 63y. G:55

Samuel d 14 Apr 1822 ae: 72y. Rev/War G:56

Thomas s/o John d 30 July 1864 ae: 4m. GSL

TOBY, Robert s/o William d 5 Aug 1806 ae: 20y. L:63

TODD, Eliza d/o Samuel & Sally d 14 Sep 1804 ae: 4y. I:26

James d 14 Apr 1884 ae: 90y. A Tomb 13

James T d 18 Feb 1899 ae: 73y.

TODD (continued)

"Died Greely Hospital" A Tomb 13

John d 22 Feb 1854 ae: 75y. A Tomb 13

Lucius s/o Royal d 30 Sep 1842 ae: 16m. GSL

Martha w/o Alexander, d/o James & Sarah Brown Milk d 25 Nov 1764 ae: 22y. E:76

Sally Shaw w/o Samuel d 23 Feb 1826 ae: 41y. I:27

Samuel d Mar 1829 ae: 51y. I:27

Sarah E d/o Royal d 16 Nov 1848 ae: 3y. GSL

Sarah R w/o Royal B d 19 Feb 1854 ae: 38y. D:7

Sarah Staniford b1797 d 3 Nov 1892 "Died Hudson, Massachusetts" A Tomb 32

Susan w/o Thomas d 9 May 1826 ae: 29y. B-5-28

Gen Thomas d 28 June 1854 ae: 56y. A Tomb 32

William d 29 Dec 1882 ae: 53y. A Tomb 32

TOLE, George Henry s/o Phineas & Pamelia d 29 Nov 1835 ae: 1y 9m. SD A-7-17

Pamelia w/o Phineas d 31 Aug 1837 ae: 34y. SD A-7-17

Phineas d 27 June 1847 ae: 47y. GSL

TOLFORD, Almira d/o Joshua & Mary d 19 Oct 1823 ae: 17y. B-5-11

Harold Mountfort s/o Joseph M d 28 July 1887 ae: 3y 9m. A Tomb 35

Joshua s/o Joshua & Mary d 29 Mar 1852 ae: 33y 3m. SB B-5-12

TOLMAN, Abigail wid/o John d 9 May 1860 ae: 73y. GSL

Jane w/o John d 1 May 1814 ae: 20y 3m. SD H:24

Mary d 5 July 1822 ae: 56y. SB I:173

Thomas d 24 Apr 1856 ae: 70y. A Tomb 54

TOMISON, Elizabeth w/o Jackman d 27 Oct 1872 ae: 78y.

TOMISON (continued)
B-14-33

George C s/o Jackman & Elizabeth d 6 Feb 1837 ae: 2y. B-14-35

Jackman d 3 Feb 1861 ae: 63y. B-14-34

TOWLE, Isabella F d/o Daniel L d 1O Sep 1854 ae: 4m. A Tomb 12

TOWNSEND, Angeline d 3 Nov 1851 ae: 18y. A-20-9

Angeline d/o Joseph d 22 Oct 1862 ae: 11y. GSL

Joseph d 19 Jan 1857 ae: 27y. GSL

TOWNSLEY, Sarah d 1 Jan 1842 ae: 48y. GSL

TRASK, George s/o Samuel & Martha F d 26 June 1826 ae: 3m. A Tomb 45

Martha F wid/o Samuel d 17 June 1839 ae: 52y. A Tomb 45

Samuel d 26 Nov 1827 ae: 5Oy. A Tomb 45

TREAT, Charles Arvida s/o Richard & Martha d 20 Apr 1842 ae: 4y. A-18-8

George William s/o James Jr d 22 Aug 1845 ae: 2y 3m 5d. GSL

TREFETHEN, Sarah H w/o Joseph d 2 Oct 1868 ae: 47y. GSL

TRETT, Capt James d Feb 1805 ae: 46y. GSL

TRIPP, Nancy w/o John d 7 Jan 1862 ae: 53y. GSL

TROTT, Charles d 31 Dec 1893 ae: 49y. "Died Marine Hospital" Civ/War: 11th Rgt New York Cav Co C. GSL

TRUE, Hannah J w/o Jonathan G, d/o Stephen Frothingham d 13 Nov 1845 ae: 21y. A Tomb 81

Henry s/o Asa W d 26 Aug 1842 ae: 7m. GSL

John d 3 Apr 1861 ae: 53y. GSL

Mary R d/o William & Rebecca d 25 Oct 1819 ae: 2y 7m. SB E:92

TRUETT, Sylvina d 14 Mar 1843 ae: 18y. GSL

TRULL, David s/o David & Submit d 22 Jan 1797 d 8 May 1808. L:66

TRUMBULL, James d 19 June 1851 ae: 63y. "Buried on the side of the hill." GSL

Mary w/o James d 9 Nov 1842 ae: 41y. GSL

TRY, Annie w/o John d 3 Aug 1879 ae: 69y. GSL

Francis A d/o John d 8 Sep 1856 ae: 2y 8m. GSL

Hannah H w/o John d 6 Dec 1841 ae: 31y. SB A-16-13

John E d 5 Jan 1839 ae: 18m. SB A-16-13

Nancy S d/o John & Hannah d 23 Dec 1858 ae: 29y 10m. SB A-16-15

TUCKER, Charles d 30 May 1842 ae: 33y. "Buried beside D Tucker's stone." NS C:111

Charles E s/o Jonathan d 11 Sep 1848 ae: 10m. A Tomb 30

Charles H s/o David d 17 May 1849 ae: 5y. GSL

Daniel d 8 Apr 1824 ae: 64y. Rev/War Privateersman C:111

Dorcas, w/o Daniel d 25 Jan 1785 ae: 21y. C:112

Eleazer C s/o Daniel & Lydia d 13 Aug 1812 ae: 14y. C:113

Eliza w/o Daniel d 18 Oct 1811 ae: 27y. SBE C:106

Elizabeth d/o Daniel & Eliza b 6 Sep 1811 d 26 Sep 1811 SBE C:106

Elizabeth d 21 July 1849 ae: 69y. "Died in Boston." GSL

Hattie M d/o David d 23 Jan 1862 ae: 6m. GSL

Jeremiah s/o Josiah d 22 Dec 1774 ae: 21y. GSL

John d 23 Apr 1852 ae: 77y. GSL

Jonathan d 1 Aug 1856 ae: 86y. SBE E:29

Julia A b 24 Aug 1820 d 24 Apr 1864 SB B-9-22

Lydia w/o Daniel d 23 Mar 1816 ae: 5Oy. C:112

TUCKER (continued)

Mary M wid/o David d 24 Aug 1858 ae: 71y. GSL

Oliver H d 22 Aug 1858 ae: 28y. "Policeman – drowned." GSL

Susan w/o Capt Jonathan d 19 Feb 1849 ae: 73y. SD E:29

Thomas s/o Thomas d 18 June 1843 ae: 3w. GSL

William C s/o David d 18 Feb 1857 ae: 1y 9m. GSL

TUFTS, Elizabeth d 21 Feb 1847 ae: 47y. SBE A–14–11

TUKESBURY, Amos B d 5 Feb 1861 ae: 40y. A Tomb 69

Charles C d 25 May 1927. "Died Boston, Massachusetts" A Tomb 69

Charlie s/o John C & Elizabeth RC d 18 Jan 1863. A Tomb 69

Dora C Sanborn w/o John C d 18 Nov 1857 ae: 26y. A Tomb 69

Elizabeth RC w/o John C d 10 May 1866 ae: 39y. A Tomb 69

Enoch D d 5 Aug 1862 ae: 51y. A Tomb 69

Herbert E s/o Amos B & Mary C d 16 Apr 1870 ae: 10y 7m. A Tomb 69

John C s/o Jonathan d 12 Apr 1891 ae: 73y 5m 15d. A Tomb 69

Jonathan b 27 Jan 1781 d 21 Apr 1866. A Tomb 69

Mary C Harding wid/o Amos B d 12 July 1863 ae: 43y. A Tomb 69

Rebecca w/o Jonathan b 1 Mar 1786 d 27 Mar 1865. A Tomb 69

Walter J s/o John C & Elizabeth RC d 1 Oct 1862 ae: 6m. A Tomb 69

TUKEY, Abigail Sweetsir wid/o John d 2 Nov 1827 ae: 95y. F:60

Benjamin s/o John & Abigail b 1749 d 26 Oct 1777. "Killed by premature discharge of a cannon while celebrating Saratoga victory." F:59B

Benjamin d 18 Feb 1833. GSL

TUKEY (continued)

Charles d 8 Nov 1853 ae: 59y. F:153

Francis s/o Stephen & Hannah d 20 Jan 1817 ae: 24y. G:31 SD

George d 7 June 1843 ae: 74y. GSL

Hannah, wid/o Stephen d 23 Dec 1837 ae: 87y. G:34

Harriet d/o George & Betsy b 29 Dec 1790 d 2 Mar 1813. F:144

Margaret A d 6 Feb 1905 ae: 95y 10m 9d. "Buried in George Adams' grave." Stone I:203A I:202

John d 4 Mar 1792. GSL

John d 19 Dec 1803 ae: 81y. F:59A

John d 19 Dec 1821 ae: 23y. F:156

Joseph d 27 Aug 1822 ae: 21y. F:155

Margaret d/o George & Betsy d 8 May 1808 ae: 16y. F:143

Mary Albertina d/o Albert d 1 Oct 1846 ae: 15m. GSL

Nabby d/o Stephen & Hannah d 7 Sep 1788 ae: 6y. SD G:30

Sarah w/o William d 2 June 1835 ae: 67y. E:20

Stephen d 8 July 1826 ae: 72y. Rev/War Sgt. G:33

Capt Stephen Jr s/o Stephen & Hannah d 20 Sep 1819 ae: 29y. G:32

William d 17 Apr 1823 ae: 31y. F:154

William b 3 Dec 1765 d 19 Mar 1858 Rev/War "Portland's oldest citizen at the time of his death." E:19 SBE

TURNER, Abigail W w/o Alpha d 5 May 1854 ae: 37y. GSL

Ann d 5 Oct 1843 ae: 50y. "Buried Strangers' Ground." GSL

Betsy d 27 May 1806 ae: 36y. SBE J:16

Cynthia w/o Thomas d 18 July 1811 ae: 36y. GSL

Elisha d 1 Feb 1816 ae: 95y. A Tomb 39

TURNER (continued)
Elizabeth J d/o William d 8 Nov 1857 ae: 1y 7m. GSL

Emma d/o William H d 9 Aug 1855 ae: 6m. Black. GSL

Harrison d 7 Aug 1845 ae: 33y. "Buried near the tool house." GSL

Janette d/o William d 2 Feb 1843 ae: 3m. GSL

Mary Ann d/o William d 13 June 1846 ae: 2y 7m. GSL

Nancy w/o John d 21 June 1858 ae: 52y. A-24-15

Sarah d 1 Feb 1815 ae: 79y. A Tomb 39

William L s/o Thomas & Betsy d 11 Sep 1805 ae: 5w 2d. SBE J:16

TWITCHELL, Dolly G w/o Thomas E d 25 May 1861 ae: 30y. A Tomb 57

TWOMBLY, Abigail wid/o Ephraim d 6 Dec 1848 ae: 71y. I:151

Ephraim d 29 July 1833 ae: 51y. SB I:153

Mary A d 18 May 1843 ae: 39y. SB I:152

TYNG, William b 17 Aug 1737 d 10 Dec 1807. Rev/War Loyalist Royal Sheriff Cumb Co. MD E:38

UPHAM, Julia w/o Edward d 22 Jan 1842 ae: 24y. "Buried John Mussey tomb." GSL

VAN, Alfred d 13 Mar 1880 ae: 56y. GSL

Mary d/o James d 4 Apr 1850 ae: 2y 5m. Black. GSL

VANBLARCOM, James d 12 July 1856 ae: 48y. SBE K:177

VANBUSKIRK, John s/o John d 27 Sep 1841 ae: 3y. GSL

VANNESS, Maj David d 14 Feb 1849 ae: 58y, 3rd Rgt US Art. A Tomb 39

VARNEY, Loring d 1 Feb 1847 ae: 54y. GSL

VARNUM, Almira Mercy d/o Phinehas & Prudence F b 5 Nov 1812 d 22 Aug 1825. A

VARNUM (continued)
Tomb 50

Charlotte Vivia d/o Phineas F & Elizabeth T b 14 Jan 1835 d 19 Apr 1870. A Tomb 50

Elias Thomas s/o Phineas F & Elizabeth T b 27 Aug 1847 d 22 Sep 1848. A Tomb 50

Elizabeth Thomas wid/o Phineas Fox b 19 Nov 1809 d 16 Feb 1908. A Tomb 50

Elizabeth Widgery d/o Phineas F & Elizabeth T b 23 May 1837 d 11 Dec 1917. A Tomb 50

Florence d/o Phineas F & Elizabeth T d 12 Aug 1851 ae: 7m. A Tomb 50

Gertrude d/o Phineas F & Elizabeth T b 17 Aug 1841 d 8 Oct 1841. A Tomb 50

John Arkwright Marshall s/o Phineas F & Elizabeth T b 12 Mar 1846 d 20 June 1916. Civ/War 33 Rgt Massachusetts Inf Co F. A Tomb 50

Lawrence Phineas s/o Phineas F & Elizabeth T b 22 Sep 1843 d 31 Mar 1930. Civ/War 25 Rgt Maine Inf Co A. A Tomb 50

Margaret Irving d/o Harry & Elizabeth Stanford, wid/o John AM b 3 May 1846 d 30 Mar 1932. A Tomb 50

Phineas Fox s/o Phineas & Prudence F b 22 Sep 1806 d 24 Jan 1892. A Tomb 50

Phineas Fox s/o Phineas F & Elizabeth T b 23 Sep 1842 d infancy. A Tomb 50

Phinehas b 21 Nov 1778 d 13 Oct 1858. A Tomb 50

Prudence Almira d/o Phineas F & Elizabeth T b 24 Dec 1837 d 14 Aug 1839. A Tomb 50

Prudence Fox wid/o Phinehas b 19 Sep 1774 d 1 Mar 1872. A Tomb 50

Prudence Harris d/o Phinehas & Prudence F b 19 June 1808 d 1 Feb 1825. A Tomb 50

Rose d/o Phineas F & Elizabeth

VARNUM (continued)
T d 24 Aug 1849 ae: 9m. A Tomb 50

Samuel d 29 Sep 1860 ae: 58y. "Killed by a bull in Westbrook, Maine." GSL

VAUGHAN, Hannah wid/o Capt William b 13 Nov 1787 d 9 Mar 1865. SD A-18-10

Capt. William b 7 Apr 1772 d 1 Aug 1842. SD A-18-9

VEAZIE, George H d 14 Aug 1858 ae: 23y. "Buried beside the fence." GSL

Isaac Jones s/o John & Rachael d 6 Jan 1809 ae: 22y. "Died at St. Bartholomew." J:108

John s/o John & Rachael d 28 Sep 1800 ae: 23y. "Died at Demarara." J:108

John d 6 Aug 1806 ae: 60y. J:107

John d 14 Jan 1863 ae: 9y 6m. GSL

Rachael w/o John d 10 Nov 1797 ae: 50y. J:108

Sarah d 11 Aug 1867 ae: 93y. J:105

Stephen s/o John & Rachael d 6 Nov 1772 ae: 3y. SB J:109

Stephen s/o John & Rachael d 1814 ae: 35y. "Lost in the Dash." J:108

VENUS, John S s/o Manuel d 3 Oct 1855 ae: 4m. GSL

VERNER, John A d 19 Aug 1840 ae: 17y. SD A-1-31

VERRILL, Augustus s/o Andrew d 22 Nov 1847 ae: 5m. GSL

Joseph s/o Andrew d 20 May 1846 ae: 2y. GSL

VERRY, Celesta M d/o John H d 1 Oct 1856 ae: 4m. "Buried at the head of Hancock St." GSL

Celesta F w/o John H d 2 June 1856 ae: 25y 1m 6d. GSL

VINCENT, Eunice wid/o John A d 18 Oct 1848 ae: 37y. Black. SD L:6

VINING, Harrison S d 14 May 1902 ae: 78y. "Died Brooklyn, New York." A Tomb 5

Helen Sherwood d/o Harrison S &

VINING (continued)
Lucy I d 30 Jan 1916 ae: 60y 6m 26d. A Tomb 5

Lucy Ilsley d 15 Nov 1893. "Died Brooklyn, New York." A Tomb 5

VINTON, Parker s/o John A & Lucretia D d 11 Mar 1824 ae: 15d. SBE I:209

VOSE, Clarissa wid/o William d 27 Apr 1859 ae: 77y. GSL

William d 28 Oct 1851 ae: 73y. GSL

WADSWORTH, Elizabeth d/o Peleg & Elizabeth B d 1 Aug 1802 ae: 22y. SBE H:15

Henry s/o Peleg & Elizabeth B Lt KIA 3 Sep 1804 ae: 20y. Barbary Wars: USN. ME H:13

WAITE, Abba d/o W d 16 Mar 1844 ae: 3y. "Buried beside A Fernald's stone." NS I:88

Abigail Wheeler wid/o Capt Stephen d 16 Sep 1796 ae: 61y. F:84

Alexander B d 7 Dec 1849. "Fell into hold of ship *Caroline C. Dow* and died of injuries." GSL

Alonzo s/o Alexander d 22 Aug 1844 ae: 11w. "Buried beside N Libby's stone." GSL

Bertha A d/o Rufus d 1 Oct 1877 ae: 3m. GSL

Carl s/o Alice L d 28 Feb 1892 ae: 1m 1w. GSL

Cordelia d/o Edward d 13 Sep 1854 ae: 10m. "Buried at foot of F Bryant's grave." NS B-8-8

Cordelia d/o Edward d 3 Aug 1857 ae: 2y. GSL

Dorcas d/o Benjamin b 2 July 1789 d 7 June 1792. SB I:93

Edward H s/o Jonathan & Alice d 26 Sep 1811 ae: 16m. F:83

Edward H b 1821 d 1850. Mmt A Tomb 34

Ellen Wildrage wid George d 8 July 1852 ae: 77y. F:26

Fanny d/o Rufus d 8 Dec 1881 ae: 8y. GSL

WAITE (continued)

Frances E d/o Stephen Jr & Martha O b 1827 d 1901. Mmt A Tomb 34

Capt George d 6 June 1805 ae: 32y. F:27

George Folsom s/o Stephen d 5 June 1854 ae: 20y. Mmt A Tomb 34

Hannah Jones d 14 Dec 1807 ae: 69y. F:24·

Capt Henry s/o John & Hannah d 12 Dec 1784 ae: 23y. F:82

Henry s/o Stephen d 17 June 1842 ae: 18m. Mmt A Tomb 34

Capt John b 6 Feb 1702 Newbury, Massachusetts d 3 Nov 1769 Peaks' Island. F:80

Col John d 20 Jan 1820 ae: 88y. Col/Wars Rev/War Sheriff, Cumb Co. F:25

Lizzie d/o Rufus H d 15 Aug 1863 ae: 8m. GSL

Lory M s/o Reuben d 3 Feb 1863 ae: 19y 9m. GSL

Lucretia Ann w/o Stephen Jr d 8 Apr 1827 ae: 28y. SBE F:91

Lucretia Ann d/o Stephen Jr & Lucretia Ann b 1824 d 1913. Mmt A Tomb 34

Lucretia Ann Folsom w/o Stephen Jr b 1799 d 1827. Mmt A Tomb 34

Margaret C w/o Isaac d 22 May 1835 ae: 19y. SBE B-1-29

Martha O Folsom d 17 May 1866 ae: 63y. Mmt A Tomb 34

Martha A d/o Rufus H d 12 Mar 1868 ae: 10y. GSL

Mary d/o Capt John & Sarah d 11 June 1756 ae: 20y. F:79

Mary w/o Stephen Jr d 7 Sep 1812 ae: 48y. F:88

Mary A w/o Stephen d 16 Jan 1890 ae: 92y 8m. Mmt A Tomb 34

Mary Emma d/o Stephen & Martha d 27 Aug 1900 ae: 64y 8m 17d. Mmt A Tomb 34

Mary Jane d 20 Aug 1847 ae: 23m. "Buried at foot of Daniel Mountfort's grave." NS D:36

WAITE (continued)

Mary M d/o Reuben d 26 Aug 1860 ae: 19y 8m. GSL

Mary S d/o Reuben d 25 Aug 1852 ae: 11m. GSL

Minnie d/o Rufus d 3 Nov 1876 ae: 1y. GSL

Nellie d/o Rufus H d 15 Aug 1863 ae: 8m. GSL

Reuben s/o Benjamin b 2 May 1791 d 7 June 1792. SB I:93

Sarah Kent wid/o Capt John b 7 Mar 1704 d 22 Jan 1775. F:81

Capt Stephen b 7 Nov 1734 Newbury, Massachusetts d 9 July 1783. Rev/War. F:85

Stephen Jr d 24 Dec 1862 ae: 67y 9m. Mmt A Tomb 34

WALDEN, Daniel s/o N d 20 Oct 1844 ae: 3y 10m. GSL

Mary w/o John d 8 Dec 1843 ae: 76y. SBE B-2-21

WALDRON, Charles, s/o Daniel d 22 May 1846 ae: 2y 8m. GSL

Daniel s/o Daniel d 21 Feb 1849 ae: 3y. GSL

Mary, widow d 8 Dec 1843 ae: 76y. "Buried by Phillips' stone." GSL

WALKER, Abby L d 12 June 1940 ae: 68y 9m 13d. "Died Pleasanton, California." Cremated. A Tomb 33

Alice Frances d/o Collingwood d 18 Aug 1861 ae: 2y. GSL

Charles E s/o Collingwood d 17 Sep 1861 ae: 1y. GSL

Charles M s/o Collingwood d 2 Sep 1857 ae: 11w. "Buried Friends' Ground." GSL

Eunice d 1 July 1826 ae: 21y. B-5-24

Isaac d 26 Aug 1817 ae: 45y. SD I:205

James d 19 Dec 1864 ae: 64y. GSL

Mary F d/o Collingwood d 25 July 1861 ae: 4m. GSL

Peter d 3 Apr 1815 ae: 34y. SD I:206

William d 30 Sep 1848 ae: 25y. "Stranger." GSL

WALL, Carrie B d/o John E d 26 Sep 1885 ae: 1y 8m. GSL

WALLACE, Betsy w/o William d 9 Jan 1849 ae: 67y. SB B-5-27

Eliza d/o Enoch d 8 Dec 1843 ae: 4y. "Buried Strangers' Ground." GSL

Enoch d 27 Jan 1863 ae: 54y. GSL

Rhoda d/o John d 21 Sep 1843 ae: 18m. GSL

WALLING, Mary E d/o Daniel d 19 Dec 1861 ae: 7m. GSL

WALSH, Almira A d/o Edward d 20 Oct 1861 ae: 22m. GSL

Franklin R s/o Edward & Lucy M d 11 Sep 1849 ae: 2y 7m. SD F:51

John s/o Edward & Lucy M d 21 Sep 1849 ae: 1y 1m. SD F:51

WALTON, Anna w/o Mark d 3 Nov 1798 ae: 27y. SD D:90

Henrietta E d/o Mark Jr d 1 Sep 1854 ae: 1y. NS D:91

Joseph B s/o Mark & Hannah d 18 Oct 1831 ae: 30y 5m. D:91

Mark d 24 Nov 1858 ae: 89y. D:91

Mark d 23 Mar 1864 ae: 56y. GSL

Moses N s/o Mark & Hannah d 22 Dec 1803 ae: 5m. D:92

Peter d 28 Mar 1733 ae: 42y. D:82

Sarah 3rd w/o Mark d 26 Jan 1844 ae: 75y. D:93

WARD, Ann w/o John d 25 July 1898 ae: 60y 1m 15d. A Tomb 33

Bridget d 30 Sep 1854 ae: 57y. "Buried at head of Elias Jacobs' wifes' stone." NS B-11-17

Charles F s/o Horace & Abbie d 22 Dec 1921 ae: 83y 5m 26d. A Tomb 33

George H s/o John P d 12 Aug 1867 ae: 15m. A Tomb 33

George W s/o Horace d 26 July 1868 ae: 30y 3m. A Tomb 33

H s/o John P d 26 Apr 1865 ae: 4y 5m. A Tomb 33

John P s/o Horace & Abbie d 18

WARD (continued)
May 1901 ae: 65y 5m 16d. "Died Biddeford, Maine." A Tomb 33

John P s/o John P & Ann P d 22 May 1926 ae: 57y. "Died Grafton, Massachusetts." A Tomb 33

Mary d 5 Jan 1850 ae: 84y. Catholic. GSL

Sophia d 10 Oct 1848 ae: 56y. GSL

WARNER, Mary wid/o Henry d 10 June 1864 ae: 69y. GSL

WARREN, inf d/o Charles A d 14 June 1860 ae: 9m 9d. A Tomb 58

Amos G s/o Thomas d 12 Sep 1868 ae: 51y. A Tomb 58

Anne P w/o Peter d 9 Nov 1811 ae: 56y. GSL

Caroline d/o John & Rebecca d 14 July 1805 ae: 1y 8m. SB J:88

Edward s/o George d 15 May 1842 ae: 10y. A Tomb 58

George H d 29 Apr 1883 ae: 69y. A Tomb 58

Huldah Ann d 29 Jan 1826 ae: 55y. I:71

Jennett w/o George d 23 Oct 1779 ae: 31y. G:28

John d 25 Feb 1805 ae: 28y. SB J:88

John H d 29 Sep 1875 ae: 50y. A Tomb 58

Lucy A d/o Thomas & Lucy d 24 Nov 1900 ae: 77y 6m 7d. A Tomb 58

Lucy Staniford wid/o Thomas d 27 Sep 1866 ae: 76y. A Tomb 58

Mary J w/o Samuel d 22 Feb 1875 ae: 81y. GSL

Robert s/o George & Jennett d 10 Sep 1778 ae: 10m. H:175

Thankful B w/o Peter d 27 Feb 1777 ae: 25y. GSL

Thomas d 21 Mar 1861 ae: 74y. A Tomb 58

Samuel d 23 Apr 1863 ae: 74y. SBE A-19-5

146

WASHBURN, Cynthia w/o Rufus
d 25 Mar 1808 ae: 38y. I:137A
Ira s/o Oliver & Nancy b 26 Mar
1814 d 6 June 1820. G:84
Priscilla w/o Cyrus d 4 Jan 1828
ae: 31y. B-3-41
Rufus B b Apr 1799 d 6 Sep 1822.
H:4

WATERHOUSE, inf ch/o George
d 28 Feb 1857 ae: 6w. "Buried
beside Lydia Cushman's
grave." GSL
Amelia J d/o late Israel d 18
Dec 1841 ae: 9y. A Tomb 51
Caroline W d/o Joshua W d 23
May 1845 ae: 6y. GSL
Charles A s/o David d 13 Nov
1853 ae: 21y. GSL
Charles Henry s/o Joshua M d 26
June 1845 ae: 10d. "Buried
beside J Downer's grave." NS
B-4-1
Charles J s/o late Israel d 15
Apr 1842 ae: 5y. A Tomb 51
Delia d/o David d 17 June 1842
ae: 23m. GSL
Eunice O d/o Jacob d 27 Mar
1846 ae: 45y. GSL
Frances d/o David d 10 Mar 1843
ae: 7y. GSL
George W s/o Elbridge G d 9 Sep
1841 ae: 13m. GSL
Hannah wid/o William d 13 Apr
1828 ae: 72y. I:74
Harry B s/o J B & C S d 3 Dec
1852 ae: 4y. GSL
Henrietta d/o late Israel d 15 Apr
1842 ae: 3y. A Tomb 51
John P d 24 May 1859 ae: 65y.
"Died in Boston." GSL
Patience w/o Capt Samuel d 7
Aug 1825 ae: 38y. SB B-14-25
Samuel d 20 Jan 1859 ae: 74y.
SB B-14-26
Sarah E w/o Capt. Samuel d 21
Dec 1846 ae: 55y. B-14-27
Susan, wid/o Joshua d 24 Aug
1865 ae: 62y. GSL
Theodotia w/o Capt Samuel d 14
June 1839 ae: 56y. SBE B-14-24

WATERHOUSE (continued)
William d 15 June 1820 ae: 55y.
SBE I:73
William S d 1 June 1850 ae: 37y.
B-14-28

WATERS, Harriet RB d/o James
d 4 Oct 1849 ae: 7m. Black.
GSL
James s/o James d 25 Sep 1843
ae: 3m. "Buried beside
Dickson's stone." Black. GSL
Kervin Lt d of wounds 15 Sep
1815 ae: 18y. War/1812 USN.
Ledger Mmt H:9
William s/o John d 20 Oct 1860
ae: 16y. Black. GSL

WATSON, Abraham d 3 Sep 1813
ae: 36y. SBE H:116
Alma A d/o Joseph B & Susan C
d 8 Sep 1846 ae: 2y. SD H:63
Emily A d/o Joseph B d 8 Sep
1846 ae: 2y. "Buried at head of
Charles Chase's child's
stone." NS H:22
Jane wid/o Abraham d 4 Oct
1819 ae: 42y. SBE H:117
Susan widow d 20 Oct 1843 ae:
37y. A Tomb 68

WATTS, John Osborn s/o Dr Ed-
ward & Mary b 5 Apr 1777 d 29
Dec 1802. H:131
Mary Oxnard d/o Thomas &
Sarah Oxnard, w/o Dr Edward d
19 Jan 1812 ae: 70y. H:133
Olive w/o John d 14 Apr 1843 ae:
45y. GSL
William s/o William & Hannah
d 12 Aug 1800 ae: 5y. SD L:33

WEAVER, Ann w/o George d 27
Sep 1830 ae: 40y. SBE A-6-1
Edward P s/o George & R W d
14 Oct 1837 ae: 11m 5d. SBE
A-6-2
Elizabeth R d/o George & RW d
30 June 1836 ae: 14m. SD A-
6-3
Margaret L d/o George d 30 July
1844 ae: 19m. "Buried Family
Range." GSL

WEBB, Abigail Knight d/o Capt
William & Nancy d 10 Nov
1837 ae: 45y. A Tomb 60

147

WEBB (continued)

Ann d/o William & Nancy d 4 Oct 1806 ae: 17m. E:67

Ann W d/o Capt William & Nancy d 18 Apr 1827 ae: 19y. A Tomb 60

Gustavus F s/o Jacob & Sarah d 3 Aug 1839 ae: 38y. SBE G:80

Hannah D w/o Capt Michael d 7 Sep 1833 ae: 38y. SBE B-7-9

Jennett N d/o Jacob & Sarah d 1 Nov 1820 ae: 21y. SBE G:82

Mary E d/o Capt William & Nancy d 28 Sep 1823 ae: 22y. A Tomb 60

Nancy wid/o Capt William d 20 Jan 1854 ae: 81y. A Tomb 60

Sarah w/o Capt Jacob d 28 Nov 1835 ae: 52y. SB G:81

Sarah J d/o Gustavus & Mary d 13 Aug 1841 ae: 5y. SBE G:79B

William s/o William & Nancy b 16 Jan 1804 d 31 Mar 1806. E:68

William s/o Capt William & Nancy d 14 Dec 1843 ae: 26y. A Tomb 60

Capt William d 1 June 1830 ae: 53y. A Tomb 60

WEBBER, Andrew s/o George d 16 Aug 1842 ae: 5y. "Buried Friends' Ground." GSL

Ephraim Lunt s/o Aaron & Augusta d 21 June 1831 ae: 13y. "Killed by lightning at Falmouth." D:63

Esther Ann d/o Solomon R d 26 Jan 1855. GSL

Jonathan d 25 Apr 1867 ae: 85y. GSL

Rosa B d/o Joseph F d 4 Oct 1872 ae: 3m. GSL

WEBSTER, Almira d/o Thomas & Mary b 1785 d 3 Apr 1807. MmtB A Tomb 85

Almira E d/o Joseph & Mary b 1827 d 6 July 1862. MmtB A Tomb 85

Ann Louisa d/o Richard C d 17 May 1855 ae: 12y. GSL

Benjamin b 1775 d 10 Mar 1815.

WEBSTER (continued)

MmtB A Tomb 85

Deborah w/o Thomas b 1777 d 7 June 1810. MmtB A Tomb 85

Edward b 1803 d 8 Apr 1819. MmtB A Tomb 85

Elizabeth wid/o Thomas b 1783 d 15 Nov 1822. MmtB A Tomb 85

Joseph b 1798 d 30 Nov 1868. MmtB A Tomb 85

Joseph S b 1835 d 2 Feb 1913. MmtB A Tomb 85

Mary w/o Thomas b 1763 d 28 Nov 1809. MmtB A Tomb 85

Mary d/o Thomas & Mary b 1793 d 6 Jan 1812. MmtB A Tomb 85

Mary C d/o Joseph & Mary b 1826 d 31 Oct 1851. MmtB A Tomb 85

Mary S w/o Joseph b 1795 d 13 Nov 1884. MmtB A tomb 85

Nathaniel d 8 Mar 1830 ae: 81y. GSL

Nathaniel d 10 Dec 1852 ae: 76y. GSL

Richard S b 1832 d 11 Sep 1900. "Died Standish, Maine." MmtB A Tomb 85

Samuel b 1796 d 3 Dec 1824. MmtB A Tomb 85

Thomas b 1756 d 4 Feb 1820. Rev/War. MmtB A Tomb 85

Thomas Jr b 1789 d 20 Feb 1809. MmtB A Tomb 85

Thomas E b 1819 d 8 Jan 1820. MmtB A Tomb 85

Thomas E s/o Joseph & Mary b 1830 d 5 Aug 1854. MmtE A Tomb 85

WEED, George B s/o Dr Samuel & Maria G d 5 Nov 1825 ae: 17m. SBE K:126

Maria G w/o Dr Samuel d 5 Nov 1835 ae: 49y. SBE K:126

Samuel, MD b 10 June 1774 d 24 Nov 1857. SBE K:126

WEEKS, Arthur McLellan s/o William Crabtree d 25 July 1833 ae: 23y. SBE D:152

Charles S s/o William d 9 Aug

WEEKS (continued)

1851 ae: 2y 8m. A Tomb 86

Daniel s/o Capt Joseph & Lois d 1815 ae: 27y. "Lost on Dash." D:146

Edward s/o Joshua d 12 Aug 1861 ae: 32y. A Tomb 79

Eliza w/o Lemuel d 22 Apr 1848 ae: 57y. A Tomb 79

George s/o Lemuel & Sarah b 6 Jan 1795 d 20 Aug 1796. D:154

George s/o Lemuel & Sarah b 23 Nov 1796 d 11 Feb 1799. D:155

George s/o Lemuel & Sarah d 28 Oct 1803 ae: 4y. SB D:156

Capt James s/o Lemuel & Sarah d 2 Sep 1809 ae: 21y 2m. "Died at St. Bartholomews." D:153

Jane wid/o William C d 31 May 1848 ae: 60y. A Tomb 86

Capt Joseph d July 1797 ae: 35y. "Died on his passage from W Indies." D:146

Capt Lemuel d 6 May 1857 ae: 73y. A Tomb 79

Lois wid/o Capt Joseph d 26 Jan 1829 ae: 69y. D:146

Mary d/o Capt Joseph & Lois d 16 Mar 1794 ae: 33m. SB D:150

William Crabtree d 29 Oct 1817 ae: 37y. SBE D:152

WELCH, Christiana d 28 July 1862 ae: 59y. GSL

Elizabeth E d/o E d 6 Dec 1844 ae: 5y. GSL

Emeline d/o Philip H d 8 Oct 1844 ae: 13m. "Buried in corner grave at foot of Mr. Cumpston's yard." GSL

Emeline d/o Philip H d 27 Feb 1846 ae: 2m. GSL

Hannah w/o Daniel d 28 Jan 1855 ae: 55y. GSL

WELLS, Ada w/o Samuel d 19 Mar 1844 ae: 29y. GSL

Clement s/o Samuel Jr d 28 Feb 1848 ae: 8y. GSL

WESCOTT, William H d 9 Jan 1861 ae: 29y. SD I:202A

WEST, Eben s/o Eben d 31 Aug 1849 ae: 17m. GSL

Manuel s/o Manuel d 25 Jan 1871 ae: 4m. GSL

WETHERBY, Harriet d/o William d 27 July 1859 ae: 2y 2m. GSL

WETHERELL, Eliza R w/o SB b 19 Mar 1835 d 25 Jan 1856. SBE A-10-15

Metcalf d 17 Dec 1806 ae: 29y. SD K:15

WEYMOUTH, Elsie J d/o Hiram d 4 Aug 1885 ae: 9m. A Tomb 1

WHARFF, Eliphalet d 16 Jan 1819 ae: 32y. C:86

WHEELER, Ann d 30 June 1856 ae: 66y. GSL

Elizabeth d 11 Sep 1774 ae: 11m. SB E:83

Elizabeth Jane w/o Job Emerson d 16 Aug 1853 ae: 65y. GSL

Francis Elizabeth W d/o Mary d 1 July 1844 ae: 13m. GSL

George s/o Harriet widow d 23 Sep 1848 ae: 8y. "Buried beside Wm Robinson's grave – 1820." NS G:103

Helena w/o G H d 25 Apr 1866 ae: 21y 5m. GSL

Henry d 16 Sep 1750 ae: 58y. SB E:82

Isabella w/o George H d 25 Sep 1870 ae: 20y 1m. GSL

Sarah w/o Henry d 31 May 1736 ae: 41y 3m. E:81

Sarah d/o Henry & Sarah d 19 Nov 1733 ae: 12y. E:79

WELLS, Gilbert W s/o George d 27 Jan 1858 ae: 6m. "Buried in Samuel Wells' lot." NS A-20-1

Helen A d/o John A & Eunice d 12 Oct 1849 ae: 8m. SB A-20-2

John A d 19 May 1850 ae: 28y. SB A-20-3

Samuel d 29 July 1845 ae: 53y. A-20-1

WELLS (continued)

Sarah wid/o Samuel d 1 Mar 1850 ae: 50y. GSL

Sarah E d/o John A & Eunice d 4 Oct 1847 ae: 5m. SB A-20-3

William d 2 Oct 1848 ae: 61y. Black. GSL

WENTWORTH, Emily Ann d/o James & Hannah d 14 Sep 1853 ae: 19m. Black. GSL

Eunice P w/o EG d 26 Mar 1851 ae: 51y. B-3-32

Margaret Hancock w/o Job S d 29 Apr 1859 ae: 59y. GSL

WESCOTT, Charlotte C d/o Robert D d 8 Mar 1869 ae: 18y 5m. GSL

Hattie E d/o William H d 13 Dec 1858 ae: 19m. GSL

Lydia d 24 Apr 1844 ae: 18y. "Buried Family Range." GSL

Mary widow d 8 Feb 1844 ae: 45y. "Buried beside Bannatyne's stone." NS A-7-1

Mary w/o Zebulon d 8 May 1844 ae: 76y. "Buried Family Range." GSL

Sarah d 26 Apr 1876 ae: 68y. "Died Windham, Maine." GSL

WHEELER, Mary d 9 Feb 1845 ae: 24y. Black. GSL

William H d 24 Aug 1783 ae: 9m. SB E:83

WHEELOCK, John N s/o AP d 24 July 1849 ae: 4y. GSL

WHILEY, Margaret wid/o James d 13 Aug 1841 ae: 74y. A Tomb 1

WHIPPLE, Lucius H d 2 Mar 1858 ae: 29y. GSL

Willis s/o Capt William H & Isabella d 15 Aug 1829 ae: 4m. SBE F:159

WHITE, ---- d/o Darius d 21 July 1842 ae: 14y. GSL

Asenath d 24 Sep 1850 ae: 66y. GSL

David d 15 Nov 1862 ae: 61y. SBE C:132

Elizabeth, widow d 19 Aug 1833 ae: 98y. A-1-13

Franklin H s/o Carlap C d 23 Sep

WHITE (continued)

1851 ae: 1y 9m. GSL

Frederick G s/o Darius d 4 Feb 1845 ae: 1y. "Buried north corner of E T Peter's fence." GSL

Hannah F wid/o John d 29 Nov 1857 ae: 81y. GSL

Harriet D w/o Horatio d 11 May 1882 ae: 77y. GSL

Horatio d 12 Aug 1873 ae: 73y. GSL

James d 18 Sep 1841 ae: 23y. GSL

Joseph S s/o Horatio & Harriet D d 8 Aug 1854 ae: 20y 10m. SD B-14-3

Martha Ann d/o Frederick d 24 Oct 1847 ae: 4m. Black. GSL

Martha L d/o Daniel d 3 Jan 1845 ae: 14m. "Buried north bank." GSL

Rachel d 23 July 1856 ae: 65y. GSL

WHITEHOUSE, Albert d 3 Jan 1828 ae: 8m. SD A-1-8

John M d 19 Dec 1855 ae: 60y. SD A-1-9

Mary w/o John M d 22 Dec 1832 ae: 32y. SBE A-1-8

William H s/o Charles d 10 Oct 1855 ae: 9m. GSL

William H s/o Mrs Hayes d 8 Sep 1852 ae: 18y. GSL

WHITMARSH, Charles d 6 Nov 1819 ae: 28y. J:110

Peter d 11 Nov 1832 ae: 31y. "Native Weymouth, Massachusetts." A-1-34

WHITMORE, Joseph d 16 May 1843 ae: 33y. GSL

Mary d/o Joseph d 11 Mar 1843 ae: 10m. GSL

WHITNEY, Abner d 14 July 1855 ae: 62y. GSL

Daniel d 19 Sep 1850 ae: 68y. SD F:14

Ellen d 13 Aug 1861 ae: 38y. GSL

George s/o John d 9 Aug 1855 ae: 1y 9m. GSL

Mrs Mary d 3 May 1846 ae: 81y. "Buried at head of Dr. Aaron

WHITNEY (continued)
Porter's grave." NS B-1-13

Olive w/o Abner d 22 Sep 1854 ae: 40y. "Buried beside Joseph Merrill." GSL

Susannah C d 15 June 1846 ae: 70y. SD F:13

WHITTIER, Elizabeth wid/o James d 3 May 1864 ae: 68y. GSL

Hannah w/o Samuel d 23 June 1844 ae: 53y. GSL

Nathan d 14 Apr 1859 ae: 56y. GSL

Samuel d 13 Apr 1848 ae: 64y. "Fell dead in the street." GSL

WHYLEY, Mary w/o John R d 28 Mar 1838 ae: 57y. A-9-11

WIDGERY, Ann L w/o John d 17 Dec 1867 ae: 70y. A Tomb 50

Elizabeth Randall wid/o William d 11 Mar 1834 ae: 85y. A Tomb 62

John d 2 Aug 1873 ae: 71y. A Tomb 50

Susan d 11 Mar 1843 ae: 72y. GSL

William b 1753 d 31 July 1822. Rev/War. A Tomb 62

WIGGIN, Henry s/o Nathaniel & Jane d 1 Oct 1814 ae: 15y. K:55

James L d 21 Feb 1857 ae: 24y. GSL

Mary d 27 May 1871 ae: 79y 6m. SBE K:127

Nathaniel d 21 Dec 1849 ae: 92y. "Died at the Alms House." GSL

WIGGINS, David d 23 Sep 1834 ae: 22y. B-8-3

WILBER, Col Ephraim d 27 Mar 1829 ae: 39y. War/1812 Sgt. GSL

Joseph H s/o Ephraim & Dorcas d 28 Nov 1821 ae: 21m. SD D:126

WILBUR, Capt Gideon G d 2 Aug 1855 ae: 48y. SBE K:60

Harriet w/o Capt Gideon G d 17 Dec 1885 ae: 79y. SBE K:60

Harriet N w/o Rufus d 1 Aug

WILBUR (continued)
1848 ae: 28y. GSL

Julia Page d/o Capt Gideon G & Harriet d 11 Apr 1848 ae: 16m. GSL

Samuel B d 19 May 1856 ae: 38y 6m. "Died in Boston." GSL

WILCOX, Clarence N d 17 Mar 1853 ae: 5m. GSL

Harriet d/o William d 11 July 1849 ae: 2y. GSL

Harriet P d/o William d 1 Sep 1846 ae: 1y. GSL

Mary L d/o late William d 29 Nov 1850 ae: 8y. GSL

William S s/o William A & Harriet d 1 Oct 1923 ae: 70y. NS B-9-39

WILDER, Thomas S d 25 Oct 1828 ae: 23y. SD B-14-14

William d 17 Sep 1805 ae: 26y. "Formerly of Lancaster, New Hampshire." J:19

WILDES, Judith B w/o Francis L d 4 Aug 1854 ae: 31y. SBE A-5-14

WILDRAGE, Capt Alexander d 7 Sep 1806 ae: 37y. H:115

Ann L d/o John & Ann d 26 Apr 1846 ae: 24y 8m. SD H:119

Ann Thurlo d/o John & Rebecca Thurlo, wid/o John d 4 May 1861 ae: 83y. SD H:120

Edward M d 6 Jan 1868 ae: 57y. SB H:113

Isabella w/o Capt James b 1740 d 23 Sep 1789. "Born at the Island of South Ronaldsha, North Briton." Interesting stone. H:114

John d 23 Apr 1831 ae: 59y. SD H:118

Margaret Flett wid/o Capt John d 1 Jan 1849 ae: 82y. H:112

WILKES, Annie w/o Thomas d 21 Nov 1880 ae: 38y. GSL

WILLACY, William R s/o William R & Nancy d 10 Aug 1833 ae: 18m. J:18

WILLARD, Charles M s/o Daniel d 9 Sep 1857 ae: 1y 13d. GSL

Sarah E d/o William & Sarah R d

WILLARD (continued)

2 Apr 1854 ae: 3d. SD I:184

Sarah E d/o William & Sarah R d 20 Sep 1856 ae: 10m 7d. SD I:183

Sarah R d 8 May 1880 ae: 58y. I:182

Capt William d 10 May 1877 ae: 56y. I:181

WILES, Israel d 1 Mar 1843 ae: 30y. GSL

WILLEY, Charlotte J w/o John T d 1 Jan 1857 ae: 20y. SD E:84

WILLIAMS, ---- gr s/o Capt John d 16 July 1850 ae: 4d. MmtE A Tomb 14

Adam Wallace Thaxter s/o Capt John & Catherine. A Tomb 14

Caroline F d/o Capt Charles F & Dolly d 29 Apr 1896 ae: 85y 4m 24d. MmtE A Tomb 14

Cally M d/o Capt Robert & Caroline F d 19 Sep 1855 ae: 24y 3m. MmtE A Tomb 14

Catherine w/o Capt John b 9 May 1787 d 2 June 1863. MmtE A Tomb 14

Catherine d/o Capt. John & Catherine d 19 July 1836 ae: 20y. MmtE A Tomb 14

Charles F s/o Charles F & Caroline d 22 Apr 1844 ae: 1y 15d. MmtE A Tomb 14

Capt Charles F d 9 Feb 1873 ae: 58y. MmtE A Tomb 14

David d 24 Dec 1835 ae: 65y. D:80

Elizabeth d/o Capt. Benjamin Davis of Ipswich, w/o Capt Joseph d 33 Apr 1823 ae: 62y. J:177

Eugene C d 17 Dec 1931 ae: 79y 5m 7d. MmtE A Tomb 14

George s/o Gordon d 15 Aug 1862 ae: 19y. GSL

Gordon d 11 Sep 1868 ae: 51y. GSL

Harriet H d/o John & Sarah d 8 Oct 1843 ae: 20y 5m. "Buried Strangers' Ground." G:24

Henry Brazier s/o Capt John & Catherine d 16 Oct 1828 ae:

WILLIAMS (continued)

22y. MmtE A Tomb 14

Henry P s/o Judson d 25 Sep 1849 ae: 2y. GSL

James d 21 May 1846 ae: 56y. Black. GSL

James F s/o William d 10 Feb 1879 ae: 28y. MmtE A Tomb 14

Jane S d/o Capt John Jr & Jane S d 23 July 1843 ae: 16y. SBE J:166

John Capt s/o Capt John & Catherine d 18 Aug 1845 ae: 41y. "Lost overboard." MmtE A Tomb 14

John Capt b 15 July 1783 d 1 Oct 1846. "Born in Boston." MmtE A Tomb 14

John H d 18 July 1875 ae: 58y. GSL

Josiah nd. SD B-10-11

Lydia w/o Charles L d 4 Sep 1854 ae: 33y. SBE J:210

Mary w/o Josiah d 6 Mar 1825 ae: 27y. B-10-10

Mary Adelaide d/o John H d 21 Sep 1846 ae: 8m. GSL

Mary Louisa d/o Capt John & Catherine d 21 Aug 1839 ae: 21y. MmtE A Tomb 14

Nelson s/o John & Sarah d 11 June 1837 ae: 17y 3m. "Buried Strangers' Ground." G:24

Peter d 27 Aug 1858. aka William Harvey "Hanged at Auburn, Maine for murder on the high seas." GSL

Rebecca w/o Gordon d 2 Nov 1862 ae: 44y. GSL

Richard d 18 Oct 1842 ae: 33y. GSL

Robert Capt s/o Capt John & Catherine d 1 Feb 1833 ae: 25y. "Died Wilmington, North Carolina." A Tomb 14

Robert d 30 Mar 1868 ae: 67y. GSL

Robert T d Nov 1902 ae: 69y 5m 27d. "Died Boston, Massachusetts." MmtE A Tomb 14

Rufus R d 31 Oct 1845 ae: 32y.

WILLIAMS (continued)

"Buried near James Deering's tomb." GSL

Samuel Thaxter d 19 Apr 1865 ae: 52y. MmtE A Tomb 14

Samuel W s/o David & Tryphena d 12 July 1830 ae: 19y. D:80

Sarah D w/o John d 18 Aug 1874 ae: 67y. A Tomb 33

Typhenia wid/o David d 5 Aug 1854 ae: 79y. GSL

William H d 22 Mar 1854 ae: 34y. MmtE A Tomb 14

WILLIS, Benjamin b 5 Mar 1768 d 1 Oct 1853. A Tomb 76

Caroline E w/o George d 1 Sep 1821 ae: 22y. A Tomb 76

Clarissa d/o George d 12 Jan 1840 ae: 11y. A Tomb 76

Clarissa M wid/o George d 17 Apr 1858 ae: 59y. A Tomb 76

Elizabeth S w/o Benjamin d 5 Mar 1823 ae: 25y. A Tomb 76

Emily M b 21 July 1839 d 3 May 1860. A Tomb 76

George s/o Benjamin b 16 June 1797 d 24 Oct 1844. A Tomb 76

Hannah B d 18 Dec 1824 ae: 27y. A Tomb 81

Mary w/o Benjamin b 17 Aug 1770 d 14 F 1847. A Tomb 76

Thomas s/o Benjamin & Mary d 20 July 1811 ae: 11y. A Tomb 76

WILLSON, Margaret, w/o Robert d 7 Oct 1818 ae: 28y. L:37

WILSON, Colin F d 3 Apr 1857 ae: 76y. Black. GSL

Eliza d 10 Jan 1843 ae: 30y. GSL

Francis HG s/o George H d 11 Apr 1859 ae: 7m. GSL

George G s/o John S d 23 Dec 1848 ae: 3y. GSL

John S d 3 Aug 1852 ae: 25y. GSL

John S Col d 30 June 1857 ae: 43y. SBE A-6-7

John M s/o John S d 10 Apr 1873 ae: 30y, Civ/War 2d Rgt Maine Cav Co D. ND A-6-7

WILSON (continued)

John T s/o John S & EM d 22 Dec 1848 ae: 3y. SD A-6-6

Jonathan d 1720. Interesting stone. F:131

Joseph d 27 Aug 1820 ae: 51y. SD A-6-6

Lucy w/o Joseph d 28 Oct 1836 ae: 64y. SD A-6-6

Maria w/o Colin F d 5 Feb 1845 ae: 71y. Black. GSL

Mary Ann d/o Adam & Sally d 2 Sep 1837 ae: 1y 9m. SD E:2

Mary Ann d/o Archibald d 3 June 1862 ae: 13m. GSL

Mary Ann d/o Archibald & Mary d 30 Mar 1863 ae: 13m 15d. SB J:203

Sarah B d/o JB d 29 Nov 1865 ae: 17y 5m. A Tomb 20

WINSLOW, Caroline d/o Albert H & Elizabeth H nd. Mmt A Tomb 8

Elizabeth H wid/o Albert H b 1855 d 1933. Mmt A Tomb 8

Frank H s/o James N d 17 Sep 1849 ae: 3y. A Tomb 14

John A d 6 Nov 1846 ae: 22y. GSL

Louis M s/o Albert H & Elizabeth H d 13 Sep 1936 ae: 47y 7m 6d. Cremated. Mmt GSL

Capt Moses d 13 May 1819 ae: 40y. G:39

Nancy C d/o Albert & Sophia d 28 Dec 1835 ae: 26y 1m. Mmt A Tomb 8

Sophia w/o Albert d 27 Feb 1861 ae: 72y 11m. Mmt A Tomb 8

Weltha A d/o John d 18 Mar 1846 ae: 10m. GSL

William H s/o Albert & Sophia d 21 Oct 1840 ae: 29y 1m 21d. Mmt A Tomb 8

WISWELL, Enoch d 4 Sep 1839 ae: 60y. SD C:205

Enoch d 26 Oct 1843 ae: 56y. "Buried by their stone." GSL

Eugene s/o Henry d 27 May 1854 ae: 15m. GSL

Georgianna d/o Henry d 20 Nov 1842 ae: 2y 9m. GSL

WISWELL (continued)

Henry B s/o Henry d 30 Oct 1845 ae: 10m. GSL

Juliet d/o Henry d 25 Feb 1856 ae: 10y 8m. GSL

Margaret d 20 Sep 1823 ae: 18y. SB I:174

Richard d 29 Nov 1851 ae: 70y. GSL

Stephen R d 10 Feb 1837 ae: 21y. A-24-1

WITHAM, Ann Chadwick d 3 July 1836 ae: 75y. H:153

Hattie F d/o Albion d 1 Feb 1857 ae: 4y 3m. GSL

James d 5 Jan 1863 ae: 66y. GSL

Joanna w/o Charles d 16 Oct 1848 ae: 48y. GSL

Judith wid/o Obadiah d 20 Feb 1846 ae: 84y. "Buried at head of Josiah Norton's grave." NS B-10-18

WITHERELL, Eliza w/o SB d 25 Jan 1856 ae: 20y 10m. "Buried in George Ropes' lot." NS A-10-14

WITHINGTON, Elizabeth C d/o William & Lydia d 15 Sep 1842 ae: 20y. SB J:170

Hannah Mendon wid/o William d 24 Nov 1863 ae: 79y 4m. GSL

Jane d/o William & Lydia d 18 July 1831 ae: 18y. J:168

Mary O w/o Henry d 28 July 1839 ae: 20y. SBE J:169

William d 15 Oct 1862 ae: 77y. GSL

WOOD, Elbridge J s/o Samuel d 2 Nov 1844 ae: 2y. GSL

Ellen M d/o John G d 6 May 1857 ae: 1w. GSL

Frances Ellen d/o John Try, w/o John P d 8 June 1853 ae: 20y 3m. SBE A-16-14

George s/o John G d 12 May 1863 ae: 6y. GSL

James M s/o John G d 30 Apr 1863 ae: 1y 8m. GSL

John G d 30 May 1908 ae: 81y. F:18A

Lucy Ann d/o Edward T d 3 Nov 1844 ae: 15y. GSL

WOOD (continued)

Mary J w/o John G b 1833 d 1903. F:18A

Matthew S s/o William & Susan d 15 Mar 1827 ae: 20y. MmtD A Tomb 19

Patience w/o Edward d 15 June 1844 ae: 36y. GSL

Susan wid/o William d 15 May 1843 ae: 57y. MmtD A Tomb 19

William d 16 Dec 1833 ae: 51y. MmtD A Tomb 19

WOODBRIDGE, Thomas b 9 Feb 1796 d 25 Apr 1885. SB C:25

WOODBURY, Caroline A d/o Joseph & Elizabeth b 1835 d 1837. A Tomb 38

Eliza d/o Almer d 20 Oct 1843 ae: 4y. GSL

Elizabeth d/o William & Mary Woodbury, w/o Joseph b 1802 d 27 June 1875. A Tomb 38

Elizabeth M d/o Joseph & Elizabeth d 11 Dec 1910 ae: 77y 6m 13d. A Tomb 38

Frank s/o Freeman & M B d 30 Apr 1857 ae: 8y 7m. SBE B-11-25

Freeman d 7 Apr 1863 ae: 57y. SD B-11-24

Granville s/o Hollis & S W d 26 May 1862 ae: 3w. SD B-11-24

Harriet R d/o Joseph & Elizabeth b 1843 d 1852. A Tomb 38

Herbert s/o William W d 16 Sep 1851 ae: 9m. A Tomb 38

John d 19 Dec 1860 ae: 69y. SD B-7-23

Julia C d 15 May 1910 ae: 69y 5m 15d. A Tomb 38

Lucia O d/o William W d 11 Oct 1849 ae: 2y. A Tomb 38

Martha D d/o William & Mary b 1815 d 23 Oct 1879. A Tomb 38

Mary d/o William Houle, wid/o William b 1778 d 17 Sep 1870. A Tomb 38

Mary H d/o William & Mary d 28 Mar 1892 ae: 93y 1m 11d. A Tomb 38

WOODBURY (continued)
Octavia w/o William W d 12 Oct 1858 ae: 47y. A Tomb 38
William b 1772 d 29 Apr 1861. A Tomb 38
William L s/o William W d 6 Oct 1849 ae: 5y. A Tomb 38
WOODLEY, Sarah Stockman w/o Charles d 14 Nov 1856 ae: 41y. A Tomb 29
WOODMAN, Aaron d 23 Feb 1856 ae: 65y 4m. A Tomb 66
Anna w/o Aaron d 22 Nov 1874 ae: 88y 9m. A Tomb 66
Capt Benjamin d 30 Apr 1789 ae: 35y 8m. D:15
John d 22 Mar 1832 ae: 50y. D:17
Martha wid/o William H d 22 May 1860 ae: 35y. GSL
Mary wid/o Capt Benjamin d 11 Feb 1811 ae: 59y. SBE D:16
Samuel d 20 Nov 1825 ae: 36y. I:123
WOODS, Capt Francis d 26 Sep 1841 ae: 67y. SB A-16-7
Hattie d/o John G d 31 Mar 1870 ae: 5y. GSL
Jane w/o Capt Francis d 29 June 1854 ae: 79y. SB A-16-8
John s/o Francis & Margaret d 29 July 1835 ae: 3y 6m. Catholic. B-8-20
Mary d/o Francis & Margaret d 28 Sep 1835 ae: 18m. Catholic. B-8-20
Mary A Q d/o Samuel M & Sarah Quincy d 29 Apr 1896 ae: 84y 1m 13d. NS C:159
WOODSMAN, William H d 23 Oct 1852 ae: 38y. SB B-8-10
WOODSOM, Charles s/o Fitz d 6 Sep 1843 ae: 20m. A Tomb 5
Ezra B d 14 Feb 1893 ae: 76y. Civ/War 5 Rgt Maine Inf Co F. GSL
WOODWARD, Smith d 25 Feb 1832 ae: 67y. "Of Dorchester." G:35
WOOLSGROVE, George d 10 Dec 1846. "Of Friendship, Maine." "Buried at the end of the

WOOLSGROVE (continued)
hearse house." GSL
WORCESTER, Henry A Rev d 21 May 1841 ae: 38y. SBE A-10-11
WORK, John d 22 Oct 1873 ae: 40y. Civ/War 32 Rgt Maine Inf Co C. SBE J:204
WRIGHT, Abigail w/o Christopher b 1 Aug 1787 d 22 Mar 1866. "Born Portland, Maine." Mmt A Tomb 12
Ann d/o David d 5 Apr 1844 ae: 7y. GSL
Christopher b 7 Apr 1782 d 6 July 1869. "Born Marshfield, Massachusetts." Mmt A Tomb 12
Christopher s/o Christopher & Abigail b 20 Aug 1814 d 23 Nov 1842. Mmt A Tomb 12
Franklin s/o Christopher & Abigail b 10 May 1809 d 20 Nov 1883. Mmt A Tomb 12
Harriet S d/o Christopher & Abigail b 16 May 1806 d 18 Sep 1807. Mmt A Tomb 12
Henry B b 1 Dec 1810 d 24 Dec 1853. Mmt A Tomb 12
James R s/o Christopher & Abigail b 17 May 1823 d 29 Nov 1845. Mmt A Tomb 12
Mary A w/o Sylvanus d 18 Sep 1866 ae: 42y 6m. GSL
John R s/o J & A F d 8 Dec 1854 ae: 2m. SD A-6-4
Sarah wid/o Robert d 28 July 1823 ae: 71y. B-11-9
WYER, Capt Daniel d 20 Sep 1805 ae: 60y. Rev/War. C:81
Eleazer d 1 Mar 1848 ae: 62y. "Buried in Wyer tomb." GSL
Esther P d/o Jonathan & Sally d 19 July 1813 ae: 9m. SD I:167
John T d 5 Aug 1849 ae: 27y. "Buried in his father's tomb." GSL
Lydia W d/o David & Lydia d 19 Sep 1802 ae: 9m. SD I:37
Mary wid/o Daniel d 30 Aug 1808 ae: 57y. C:80
Robert s/o David & Lydia d 28 June 1800 ae: 6d. SD I:37

WYLIE, Samuel d 1 Apr 1872 ae: 74y. GSL

YATEN, David d 5 May 1821 ae: 21y. Black. GSL L:7

YEATON, Mary d/o John d 26 Oct 1843 ae: 16y 8m. "Buried beside her mother's stone." GSL

Nancy d 1 Dec 1855 ae: 72y. GSL

YORK, Betsy wid/o Levi d 10 Nov 1862 ae: 56y. GSL

Charles d 20 Sep 1854 ae: 27y. GSL

Charles d 14 Dec 1861 ae: 4y. GSL

Eliza d 9 Aug 1860 ae: 24y. "Buried at the head of the Friends' Ground." GSL

Elizabeth w/o Reuben G d 17 Nov 1833 ae: 47y. C:31

Emeline J d/o Reuben G & Elizabeth d 18 Oct 1820 ae: 11m. SB C:29

Fannie P d 23 June 1868 ae: 71y 4m. SBE B-7-3

Fanny W d/o Reuben G & Elizabeth d 9 Oct 1822 ae: 1d. SB C:29

James H s/o John L d 15 Sep 1862 ae: 1y 6m. GSL

Katy d/o Charles L d 7 Feb 1865 ae: 5y 5m. GSL

Margaret D d/o Reuben G & Elizabeth d 11 Dec 1822 ae: 2m. SB C:29

Olive d/o Reuben G & Elizabeth d 17 Nov 1828 ae: 1y 8m. SB C:29

Sarah E w/o James B d 24 Nov 1848 ae: 33y. MmtE A Tomb 25

YOUNG, inf d/o James F & Nancy W d 5 Aug 1839. SB I:18

Dorcas w/o John d 16 Aug 1845 ae: 38y. "Buried near the hearse house." GSL

George s/o Jesse d 7 Aug 1843 ae: 2y 7m. "Buried at the head of Rev Mr Bisbee." NS B-4-19

George d 23 Feb 1851 ae: 27y. "Died at the Marine Hospital." GSL

Hannah w/o Joseph d 30 Jan 1848 ae: 76y. B-4-29

Mary I d 19 June 1824 ae: 69y. SB H:78

William A s/o Dr James F & Nancy W d 26 Aug 1841 ae: 10w. SB I:18

William A s/o Dr James F & Nancy W d 27 Aug 1845 ae: 6m. GSL

Alms House Yard – 1858–1875

Stranger, Unknown – Frenchman d 15 Jan 1873 ae: 55y. "Died insane."

ABBOTT, Louisa d 22 May 1872 ae: 78y.

ADAMS, Jane d 14 D 1872. "Died Pest House, Small Pox."

AGERY, Eliza d/o James d 30 Mar 1866 ae: 3m.

ANDERSON, Mary E d 30 Aug 1871 ae: 19y.

Peter d 24 Jan 1873 ae: 26y. "Died Pest House, Small Pox."

ANDREW, William A s/o John d 26 Feb 1869 ae: 2m.

AUSTIN, John T d 5 May 1869.

BAKER, James s/o Jane d 13 Mar 1872 ae: 4w.

Reziah w/o Charles d 2 Jul 1873 ae: 74y.

BARTON, John d 17 May 1872 ae: 80y.

BATTIS, Susan d 28 Jan 1874 ae: 63y.

BEAN, Abiertha d 6 Jan 1865 ae: 68y.

BETTER, Joseph d 1 Dec 1872 ae: 36y. "Died Pest House, small pox."

BLACK, Charles s/o Mary J. d 25 Oct 1871 ae: 2y.

Mary Ann d 5 Nov 1865 ae: 33y.

BREWER, Caroline d 28 Sept 1866 ae: 65y.

BROWN, George A d 1 Aug 1873 ae: 64y.

George E d 1 Aug 1873 ae: 69y.

BROWNE, Matilda d 15 Jan 1870 ae: 76y.

BURGESS, John d 7 Jan 1868 ae: 85y.

BURKE, Miles d 22 Feb 1873 ae: 75y.

CAIN, Patrick d 3 Apr 1868 ae: 4y.

CANTWELL, Patrick d 22 Dec 1866.

CARR, John d 10 Apr 1873 ae: 55y.

John Jr d 7 Aug 1870 ae: 2m.

CARY, Eben M s/o Michael d 24 Jan 1873 ae: 5y. "Died Pest House, small pox."

Patrick s/o Michael d 28 Jan 1873 ae: 11m. "Died Pest House, small pox."

CASH, Sally d 27 May 1864 ae: 74y. "Died Pest House, small pox."

CAVINDEN, Peter d 13 May 1864 ae: 90y. "Died Pest House, small pox."

CHESTNUT, Robert d 20 Sept 1866 ae: 6m.

CLANCY, John d 16 Nov 1870 ae: 32y.

CLAPP, Oliver d 8 Oct 1868 ae: 73y.

CLARK, Mary E d 5 Mar 1873 ae: 50y.

COFFEE, Dennis d 11 Nov 1870 ae: 46y.

COOK, Samuel s/o Francis d 21 Nov 1869 ae: 1y.

COOLEY, Bridget d 13 Sept 1872 ae: 45y.

COOPER, Mrs. Phillis d 15 Oct 1858 ae: 65y. Black.

COVEL, Ann d 12 Sept 1869 ae: 68y.

157

CROSBY, William d 25 May 1870 ae: 67y.

CURRIN, Thomas s/o Michael d 28 Dec 1865 ae: 11m.

DEAN, Mary d/o Mary d 16 Feb 1873 ae: 1y. "Died Pest House, small pox."

DEERING, Mary d/o Thomas d 17 Jan 1873 ae: 15y. "Died Greely Hospital."

DELANO, Lydia A d 17 Aug 1866 ae: 35y.

DELANY, Ann d 15 May 1866 ae: 1y.

DODGE, William s/o Mary d 11 Jan 1872 ae: 15y. "Died Pest House, small pox."

DOHERTY, Bridget d 30 Sept 1873 ae: 45y.

DOLAN, Patrick d 18 Jan 1871 ae: 29y.

DRISCOLL, Kate d 12 May 1865 ae: 45y.

DUNCAN, John Jr d 4 Aug 1870 ae: 6m.

DYER, Anah d 7 Oct 1858 ae: 75y.

ELDRIDGE, Charles H d 31 Aug 1870 ae: 10m.

ESTELL, George d 3 Aug 1873 ae: 70y.

FIELDS, Alvin d 21 Jan 1865 ae: 62y.

FITZPATRICK, Daniel d 31 May 1870 ae: 21y.

FLOYD, Olivia d 6 Apr 1872 – insane.

FRATES, Manuel d 23 May 1872 ae: 69y. "Died Pest House, small pox."

GAMMON, Patrick d 11 Apr 1872 ae: 29y.

GILLESPIE, Frank d 3 Oct 1869 ae: 6m.

GILLEY, Jane d 25 Feb 1874 ae: 30y.

GLEDELL, George s/o Ann d 3 Apr 1868 ae: 6m.

GRANY, Catherine d 7 Feb 1869 ae: 65y.

GREEN, Daniel d 4 Aug 1865 ae: 63y.

GREEN (continued)
Joseph d 27 June 1873 ae: 60y.

Mary d/o Joseph d 12 Mar 1869 ae: 32y.

GRIFFIN, Lizza d/o Richard d 28 Jan 1873 ae: 18m. "Died Pest House, small pox."

HALEY, John s/o Nate d 23 Jul 1873 ae: 1m.

HARDING, Sarah d 9 Nov 1872 ae: 39y.

HARRIS, Mattie d 31 Aug 1870 ae: 21y.

HENDER, Fannie d/o Mary d 24 Mar 1872 ae: 4m.

HIGHLAND, James d 2 Nov 1869 ae: 53y.

HILL, Statira d 11 Dec 1858 ae: 18y. Black.

HODGKINS, Stephen d 16 Jul 1870 ae: 76y.

HOLLY, P d/o John d 23 Feb 1873 ae: 7y. "Died Pest House, small pox."

HOLMES, John d 13 Sept 1870 ae: 4m.

HORR, Anna d/o Kenneth McLoude d 2 Feb 1873 ae: 32y. "Died Pest House, small pox."

HOWARD, Augusta d 17 Aug 1870 ae: 20y.

HURLEY, Abba d/o Patrick d 9 Apr 1868 ae: 2y.

HUSE, Mrs. d 25 Apr 1873 ae: 45y.

JACKSON, Clara w/o Frederick 8 May 1864 ae: 28y.

Orville d 6 Aug 1866 ae: 28y.

JOHNSON, Ann d 16 May 1866 ae: 5m.

Arthur d 6 Oct 1871 ae: 48y.

Ellen F w/o Leonard d 20 Nov 1869 ae: 49y.

Emma G d/o Jeremiah d 19 Dec 1872 ae: 1y. "Died Pest House, small pox."

JONES, Matilda d 13 Nov 1864 ae: 19y.

JOSEPH, Antonio d 9 Feb 1873 ae: 24y. "Died Pest House, small pox."

JOSEPHS, Patty w/o Frederick d 19 Jul 1864 ae: 94y.

JOYCE, Annie d 1 Feb 1874 ae: 28y.

KARVIN, William d 31 May 1869 ae: 29y.

KEITH, James d 20 Nov 1869.

KELLEY, J d 18 May 1870 ae: 22y.

Mark d 31 Oct 1869 ae: 6m.

KILGORE, Leander d 24 Feb 1874 ae: 40y.

LANE, William d 16 Sept 1870 ae: 40y.

LIFTON, Nancy d 11 June 1864 ae: 55y.

LITTLEJOHN, Sarah d 25 May 1872 ae: 50y. "Died Pest House, small pox."

LUDKINS, Welcome d 27 May 1864. "Died Pest House, small pox."

MALLOY, John s/o John d 14 Mar 1873 ae: 14y. "Died Pest House, small pox."

MARSH, John d 6 Sept 1868 ae: 85y.

MARSTON, Greenleaf d 2 Jan 1866 ae: 63y.

MASON, John E s/o James S & Mary E d 28 Jan 1873 ae: 24y. "Died Pest House, small pox."

MATTHEWS, Henry d 17 June 1864 ae: 55y.

McCLAFFERTY, John s/o James d 22 Feb 1873 ae: 22y. "Died Pest House, small pox."

McCLOUD, David d 19 Nov 1869 ae: 2y 7m.

McDONALD, Daniel d 30 Apr 1864 ae: 25y. "Died Pest House, small pox."

McFEE, John d 25 Dec 1872 ae: 20y. "Died Pest House, small pox."

McGEE, James d 17 Dec 1866.

McGILL, Benjamin d 4 Mar 1859 ae: 50y.

McKAY, Frederick s/o James d 23 Aug 1864 ae: 7m.

McKEY, William d 14 Dec 1871. "Died Pest House, small pox."

McLEOD, Daniel s/o Malcolm d 7 Aug 1873 ae: 4y.

MESERVE, Eliza d 8 Oct 1868 ae: 66y.

MILLER, James d 12 Aug 1865 ae: 78y.

MITCHELL, David d 16 Jan 1871 ae: 33y.

MORRIS, Thomas d 24 Nov 1869 ae: 6m.

MORSE, James d 4 Oct 1866 ae: 67y.

MOULTON, Jane w/o John d 12 Oct 1866 ae: 65y.

MULLOY, Mary d/o John d 19 Feb 1873 ae: 3y. "Died Pest House, small pox."

MURPHY, John s/o Bernard d 5 Apr 1873 ae: 1yr. "Died Pest House, small pox."

NEWHALL, James B d 29 Nov 1873 ae: 70y.

NICKERSON, T W S d 25 Dec 1872 ae: 35y. "Died Pest House, small pox."

NILES, George d 15 Dec 1872. "Died Pest House, small pox."

O'DONNELL, David d 7 Jan 1865 ae: 72y.

Gerard d 24 May 1864 ae: 55y.

OLIVER, Benjamin d 10 Jul 1873 ae: 43y.

OLLINER, Perry d 10 Jul 1873 ae: 43y.

O'NEAL, Martha d 20 Mar 1873 ae: 37y.

PAGE, Eva Gertie d 25 Aug 1873 ae: 2m.

PARKS, John d 23 Oct 1864 ae: 66y.

PETTINGILL, Eliza w/o Wm d 24 D 1872 ae: 55y. "Died Pest House, small pox."

Elthea d/o Wm Jr d 2 Jan 1873 ae: 21y. "Died Pest House, small pox."

PLUMMER, George H s/o Mary A d 14 Apr 1868 ae: 5y.

PORTER, Henry d 14 May 1870 ae: 70y.

PRESLEY, Abigail d/o Wm d 16 Apr 1868 ae: 11m.

PROSPECT, John O d 22 June 1864 ae: 3m.

RADIGAN, Mary d 16 Feb 1865 ae: 27y.

RAYNER, George d 20 Jan 1865 ae: 81y.

READ, John s/o Sarah Gray d 30 Jan 1873 ae: 21y. "Died Pest House, small pox."

REED, James O d 20 Feb 1869 ae: 58y.

REEVES, Robert C s/o Martha d 31 Oct 1870 ae: 5y 4m.

REGAN, James d 28 Dec 1873.

RICH, Joseph d 12 Aug 1865 ae: 68y.

ROBBINS, William S d 14 Apr 1872 ae: 20y. "Died Pest House, small pox."

William T d 15 Apr 1872. "Died Pest House, small pox."

ROOT, Rev N W T d 14 Dec 1872. "Died Pest House, small pox."

RYAN, Margaret d 24 Sept 1869 ae: 65y.

SAWYER, Isaac d 25 Mar 1873 ae: 74y. "Died Pest House, small pox."

SEAVY, Charles d 11 Feb 1864 ae: 20y. "Died Pest House, small pox."

SENLEY, Sarah d 21 Dec 1869 ae: 83y.

SHERRY, Patrick d 24 Nov 1872 ae: 38y. "Died Pest House, small pox."

SMITH, Ada d/o F O J d 27 Dec 1875 ae: 6w.

Kate d 5 Aug 1865 ae: 22y.

Malcolm d 24 Dec 1872 ae: 27y. "Died Pest House, small pox."

Margaret d 30 Jul 1872 ae: 18y.

SPRING, William d 29 Aug 1864 ae: 9m.

STUART, Emma d 9 Oct 1872 ae: 104y.

SULLIVAN, Margaret d 20 Nov 1865 ae: 32y.

Michael d 25 Apr 1873 ae: 60y.

SWEETSER, Mrs d 21 Mar 1864. "Died Pest House, small pox."

TAPE, William d 19 Dec 1873 ae: 53y.

TAYLOR, George d 21 Nov 1872 ae: 21y. "Died Pest House, small pox."

TENNEY, John d 26 Dec 1871 ae: 65y.

THOMPSON, Joseph M d 6 Jan 1865 ae: 28y.

TOWNSEND, Peter d 10 Sept 1871 ae: 23y.

TROW, A d 29 Aug 1864 ae: 60y.

WALLWORTH, Charles s/o Thomas d 13 May 1864 ae: 1d.

Thomas s/o Thomas d 28 June 1864 ae: 5m.

WARD, Frank d 4 Dec 1873 ae: 45y.

WATERHOUSE, Samuel d 31 Oct 1858 ae: 70y.

WHITE, Mary d 27 Feb 1869 ae: 54y.

WILSON, Mary Elizabeth d/o Nellie d 13 Sept 1873 ae: 2m.

WOODS, John P d 6 Jan 1871 ae: 52y.

YEATON, David d 29 Jan 1863 ae: 32y. "Died Pest House, small pox."

YORK, Jessie P C d/o Jessie H d 4 Apr 1873 ae: 2m. "Died Pest House, small pox."

Individuals consigned to the Maine Medical School
for anatomization purposes between 1891 and 1920

Unknown man d 26 Mar 1907 ae: c35y.

Unknown man found 17 Mar 1917 at Merrill's Wharf, drowned.

ALWARD, stillborn ch/o Arthur A & Sadie E d 19 Jan 1909.

ARCHAMBEAU, Joseph d 11 Nov 1918 ae: 75y. "Died Waterville, ME."

AUBENS, Albert G d 6 May 1899 ae: 39y 3m 3d.

BAILEY, Lizzie d 18 Mar 1896 ae: 65y. "Died Greely Hospital."

BEAN, Mildred d 18 Dec 1902 ae: 5d. "Died Greely Hospital."

BURD, John s/o Joseph & Mary d 13 Feb 1920 ae: 61y. "Died City Hospital."

CASEY, stillborn s/o Timothy & Margaret d 28 Dec 1911. "Died City Hospital."

CLARK, stillborn s/o Chiever N & Eva E d 15 Mar 1915.

CLOUTIER, J d 27 Oct 1914 ae: c40y.

COBURN, Albert s/o John d 5 Nov 1909 ae: 59y.

CONNERS, Charles d 25 Apr 1912 ae: 55y.

CROSS, Robert S d 24 Oct 1907 ae: c50y.

CROSSMAN, infant s/o Grace d 6 Feb 1915.

DAVIS, Levi T s/o Ezra & Rebecca d 4 Feb 1919 ae: 73y. "Died City Hospital."

DOLLOFF, Joseph d 30 Jan 1911 ae: 58y.

DWYER, William d 21 Apr 1915

DWYER (continued) ae: c 50y.

EDWARDS, Daniel d 17 July 1908 ae: 27y. "Died City Hospital."

ELWELL, Elnora May d/o Elmer B & Mary d 2 Nov 1917 ae: 3d.

FERGUSON, Peter d 1 May 1892 ae: 58y. "Native of Scotland." "Died Greely Hospital."

FEUSTODO, Michael d 15 Dec 1897 ae: 30y. "Died Malaria."

GARNIER, Thomas d 15 Jan 1907 ae: c60y. "Died Greely Hospital."

GILMORE, Thomas E s/o Martin & Winnifred d 30 Sep 1908 ae: 48y 4m.

GOULD, Watson E s/o Samuel & Susan d 25 Oct 1905 ae: 67y.

GRANT, Annie d/o Stephen d 12 July 1897 ae: 28y. "Died Greely Hospital."

GRINNELL, Palmer L s/o Richard R & Harriet d 9 Aug 1905 ae: 56y.

HALE, T F d 4 June 1905 ae: c 40y. "Suicide-gun shot."

HARDING, Thomas d 2 Dec 1914 ae: c50y.

HAYES, Patrick d 1 Sep 1897 ae: 87y. "Died Greely Hospital." "Buried Calvary Cem."

HOLMAN, Niles d 19 Mar 1906 ae: 30y.

HUDSON, George W d 15 Mar 1908 ae: 55y. "Died City Hospital."

HUDDLESTON, Hazel d 4 Apr 1891 ae: c30y. "Died Greely Hospital."

JACKSON, Nellie d/o Robert & Florence d 7 Nov 1913 ae: 3m 27d.

JOHNSON, James d 12 May 1908 ae: 51y. "Died City Hospital."

JONES, stillborn d/o Wallace S & Phoebe d 8 Feb 1912.

KELLEY, Sarah J w/o Larry d 21 Mar 1908 ae: 58y.

KELLY, John s/o John & Bridget d 20 Dec 1897 ae: 51y. "Died Greely Hospital."

KOTLOWSKI, Joseph d 26 Oct 1915 ae: c60y. "Died City Hospital."

LALLY, Bridget d/o John d 16 Feb 1906 ae: 37y. Buried Forest City Cem., 21 June 1906.

LARRABEE, William s/o Nathaniel & Ellen d 21 Oct 1910 ae: 73y. "Died City Hospital."

LEARY, Edward d 19 June 1907 ae: 54y. "Died City Hospital."

LEONARD, Edwin s/o Leslie & Isabelle d 1 July 1907 ae: 51y. "Died City Hospital."

John d 13 Mar 1906 ae: 22y. "Died City Hospital."

LINNEHAN, Honora d 14 Mar 1900 ae: 83y. "Died Greely Hospital."

LITTLE, Lavina d 30 June 1904 ae: 76y. "Died Greely Hospital."

MADOR, William s/o Albert & Delmanis d 18 Apr 1913 ae: 26y. "Died City Hospital."

MAIER, Charles s/o Martin d 10 June 1914 ae: 22y. "Died City Hospital."

MALONEY, James d 4 June 1901 ae: 31y. "Died Gorham-suicide."

MARTIN, William d 11 Apr 1913 ae: 31y. "Died City Hospital."

William d 26 Dec 1916 ae: 65y. "Died City Hospital."

MERKELBERK, Peter "sailor" s/o Harry & Mary F d 18 Jan 1916 ae: 49y.

MOULTON, John d 23 May 1907

MOULTON (continued) ae: 24y. "Died City Hospital."

MULLER, Frederick "shoemaker" d 10 Oct 1914 ae: c80y. "Died City Hospital."

PELLERIN, Alfred d 23 Nov 1918 ae: 56y.

PIERCE, Frank aka McKearney d 15 Sep 1914 ae: 70y.

POMARO, Daniel A aka William Bradley d 27 Aug 1904 ae: 23y. "Found dead in MCRR car."

RICHARDSON, Daniel F d 18 Feb 1918 ae: 48y.

RILEY, James s/o Michael & Margaret d 28 Oct 1918 ae: 73y. "Died City Hospital."

SEACOTT, John d 14 Apr 1913 ae: 74y. "Died City Hospital."

SHADE, Herman d 24 Feb 1906 ae: 47y.

SHERWOOD, James d 4 May 1904 ae: 45y.

SKETUP, George d 23 June 1913 ae: c60y. "Died City Hospital."

SMITH, James s/o John & Mary d 23 May 1898 ae: 55y. "Died Greely Hospital."

Simeon s/o John & Mary d 21 July 1897 ae: 60y. "Died Greely Hospital."

William s/o Charles & Mary d 30 Sep 1916 ae: 56y 8m 22d. "Died City Hospital."

SPEAR, James d 16 Apr 1914 ae: 67y.

STAPLES, Elmira d 23 Jan 1909 ae: 76y.

STEVENS, Albion H d 3 Sep 1897 ae: 27y.

STONE, Elizabeth W d 13 May 1901 ae: 77y 1m 9d.

SULLIVAN, Bridget d 4 Jan 1899 ae: 65y. "Died Greely Hospital."

SWATOY, Dennis d 24 July 1914 ae: 29y.

TAYLOR, Margaret "cook" w/o Randall d 25 Dec 1913 ae: 35y.

TEENER, Auguste d 28 May 1892 ae: c65y. "Died Greely Hospi

TEENER (continued)
tal."

THOMAS, Charles C d 1 Oct 1898 ae: 57y 7m. "Suicide-drowned."

TINKHAM, Ephraim d 18 Nov 1914 ae: 73y. "Died City Hospital."

TOOMEY, Frank J d 20 Feb 1906 ae: 45y. Buried Forest City Cem., 21 June 1906.

WALTER, Frederick s/o Fred & Mary A d 26 Aug 1903 ae: c54y. "Died Greely Hospital." Buried Forest City, 16 Dec 1903.

WEHLER, Randolph d 18 May 1907 ae: 81y 3m. "Died City Hospital."

WHITNEY, infant s/o Raymond R & Lucy L d 26 Jan 1915 ae: 3h.

WILLIAMS, Estelle Black d 29 Jan 1915 ae: c36y.

Bohemian shipwreck victims, Cape Elizabeth, 22 Feb 1864.
Burial Records, City of Portland.

CASSIDY, James (Calvary Cemetery)

CANAVAN, Barbara ae: 6y. (Taken by family) (Calvary Cemetery)

CLARK, A ae: 30y. Fireman, Bohemian (Calvary Cemetery)

CONLEY, Ellen (Calvary Cemetery)

Mrs (Calvary Cemetery)

FLAHERTY, Ellen ae: 18y. (Calvary Cemetery)

GREIG, James Forest City Cemetery, strangers' Ground

HONEYCHURCH, Begen ae: 30y. Forest City Cemetery, strangers' ground

KANE, John Taken to Boston, Massachusetts

Thomas s/o John Taken to Boston, Massachusetts (BV)

KEELAN, Thomas (Calvary Cemetery)

KELVEY, Mr Forest City Cemetery, strangers' ground

MATTHEWS, James Forest City Cemetery, strangers' ground

MCDONOUGH, Mary ae: 34y. (Calvary Cemetery)

Mary ae: 7m. (Calvary Cemetery)

Patrick ae: 12y. (Calvary Cemetery)

Thomas ae: 6y. (Calvary Cemetery)

Thomas (Calvary Cemetery)

MULLER, Ann ae: 18y. Brooklyn, New York

NOLAN, Mary (Calvary Cemetery)

O'CONNOR, Mrs (Calvary Cemetery)

PURCELL, Mr (Calvary Cemetery)

Mrs body lost

child body lost

child (Calvary Cemetery)

Soldier, unknown Forest City Cemetery, strangers' ground

Unknown female child (Calvary Cemetery)

Unknown woman (Calvary Cemetery)

Five unknown men Forest City Cemetery, strangers' ground

Five unknown women Forest City Cemetery, strangers' ground

Two unknown children Forest City Cemetery, strangers' ground

Unknown male child Forest City Cemetery, strangers' ground

Victims of the Portland Fire - 1866

BLUEFIELD, Susan w/o Simon d 4 July 1866 ae: 36y. "Her body was entirely consumed in the house in which she lived on Fore Street. Affidavit of Ephraim G. Webster and Elizabeth J. Webster, 11 Feb 1891."

CHICKERING, Elizabeth d/o Zabrina d 5 July 1866. Burned to death.

Zabrina d 5 July 1866. Burned to death.

Individuals consigned to the Portland Medical School
for anatomization purposes between 1900 and 1920.

Unknown man d 23 Aug 1901, killed in railroad accident, North Yarmouth.

Unknown infant d 5 Mar 1910, found in Eastern Cemetery.

Unknown man found 10 June 1916, drowned - Portland Pier.

Unknown man found 8 July 1916 ae: about 30y, drowned Commercial Wharf.

ABBOTT, Margaret w/o Andrew A, d/o Thomas McGeorge d 9 Ap 1917 ae: 82y.

ANNIS, Ervin E d 15 July 1908 ae: 48y 5m. "Died City Hospital."

ARCHIBALD, James E d 19 Oct 1920 ae: 43y. "Died City Hospital."

John C s/o Graney & Margaret d 20 Sept 1917 ae: 68y. "Died City Hospital." (MSC2)

ATUS, Sewall d 8 Dec 1902 ae: 44y. "Died Greely Hospital."

AVERY, Simon d 5 Jan 1907 ae: 52y. "Died City Hospital."

BARNES, William H s/o George W d 25 Nov 1908 ae: 58y.

BERRYMAN, Sarah d 16 Nov 1907 ae: 47y. "Died City Hospital."

BICKFORD, Walter d 25 Aug 1900 ae: 16y. Buried Forest City Cem 21 Dec 1902.

BOARDMAN, Ellen M, d/o Sewall d 2 Nov 1908 ae: 63y. "Died City Hospital."

BOWLER, John d 7 July 1911 ae: 38y.

BRICKLEY, June d 18 Jan 1917

BRICKLEY (continued) ae: 40y. (MSC2)

CALLAHAN, Jeremiah d 23 Dec 1902 ae: 65y. "Died Greely Hospital." Buried Brunswick, Maine 25 Mar 1903.

CLINTON, Peter d 8 June 1903 ae: about 60y. "Died Greely Hospital." Buried Forest City Cem 16 Dec 1903.

CONEY, Alice Mary, d/o Louisa d 14 Dec 1917 ae: 2d. "Died City Hospital."

CONNELL, Sylvester d 9 Oct 1901 ae: 58y. "Died Greely Hospital." Buried Brunswick, Maine.

CRILLEY, Edward s/o Thomas & Mary d 12 Nov 1911 ae: 45y. "Painter." "Died City Hospital."

DONAHUE, Patrick s/o Morgan d 16 July 1916 ae: 35y.

DREW, Herbert S s/o Henry d 3 Aug 1905 ae: 37y. "Died Greely Hospital."

DRUMMOND, Alexander d 10 F 1913 ae: 53y.

FLINT, George s/o Hiram d 21 Sept 1907 ae: 18y. "Died City Hospital."

GASSETT, Ira d 17 Nov 1917 ae: 63y. "Died City Hospital."

GREENAWAY, William d 14 Dec 1900 ae: 89y. "Died Greely Hospital." Buried Forest City Cem 20 Dec 1902.

HAMMOND, Charles J s/o William S & Narcissa d 23 Dec 1917 ae: 74y. "Died City

HAMMOND (continued)
Hospital."

HASKELL, Thomas d 19 Jan 1912 ae: 65y. "Died City Hospital."

HERBERT, Arthur d 2 Jan 1905 ae: 20y. "Died Greely Hospital."

HUNNEWELL, inf c/o Franklin d 1 Dec 1904 ae: 1h.

JOHNSON, Emil d 7 Dec 1907 ae: 25y. "Died City Hospital."

William d 18 April 1914 ae: 78y. "Died City Hospital."

LEE, Walter d 28 June 1903 ae: 27y 11m 14d. "Died Greely Hospital." Buried Forest City Cem 16 Dec 1903.

LEIGHTON, Joel d 29 Jan 1903 ae: 68y. "Died Greely Hospital."

MacBETH, Albert s/o David & Jane d 31 May 1916 ae: 57y. "Died City Hospital."

MANISKY, Peter s/o Tedal d 24 June 1916 ae: 51y. "Died City Hospital."

MANN, Emeline Hamlin d/o John Hamlin d 14 July 1911 ae: 74y. "Died City Hospital."

MASKILL, Thomas Jr b Eastport, Maine d 19 Jan 1912 ae: 66y. "Pedlar." "Died City Hospital." Civil War: 29th Regt Maine Infantry Co E.

MILES, Frances d 2 Aug 1900 ae: 84y. "Died Greely Hospital." Buried Forest City Cem 20 Dec 1902.

MILLIKEN, Daniel Edward s/o John F & Louise d 23 April 1905 ae: 24y 8m.

MITCHELL, Thomas d 12 Oct 1904 ae: 66y. "Died Greely Hospital."

MOORE, Frank d 21 Oct 1920 ae: 41y. "Died City Hospital."

MOREY, Frank G found dead 12 April 1906 ae: about 55y. Buried Forest City Cem 24 June 1906.

MORSE, John K d 19 Sept 1907 ae: 75y.

NAZUTO, Lorenzo s/o Antonio & Rose d 4 Oct 1920 ae: 26y 6m 19d. "Died Fairfield, Maine."

NELSON, William H d 22 May 1912 ae: 80y. "Carpetmaker." "Died City Hospital."

PESCE, Filomena d/o Tony & Rosa d 18 Nov 1911 ae: 17y 2m 4d. "Died City Hospital."

RAIDEX, John d 21 Sept 1904 ae: 87y. "Died Greely Hospital."

ROSARIO, Vinnie d/o Emilio & Jennie d 1 Jan 1907 ae: 2h.

SMITH, Charles E s/o Edward & Bridget d 3 April 1911 ae: 26y. "Died City Hospital."

William d 12 Aug 1907 ae: 47y. "Died City Hospital."

WALSH, Gertrude found dead 1 April 1902 ae: 27y. Buried Forest City Cem.

YORK, Gustavus d 8 Aug 1912 ae: 53y.

YOUNG, Bridget d 24 May 1901. "Died Greely Hospital."

City Tomb

List of bodies placed in the City Tomb (built 1849). Subsequent place of burial is unrecorded in the city burial records.

Child found in Portland harbor, d 16 Feb 1863.

Unknown man found drowned 8 Mar 1869.

ABBOTT, Guy Burbank s/o Richard d 1 Mar 1871 ae: 2y 10m 4d.

ADAMS, Augustus d 15 Mar 1856 ae: 69y.

Carrie d/o Augustus d 18 Dec 1859 ae: 21y.

Frederick Leaman s/o A K d 20 Feb 1876 ae: 5y.

Mary Gertrude d/o Frederick R d 13 Sep 1883 ae: 4m.

ADDITION, Lloyd W d 19 Jan 1856 ae: 36y. "Died Calais, Maine."

AINSWORTH, Margaret d 18 Mar 1892 ae: 72y. "Died Greely Hospital."

ALLEN, Abby d/o D W d 25 Jan 1863 ae: 4m 2d.

Bertie s/o Frank H d 12 Oct 1882 ae: 6m.

Francis M d 8 Dec 1859 ae: 24y.

Horace N d 21 Jan 1882 ae: 46y. "Died Boston, Massachusetts."

ANDERSON, Axel Elmore s/o Axel d 2 Feb 1885 ae: 10w.

Charles W s/o George W d 27 Dec 1872 ae: 2y.

Victor L s/o Axel & Clara d 16 Mar 1891 ae: 6y 10m.

ANGLON, Timothy s/o Timothy d 15 Mar 1856 ae: 1y 6m 8d.

ANTONIO, Caleb d 27 Dec 1855

ANTONIO (continued) ae: 70y. "Native of Venice, Italy."

ARMSTRONG, Edward C d 19 Jan 1870 ae: 11y.

ASBURY, Caldwell d 29 Jan 1862 ae: 24y.

ATKINSON, Elizabeth d 2 Jan 1880 ae: 27y.

AYER, Frederick E s/o John d 27 Jan 1867 ae: 10w.

AYERS, Joseph N d 12 Jan 1859 ae: 35y.

BABCOCK, Augusta M d/o Alvin d 19 Jan 1853 ae: 14m 20d.

BACHELDER, Mary d 29 Jan 1872 ae: 71y.

BAILEY, Thomas E s/o Thomas d 22 Mar 1856 ae: 8y 6m.

BAKER, Emma F w/o John E d 15 Dec 1877 ae: 19y.

BALL, Janmes F s/o Janmes G d 25 Dec 1876 ae: 15y.

BANKS, William H s/o late Josiah d 2 Mar 1862 ae: 20y.

BARKER, Esther Jane w/o Peleg d 27 Feb 1857 ae: 24y 6m.

Mary L w/o JC d 15 Mar 1860 ae: 22y 1m 13d.

Winfield Scott s/o Nathan d 23 Jan 1858 ae: 10y 4m.

BARR, Nancy d/o Alexander d 24 Sep 1857 ae: 70y. "of North Yarmouth."

BARTLETT, Clorina w/o Alexander P d 25 Jan 1850 ae: 30y.

George E d 21 Jan 1873 ae: 19y.

Mercy widow d 4 Feb 1859 ae:

BARTLETT (continued)
80y.

BASSIT, Mary Ann d 26 Jan 1857 ae: 48y 6m.

BASTON, Hiram d 13 Dec 1883 ae: 72y.

BATTY, Charles s/o John V & Georgia E d 20 Feb 1887 ae: 5w.

BEACH, George W s/o George W d 12 Nov 1865 ae: 6y.

Margaret E d/o Charles & Matilda d 19 Apr 1852 ae: 6m.

BEAL, Nellie G d/o John N d 2 Jan 1866 ae: 2w.

BEALES, Charles B s/o late William d 18 Mar 1856 ae: 21y.

BECKETT, Charles F s/o Charles C d 21 Jan 1850 ae: 3y.

BECKWITH, Morton s/o Asa d 8 Nov 1865 ae: 17y.

BEECH, Charles d 16 Feb 1852 ae: 31y. "Of Prince Edwards Island."

BEECHER, Harriet J w/o William d 28 Mar 1887 ae: 40y.

BEEMAN, Mary P d/o John F d 7 Jan 1852 ae: 1y.

BELL, Elizabeth w/o Hugh d 11 Feb 1865 ae: 41y.

BENJAMIN, Margaret d 19 Jan 1879 ae: 86y.

BENNETT, Elizabeth S d 18 Apr 1885 ae: 78y 10m.

John d 11 Dec 1863 ae: 68y.

BERRY, John d 11 Jan 1851 ae: 35y.

BETTS, John d 1 Jan 1862 ae: 28y. "Drowned from the steamship *Norwegian*."

BICKFORD, Levi S s/o Frank W d 18 Jan 1883 ae: 6m.

BILLINGS, Reuben F d 12 Dec 1860 ae: 40y.

BLACK, Mary Eliza d/o Henry S d 8 Dec 1869 ae: 13y.

BLACKBURN, inf/o James E d 27 Feb 1856 ae: 3d.

BLACKSTONE, Charles H s/o Albion d 13 Feb 1862 ae: 18m.

BLONDEIM, Charles W d 16 Feb

BLONDEIM (continued)
1883 ae: 66y.

BODKIN, Christiana d/o Peter d 8 Feb 1870 ae: 14y.

BOLLIN, John E s/o John d 19 Mar 1851 ae: 9m.

BOND, Mary d 23 Feb 1884 ae: 67y.

Thankful S wid/o Elias d 4 Mar 1864 ae: 56y.

BOOTHBAY, Horatio s/o Horatio d 24 Mar 1863 ae: 1y 5m.

BOTTS, George d 24 Jan 1856 ae: 22y. "Native of Germany."

BOWEN, Alive d/o M d 7 Mar 1863 ae: 2m 4d.

Hiram A d 15 Apr 1869 ae: 25y.

BOWER, Addie M d/o Augustus d 10 Mar 1873 ae: 2y.

Leontel R d/o John S d 20 Feb 1858 ae: 3y 7d.

BOYCE, Elizabeth d/o Neal d 24 Jan 1851 ae: 9y.

BOYD, James R d 18 Sep 1876 ae: 45y.

Samuel G d 5 Mar 1883 ae: 44y. "Died St Louis, Missouri."

BRACKETT, Benjamin H d 8 Jan 1864 ae: 26y.

BRADBURY, Marion Elizabeth d/o Edward & Ellen C d 16 Dec 1870 ae: 1y 1m 25d.

BRADFORD, Mary d 26 Feb 1876 ae: 71y.

Ruth w/o William d 7 May 1851 ae: 53y. "Of Minot."

BRADISH, Josephine F d/o Henry C d 21 Feb 1861 ae: 3y.

BRADLEY, Benjamin V s/o JV d 28 Feb 1870 ae: 2y 6m.

Robert d 3 Mar 1875 ae: 40y.

BRAGDON, Ann d 10 Apr 1875 ae: 77y.

BRECKET, George E s/o George C d 30 Jan 1852 ae: 4y 29d.

BRICKELL, Frank R s/o Alonzo B d 17 Aug 1860 ae: 7w.

BRIGGS, Noble d 4 Feb 1857 ae: 53y. "Native Shrewsbury, Massachusetts" "Died at the Marine Hospital."

BRIGHAM, Dennis s/o John A d

BRIGHAM (continued)
3 Jan 1857 ae: 2y 4m.
BROOKINGS, Emma L d/o A d 29
Feb 1872 ae: 1y.
BROWN, Arthur G s/o FW d 21
Mar 1890 ae: 10d.
Benjamin d 11 Jan 1882 ae: 86y.
Benjamin F d 2 Apr 1870 ae:
37y.
Carrie J d/o Charles E d 24 Feb
1858 ae: 1d.
Cecil F s/o FW d 15 Apr 1890
ae: 1y 3m.
Charles C d 6 June 1902 ae: 79y.
Daniel d 3 Mar 1875 ae: 50y.
Edward d 24 Apr 1886 ae: 41y.
"Died Augusta State Hosp."
Eliza S w/o James H d 27 Mar
1882 ae: 62y.
Elizabeth H w/o George d 6 Feb
1859 ae: 69y.
George A s/o Thomas d 23 Feb
1866 ae: 1y 2m.
Harriet d 25 Feb 1876 ae: 55y.
J Everett d 14 Jan 1877 ae: 43y.
John d 10 Dec 1877 ae: 55y.
Nathaniel d 25 Feb 1869 ae: 82y.
William d 5 Mar 1871 ae: 38y.
William C s/o Augustus d 2 Feb
1876 ae: 1y.
BRUCE, Mary w/o Peter d 21 Jan
1856 ae: 64y.
BRUNDAGE, John s/o Daniel d 6
Apr 1885 ae: 3d.
BRYANT, Charles W d 15 Dec
1877 ae: 17y.
BUCHANAN, Rebecca w/o
George d 10 Mar 1859 ae: 38y.
BUCHER, Tammy d 2 Jan 1873
ae: 29y.
BURGESS, Henry S d 22 Feb 1879
ae: 69y.
BURGIN, Emmeline G d/o E A d
9 Feb 1856 ae: 5m.
BURKE, Emily s/o James d 5
Feb 1871 ae: 1m.
BURNELL, William E d 22 Sep
1881 ae: 24y.
BURNS, Anne Dicks d/o Chandler
d 9 Feb 1862 ae: 5y.
Eliza w/o George d 30 Jan 1850
ae: 50y.

BURNS (continued)
Mena d/o Christian d 2 Jan 1882
ae: 1y.
BURTON, Jane M d/o A M d 8
Jan 1860 ae: 3d.
BUZZELL, John d 3 Jan 1878 ae:
56y.
Luella d/o Silas d 21 Dec 1871
ae: 6y.
CADDELL, Manard s/o John d 14
Mar 1881 ae: 1y.
CAMPBELL, Elizabeth A d 9 Apr
1867 ae: 30y.
CANNON, Ann d/o Peter d 18 Dec
1856 ae: 3y.
CAREY, Adeline F d 16 Jan 1884
ae: 65y.
CARLTON, Corabell d/o SL d 26
Feb 1860 ae: 11m.
CARNEY, John W d 30 Jan 1891
ae: 50y 6m.
CARR, Henry K s/o Charles H d 3
Mar 1862 ae: 22m.
CARROLL, Charles s/o Peter d
28 Feb 1876 ae: 7m.
CARTER, Betsy d 6 Feb 1859 ae:
66y.
CHURCH, Izora Isabella d/o
John & Annie L d 10 Feb 1888
ae: 4y 1m.
CENTER, Isaac d 28 Feb 1862
ae: 32y.
CHAMBERLAIN, Ella d/o AG d
19 Mar 1875 ae: 12h. "Died
Norwood, Massachusetts."
Forest W s/o William d 6 Mar
1861 ae: 3y 11m.
Rosanna d 1 Jan 1894 ae: 84y
9m.
CHASE, Alice wid/o William d 3
Mar 1859 ae: 86y 10m.
Edward s/o Edward d 20 Jan
1858 ae: 9m.
Eliza A w/o Robert d 26 Feb
1859 ae: 42y.
George W s/o George W d 11
Jan 1858.
Henry W s/o Elias d 21 Aug
1878 ae: 20y.
Lodemia L w/o John d 14 Feb
1859 ae: 51y.
Sarah O J w/o Andrew J d 6 Apr

CHASE (continued)
1864 ae: 29y 6m.

CHELLICE, Betsy d 4 Feb 1862 ae: 75y.

CHENERY, Hattie E d/o Solomon d 25 Jan 1884 ae: 17y.

CHICK, Herman L s/o William M d 24 Dec 1872 ae: 3y.

CHOATE, Ernest Z s/o Horace d 15 Aug 1871 ae: 14m.

CHURCH, James s/o John C d 30 Mar 1880 ae: 16y.

CLAPP, Emily H d/o John d 15 Feb 1873 ae: 7m.

CLARK, Francis d 25 Feb 1876 ae: 86y.

Philena G w/o George W d 14 Mar 1863 ae: 20y.

Thomas d 11 Feb 1885 ae: 74y.

CLARRY, Ruth E w/o Robert d 22 Jan 1869 ae: 63y.

CLEAVES, Capt William d 14 Feb 1871 ae: 63y.

COBB, Eliza w/o Rufus d 1 Jan 1851 ae: 33y.

Mary T w/o Josiah C d 19 Feb 1875 ae: 51y.

Olivia E d/o Benjamin d 16 Dec 1860 ae: 4m.

COCHRAN, Inf ch/o John d 24 Feb 1857 ae: 4m.

COLE, George W d 9 Feb 1879 ae: 46y.

Helen A d/o William G Davis d 18 May 1872 ae: 22y.

COLLIER, Lucy W d/o William d 5 Mar 1857 ae: 1y.

COLLINS, Jane d/o J W d 27 Feb 1858 ae: 9d.

COOMBS, Hannah d 23 Dec 1861 ae: 96y.

CONLEY, John s/o John d 31 Dec 1855 ae: 9m.

Mary d 8 Dec 1883 ae: 75y.

COOK, child d 11 Feb 1858 ae: 4d. "Died on board the British steamer."

Augusta J w/o AG d 20 Dec 1893 ae: 46y. "Died Boston, Massachusetts."

Melvino d 1 Jan 1877 ae: 16y.

COOLBROTH, Frederick R W s/o William d 24 Dec 1867 ae: 8y 2m.

COOLIDGE, William d 28 Mar 1856 ae: 63y.

COUILLARD, Elijah s/o Elijah d 17 Jan 1856 ae: 1d.

Lydia Jane w/o Elijanh d 20 Jan 1856 ae: 31y.

CRAFTS, Hiram d 6 Jan 1861 ae: 23y. "Died from fumes of brimstone aboard schooner at Burnham's wharf." "Native of Carlton, New Brunswick."

CROCKETT, Horace F s/o John Jr d 21 Mar 1884 ae: 2m.

CROOK, Mary Delia d/o d 17 Mar 1873 ae: 1y.

CROOKER, Elizabeth E d/o John d 20 Sep 1860 ae: 1y.

CROSS, Cynthia K d 29 Jan 1867 ae: 85y.

CROSSMAN, Annie H w/o Smiten P d 30 Mar 1882 ae: 63y.

CROSSTON, Anna S w/o Gregory d 3 Mar 1862 ae: 33y.

CROW, William d 22 Feb 1856 ae: 45y.

CUMMINGS, Elizabeth w/o Jancob A d 24 Dec 1867 ae: 86y 9m.

CUNNINGHAM, Adrianna d/o W B d 21 Jan 1851 ae: 19m.

CURTIS, Ernest C s/o Hattie B d 24 Dec 1884 ae: 2y.

CUSHING, Abigail w/o Emery d 7 Mar 1856 ae: 41y.

Maud Louisa d/o Geo T d 28 July 1876 ae: 6m.

CUSHMAN, Catherine d 19 Jan 1875 ae: 73y.

Mary E d 22 Mar 1884 ae: 57y. "Died Greely Hospital."

CURRY, Maria A w/o James d 28 Feb 1856 ae: 38y.

CUTLER, Ethelbert N d 14 Jan 1866 ae: 38y.

DAIN, George H s/o John P d 1 Feb 1852 ae: 2y 9m.

DANFORTH, Amelia B d/o B d 8 Apr 1862 ae: 16y 1m 3d.

DARRAH, Ella Maud d/o Edward d 5 Mar 1873 ae: 7m.

DAVIS, Carrie M d/o A M d 17 Jan 1870 ae: 53y.

Dana s/o Nathaniel d 10 Jan 1880 ae: 3y.

Eliza A w/o Charles P d 4 Feb 1859 ae: 30y 9m.

Emmeline d/o Isaac d 29 Feb 1856 ae: 36y.

Fannie E w/o Janson H d 30 Sep 1871 ae: 31y 3m.

George H s/o Charles H d 28 Nov 1876 ae: 3m.

Harriet J d/o George R d 20 Feb 1858 ae: 6m.

Helen M w/o James W d 21 Feb 1887 ae: 34y 3m.

Mary Berry w/o Solomon d 6 Jan 1892 ae: 80y 4m 18d.

Mary N d/o George H d 23 Jan 1886 ae: 4y 5m.

Nathaniel d 21 Feb 1870 ae: 2m.

DAY, Catherine M d/o Josiah F Jr d 13 Dec 1863 ae: 13m.

Nelson S d 2 Mar 1875 ae: 67y.

DEANE, Fanny H wid/o George d 29 Dec 1893 ae: 59y.

George d 12 Jan 1890 ae: 58y.

Margaret d 17 Dec 1859 ae: 14y 7m.

Perley T s/o Robert d 21 Feb 1881 ae: 1y.

Robert d 21 Dec 1883 ae: 28y.

DEARBORN, Cora E d/o John E d 6 Nov 1861 ae: 9m.

DEERING, Francis W s/o Rufus d 21 Sep 1856 ae: 4m.

DELAND, Ruth w/o Stephen d 24 Feb 1867 ae: 54y.

DELANO, Abbie B d 16 Feb 1873 ae: 60y.

DENNIS, James d 2 Apr 1873 ae: 30y.

DOANE, Henry d 21 Feb 1884 ae: 61y.

DODGE, Elizabeth d 12 Nov 1871 ae: 61y.

DOGGETT, Maud d/o John A d 10 Feb 1889 ae: 2m.

DOHERTY, Daniel s/o John d 25 Feb 1856 ae: 8m.

DORMAN, Eunice M d 13 Mar 1893 ae: 69y 10m.

DOUGLASS, Batheline w/o Henry d 31 Jan 1882 ae: 35y.

Etta M d/o Henry d 20 Mar 1877 ae: 1y.

DOW, Harriet d/o Josiah d 22 Feb 1869 ae: 62y.

DRAKE, Lillian S d 27 Jan 1884 ae: 11y.

DRESSER, Caroline H d/o Robert d 6 Feb 1850 ae: 10y.

Margaret w/o Stephen d 9 Feb 1875 ae: 34y.

Sophia d/o Stephen G d 18 Feb 1860 ae: 7w.

DREW, Charles A s/o Charles A d 22 Dec 1876 ae: 11m.

DUDLEY, Harry d 2 Jan 1877 ae: 3y.

DUFFY, James d 7 Jan 1888. "Died Marine Hospital."

DUNN, Edward s/o D M C d 16 Dec 1851 ae: 1y 9m.

Joseph M d 5 Mar 1852 ae: 40y.

Sarah Scott d/o D M C d 20 Nov 1851 ae: 4y 6m.

DUNPHY, Georgianna d/o Abel d 24 Dec 1862 ae: 11m.

Sarah E d/o Charles d 1 Apr 1867 ae: 5y.

DUNSIER, Catherine d 15 Dec 1855 ae: 73y. "Native of England."

DURGIN, Kenneth s/o John & Clara d 4 Oct 1901 ae: 8d.

DYER, Betsy d 19 Feb 1880 ae: 71y.

Catherine d/o William d 5 Apr 1857 ae: 4w.

Lewis W s/o Edward L d 21 Jan 1889 ae: 21y.

Lucy H d/o Samuel T d 10 Jan 1863 ae: 3m.

EASTMAN, ch s/o William d 3 Oct 1857 ae: 1w.

Mary H d/o Joseph W d 2 June 1861 ae: 2m.

Malhon s/o Joseph d 7 Feb 1867 ae: 2m.

EATON, Charles C d 14 Jan 1860 ae: 27y.

EATON (continued)

Elizabeth W w/o George d 27 Feb 1875 ae: 74y.

William s/o Benjamin d 14 Feb 1857 ae: 1y.

EBBESON, George W d 24 Jan 1877 ae: 2y.

EDDY, George W s/o George W d 9 Feb 1862 ae: 7w.

EDWARDS, James W d 18 Mar 1879 ae: 72y.

John d 26 Dec 1851 ae: 68y.

William d 21 Jan 1880. "Died Augusta, Maine."

ELDER, Frederick W s/o Gideon d 12 Apr 1873 ae: 20y.

Anna K d/o Gideon G d 12 Dec 1851 ae: 18m.

EMERSON, Amos d 4 Jan 1852 ae: 77y.

Emily gr/d Abraham Strout d 11 July 1860 ae: 5w.

ENFER, Gustave A, s/o Pauline d 22 Jan 1880 ae: 3y.

FABYAN, John d 19 Feb 1856 ae: 55y.

FALBY, George S s/o Andrew J d 26 Feb 1872 ae: 2m 10d. "Died Boston."

FALBEY, Mamie d/o Andrew N d 17 Jan 1879 ae: 11y.

FARR, David A d 4 Aug 1877 ae: 51y. "Died Boston."

Elizabeth C d/o SF d 1 Oct 1857 ae: 5w.

Freelove E d/o James d 9 Feb 1863 ae: 5y 5m.

Laura I d/o George H d 1 Mar 1853 ae: 6y.

FARRINGTON, Harriet E w/o Ira P d 26 Jan 1853 ae: 22y.

FARROW, Sarah w/o John d 19 Jan 1862 ae: 55y.

FAULKNER, Hugh d 11 Jan 1871 ae: 36y 10m.

FAUNCE, Mahala wid/o Ansel d 12 Feb 1856 ae: 39y.

FELIN, Catherine d/o Patrick d 2 Mar 1852 ae: 2m.

FERNALD, Abba W d/o Alfred d 7 Dec 1872 ae: 3y.

Isaac Henry s/o Isaac d 20 May

FERNALD (continued)

1860 ae: 19y 2m.

FERRIMAN, Isaac s/o Robert d 19 Feb 1859 ae: 17y.

FICKETT, Hannah Waterhouse d/o John d 5 Mar 1865 ae: 87y.

FIELD, Anna M w/o Levi C d 7 Dec 1859 ae: 29y.

Henry s/o William d 6 Apr 1861 ae: 6w.

Moses d 10 Apr 1870 ae: 66y.

Nelson d 18 Mar 1861 ae: 27y.

FIELDS, Abner W s/o Levi d 3 Jan 1857 ae: 3w.

Lydia A d/o Moses d 18 Nov 1861 ae: 17y.

FINNON, Rebecca w/o Geo T d 1 Mar 1891 ae: 35y 10m.

FITZ, William d 22 Feb 1871 ae: 40y.

FITZGERALD, Ellen d 20 Jan 1856 ae: 9m.

George E s/o James F d 13 Sep 1892 ae: 24y 3m 2d.

James d Dec 1876 ae: 40y. "Died Boston, Massachusetts."

FLING, Charles A s/o Charles H d 25 Apr 1860 ae: 6y 2m.

FOGA, Ann E H d/o Charles N d 19 Feb 1862 ae: 7y.

FOLEY, John d 25 Mar 1856 ae: 20y.

FOLLETT, Alice G d/o Wm E d 20 Mar 1882 ae: 2y.

Frank J d 27 Dec 1871 ae: 43y.

FOOTE, James M d 8 Feb 1872 ae: 65y.

FORDE, Alice Robinson d/o John W d 13 Jan 1856 ae: 1w.

FORSHAY, Charles d 19 Feb 1890 ae: 38y 8m.

FOUNTAIN, Sarah C w/o Edward d 22 Feb 1861 ae: 25y.

FOYE, Edwin Augustus s/o Wm A d 12 Mar 1860 ae: 18y 10m.

Joseph T d 30 Mar 1864 ae: 77y.

FRANCIS, Thomas d 1 Jan 1856 ae: 28y. "Died in the Work House."

FRANK, Charles s/o John d 9 May 1878 ae: 9m.

Elizabeth Ann w/o Isaiah d 14

FRANK (continued)
Mar 1890 ae: 70y.
FRASER, Alexander d 29 Mar 1862 ae: 67y.
FRATES, John A s/o John A d 26 Mar 1891 ae: 2m.
FRITH, Foster C d 7 Mar 1861 ae: 36y.
FROST, Alice d 25 Aug 1861 ae: 1m.
Alphonso s/o Orange C d 3 May 1850 ae: 2y 1m.
Jacob s/o Nathaniel d 4 Mar 1867 ae: 57y 8m.
FRYE, Nancy S d/o John d 23 Dec 1858 ae: 29y.
FULLER, Job Emerson d 28 Mar 1852 ae: 27y.
Susan d 5 Feb 1863 ae: 89y.
FURLONG, Benjamin d 14 Jan 1856 ae: 61y.
Edmund J s/o George W d 18 Dec 1859 ae: 9m 15d.
Sarah H w/o Mathias d 3 Jan 1871 ae: 66y 6m.
GAMMON, Frederick s/o Samuel d 15 Feb 1867 ae: 2y.
Sereno s/o Charles d 25 Jan 1852 ae: 9y 6m.
GARDINER, William J d 8 Feb 1871 ae: 32y 10m.
GATES, Nancy H d 30 Jan 1878 ae: 93y.
GERRISH, George Curtis s/o William H d 3 Jan 1861 ae: 4m.
GILMAN, Ellen M d 16 Feb 1864 ae: 40y. "Died in Boston."
Frank s/o N J d 7 Mar 1864 ae: 6y.
GOLDSMITH, Henry s/o George d 2 July 1883 ae: 5d.
GOODHUE, Lizzie d/o Thomas d 11 Feb 1863 ae: 18m.
GOODING, Mary Ann w/o Charles d 25 Mar 1853 ae: 24y.
William C d 1 Apr 1858 ae: 1y 5m.
GORDON, Joshua d 23 Mar 1857 ae: 73y.
GOULD, Daniel d 28 June 1863. Accidentally killed on the

GOULD (continued)
"Rebel Pirate *Archer*."
Eleazer d 15 Jan 1852 ae: 67y.
GOVERNOR, John d 23 Jan 1859 ae: 37y. "Native of Toronto, Canada."
GRACE, Frederick A d 4 Nov 1861 ae: 64y.
Martha w/o Jeremiah d 21 Apr 1870 ae: 27y 11m.
GRANT, James A d 4 Feb 1863 ae: 20y.
Jotham S s/o John d 14 Dec 1866 ae: 55y 4m.
GRAVES, Annie T d/o William W d 19 Mar 1856 ae: 3w.
GRAY, Charles H s/o Marshall d 2 Feb 1858 ae: 4m.
Edward d 29 Dec 1851 ae: 48y.
GREEN, Caroline d/o George C d 22 Jan 1852 ae: 2y 11m.
Clara E B w/o Benjamin d 11 Feb 1879 ae: 21y.
George d 28 Jan 1879 ae: 58y.
James A s/o Andrew d 3 Mar 1859 ae: 6m.
Mary A w/o Benjamin d 6 Mar 1862 ae: 35y.
Sarah F w/o James L d 3 Mar 1875 ae: 33y.
GREER, Edward H s/o John d 24 Dec 1856 ae: 3m.
GREGORY, Bertha L d/o Mathias & Caroline d 5 Mar 1888 ae: 14y 10m.
GRIFFIN, Adda d 2 Feb 1856 ae: 3y.
Benjamin s/o Benjamin d 12 Aug 1862 ae: 7w.
George H s/o Charles d 28 Jan 1879 ae: 4y.
Ellen d/o Samuel d 28 Mar 1882 ae: 11m.
GROVER, Walter M d 26 Dec 1849 ae: 16y.
GUILFORD, Henry L s/o Joseph d 28 Jan 1869 ae: 5y.
GRIMES, Joseph d 15 Nov 1883 ae: 78y.
GULLIVER, John M s/o Charles d 19 Mar 1856 ae: 26y.

GUPTILL, Charles H s/o Humphrey d 2 Feb 1852 ae: 1y 7m.

GURNEY, Patrick s/o Patrick d 11 Mar 1858 ae: 12d.

HACKETT, Charlie H s/o Jonathan d 2 Apr 1878 ae: 2y.

HAGGETT, Fanny d/o Charles H d 2 Jan 1862 ae: 3m.

HALL, Clara B d/o Clarence B d 23 Dec 1888 ae: 1y 1m.

Mrs Mary F d 2 Jan 1859 ae: 42y.

Sarah L wid/o Paul d 23 Feb 1865 ae: 61y.

HALLOWELL, Henry F d 20 Feb 1867 ae: 47y.

HALSE, William d 29 Dec 1890 ae: 83y 10m.

HAMEL, Kate d/o Thomas d 25 Dec 1890 ae: 14y 8m.

HAMILTON, Jane w/o William d 11 Jan 1877 ae: 86y. "Died Gray, Maine."

Lucy d 20 Mar 1861 ae: 70y.

Mellen s/o Mellen d 18 Oct 1890 ae: 6d.

HAMLIN, Mary S d/o Alonzo d 2 Mar 1856 ae: 20m. "Died Westbrook."

HAMMETT, Mary d/o John d 24 Sep 1870 ae: 5m.

HANNAFORD, Margaret J d/o Robert d 25 Feb 1856 ae: 17y.

Sarah Ann w/o Benjamin W d 15 Dec 1851 ae: 23y.

HANS, Ann d 27 Mar 1862 ae: 22y.

HANSCOMB, Anna A d/o Whiteley d 25 Dec 1876 ae: 7m.

HANSEN, Franz d 29 Jan 1891 ae: 36y.

HANSON, Marion d/o Charles d 19 Mar 1882 ae: 7w.

Mary E d/o Josiah d 16 Nov 1850 ae: 2y.

HARDENBROOK, Helen d/o John d 5 Feb 1866 ae: 14m 12d.

HARFORD, Charles d 10 Jan 1883 ae: 17y.

HARMON, Joseph A s/o John d 10 Oct 1852 ae: 17m.

HARMON (continued)
Melville s/o George d 23 Mar 1862 ae: 5y.

William s/o John d 24 July 1869 ae: 14y.

HARPER, Lucy d/o Charles d 3 Feb 1868 ae: 3y 8m.

Mary A R d/o Charles d 11 Feb 1868 ae: 3y 8m.

HARRIS, Charles E s/o Edwin R d 15 Jan 1872 ae: 14w.

Lillie D d/o George W d 20 Jan 1879 ae: 1y.

Robert B s/o Thomas d 17 Jan 1856 ae: 3y 8m 16d.

HARROLL, George H d 23 Dec 1856 ae: 30y. "Native of England."

HART, Maudie M d/o Wm d 23 Mar 1884 ae: 6y.

HARWOOD, Henrietta d/o late Capt Otis d 19 Mar 1862 ae: 26y. "Died Brooklyn, New York."

HASKELL, Hannah wid/o A P d 13 Mar 1887 ae: 60y.

HASTINGS, Rebecca A wid/o Samuel d 12 Jan 1851 ae: 75y.

HATCH, Albert W s/o Geo A d 17 Jan 1879 ae: 3y.

Juliet S d/o Harriet M d 8 Mar 1867 ae: 13y 5m.

Mary D w/o Wm Jr d 10 Jan 1851 ae: 31y.

HAWES, George H s/o C A d 12 Oct 1861 ae: 10w.

HAY, Appleton s/o John d 28 Feb 1866 ae: 64y.

HAYES, Amelia A d/o David d 4 Feb 1880 ae: 8y.

HEALD, Rebecca d 7 Mar 1883 ae: 86y.

HEARN, George S s/o Capt George d 22 Mar 1851 ae: 2y.

HELSON, Jennie d 30 Sep 1876 ae: 22y.

HENLEY, Charles G d 10 Dec 1877 ae: 21y.

HENNESSY, Mary E d/o Wm d 9 May 1881 ae: 29y.

HENNY, Elizabeth d/o Thomas d 27 Feb 1862 ae: 7d.

HENRY, Inf ch/o RB d 27 Mar 1857 ae: 6d.

Margaret w/o Albert d 12 Mar 1881 ae: 23y.

HERBERT, Susannah d/o William d 15 Feb 1866 ae: 3y 5m.

HIGGINS, William C s/o Charles W & Annie F d 21 Mar 1888 ae: 11d.

HILL, Flora A w/o John M d 24 Dec 1879 ae: 30y.

Mary E w/o Abner C d 20 Aug 1871 ae: 28y 4m.

HILLMAN, Henry d 31 Dec 1876 ae: 71y.

HILTON, Alvenus s/o Alvenus d 12 Dec 1860 ae: 8w.

HILTZ, John d 24 Mar 1884 ae: 29y.

HOAR, William H s/o John d 19 Dec 1856 ae: 4y.

HODGES, William s/o William d 30 Jan 1860 ae: 16y.

HODGKINS, Mary A d/o William B d 29 Dec 1863 ae: 9d.

Sarah E d/o Chitman d 14 Jan 1850 ae: 1y.

Sarah P w/o Charles d 29 Jan 1872 ae: 30y.

HOLBROOK, George M s/o James A d 1 Mar 1872 ae: 23y.

HOLLAND, William d 8 Jan 1884 ae: 35y.

HOOPER, Peter d 21 Mar 1861 ae: 48y.

HOSSACK, Susan M d 17 Jan 1888 ae: 47y 6m.

HOWARD, Thomas W d 9 Jan 1871 ae: 41y.

HOWE, Edward d 12 Jan 1877 ae: 93y.

George F d 22 Sep 1891 ae: 38y.

James R d 10 Feb 1863 ae: 33y 6m.

HOWES, Leon C s/o George d 3 Mar 1880 ae: 1y.

HOYT, Helen d/o Wm G d 30 Jan 1863 ae: 19y.

HUBBS, Charles G s/o Capt Alexander d 17 Feb 1858 ae: 29y.

HUDSON, Clara J d/o George d

HUDSON (continued) 18 Nov 1856 ae: 13m.

Frank H s/o James O d 13 Mar 1858 ae: 4m.

Frederick W s/o James O d 9 Jan 1857 ae: 1y 4m.

HUGHES, Henry d 12 Jan 1877 ae: 43y.

HUMPHREY, Henry S s/o Wm d 9 Mar 1894, 51y. "Died Greely Hospital - Insane."

HUNTER, Edith E d 27 Dec 1879 ae: 3y.

Robert R d 1 Mar 1871 ae: 23y 7m.

HURLEY, Thomas B s/o Alexander d 17 Oct 1860 ae: 3m.

HUSE, William Henry s/o William d 26 Feb 1856 ae: 9w.

HUSTON, Abigail w/o Deacon Robert d 4 Jan 1857 ae: 76y. "Native of Eastport, Maine."

Charles B d 27 Oct 1862 ae: 45y.

George F s/o Paul d 18 Dec 1850 ae: 4y.

HUTCHINS, Charlotte W d 1 Mar 1860 ae: 72y.

Elizabeth d 19 Nov 1862 ae: 64y.

HUTCHINSON, Jennie d 28 Apr 1873 ae: 76y.

Ruthie d 7 June 1880 ae: 5m.

JACK, Charles L d 11 Mar 1875 ae: 24y.

Frank s/o Edward d 25 Feb 1876 ae: 20y.

JACKMAN, Woodbury L d 20 Jan 1877 ae: 34y. "Died Gorham, New Hampshire."

JACKSON, Harriet d/o John Black d 14 Jan 1857 ae: 8y.

Pearl L d/o John M d 16 Dec 1882 ae: 5m.

JENSEN, Henry B s/o Henry d 26 Feb 1884 ae: 7w.

William E s/o Anthon & Maggie d 24 Jan 1891 ae: 10d.

JEWELL, Llewellyn d 1 Feb 1856 ae: 62y.

JEWETT, Lewis Blaine s/o George & Alice d 12 Feb 1889 ae: 9m.

JOHNSON, Alice M d 13 Jan 1871

JOHNSON (continued)
ae: 6m.

Almira M d/o Wm D d 15 Dec 1880 ae: 1y.

Amelia d 9 Nov 1899 ae: c70y.

Bertie F s/o Peter B d 23 Jan 1880 ae: 5d.

Charlotte J d/o Wm d 25 Jan 1879 ae: 1y.

Josephine M w/o John J d 24 Jan 1898 ae: 26y 7m.

Margaret H d/o Frank d 28 Feb 1877 ae: 8m.

Robert d 30 Dec 1859 ae: 30y. "Native of London, England."

Robert d 5 Feb 1884 ae: 35y. "Died Greely Hospital."

Rose E d/o David d 22 Jan 1875 ae: 6y.

Stephen s/o Mary E d 9 Jan 1892 ae: 8m 10d.

Susan d 27 Jan 1881 ae: 84y.

Wealthier d 22 Apr 1882 ae: 16y.

William H d 23 Feb 1891 ae: 58y 22m.

JOHNSTON, Charlotte d 2 Jan 1879 ae: 43y.

JONES, Emma d 26 Feb 1870 ae: 9y.

Frances E d/o Charles d 27 Feb 1862 ae: 17y.

Frank L s/o David d 18 Feb 1868 ae: 37y.

Henry d 11 Mar 1876 ae: 60y.

James s/o O C d 6 Jan 1869 ae: 17y.

Margaret d/o David P d 12 Feb 1870 ae: 7y 5m.

Mary A w/o Daniel S d 23 Dec 1879 ae: 52y.

Oliver d 28 Feb 1870 ae: 39y.

JORDAN, Adaline M w/o Wm P d 5 Feb 1861 ae: 32y.

Ernest S s/o Charles H d 2 Jan 1879 ae: 1y.

Frances L d/o Richard L d 8 Mar 1862 ae: 13m.

JOSEPH, Eliza Ann w/o Benjamin d 3 Feb 1879 ae: 66y.

JOSSELYN, Abby Cora d/o Moses F d 16 Sep 1861 ae: 3w.

Samuel R s/o Moses F d 29 Mar

JOSSELYN (continued)
1862 ae: 5y 11d.

JOYCE, Hannah L d 4 Sep 1878 ae: 57y.

JUNKINS, Mabel d/o Henry d 6 Sep 1879 ae: 10m.

KALLOCK, Amaziah d 27 Dec 1884. "Died Marine Hospital."

KELLEY, Mary Ann d/o Michael d 23 Jan 1856 ae: 2y.

KELSEY, Fobes L s/o Samuel M & Maria M d 29 Dec 1887 ae: 1y 7m.

KENTON, Mary d/o Thomas d 4 Feb 1852 ae: 12y.

KILBY, Mary Ann w/o William d 13 Jan 1852 ae: 25y.

KIMBALL, Joseph s/o John d 9 Mar 1861 ae: 49y.

William A s/o William E d 5 Mar 1861 ae: 24y 5m.

KNIGHT, David s/o Daniel d 28 Feb 1859 ae: 1m 14d.

Edward s/o F C d 10 Apr 1862 ae: 1y 6m.

Frances E d/o Eben d 18 Apr 1862 ae: 19y.

John s/o Daniel d 1 Mar 1859 ae: 1m.

John R d 3 Jan 1881 ae: 46y.

KNOX, Mary d 14 June 1882 ae: 84y.

KYLE, Samuel d 7 Feb 1888 ae: 61y.

LANE, Elizabeth d 5 Mar 1881 ae: 72y.

LANG, Nathaniel N d 27 Jan 1861 ae: 38y.

LARRABEE, Charles F s/o William P d 30 Dec 1865 ae: 22y.

Mary E d/o Samuel W d 9 Mar 1856 ae: 1y 8m.

William P s/o S W d 6 Mar 1857 ae: 9m.

LAWRENCE, George d 16 Dec 1880 ae: 19y. "Died Boston, Massachusetts."

LEATHERBORO, Albert s/o John d 8 Feb 1880 ae: 6y.

LEAVITT, L B d/o James A d 9 Dec 1861 ae: 9m.

LEIGHTON, Ann wid/o Samuel d

LEIGHTON (continued)
6 Apr 1886 ae: 54y. "Died Greely Hospital."
Emma F s/o John L d 10 Jan 1880 ae: 1y.
Ernest B s/o Orlando d 20 Aug 1866 ae: 9m.
LELAND, Edward N d 20 Dec 1879 ae: 43y. "Died Greely Hospital."
LEMONT, George M s/o William d 10 Jan 1879 ae: 10m.
LEONARD, Ernest L s/o William L d 6 Feb 1885 ae: 2y.
LEWIS, Elizabeth d 4 Feb 1880 ae: 77y.
LIBBY, Mary E d/o L D d 20 Mar 1857 ae: 3w.
LINDEMAN, Henry F s/o Frank d 25 Jan 1868 ae: 1y 10m.
LINDSEY, Hattie E d 27 Feb 1873 ae: 24y.
LISCOMBE, Frank s/o John d 20 Sep 1857 ae: 5w.
LITTLEFIELD, Thomas d 22 Mar 1875 ae: 45y.
LORD, Clarence s/o George H d 17 Dec 1882 ae: 2y.
George E s/o E Milton d 1 Feb 1887 ae: 33y 3m.
Mary w/o Fred d 9 Mar 1904 ae: 39y.
LORING, Elizabeth d 27 Mar 1857 ae: 42y.
Levi S s/o Sylvester R d 30 Jan 1850 ae: 8y.
LOTHROP, Horatio J d 11 Mar 1852 ae: 5 1/2m.
LOUD, William d 1 Nov 1858 ae: 61y.
LOVEJOY, Annie EH d/o Charles N d 16 Jan 1862 ae: 7y.
LOVETT, William s/o William d 7 Nov 1861 ae: 3y.
LOW, Charles E s/o William A d 10 Apr 1872 ae: 2y 2m.
LOWELL, Thomas W s/o Abner d 4 Mar 1856 ae: 2y 5m.
LOWRE, Ellen d/o William d 28 Mar 1862 ae: 13m.
LUNT, Judah d 10 Mar 1860 ae: 71y. "Died Chelsea, Mass."

LUNT (continued)
Mary J w/o G W B d 23 Feb 1879 ae: 50y.
LUSCOMB, Esther Duffie d/o Capt John d 20 Oct 1858 ae: 2y 6m.
LUTES, John d 12 Dec 1855 ae: 31y. "Native Prince Edwards Island."
LYNDS, James s/o Silas C d 4 Jan 1863 ae: 6y 3m.
MANAGAN, Nancy w/o John d 27 Jan 1850 ae: 31y.
MANCHESTER, George C s/o Isaiah d 27 Dec 1864 ae: 4y 3m.
MANGERSON, William d 18 Jan 1892 ae: 58y. "Died Greely Hospital."
MANSFIELD, Annis s/o Elias d 30 Dec 1857 ae: 3y 2m.
Joseph W d 13 Mar 1878 ae: 60y.
MARINER, Margaret S d/o John B d 2 Feb 1856 ae: 2m.
MARKS, Dominica d/o Bartholomew d 19 Jan 1857 ae: 12y.
MARSTON, Carrie O d/o Samuel H d 23 Feb 1868 ae: 8m.
MARTIN, Charles E s/o Robert d 6 Feb 1851 ae: 3w.
Frank A s/o E d 29 Dec 1861 ae: 1y.
George A s/o Robert d 11 Feb 1852 ae: 3y.
MASON, Caroline B d 5 Mar 1884 ae: 45y.
George A d 16 Nov 1882 ae: 54y.
Irene A w/o William d 10 Feb 1890 ae: 49y.
Leroy s/o George W B d 15 Jan 1877 ae: 1y.
Mary w/o James d 7 Jan 1862 ae: 45y.
MATTHEWS, Isabella d/o William d 11 Feb 1863 ae: 11y 2m.
MAXNER, Henry A d 27 Jan 1891 ae: 46y 8m.
MAYBERRY, Lavinia d 14 Jan 1862 ae: 83y.
MAYNARD, Cornelius d 9 Mar 1856 ae: 63y. "Died in Bos-

MAYNARD (continued)
ton."

Frances W w/o Cornelius D d 4 Mar 1853 ae: 62y.

John W s/o C D d 25 Feb 1851 ae: 13y.

MCALONEY, Annie Viola d/o N Grant d 12 Feb 1892 ae: 1y 5m.

MCAULEY, William d 12 Apr 1883 ae: 14m. "Died Greely Hospital."

MCBANTY, Bridget d 21 Jan 1857 ae: 26y.

MCCOCHRAN, Nehemiah d 15 Mar 1862 ae: 54y.

MCCORMICK, Lizzie B d 28 Jan 1876 ae: 2w.

Robert Francis s/o John d 17 Feb 1860 ae: 2y 3m.

MCDONALD, Charles A s/o Oliver d 5 Jan 1882 ae: 1y.

Simeon E d 7 Feb 1880 ae: 33y. "Died Bartlett, New Hampshire."

MCDONALES, John A d 24 Jan 1875. "Died Russell, Kansas."

MCDOWELL, Rachel wid/o James d 8 Feb 1862 ae: 81y.

MCFARLAND, Edward d 23 Mar 1881 ae: 38y.

Julia I d/o William d 3 Mar 1871 ae: 22y 6m.

MCGEE, Margaret d Dec 1876 ae: 28y. "Died South Boston, Massachusetts."

MCGOWEN, Eva S s/o James d 5 Feb 1875 ae: 9m.

MCGRADY, Marion A d/o Robert E d 14 Feb 1872 ae: 2y 7m.

MCGRAW, James d 7 July 1900 ae: 55y. "Died Greely Hospital."

MCINTOSH, Frederick T s/o George T d 4 Jan 1878 ae: 9m.

MCKENNEY, Ella Mary d/o Moses d 27 Feb 1876 ae: 1y.

MCNEIL, Ella Jane d/o Levi & Ella d 18 Mar 1890 ae: 11y 4m.

MCRAE, Margaret w/o William d 14 Mar 1856 ae: 27y.

MCVICKEN, Jenny d/o John d 28 Jan 1864 ae: 22d.

MEANS, Francis H d/o Thomas d 10 Feb 1851 ae: 5m.

MEGGUIRE, Mattie A w/o John O d 11 Dec 1877 ae: 33y.

MENUS, Mary E d/o Manuel d 26 Sep 1858 ae: 6w.

MERRILL, Henry G s/o William G d 12 Jan 1862 ae: 5y.

Ida F d/o William d 10 Mar 1860 ae: 1y 1m 17d.

Mary W w/o John d 21 Jan 1875 ae: 71y.

MERRY, George A d 11 Feb 1884 ae: 50y.

MESERVY, Charles W s/o Curtis d 21 Feb 1851 ae: 17y.

Isabella d/o John d 25 Jan 1852 ae: 6y.

METCALF, Lillian Mary d/o Nathan H d 6 Jan 1891 ae: 1y 6m 8d.

MILLER, Angus s/o James d 7 Mar 1883 ae: 30y.

Charles B s/o Charles G d 29 June 1862 ae: 14m.

MILLIKEN, Charles s/o Warren d 11 Feb 1872 ae: 14y.

Francis s/o Phineas d 25 Mar 1877 ae: 77y.

MITCHELL, Maria E d 28 Oct 1866 ae: 36y.

Sarah E S d/o Lewis d 15 Mar 1851 ae: 1y.

William B s/o Ephraim d 28 Feb 1869 ae: 5y 3m.

MONTEITH, William d 28 Mar 1890 ae: 80y.

MONTGOMERY, Nellie E S d/o Charles W d 28 Jan 1871 ae: 9m 14d.

MOORE, Abbie D d/o Harry d 20 Nov 1864 ae: 3y 5m.

MORGAN, Inf ch/o John d 23 Dec 1861 ae: 3d.

Sarah Sophia d/o Theophilas d 28 Jan 1862 ae: 3y 9m.

MORRISON, Clarence B d 31 Mar 1891 ae: 11m.

Hannah E w/o William E d 17 Feb 1882 ae: 41y. "Died Bos-

MORRISON (continued)
ton, Massachusetts."
Lenore L d/o Martin d 18 Aug 1866 ae: 3w.
MORSE, Charles B s/o Jonathan K d 4 Dec 1851 ae: 20y 9m.
Ephraim d 16 Mar 1869 ae: 4y 7m.
Frances E d/o David C d 27 Dec 1851 ae: 9m.
Sarah E d 11 Jan 1859 ae: 22y.
MORTON, James E d 6 Dec 1882 ae: 75y.
MOTHERWELL, Ellen w/o John d 10 Feb 1865 ae: 18y 4m.
MOULTON, James W d 16 Jan 1862 ae: 37y.
William d 26 Jan 1859 ae: 33y. "Died at the hospital."
MUNROE, Eva d/o William H d 30 Apr 1885 ae: 30y.
MURPHY, Ida d/o John d 22 Jan 1864 ae: 1y 5m.
MURRAY, John s/o John d 21 Feb 1856 ae: 11m.
William d 27 Dec 1883 ae: 50y.
MUSANS, Alice R w/o Capt C F d 17 Nov 1856 ae: 36y.
Charles F s/o Charles d 17 Feb 1857 ae: 6m.
NASON, Amy A w/o William d 2 Jan 1879 ae: 54y.
NELSON, Andrew P d 6 Mar 1891 ae: 50y. "Died Worcester, Massachusetts."
John W d 18 Jan 1864 ae: 46y.
NEWBEGIN, Charles W d 13 Dec 1851.
Samuel B s/o Capt David d 16 Jan 1861 ae: 37y.
Theodore C s/o David d 11 Dec 1851 ae: 2y 7m.
NEWMAN, Ellen d 25 Jan 1871 ae: 81y.
NEWTON, Rev Gideon J d 17 Feb 1859 ae: 71y 6m.
Willie E s/o Charles B d 22 Feb 1876 ae: 1w.
NICHOLS, Grenville Cornelius s/o N Gilman d 22 Apr 1860 ae: 13m.
Hattie B d/o Frederick W d 10

NICHOLS (continued)
Jan 1868 ae: 13m.
NICHERSON, Charles C s/o Leander C d 21 Jan 1860 ae: 3m.
NICKOLS, Jacob d 23 Feb 1876 ae: 64y.
NIELSON, Kreston d 24 Jan 1888 ae: 52y.
NIXON, George S d 30 Dec 1876 ae: 59y.
William E s/o George d 22 Jan 1880 ae: 2y.
NOBLE, Lizzie d/o A A d 9 Feb 1863 ae: 3m 27d.
NORRIS, Betsy A d 15 Mar 1852 ae: 3m.
Ella d/o Lucas d 3 Mar 1856 ae: 10m 9d.
NOWELL, Patty w/o Moses d 7 Jan 1852 ae: 78y.
William G s/o Cyrus & Henrietta d 12 Sep 1857 ae: 5m.
NOYES, James L s/o Moses d 3 Mar 1859 ae: 65y.
O'BRIEN, Joseph F s/o Ella d 18 Mar 1886 ae: 1y. "Died in the Alms House."
OFFEN, Ethel M s/o Albert C d 16 Feb 1880 ae: 10m. "Died Greely Hospital."
George E s/o Robert C & Mary A d 29 Jan 1889 ae: 12d.
O'HARA, Margaret w/o William d 9 Jan 1864.
O'HAREN, Fanny d 7 Mar 1859 ae: 8y.
OLES, David d 6 Jan 1851 ae: 42y. "Died in Boston."
ORCHARD, Elizabeth A w/o John d 5 Dec 1882 ae: 56y.
ORR, Charles C d 9 Feb 1880 ae: 3y.
OTIS, Frank s/o John d 8 Nov 1860 ae: 7m 9d.
OWEN, Rebecca d 22 Jan 1862 ae: 79y.
PAGE, Mary d 28 May 1883.
William W s/o Julia A d 12 Mar 1863 ae: 14y 5m.
PARKER, Annie L d/o Eleazer H d 8 Apr 1861 ae: 8y 8m.

PARKER (continued)

Chester Harris s/o Nathaniel d 23 Apr 1861 ae: 19m.

Edgar d 4 Jan 1859 ae: 29y.

Nathalia d/o Nathaniel d 22 Apr 1856 ae: 2y 9m.

Sarah J w/o Charles d 17 Mar 1882 ae: 34y.

PARSONS, Joseph B s/o Samuel N d 8 Apr 1873 ae: 45y.

Mary Ellen d/o Thomas B d 2 Jan 1861 ae: 15m.

PEACHY, Lavina w/o Peter d 9 Feb 1865 ae: 49y.

PEARSON, Judson S s/o Jacob d 24 Nov 1858 ae: 26y. "Died at Niagara Falls."

PENNELL, Anna d/o William d 15 Jan 1866 ae: 10d.

Caroline w/o Charles d 9 Jan 1857 ae: 25y.

Charles W d 23 Sep 1851 ae: 38y.

Margaret A w/o George H d 19 Dec 1861 ae: 27y.

PERKINS, Lucy A w/o John d 6 Jan 1884 ae: 60y.

PERLEY, Charles s/o John d 29 Jan 1852 ae: 1y.

Joseph H s/o Joseph H d 18 Dec 1862 ae: 20y.

PETERS, Arelia d/o WmW d 19 Feb 1863 ae: 23y.

PETERSON, Christina M d/o O W d 18 Dec 1880 ae: 3y.

George S s/o Nelson d 22 Mar 1877.

PETTES, Capt John d 9 Mar 1856 ae: 70y.

PHARO, Ephraim d 8 Dec 1863 ae: 32y. "Died in New York."

PHELPS, Abigail d 19 Mar 1863 ae: 30y.

PHENIX, John H s/o John C d 18 Dec 1857 ae: 13m.

PHILLIPS, Jordan J s/o Leander d 15 Feb 1876 ae: 6w.

PIERCE, Melvina d/o James Carter d 2 Mar 1894 ae: 48y 10m.

PILLSBURY, George L d 14 Jan 1877 ae: 25y.

PINE, Lena M s/o James A d 25 Sep 1880 ae: 1y.

PLIMPTON, Elias M d 8 Apr 1876 ae: 68y.

PLUMMER, Mary wid/o Joseph d 28 Jan 1856 ae: 90y 6m.

Mary Isabel d/o Charles M d 19 Feb 1856 ae: 6y 8m.

William d 24 Feb 1854 ae: 53y.

POND, John B d 8 Feb 1860 ae: 37y.

POOLE, Maggie C d/o John C d 6 Mar 1858 ae: 10m.

POOR, Frank M s/o Charles B d 1 Jan 1877 ae: 6m.

PORTER, Clifford E s/o John d 4 Apr 1875 ae: 3y. "Died Cambridge, Massachusetts."

Frederick D s/o Albert W d 30 Mar 1864 ae: 10m.

POTTER, Henry Reed d 2 Jan 1862 ae: 34y.

POWERS, Ishabod d 20 Dec 1851 ae: 30y.

Lizzie H d/o William d 23 Feb 1876 ae: 10m.

PRATT, Betsy C d 3 Feb 1871 ae: 88y 9m.

PRESLEY, William H d 29 Jan 1875 ae: 17y.

PRICHARD, Augusta w/o Joseph d 27 Dec 1864 ae: 27y 10m.

PRIDHAM, Walter EW s/o James H d 21 July 1871 ae: 11m.

PRIME, Thomas H A d 28 Jan 1859 ae: 35y.

PRINCE, Harriet C d 28 Feb 1869 ae: 36y 3m.

Mary E d/o Albion d 7 Mar 1861 ae: 20y.

Matilda W w/o William H d 18 Jan 1870 ae: 70y.

QUILL, Mary d/o John d 25 Jan 1857 ae: 1y 9m.

QUIMBY, Anne M w/o William M d 9 Jan 1857 ae: 25y.

Henrietta d/o Charles O d 19 Sep 1858 ae: 2y.

William B s/o William M d 1 Jan 1857 ae: 21d.

QUINCY, Caroline M d/o Samuel

QUINCY (continued)
d 19 Jan 1869 ae: 66y.
Henry d 28 Jan 1879 ae: 78y.
QUINN, Sarah w/o John d 27 Dec
1876 ae: 78y.
RAMSDELL, Carrie E d/o Joseph
d 11 Jan 1872 ae: 3w.
RAND, Edward W A d 19 Feb
1885 ae: 37y.
RANDALL, George E s/o Samuel
W d 13 Feb 1885 ae: 21y.
John d 1 Mar 1871 ae: 57y.
Sumner C s/o John C d 19 Mar
1858 ae: 16y.
RANSON, Josephine d/o John d 9
Feb 1857 ae: 4m.
RAY, John Joseph d 15 Dec 1859
ae: 1w.
READ, Rufus d 12 Feb 1879 ae:
83y.
REDLON, Mehitable d 10 Feb
1858 ae: 81y.
REED, Earle G s/o Helen d 5 Jan
1873 ae: 2y.
James W s/o Edward d 2 Feb
1878 ae: 1y.
REMICK, George d 27 Dec 1879
ae: 75y.
Lydia May d/o A M d 17 Dec
1886 ae: 2m 22d.
RHODES, Grace C s/o Anthonie d
12 Mar 1881 ae: 9m.
Harriet J Wilson w/o William K
d 16 Jan 1861 ae: 28y.
Lizzie d 16 July 1884.
RICE, George A d/o late Luther d
24 Mar 1862 ae: 21y.
RICH, Rosanna w/o Joseph C d 5
Mar 1852 ae: 50y.
RICHARDS, Dora Butler d/o Vin-
cent d 14 Mar 1882 ae: 6y.
Lydia M d/o Samuel d 29 Feb
1856 ae: 8y.
RICHARDSON, Alice Florence d
10 Oct 1858 ae: 1y 7m.
Elizabeth L w/o James A d 6
Jan 1875 ae: 45y.
Sarah d 22 Mar 1884 ae: 42y.
"Died Greely Hospital."
RICHTER, Susannah P d 29 Dec
1890 ae: 84y 6m.
RICKER, Ezra W s/o Andrew J d

RICKER (continued)
8 Sep 1871 ae: 1y 14d.
Frank Hall s/o Robert E d 3 Mar
1860 ae: 2y 11m.
Richard M s/o Erastis d 26 Mar
1869 ae: 33y.
RIGGS, Thomas H s/o James H d
16 Jan 1883 ae: 2y.
RILEY, Barney d 16 Dec 1859 ae:
71y.
Thomas s/o Patrick d 18 Jan
1860 ae: 16d.
ROACH, James d 5 Mar 1891 ae:
47y.
ROBERTS, Mary Angeline d/o
Charles W d 18 Feb 1856 ae: 4
1/2y.
Mary W d/o Elizabeth Wiswell,
w/o Charles W d 14 Feb 1859
ae: 38y 5m.
Thomas J d 12 Mar 1870 ae: 46y.
William H d 26 Fen 1875 ae:
47y.
ROBERTSON, Charles s/o James
& Agnes d 17 Apr 1892 ae:
18d. "Murdered."
David W s/o Frank d 16 Feb
1880 ae: 7m. "Died Greely
Hospital."
Harriet A d/o Alfred d 2 Mar
1856 ae: 7w.
ROBINSON, Bessie M d/o WmF
d 25 Mar 1884 ae: 2y.
Elizabeth w/o William d 15 Feb
1867 ae: 27y.
ROGERS, Mary Jane d/o Daniel d
18 Feb 1860 ae: 8d.
Sarah d/o George W d 2 Feb
1860 ae: 32y.
ROLF, Cora Isabel d/o William d
4 Nov 1871 ae: 1y 2m 14d.
ROLLINS, Priscilla d 8 Jan 1860
ae: 54y.
RONSOR, Frederick s/o Joseph d
17 Dec 1850 ae: 5y.
ROSS, Ernest s/o Martha J d 24
Jan 1875 ae: 5d.
Thomas T s/o late John d 31
Mar 1856 ae: 17y.
RUGGS, George s/o William d 11
Sep 1860 ae: 2y.
RUMERY, Abby H w/o James L

RUMERY (continued)
d 6 Mar 1860 ae: 31y.

RUSSELL, Joseph s/o Joseph d 10 Mar 1852 ae: 11d.

RYALL, Charles J s/o William & Abbie d 27 Feb 1890 ae: 1d.

SABINE, Nancy E w/o WmA d 26 Jan 1860 ae: 31y.

SAMPLES, Rufus s/o Francis d 4 Mar 1863 ae: 1y 4m.

SANBORN, Carrie May d/o Winfield & Susie d 9 Mar 1888 ae: 6y 1m.

SANFORD, Thomas d 1 Mar 1860 ae: 60y.

SARSTROFF, Henry d 3 Mar 1853 ae: 55y.

SAWYER, Abraham d 20 Feb 1877 ae: 65y.

Alice W d/o Joshua W d 22 Mar 1862 ae: 2y.

Ellen d 27 Feb 1881 ae: 73y.

Hannah w/o William d 22 Mar 1856 ae: 62y.

Hattie d/o George F d 15 Feb 1870 ae: 4w.

Minnie H d/o Melville d 28 Jan 1880 ae: 5m.

Philip Bryant s/o George d 4 Mar 1891 ae: 11w.

William H s/o Moses H d 24 Oct 1862 ae: 9m 19d.

SCHAEFFER, Carrie L w/o George H d 4 Dec 1890 ae: 36y.

SCOTT, James L d 20 Mar 1875 ae: 25y.

Mary w/o William d 8 Feb 1858 ae: 38y.

Olive E d 12 Mar 1875 ae: 4m.

SEARLE, Charles Francis s/o Frank W d 30 Apr 1893 ae: 4d.

SEARS, Henry L s/o Emma A d 29 Mar 1883 ae: 5d. "Died Greely Hospital."

SENATE, Franklin s/o John d 22 Jan 1850 ae: 4y.

SHARPS, William d 7 Feb 1884 ae: 25y.

SHAW, Benjamin M S s/o Alvah T d 13 Jan 1862 ae: 5y 10m.

John C d 6 Mar 1852 ae: 47y.

SHERWOOD, Mabel d/o Charles d 27 Jan 1880 ae: 1y.

Maggie d/o Charles d 24 Jan 1880 ae: 4y.

SILUS, Lovina d/o William d 2 Mar 1860 ae: 10d.

SIMPSON, Albert s/o George d 5 Oct 1862 ae: 1y.

Robert s/o George d 4 Oct 1862 ae: 1y.

SKELTON, Burton M s/o David J d 8 Mar 1877 ae: 2y. "Died Boston, Massachusetts."

SKILLIN, Otis H d 4 Mar 1887 ae: 48y. "Died Boston, Massachusetts."

SKILLINGS, Albert T s/o John d 9 Oct 1861 ae: 3m.

Amos B s/o Ebenezer d 19 Jan 1862 ae: 17y.

Edward P s/o Silas d 25 Mar 1863 ae: 3y 6m.

George S s/o Joseph T d 17 Jan 1856 ae: 8y 6m.

SLIGHT, Martha Florence d/o Geo C d 23 Oct 1860 ae: 4y 7m.

SMALL, Abby d/o Charles d 8 Feb 1878 ae: 9y.

Harold G s/o John d 10 Apr 1876 ae: 9m.

Peter H s/o E H d 5 Feb 1871 ae: 47y 20d.

SMITH, Albert G d 7 Sep 1849 ae: 27y. "First body placed in City Tomb."

Charles D s/o Frank A d 27 Feb 1871 ae: 7y 1m.

Charles N d 30 Jan 1878 ae: 20y.

Eliza J w/o Thomas d 1 Feb 1891 ae: 53y 2m.

Ellen w/o Charles d 10 Mar 1873 ae: 53y.

SOMERS, George T s/o John & Anna d 12 Feb 1880 ae: 5y. "Died Greely Hospital."

SOULE, Ernest s/o Enoch d 18 Sep 1867 ae: 10m.

George W s/o Wm H d 15 Dec 1876 ae: 8m.

SPAULDING, John D d 7 Mar 1880 ae: 78y.

SPOFFORD, Nancy J d/o Joseph d 20 Mar 1856 ae: 19y.

SPOONER, Dolly d 1 Mar 1853 ae: 80y.

SPRAGUE, Manuel d 30 Jan 1873 ae: 4m.

SPRING, Mary A w/o William GJ d 15 Jan 1863 ae: 42y.

STACKPOLE, James d 7 Apr 1862 ae: 70y.

STANORTH, Charles W s/o Joseph F d 19 Mar 1863 ae: 4y 9m.

STAPLES, Charles d 20 Jan 1877 ae: 63y.

George A s/o Nelson A d 27 Dec 1879 ae: 4m.

STARBIRD, Thomas E s/o Thomas d 23 Jan 1859 ae: 5m 9d.

STEARNS, Josephine G d/o Wm B d 3 Sep 1856 ae: 2y.

STEEL, James d 11 Jan 1864 ae: 43y. "Native of Scotland."

STEELE, Lewis A d/o Thomas L d 8 Mar 1875 ae: 3m.

STEVENS, Eben R s/o Edward d 5 Nov 1861 ae: 15y.

Mary E d/o Isaac d 1 Mar 1861 ae: 1y 5m.

Nancy W w/o Luther G d 22 Dec 1858 ae: 59y 9m.

Sally wid/o Samuel d 13 Jan 1856 ae: 65y.

Sophia B w/o Isaac d 29 Mar 1862 ae: 36y.

STEVENSON, Janet d 18 Jan 1883 ae: 55y.

STEWART, Bertha d 12 Apr 1886 ae: 20y. "Died Greely Hospital."

Bertie R s/o Wm H d 12 Jan 1880 ae: 2y.

STINSON, Alexander d 28 Mar 1884. "Died Greely Hospital."

STRATTON, Mary Ann d/o Wm T d 21 Jan 1863 ae: 7y.

STROUT, John W s/o Charles d 13 Dec 1862 ae: 2y 4m.

STUBBS, Mary E w/o Alexander A d 4 Feb 1867 ae: 36y.

STURDIVANT, Willie Fulton s/o

STURDIVANT (continued)
Henry W & Anna L d 21 Jan 1871.

STYLES, James d 25 Dec 1867 ae: 68y.

SURRAT, William M d 6 Jan 1884 ae: 42y.

SWETT, ch/o Mrs Clara d 27 Dec 1860 ae: 3w.

Fanny S d/o George d 4 Mar 1862 ae: 11m.

Rufus O s/o Rufus d 1 Feb 1872 ae: 21y.

Thomas s/o George L d 22 Feb 1862 ae: 11m.

SYLVESTER, Asbury C d 17 Feb 1891 ae: 49y.

Helen Frances d/o David M d 16 Mar 1869 ae: 4y 7m.

SYMONDS, Annie E d/o Samuel T d 10 Aug 1857 ae: 11m 17d.

Nelly d/o James d 27 Dec 1858 ae: 16m.

TALBOT, Benjamin A s/o Elbridge P d 18 Feb 1857 ae: 6y 7m.

Emeline L d/o Elbridge T d 25 Jan 1864 ae: 16y.

Mary w/o Abraham d 27 Feb 1857 ae: 59y. Black.

TANNER, Kate d 17 Feb 1880 ae: 3m. "Died Boston, Massachusetts."

TARBOX, Flora E d 6 Jan 1880 ae: 25y.

TAYLOR, Eliza d 6 Dec 1880 ae: 41y. "Died Chelsea, Massachusetts."

TEATSON, Willie E s/o Algernon D d 3 Mar 1873 ae: 2y.

THATCHER, Harriet H d 19 Feb 1883 ae: 74y.

THOMAS, Henry C s/o Charles D d 10 Jan 1856 ae: 8y 9m.

John J s/o William d 12 Feb 1870 ae: 1y 8m.

Porter G s/o Frank E d 15 Feb 1879 ae: 3m.

THOMPSON, Frank H d 13 Jan 1860 ae: 7w.

Freddie s/o Elisha d 13 Jan 1873 ae: 6d.

THOMPSON (continued)

James d 25 Feb 1857 ae: 70y. "Native of London, England."

Lois A d/o Lydia A Furbush, w/o William d 14 Dec 1856 ae: 25y.

Mary d/o Nathaniel d 23 Dec 1851 ae: 2y 6m.

Mary w/o Nathaniel d 19 Feb 1852 ae: 29y 8m.

THORNDIKE, Mary E d/o Joseph H d 14 Feb 1871 ae: 3y 8m.

TIBBETTS, Charles d 21 Dec 1883 ae: 83y.

TIFTON, Nicholas d 4 Dec 1871 ae: 68y 9m.

TILDEN, Henry B d 7 Apr 1870 ae: 70y.

TILSON, Joseph d 18 Jan 1885 ae: 76y.

TODD, Sarah Tappen w/o John d 1 Apr 1872 ae: 88y.

T S s/o Royal B d 26 Jan 1871 ae: 6y 6m.

TOLMAN, Cordelia d/o Horace d 10 Jan 1852 ae: 14y.

Sarah d 4 Mar 1856 ae: 77y.

TORREY, Charles Henry s/o Mary Ann d 17 Feb 1861 ae: 10d.

TRAVERS, Linwood C s/o Lemuel d 25 Feb 1868 ae: 1y 26d.

TREFETHEN, Joseph d 23 Mar 1884 ae: 69y.

Nathan W s/o John d 17 Jan 1886 ae: 1y 10m.

Robert W d 22 Feb 1862 ae: 21y.

TROTT, Charles d 31 Dec 1893 ae: 49y. "Died Marine Hospital."

TRUE, Arthur L s/o Charles H d 4 July 1882 ae: 1y. "Died Old Orchard, Maine."

TRUNDY, Albert E s/o Hannah d 16 Dec 1876 ae: 5m.

TUKESBURY, Georgianna E w/o Erwin M d 4 June 1882 ae: 36y.

TURNER, Annie E w/o Roy P d 1 Jan 1894 ae: 23y.

Helen H d/o Henry K d 13 Feb 1859 ae: 6y 10m.

VAN, James Black d 23 Mar 1858 ae: 40y.

VANKLEEK, Joanna d 12 Oct 1857 ae: 64y.

VEAZIE, Albert E d 11 Feb 1884 ae: 41y.

VERRILL, Eleanor M d/o Charles d 20 Sep 1878 ae: 7w.

WADE, Annie M d/o Samuel R d 16 Dec 1883 ae: 7m.

WAITE, Frank s/o Reuben d 1 Jan 1869 ae: 19y.

Nancy w/o Solomon d 22 Mar 1852 ae: 57y.

WALKER, Andrew J d 2 Jan 1866 ae: 29y.

Mary K wid/o Robert d 27 Jan 1866 ae: 67y.

WALSH, Hannah M w/o Thomas d 22 Apr 1876 ae: 70y.

WALTON, Martha E d/o Simeon d 21 Jan 1852 ae: 6m.

WARREN, Patrick d 24 Mar 1883 ae: 35y. "Died Greely Hospital."

WASHINGTON, Elizabeth A d/o George I d 4 Mar 1877 ae: 19m.

WATERHOUSE, Franklin s/o Nathaniel d 19 Dec 1857 ae: 6y.

Leon S s/o Winfield S d 5 Feb 1873 ae: 18m.

WATERMAN, Anthony d 17 Apr 1860 ae: 56y.

WATSON, Ivy E d/o George W & Sarah E d 10 Mar 1888 ae: 1y 3m.

WEBBER, Betsy w/o Jonathan d 15 Feb 1866 ae: 72y.

WEBSTER, George T s/o Charles F d 18 Dec 1849 ae: 6y.

WEEKS, Mary M w/o Joseph d 18 Jan 1875 ae: 32y.

WELKEN, John C d 4 Jan 1864 ae: 60y. "Died on board SS *North America*."

WENTWORTH, Henry S d 27 Dec 1859 ae: 14y.

Thomas C S Black s/o Job L d 15 Feb 1858 ae: 15y 10m. "Died New Gloucester, Me."

WESCOTT, Charles H s/o William H d 2 Mar 1861 ae: 2m.

George A s/o David d 1 Mar 1859 ae: 3y 6w.

Willie J s/o John d 31 Jan 1881 ae: 20y.

WEST, William E s/o Manuel d 16 Oct 1857 ae: 6m 16d.

WESTON, Isaac Henry d 1 Feb 1861 ae: 31y 7m.

William T s/o Wm d 5 Apr 1868 ae: 5m.

WHEELER, Willard d 22 Jan 1885 ae: 25y.

WHITE, Charles d 6 Mar 1884 ae: 50y.

Henry s/o Frank E d 5 Aug 1871 ae: 5m.

Robert S d 12 Dec 1880 ae: 59y.

Sarah J d/o Tristram d 21 Dec 1864 ae: 4w.

WHITTIER, George W d 27 Dec 1872 ae: 30y.

WIGGINS, Greenleaf d 23 Dec 1851 ae: 45y.

WIGHT, Robert s/o James R d 5 Feb 1880 ae: 5m.

WILBER, Charles A s/o Rufus A d 3 Dec 1862 ae: 2y 9m.

WILDER, Alice A C d/o Henry H d 15 Mar 1869 ae: 7m 14d.

WILKINSON, Joseph B s/o DR d 10 Mar 1891 ae: 7m.

WILLARD, Rhoda F w/o Daniel d 26 Feb 1858 ae: 20y 8m.

WILLEY, Sabra A d 12 Mar 1878 ae: 83y. "Died Chelsea, Massachusetts."

WILLIAMS, Althea s/o James C d 9 Mar 1877 ae: 4y.

John W d 11 Jan 1883 ae: 56y.

Louisa M w/o Jancob d 7 July 1857 ae: 35y.

Royal d 28 Jan 1882 ae: 73y. "Died Brooklyn, New York."

WILSON, Isabella d/o Janson d 11 Dec 1851 ae: 3y.

Rebecca w/o James d 18 Feb 1856 ae: 66y. "Died Cape Elizabeth, Maine."

WINCH, Mary E w/o Benjamin M d 9 Feb 1880 ae: 41y.

Robert s/o James d 19 Mar 1875 ae: 4d.

WINSHIP, Samuel F s/o Edward d 21 Nov 1860 ae: 13m.

WINSLOW, Charles d 3 Mar 1856 ae: 42y.

WITHAN, John W s/o Asa H d 27 Feb 1864 ae: 3y.

WOOD, Elizabeth A d 10 Jan 1876 ae: 52y.

Georgie T s/o John G d 22 Jan 1880 ae: 3y.

WOODWARD, Almira wid/o Moses d 12 Mar 1862 ae: 49y.

Moses d 18 Dec 1852 ae: 40y 1m 27d.

WOODWORTH, Silas M d 25 Mar 1876 ae: 24y.

WRIGHT, Charles H s/o Dr Kendall d 10 Oct 1857 ae: 4y 6m.

Sarah w/o Joshua d 17 Feb 1886 ae: 26y. "Died Cushing's Island."

YEATON, ch/o John d 29 Jan 1861 ae: 3m.

YORK, Eleanor w/o Charles d 10 Jan 1888 ae: 85y 6m.

James K d 21 Mar 1875 ae: 44y.

Levi d 28 Jan 1860 ae: 57y.

YOUNG, Elizabeth d 21 Jan 1884 ae: 82y.

Mary d 9 Dec 1876 ae: 55y. "Died Dexter, Maine."

INDEX

This cross-index lists people buried in the main text and the appendices. When looking for a name, check the alphabetized main text and each appendix as well as this index.

COX, Dorcas 94 Kerenhappuck
(Happy) 137
COYLE, J B 35 97
CRANDALL, Philip 50
CROCKETT, Benj 92 Daniel 130
CROOKER, Alden 68 Delphina 68
CUMPSTON, Mr 149
CUSHING, Miss 22
CUSHMAN, Lydia 147
DANA, David 2 N L 126
DAVIS, Ebenezer 89 Mehitable
Griffin 89
DEAN, J 90
DEANE, Sarah P 136
DEERING, Anna Dunn 91 James
153
DENNISON, John 17 37 Mary 93
DODGE, Ruth 125 Thomas 125
128
DOWNER, J 147
DRINKWATER, Frances C 27
DUBOIS, Charlotte A 137
DUGUID, Elizabeth 119
DUPREE, Henry F 31 J S 31 John
31
EUSTIS, Mary 2
EVANS, Caroline E 20 Estwick 20
Sally 20
EVERETT, O 95
FERNALD, A 121 144
FESSENDEN, Samuel 45
FICKETT, Elliot 126
FINLEY, Matthew 76
FINNEY, Mother 3
FLETT, John 89 Margaret 151
FLOYD, Gardner 11 Hannah 11
Harriet Lavina 11
FOLSOM, Lucretia Ann 145 Mar-
tha O 145
FORD, Emma 41 Nabby 41
FOSDICK, Sarah A 38
FOSTER, Eleanor 27 Mr 41
FOWLE, John 48 Mary 48
FOX, Jabez 102 Mary 102
Prudence 143
FREEMAN, James 62 Mary 22
Rev 46 Thos 127
FRENCH, C 67 98
FROTHINGHAM, Hannah J 141 J
58 John 114 Stephen 141
FURBUSH, Lois A 188 Lydia A
188

GAGE, Lucy 67
GOODWIN, Emily 109
GOOLD, R 55
GRAY, Sarah 160
GREELY, E 19
GREENLEAF, Sarah 30
GRIFFIN, Edward 140 Mehitable
89
HALEY, Joel 105
HALL, Harriet 39
HAMLIN, Emeline 170 John 170
HANCOCK, Margaret 150
HARDING, Mary C 142 William
35
HARMON, A 128
HARRIS, Prudence 143
HARTSHORN, Caroline E 88 Wil-
liam 88
HARVEY, William see WIL-
LIAMS Peter 152
HASKELL, Alexander N 105
Elizabeth 105 Georgianna 105
HAYES, Mrs 150
HERRICK, Miss 121
HEWITT, Catherine 45 Dr 45
HILL, John C 77 Olive 77
HOBSON, Mary 4
HOLT, Mary 58 Moses Jr 58
HOOD, Elmira K 121
HOULE, Mary 154 William 154
HOY, William 126
HOYT, Sarah 56
HUDSON, Martha 29
ILSLEY, Elizabeth 48 Enoch 48
Lucy 144
IRISH, Mary 110
JACOBS, Elias 146
JERRIS, Wm 71
JONES, Ann Hodge 47 Elizabeth
48 Hannah 145 Pierson 48
JORDAN, James 83 90 Olive
Plaisted 128
KENT, Sarah 145
KING, Mary 12
KNAPP, Anthony 137 Dolly 137
Hannah M 137
KNIGHT, Abigail 147 Benjamin
89 Harriet E 89 Isabella H 44
Mary 89 Mary J 106 William
76
LEONARD, C E 48
LEWIS, Nabby C 52

LIBBY, Elliot 42 N 144
LONGFELLOW, Tabitha 131
LORD, Samuel 34
LORING, A 82 Betsy 98
LOWELL, Lydia 68
MACK, Andrew 125 Arthur 69
MARBLE, Nancy 96
MARSTIN, G R 53
MARSTON, Z 20
MARTIN, J 40 Sarah 30 William 45
MARWICK, Nancy 98
MASON, Hannah 105 Johanna 72 Joseph 72 Josie M 72
MCGEORGE, Margaret 169 Thomas 169
MCKEARNEY, Frank see PIERCE Frank 162
MCLEAN, Allon 46
MCLELLAN, Elizabeth Ann 34 Jane 47 Thomas 34
MCLOUDE, Anna 158 Kenneth 158
MCMANNUS, Harriet 2
MENDON, Hannah 154
MERRILL, Joseph 151
MILK, Abigail 70 James 140 Martha 140 Sarah Brown 140
MILLICAN, Alexander 63 Mary A 63 Sarah 63
MILLS, Mrs Jonas 131
MINOT, Thomas 92
MITCHELL, Elizabeth 54 James R 55 136 Lucretia 33 Olive 39 Rebecca 4 Sophia A 136
MOODY, Daniel S 19 59 Dorcas 114 Lucy 79 Mary 96
MOTLEY, Emma 3 Mrs 81
MOUNTFORD, Daniel 145
MULLEN, Catherine 90
MURCH, Harriet A 95 Judith I 35
MUSSEY, Elizabeth 58 John 143 Mary 96
NEWALL, Harriet 107
NILES, Abraham 22
NOBLE, John 117
NORTH, Elizabeth 112
NORTON, Aaron 20 Josiah 135 154 Mary E 108 Thomas 108
NOYES, Elizabeth 85 Jacob 133
OSTINELLI, Sophia 63
OXNARD, E 132 M 24 Mary 147

OXNARD (continued)
Sarah 147 Thomas 84 147
PAINE, Mercy 83
PATTEN, Ezekiel 62
PAYSON, Ann Louisa 113
PEARSON, Anne 140 Eunice 36 Lois 48
PENNELL, Cynthia E 15 J 105
PETER, E T 150
PHILLIPS, John 85 Wm 107
PITT, Mary D 45 William 45
PLUMMER, Abigail 37 Francis 81 Mary Ann S 37 Moses 37
POLAND, Joseph 64
POOLE, J 128
PORTER, Aaron 150 151
POTE, Mary 101
PREBLE, J 30 Jedediah 102 Martha 102 Mehitable 116 Statira 27
PRENTISS, Sarah 101
PRINCE, Irene 5 Tristram G 5
QUINCY, Ann 108 Elizabeth Wingate 24
RACKLEFF, James 112
RAMSEY, Mary L 15
RANDALL, Elizabeth 151 Job 10
REA, Mrs 115
REED, Abbie Rollins 16 Hiram 16 Lucy 74 Mary A 16
RIGGS, Jacob 71 136 137
ROBINSON, Mrs 66 Wm 149
ROGERS, Patience 48
ROPES, George 154
RUSSWURM, John 19
SANBORN, Dora C 142
SENTER, John 49
SHAPLEY, Prince 73
SHAW, Lucy 94 Sally 140
SHERWOOD, Helen 144
SIMONTON, James 25 Lucy 25 Mary 25
SMITH, David 17 Eliza S 130 Moses 75 131 Sarah 27 Thomas 27
SOULE, Timothy 22
SOUTHGATE, Mary King 12
STACY, Mrs 34
STANFORD, Elizabeth 143 Harry 143 Margaret Irving 143
STANIFORD, Lucy 146 Sarah 140
STANORTH, Capt 130

STARBIRD, John 35 Mary 35
STARBUCK, Molly 84
STETSON, Lewis 129
STEVENS, Eliza 23 Mary A 9
STEWART, Jonathan 49
STOCKMAN, Sarah 155
STROUT, Abraham 176
STURDEVANT, Cyrus 135
STURDIVANT, Isaac 28 J 38
SWANTON, Mary 109
SWEETSIR, Abigail 142
SWIFT, Martha 15
TATE, Ann 70 Elizabeth 2
THACHER, Fear 52
THATCHER, Sarah 54
THAXTER, Joseph 8 Mr 32
THOMAS, Elizabeth 143 William
41
THORPE, Elizabeth A 7 Stillman
7
THURLO, Ann 151 Fanny 80 John
151 Rebecca 151
TITCOMB, Anne 61 Benjamin 61
Elizabeth 61 Henry 91 116
Sarah 105 William 105
TODD, Sarah 49 Susan 133
TORREY, Mary Ann 77 78 Mary
Ann Griffin 77 78 Midian 77 78
TREAT, J 54
TUCKER, D 141 Daniel 66 Dorcas
66 109 Lydia 66
TYNG, Sarah 128
WADSWORTH, John 98 Sarah 98
WAITE, Emma 96 John 96
Rebecca 139
WALSH, E 100

WARREN, Jennet 8
WASHBURN, Priscilla 99
WATERHOUSE, Alice Ilsley 32
Hannah 176 Israel 32 J M 108
Wm 133
WATTLES, Sophia 110
WEBB, Mary 39
WEBSTER, Elizabeth J 167 Eph-
raim G 167 Nathan 43
WEEKS, Ann 94 J F 37 Joshua 6
Lemuel 96 Sally 96
WELLS, Samuel 149
WENTWORTH, E G 19
WHEELER, Abigail 144 Ann 135
WHITE, Ann Maria 39 Hannah 39
John 39
WHITTIER, S 115 Samuel 121
WIDGERY, Elizabeth 137 138 143
Elizabeth R 137 William 137
WILDRAGE, Ellen 144
WILLIAMS, Catherine 99 David
80 Frances Ellen 99 John 99
Sara G 80 Tryphena 80
WINGATE, Elizabeth 24 Snell 42
WISWELL, Elizabeth 185 Mary
W 185
WOODBURY, Hannah H 92 Mary
92 William 92
WOODMAN, Olive J 112
WOODS, F 86
WRIGHT, Mary 48
YORK, Margaret R 90 Mary 90
Robert 90